J. C. Wilson

The complete medical pocket-formulary and physician's

vade-mecum

collated for the use of practitioners

J. C. Wilson

The complete medical pocket-formulary and physician's vade-mecum
collated for the use of practitioners

ISBN/EAN: 9783742832931

Manufactured in Europe, USA, Canada, Australia, Japa

Cover: Foto ©Thomas Meinert / pixelio.de

Manufactured and distributed by brebook publishing software
(www.brebook.com)

J. C. Wilson

The complete medical pocket-formulary and physician's vade-mecum

/

Complete Medical Pocket-Formulary

AND

PHYSICIAN'S VADE-MECUM:

CONTAINING UPWARDS OF **2500** PRESCRIPTIONS, COL-
LECTED FROM THE PRACTICE OF **PHYSICIANS
AND** SURGEONS OF EXPERIENCE, AMERICAN
AND FOREIGN, ARRANGED FOR READY
REFERENCE UNDER AN ALPHABET-
ICAL LIST OF DISEASES;

Also a Special List of New Drugs, with their Dosage,
Solubilities, and Therapeutical Applications;

TOGETHER WITH

A TABLE OF FORMULÆ FOR **SUPPOSITORIES**; A TABLE OF FOR-
MULÆ FOR **HYPODERMIC MEDICATION**; A LIST OF DRUGS
FOR INHALATION; **A TABLE OF** POISONS, WITH THEIR
ANTIDOTES; A **POSOLOGICAL TABLE**; A LIST OF
INCOMPATIBLES; A TABLE OF METRIC EQUIV-
ALENTS; A BRIEF ACCOUNT OF EXTERNAL
ANTIPYRETICS, DISINFECTANTS, MED-
ICAL THERMOMETRY, THE URI-
NARY TESTS; AND MUCH
OTHER USEFUL IN-
FORMATION.

COLLATED FOR THE USE OF PRACTITIONERS

BY

J. C. WILSON, A.M., M.D.,

Physician to the German Hospital, Philadelphia, etc., etc.

PHILADELPHIA:
J. B. LIPPINCOTT COMPANY.
1892.

PRINTED BY J. B. LIPPINCOTT COMPANY, PHILADELPHIA.

PREFACE.

No apology is offered for presenting to the profession The Complete Medical Pocket-Formulary. The value of such a manual for ready reference at all times has been fully established, and is understood not only by the oft-referred-to busy practitioner, but also by every physician at the outset of his professional labors. Nor, indeed, will those who are more experienced and critical in all instances deny the immediate value of suggestions found between its covers.

This little book is not intended to take the place either of treatises on practice or of hand-books of therapeutics. Nor is it designed to eke out the defects of an imperfect medical education.

Its true office will consist in bringing to the attention of the practitioner, when most needed, the results of the experience of the profession at large, in rendering available a wider range of therapeutic knowledge than most possess, and in refreshing the memory with facts which from disuse are often difficult to recall at once. Those who use it rightly will avoid the error of forcing their individual cases to fit the requirements of formal recipes; they will, on the contrary, so modify the suggestive formulæ as to render them available for each case in turn, and will find throughout its pages, often usefully referred to in haste, the starting-point for valuable reading and investigation at leisure.

PHILADELPHIA, July 4, 1891.

CONTENTS.

AUTHORITIES.

Diday.
Diederichs.
Douell.
Dobronravoff.
Dochmann.
Donavan.
Donnelly.
Dowell.
Doyon.
Drasche.
Drescher.
Druitt.
Dubief.
Duchenne.
Duckworth.
Duguet.
Duhring.
Dujardin-Beaumetz.
Dukes.
Dumas.
Duncan.
Dunglison.
Dunn.
Duparc.
Dupasquier.
Dupont.
Dupuytren.
Durand.

Easby.
Eberle.
Ebstein.
Echeverria.
Eillard.
Eisenhart.
Eitelberg.
Elieaume.
Eller.
Elliott.
Ellis.
Elsberg.
Embleton.
Emmet.
Endler.
Erichsen.
Erlenmeyer.
Eulenburg.
Evans.
Ewald.

Fahnestock.
Fairbank.
Faust.
Fenn.
Fenwick.
Ferguson.
Fernald.
Ferriar.
Fischer.
Fisher.
Flanagan.
Fleischmann.
Fleming.
Fliesburg.
Fordyce.
Foster.
Fothergill.
Fournier.
Fowler.
Fox, G. H.
Fox, L. W.
Fox, Tilbury.
Foy.
Fraipont.
Fräntzel.
Fraser.
Free.
Frerichs.
Frey.
Fronmueller.
Frost.
Frühwald.
Fuller.
Furey.
Furlonge.

Galezowski.
Garageorgiades.
Gardner.
Garretson.
Garrod.
Georgi.
Getchell.
Gilles de la Tourette.
Gimbert.
Giné.
Giordano.
Girard.
Girwood.
Glover.
Goelet.
Gola.
Goldberg.
Gelding-Bird.
Gooch.
Goodell.
Goodfellow.
Goodman.
Goolden.
Gottschalk.
Graefe.
Grandin.
Grandmont.
Grant (Bey).
Granville.
Graves.
Green.
Greenhalgh.
Gregory.
Grieve.
Gross, S. D.
Gross, S. W.
Grossich.
Gsell-Fels.
Gubler.
Guibout.
Guichon.
Guild.
Guitéras.
Guthrie.
Guttmann.
Guy.
Guy's Hospital.

Habershon.
Haden.
Halford.
Hallopeau.
Hamilton.
Hammerschlag.
Hammond.
Hannay.
Hannon.
Hardy.
Harkin.
Harley.
Hartmann.
Hartshorne.
Hasterlik.
Haughton.
Hausmann.
Hawack.
Hawack and Arboe.
Hawkins.
Hay.
Hazard.
Headland.
Heath.
Hebersmith.
Hebra.
Hecket.
Heder.
Heinzelmann.
Henry.
Henson.
Hering.
Herrmann.
Henter.
Hicks.
Higginbottom.
Higgins.

Hildenbrand.
Hildreth.
Hill.
Hillier.
Hinsberg and Kast.
Hirsch.
Hirst.
Hirtz.
Hitchman.
Hodgson, A. L.
Hodgson, G. F.
Hogg.
Hogner.
Holloway.
Holt.
Hood.
Hooper.
Hope.
Hôpital St. Louis.
Horwitz.
Hôtel-Dieu.
Housman.
Howard.
Howe.
Huchard.
Hufeland.
Hull.
Hulse.
Hunter.
Hutchinson.
Hyde.

Icard.
Ihle.
Ingals.
Ingraham.

Jaccoud.
Jackson.
Jacobi.
Jamieson.
Janeway.
Jefferson Hospital, Phila.
Jenner.
Joffroy.
Johnson.
Johnston.
Jolly.
Jones, Wharton.
Jordan.
Joret et Homolle.
Jorissenne.
Joy.
Judkins.

Kaposi.
Kappesser.
Kassowitz.
Kennard.
Kennedy.
Kentish.
Kerner.
Kesteven.
Keyes.
Keyser.
Kilgour.
Kingdon.
King's College Hospital.
Kinney.
Kinnicutt.
Kirk.
Klapp.
Knaggs.
Knoll.
Kobert.
Kobler.
Koebner.
Kolover.
Kopp.
Kortüm.
Kossobudski.
Krafft-Ebing.
Krecke.

Kreis and Goll.
Krombholz.
Kroyla.
Krutovski.

Labbé.
Laborde.
Labric.
Lafargue.
Lailler.
Lallemand.
Lambert.
Laucereaux.
Langenbuch.
Lardier.
La Roche.
Lashkevitch.
Lassar.
Latzel.
Lawrence.
Lawson.
Lax.
Laycock.
Lazarus.
Leahy.
Lebrun.
Lecluyse.
Ledsson.
Lee
Leedom.
Le Gendre.
Legroux.
Leidy.
Leishman.
Lemare-Picquot.
Leroy.
Lettsom.
Letzerich.
Levi, Jos.
Levick.
Levis.
Lewis.
Lexton.
Leyden.
Lichtwitz.
Liebreich.
Lisfranc.
Lister.
Little.
Liveling.
Livezey.
Lodewyks.
London Hospital.
Loomis.
Lopez.
Lorens.
Lorenz.
Louis.
Lowndes.
Lublinski.
Ludlow.
Lugol.
Lunin.
Lutaud.
Luton.
Luzzato.
Lyman.

MacDonald.
Mackenzie, Morell.
MacLagan.
Madigan.
Magendie.
Magitot.
Mairet and Combe-
  male.
Maisch.
Manassein.
Mann.
Maragliano.
Marcus.
Markoe.
Marsden.
Marshall.
Martin, J. **R.**

Martin, Sidney.
Marini.
Marini and Massei.
Mason.
Mattison.
Matudsley.
Maunsell.
Mauriac.
Mays.
Mazzoni.
Meglun.
McCockle.
McDonald.
McDowell.
McLane.
Meigs.
Meigs and Pepper.
Mérière.
Metcalf.
Metzauer.
Metznier.
Meyer.
M'Gregor.
Miall.
Michou.
Milvet.
Milton.
Minot.
Mira
Mitchell, J. K.
Mitchell, R. W.
Mitchell, S. Weir.
Mitchell, T. D.
Moeli.
Moczard.
Monin.
Monoe.
Morétin.
Morse.
Merton.
Messtig-Moorhof.
Mosler.
Moure.
M'Phail.
Mündé.
Murchison.
Murrell.

Nagel.
Nakamura.
Napheys.
Neale.
Negri.
Neligan.
Neumann.
Nicot.
Niemeyer.
Nikolski.
Norton.
Nothnagel.
Noyes.
Nussbaum.

Oakes.
Oesterlen.
Oervoes.
Oxe.
Oldham.
Oliver.
Oppolzer.
Orfile.
Osbrey.
O'Shaughnessy.
Osecki.
Osler.
Otis, F. N.
Otto.

Pagenstecher.
Palmer.
Pancoast, Jos.
Pareira.
Parinaud.
Paris.
Paris Codex.

Pariset.
Parkes.
Parrish.
Parry.
Parvin.
Parzevski.
Patton.
Paul.
Pavy.
Payne.
Peabody.
Peart.
Pelletan.
Pennypacker.
Penrose.
Penzoldt.
Pepper.
Persh.
Pescheck.
Peter.
Peters.
Philadelphia Hos-
  pital.
Phillips.
Phoebus.
Physick.
Pick.
Picrquin.
Pigornet.
Pinard.
Pins.
Piorry.
Playfair.
Plumbe.
Polli.
Porcher.
Potain.
Potter.
Poulain.
Poulet.
Preston.
Pribram.
Prideaux.
Priestley.
Proctor.
Proutt.
Puche.
Pulawski.

Quain.
Quaita.
Quinlan.

Rabow.
Rademaker.
Radius.
Raison.
Raspail.
Ratier.
Rayer
Reece.
Reisner.
Reliquet.
Renou.
Rester.
Reveil.
Revillout.
Reynolds, R. G.
Rhode.
Richardson.
Richmond.
Ricord.
Ridgeway.
Riebe.
Riess.
Riggs.
Ringer.
Rivas.
Rivière.
Robert.
Robinson, **Beverley.**
Roche.
Rodet.
Rodier.
Roland.

9

Romanovsky.
Romberg
Rocca.
Roosevelt **Hospital**, N.Y.
Rosenbach.
Rosenberg.
Rosenthal.
Rothe.
Rouquette.
Roussel.
Rnault.
Rudermacher.
Rudolphi.
Ruschenberger.
Rush.
Rust.
Ryan.

Saalfeld.
Saerbs.
Sajous.
Salter.
Sands.
Sansom.
Sarzance.
Sawyer.
Scarenzio.
Schafhirt.
Schenker.
Schilling.
Schmidiger.
Schmidt.
Schneck.
Schnitzler.
Schubarth.
Schwarz.
Scott and McCormac.
Scudamore.
Sedgwick.
Sée.
Seguin.
Seifert.
Seiler.
Selkirk.
Selldéu.
Selwyn.
Semmola.
Seymour.
Shapter.
Shaw.
Shillitoe.
Shinn.
Shoemaker, J. **V.**
Silverthorn.
Simon.
Simpson.
Sinéty.
Skoda.
Smith, A. A.
Smith, A. H.
Smith, Charles.
Smith, Eustace.
Smith, F. A. A.
Smith, F. G.
Smith, H. H.
Smith, Hugh.
Smith, J. Lawrence.
Smith, J. Lewis.
Smith, Tyler.
Sobernheim.
Soden.
Sollard.
Solon.
Sonneberg.
Sonnenberger.

Soubeiran.
Soulez.
Sozinsky.
Spillmann.
Spitzka.
Squibb.
Squire, B.
Squire, P.
Starr.
Startin.
Stekoulia
Stelwagon.
Stetter.
Stewart.
Stillé.
St. Luke's Hospital, N.Y.
Stokes.
Stone.
Stowell.
Strother.
Stroud.
Stubbs.
Sturgis.
Styrap.
Suckling.
Sullivan.
Sully.
Sundelin.
Swedianr.
Sweringen.
Sylvestrini and Picchini.
Symonds.
Szadek.

Tait.
Tanner.
Tauret.
Tanturri.
Tardieu.
Taylor, R. W.
Teale.
Terrillon.
Thiersch.
Thomas.
Thomas, T. G.
Thompson, A. T.
Thompson, J. A.
Thomson, W. H.
Thor.
Thuries.
Todd.
Tortual.
Tournie.
Troilins.
Trousseau.
Trousseau et Reveil.
Truman.
Trussewitsch.
Tuke.
Turnbull.
Tutt.
Tweedy.
Tyrell.
Tyson, J.

L'Union Médicale.
University Hospital.
Unna.
Ure.
Uspenski.

Valleix.
Van Buren.

Van **Buren** and Keyes.
Van den Corput.
Van Goidtsnoven.
Van Mons.
Vanoye.
Vecchizetti.
Velpean.
Venot.
Vetlesen.
Vidal.
Vigier.
Villate.
Villemin.
Vleminckx.
Vogt.
Von Mering.
Von Ziemssen.
Vulpian.

Wankes.
Walker.
Wallace.
Walsh.
Walshe.
Walterand Blurdell.
Ward's Island Insane Asylum, N.Y.
Ware.
Warfvinge.
Waring.
Waring-Curran.
Waterhouse.
Waters.
Watson.
Waugh.
Webb.
Weber.
Weir.
Weiss.
Weller.
Wende.
West.
White, J. W.
Wieherkiewicz.
Wichmann.
Widerhofer.
Widowitz.
Wiß.
Wigan.
Wiglesworth.
Wilcox, R. W.
Wilde.
Wilkes.
Wilks.
Willard.
Williams.
Willis.
Wilson, Ellwood.
Wilson, Erasmus.
Wilson, J. C.
Winzar.
Woakes.
Wolfenden.
Wood, G. B.
Wood, H. C.
Wood, James.
Wooster.
Wright.
Wulfsberg.
Wyeth.

Young.
Yvon.

Zakrzhevski.

I.

FORMULÆ.

ABORTION THREATENED.

1—℞ Tinct. opii . . . . ℳxx–xxx.
Sig. Mix with two or three tablespoonfuls of **boiled starch**
and inject into the rectum.   PARVIN.

2—℞ Ext. viburni prunif. fld. . . . . f℥ij.
Sig. A teaspoonful in a sherryglassful of water **every four**
hours.   JENKS.

3—℞ Tinct. opii deod. . . . . ℳlx.
 Sodii bromidi . . . . ℨiij.
 Chloral. hydrat. . . . . ℨss.
 Syr. acaciæ . . . . f℥j.
 Aquæ . . . . q. s. ad f℥iij.—M.
Sig. A dessert-spoonful in water every four hours. E. WILSON.

4—℞ Chlorodyne . . . . f℥ss.
Sig. Ten minims in water every third or fourth hour.
                                                       PLAYFAIR.

5—℞ Potassii iodidi . . . . ℨj.
 • Aquæ . . . . f℥j.—M.
Sig. Twenty **to forty** drops in water or milk two or three
times a day. (*Habitual abortion. When due to syphilis.*)
                                                       J. C. WILSON.

6—℞ Mist. asafœtidæ . . . . ℨviij.
Sig. A tablespoonful several times **daily.** (*In habitual abortion.*)   NEGRI.

7—℞ Tinct. ferri chlor. . . . . ℨss.
 Potassii chloratis . . . . ℈iv
 Syr. simplicis . . . . ℨj.
 Aquæ menth. pip. . . . . ad ℥iv.—M.
Sig. A dessertspoonful in a wineglassful of water after meals.
                                                       STROTHER.

ABSCESSES.

8—℞ Iodoformi . . . . ℨiss–℥v.
 Ætheris . . . . ℥vj.—M.
Inject three to five ounces after aspirating the abscess. (*In
tubercular abscess.*)   MOSETIG-MOORHOF.

9—℞ Iodoformi . . . . ℨij.
 Glycerini . . . . ℨiss.—M.
Inject the abscess-cavity after evacuating the pus. (*In tuber-
cular abscess.*)   BILLROTH.

10—℞ Calcii sulphureti . . . . gr. vj.
 Pulveris glycyrrhizæ . . . . q. s.
Fiat massa, in pilulas no. xii dividenda.
Sig. One pill every three hours.   WAUGH.

11—℞ Calcii sulphidi . . . . gr. j.
 Sacchari lactis . . . . gr. x.
℞ Misce et fiant chartulæ no. x.
Sig. One powder every two hours.   RINGER.

12—℞ Sodii hypophosphitis . . . . ℈iv,
 Calcii hypophosphitis . . . . ℈viij.
 Syrupi simplicis . . . . f℥iss.
 Aquæ fœniculi . . . . q. s. ad f℥iv.—M.
Sig. A dessertspoonful four times a day.   CHURCHILL.

ACIDITY. (See also Pyrosis.)

13—℞ Tinct. nucis vomicæ . . . . f 3j.

Sig. Five drops a quarter of an hour before food
three times daily.　　　　　　　　　　RINGER.

14—℞ Infusi rhei . . . . f 3iss.
　　Sodii bicarb. . . . . 3iss.
　　Syr. aurantii cort. . . . . f 3vj.—M.

Sig. A teaspoonful twice daily.　　　　　EWALD.

15—℞ Pulv. ipecac. . . . . gr. ss.
　　Pulv. rhei . . . . gr. ij.
　　Sodii bicarb. . . . . gr. xij.—M.

In chartulas no. xii. dividenda.
Sig. One powder every four to six hours to an infant one year
old.　　　　　　　　　　　　J. LEWIS SMITH.

16—℞ Sodii bicarb. 　　　　　　　　　　　3j.
　　Pulv. rhei . . . 　　　　　　　　　3ss.
　　Spts. menth. pip. 　　　. . . . . f 3ij.
　　Aquæ 　　　　. . . . q. s. ad f 3iv.—M.

Sig. A tablespoonful after meals. (For acidity combined with
constipation.)　　　　　　　　Bellevue Hosp.

17—℞ Sodii bicarb. . . . . 3ij.

In pulveres no. xii dividenda.
Sig. A powder in a wineglassful of water after meals.
　　　　　　　　　　　　　ALONZO CLARK.

18—℞ Hydrargyri cum cretá 　　. . gr. iij.
　　Bismuthi subnitratis . . . 　. . gr. xij.
　　Pulveris nucis myristicæ . 　　. . gr. iij.

Misce et divide in chartulas no. vi.
Sig. One powder morning and night.　　BARTHOLOW.

19—℞ Liquoris potassæ . . . . m̨ xx.
　　Misturæ cretæ . . . . f 3j.
　　Tincturæ calumbæ . . . . f 3j.

Misce et fiat haustus.
Sig. One dose.　　　　　　　　　　HOOPER.

20—℞ Spiritus ammoniæ aromatici . . . . . . f 3iss.
　　Spiritus ætheris compositi 　　. . . . f 3j.
　　Syrupi zingiberis 　　　　　　　f 3iij.
　　Aquæ anisi . 　　　　　. 　f 3iiiss.—M.

Sig. The one-third part, frequently repeated.　DRUITT.

ACNE. (See also Skin Diseases.)

21—℞ Sulphuris iodidi . . . . 3ss.
　　Adipis . . . . 3j.—M.

Sig. Use freely over the eruption night and morning. (In acne
indurata and rosacea.)　　　　　　RINGER.

22—℞ Naphthol β 　. . . . . 3iss.
　　Sulphur. præcip. . . . . 3ss.
　　Vaselin. vel lanolin.,
　　Sapon. viridis . . . . āā 3ij.—M.

Leniter terendo fiat pasta.
Sig. Spread a thin layer on affected skin and leave for fifteen
to twenty minutes; then rub off the ointment and dust with
powdered talc.　　　　　　　　LASSAR.

23—℞ Hydrargyri biniodidi . . . . gr. v.
　　Unguenti petrolei . . . . 3j.

Misce et fiat unguentum.
Sig. Apply twice daily.　　　　　　　RINGER.

24—℞ Liq. potassæ . . . . f 3j.
　　Aquæ rosæ . . . . f 3iv.—M.

Sig. Apply with a soft sponge twice daily.　BARTHOLOW.

25—℞ Acidi nitrohydrochlorici diluti . . . . . f 3iss.
　　Syrupi simplicis . . . . f 3iss.
　　Aquæ aurantii florum . . . . . . q. s. ad f 3iv.—M.

Sig. A dessertspoonful three times a day.　DA COSTA.

26—℞ Syrupi hypophosphitum compositi . . . f 3iv.

Sig. A dessertspoonful three times a day.　DA COSTA.

27—R Syr. ferri iodidi . . . . f3j.
Sig. Ten to thirty drops in water three times a day.
J. C. WILSON.

28—R Ichthyol. . . . . 3ij.
Adipis . . . . 3j.—M.
Sig. Apply twice a day.
COHEN.

AGALACTIA

29—R Ext. pilocarpi fld. . . . . f3ij.
Sig. A teaspoonful two or three times daily. BARTHOLOW.

30—R Decocti gossypii . . . . Oj.
Sig. A wineglassful every half-hour. PHILLIPS.

31—R Ricinus communis fol. . . . . 3ij.
Aquæ bullientis . . . . f3viij.—M.
Sig. Make an infusion and apply as a fomentation to the
breasts. TANNER.

ALBUMINURIA (Bright's Disease).

32—R Liq. trinitrin. (1 per cent.) f3j.
Sig. Three drops in water three times a day. BARTHOLOW.

33—R Auri et sodii chlor. . . gr. iij.
Hydrarg. chlor. corr. gr. v.
Ext. gentian. . . . . q. s.—M.
Ft. massa et in pil. no. lx div.
Sig. One pill morning and evening. BARTHOLOW.

34—R Auri et sodii chloridi . . . . gr. j.
Micæ panis . . . . q. s.
Fiat massa et in pilulas no. xv dividenda.
Sig. One pill three times a day DA COSTA.

35—R Potassii iodidi . . . 3iss.
Syrupi simplicis . . . . . f3ss.
Aquæ cinnamomi . . . . q. s. ad f3ij.—M.
Sig. A teaspoonful three times a day. GOLDBERG.

36—R Tincturæ ferri chloridi . . . . f3iij.
Acidi acetici diluti . . . . f3ij.
Syrupi simplicis . . . . f3iss.
Liquoris ammonii acetatis . . . . q. s. ad f3iv.—M.
Sig. A dessertspoonful every six hours. BASHAM

37—R Ferri sulph. . . . . gr. xv.
Magn. sulph. . . . . 3ij.
Potass. bicarb. . . . . 3iij.
Infusi buchu . . . . f3viij.—M.
Sig. A tablespoonful once or twice a day in a tumblerful of
water. (When constipation exists.) FOTHERGILL.

38—R Acidi gallici . . . . 3j-ij.
Acidi sulphurici dil. . . . . . . f3ss.
Tinct. lupuli . . . . f3j.
Infusi lupuli . . . . ad f3vj.—M.
Sig. A tablespoonful thrice daily. (If urine is smoky.)
AITKEN.

39—R Ferri sulphat. 3j
Ext. nucis vom. . . . . gr. x-3j
Pil. galbani co. . . . . 3ij-iij.—M.
Ft. massa et in pil. no. xx div.
Sig. A pill twice or thrice daily. (When dyspeptic symptoms
arise.) GOODFELLOW.

40—R Tinct. strophanthi hisp. (1-20) . . . . . . f3ss.
Sig. Five to ten drops in water three times daily. (When
there is a weak rapid pulse, scanty secretion, and dyspnœa.)
PYE.

41—R Ol. erigerontis . . . f3ss.
Sig. Five drops on a lump of sugar every three or four hours.
(In the chronic forms.) BARTHOLOW.

42—℞ Sodii iodidi . . . . gr. xv.
Sodii phosphat. . . . . 3ss.
Sodii chloridi . . . . 3ij.
Aquæ . . . . q. s. ad ft. sol.—M.
Sig. To be taken in the course of the twenty-four hours.
SEMMOLA.

ALCOHOLISM.

43—℞ Hydrarg. chl. mitis . . . . gr. j.
Sacch. lactis . . . . gr. iij.
M. et in chtt. no. vi div.
Sig. One powder every hour. J. C. WILSON.

44—℞ Codeinæ . . . . gr. iij.
Camphor. monobrom. . . . . gr. xlj.
M. et in pil. no. xii div.
Sig. One pill every two or three hours. J. C. WILSON.

45—℞ Paraldehydi . . . . f3vj.
Mucilag. acaciæ,
Spts. vini gallici . . . . ãã f3ij.—M.
Sig. Shake the vial. A tablespoonful to induce quiet and
sleep; repeat in an hour if necessary. J. C. WILSON.

46—℞ Spts. ammon. aromat. . . . . f3ij.
Tinct. camphoræ . . . . f3iss.
Tinct. hyoscyami . . . . f3iss.
Spts. lavandulæ co. . . . . . . q. s. ad f3ij.—M.
Sig. A teaspoonful every hour till relieved. Then give—

47—℞ Pulv. capsici . . . . gr. ij.
Quininæ sulph. . . . . gr. iij.—M.
Ft. pulv. no. i.
To be taken before each meal for several days. If sleepless-
ness, then give—

48—℞ Sodii bromidi . . . . 3ss.
Chloral. hydrat. . . . . 3iss.
Syr. aurantii cort. . . . . f3ss.
Aquæ . . . . ad f3iv.—M.
Sig. A tablespoonful at night. Repeat if necessary. AITKEN.

49—℞ Tinct. gentianæ co.,
Tinct. calumbæ co. . . . . ãã f3ij.
Tinct. nucis vom. . . . . ♏lxxx.—M.
Sig. A dessertspoonful before each meal. LOOMIS.

50—℞ Strychninæ sulph. . . . . gr. j.
Aquæ font. . . . . 3j.—M.
Sig. Five minims, increased cautiously to twenty minims,
hypodermically twice daily. (In both acute and chronic
forms.) DOBRONRAVOFF.

51—℞ Zinci oxidi . . . . 3j.
Piperinæ . . . . 9j.
Misce et fiant pilulæ no. xx.
Sig. One pill three or four times a day. CHAPMAN.

52—℞ Sol. nitro-glycerin. (1 per cent.) . . . . . f3ij.
Sig. One drop every two hours. (In acute form, with cerebral
anæmia and intense depression.) VAN GOIDTSNOVEN.

ALOPECIA.

53—℞ Spts. æther. 110.00
Tinct. benzoin. . . . . 15.00.—M.
Sig. Apply once a day. HEBRA.

54—℞ Tinct. capsici . . . . f3ss.
Tinct. saponariæ quil. . . . . f3j.
Glycerini . . . . 3ij.
Tinct. cantharidis . . . . f3ij.
Spiritus rosmarini . . . . f3iss.
Aquæ rosæ . . . . ad f3viij.—M.
Sig. Drop on the hair night and morning. SHOEMAKER.

55—℞ Quininæ sulphatis . .   gr. xl.
     Tincturæ cantharidis . . .   f 3j.
     Spiritus ammonii aromatici   f 3j.
     Olei ricini . . .   f 3iss.
     Spiritus myrciæ   f 3vss.
     Olei rosmarini   gtt. vj.

Fiat mistura.
Sig. Shake well. Apply once a day.   J. C. WILSON.

56—℞ Tincturæ cantharidis   f 3j.
     Glycerini . . . .   f 3ss.
     Spiritus ammoniæ aromatici . . .   f 3ss.
     Aquæ rosmarini   . . . .   f 3vij.—M.

To be used with a wet brush once or twice a day.   STARTIN.

57—℞ Tinct. cantharidis . . . . f 3iss.
     Tinct. capsici . . . . ℳxx.
     Glycerini . . . . f 3ss.
     Spts. odoratæ . . . . ad f 3vj.—M.

Sig. Apply to the head two or three times daily.   GROSS.

58—℞ Tinct. macis   f 3iss.
     Olei olivæ   . . . . ad f 3ij.—M.

Sig. Apply two or three times daily to affected spots. HEBRA.

59—℞ Quininæ sulphat. . . . . 3iv.
     Spiritus vini rectif. . . . . f 3iv.
     Tinct. capsici,
     Tinct. cantharidis,
     Spts. ammon. arom. . . . . āā f 3ss.
     Glycerini . . . . f 3iv.
     Aquæ. . . . . q. s. ad ft. Oj.—M.

Sig. Apply locally.   BRIXTON.

60—℞ Tinct. cantharidis . . . . f 3ss.
     Olei ricini . . . . f 3iv.—M.

Sig. Rub well into roots **of hair night and morning.** WARING.

61—℞ Aquæ ammoniæ . . . . f 3ss.
     Olei terebinthinæ . . . . f 3ij.
     Aquæ. . . . . f 3x.—M.

Ft. lotio.
Sig. Apply **locally, alternating with small flying blisters.**
                    HALLOPEAU.

62—℞ Hydrarg. sulphat. flav.,
     Sulphuris loti . . . . āā 3j.
     Vaselini   . . . . 3x.—M.

Ft. ungt.
Rub in the affected spots, after washing with soap and warm
   water, thrice daily. When nearly well, use the following:

63—℞ Acidi boracici .   . . . 3ij.
     Spts. camphoræ,
     Olei terebinthinæ . . . . āā f 3xiiss.
     Aquæ coloniensis . . . . f 3iv 3vj.—M.

Ft. lotio.
Rub in locally **morning and evening.**   ROUQUETTE.

AMAUROSIS (Functional).

64—℞ Strychninæ sulphatis   . . . . gr. j.
     Confectionis rosæ   . . . .   . q. s.

Fiat massa, in pilulas no. xxx dividenda.
Sig. One pill after each meal.   MAGENDIE.

65—℞ Strychninæ sulph.   gr. j.
     Alcoholis . .   . f 3j.
     Aquæ destillatæ   . . . . . . ad f 3iv.—M.

Sig. A teaspoonful thrice daily before meals.   NAGEL.

66—℞ Potassii iodidi . . . . 3j.
     Aquæ   . . . . f 3j.—M.

Sig. **Twenty to forty drops in water** three times a day. LEVIS.

67—℞ Pilocarpinæ muriatis . . . . gr. j.
In pil. no. viii div.
Sig. One pill **every three hours.** .   LEVIS.

68—℞ Manganesii **binoxidi** . . . . ℨj.
Fiat massa et in pil. no. xxx div.
Sig. One pill three times daily after meals.   P. BARKER.

69—℞ Ext. aloč aq. . . . . ℨj.
       Ferri sulph. **exsic.** . . . . ℨij
       Asafœtidæ . . . . ℨiv.—M.
Ft. massa et in pilulæ no. c div.
Sig. One pill after each meal, gradually increased to three.
                                                GOODELL.

70—℞ Tinct. ferri muriat. . . . . **ℨij.**
       Tinct. cantharidis . . . . **ℨj.**
       Tinct. guaiaci ammon. . . . . **ℨss.**
       Tinct. aloës. . . . . **ℨss.**
       Syrupi . . . . q. s. ad **ℨvj.**—M.
Sig. A tablespoonful thrice daily.   DEWEES.

71—℞ Myrrhæ . . . . **gr. viij.**
       Pulveris jalapæ . . . . **gr. xv.**
       Ferri sulphatis exsiccatæ,
       Pulveris aloës et canellæ . . . . . . āā **ℨj.**
       Syrupi simplicis . . . . **q. s.**
Fiat massa et divide in pilulas l.
Sig. Two or three pills at bedtime, for several nights succes-
sively.   CHAPMAN.

72—℞ Potassii **carbonatis** . . . . ℨss.
       Myrrhæ . . . . ℨj.
Tere simul, dein adde—
       Ferri sulphatis,
       Sacchari albi . . . . āā ℨss.
Fiat massa **et divide in pilulas xl.**
Sig. Two **or three pills three times a day.**   HULSE.

73—℞ Pulveris cantharidis . . . . **gr. ij.**
       Pulveris sabinæ . . . . **ℨj.**
Misce et divide in pulveres no. iv.
Sig. One every night on going to bed, watching its effects.
                                                GOLDBERG.

74—℞ Pulveris sabinæ,
       Pulveris zingiberis . . . . āā gr. vj.
       Sodii biboratis . . . . gr. xv.
Misce et fiat pulvis.
Two powders daily, morning and evening.   THOMSON.

75—℞ Iodi . . . . ℈ij.
       Spiritus lavandulæ compositi . . . . . f ℨij.
       Spiritus vini . . . . f ℨj.
Fiat tinctura.
Sig. From five to ten drops in sweetened water twice a day,
gradually and cautiously increasing the dose. S. G. MORTON.

76—℞ Pulv. resin. guaiaci . . . . ℨij.
In chartulas no. xii div.
Sig. A powder in **a** wineglassful of milk **before** breakfast.
                                                J. SAWYER.

77—℞ Acidi oxalici . . . . gr. xx.
       Syr. aurantii cort. . . . . ℨij.
       Aquæ ferv. . . . . ad ℨviij.—M.
Sig. A tablespoonful every hour at the time of the usual menstrual period.   POULET.

78—℞ Tinct. aconiti radicis . . . . ℨss.
Sig. One drop every hour. (*When checked by cold.*) RINGER.

79—℞ Salicini . . . . gr. xv.
       Pulv. rhei . . . . gr. vijss.
       Confect. rosæ . . . . q. s. ut ft. massa.—M.
Ft. massa et in **pil. no. x div.**
Sig. One thrice **daily.**   DE MUSSY.

80—℞ Terebinthinæ **alb.,**
       Pulv. aloës,
       Ferri sulph. exsic. . . . . āā ℈j.—M.
Ft. massa et in pil. no. xx div.
Sig. One thrice daily.   PARVIN.

81—℞ **Ferri sesquibromidi** . . . . ʒj.
Fiant capsulæ no. xii.
Sig. A capsule after meals. **HECKET.**

82—℞ Hydrarg. chlor. corr. . . . . gr. i-ij.
Liq. arsenici chlor. . . . . ʒj.
Tinct. ferri chlor. . . . . ʒiv.
Acidi hydrochlor. **dil.** . . . . ʒiv.
Syrupi . . . . ʒiij.
Aquæ . . . . ad ʒvj.—M.

Sig. A dessertspoonful in a wineglassful of water after
meals. A. H. SMITH.

83—℞ Strychninæ sulphatis . . . . gr. j.
Acidi arseniosi . . . . gr. ij.
Extracti belladonnæ . . . . gr. v.
Quininæ sulphatis,
Pulveris ferri . . . . āā ʒij.
Extracti taraxaci . . . . ʒss.

Misce et fiant pilulæ no. xl.
Sig. One pill after each meal. FRANCIS GURNEY SMITH.

84—℞ Ferri sulphatis,
Quininæ sulphatis,
Extracti anthemidis . . āā ʒj.
Olei anthemidis . . . . ℳvj.
Fiat massa et in pilulas xx dividenda.
Sig. One pill three times a day. GOLDING-BIRD.

85—℞ Syrupi ferri iodidi . . . . f ʒij.
Syrupi zingiberis . . . . f ʒj.
Aquæ destillatæ . . . f ʒv.—M.
Sig. A tablespoonful three times a day. R. M'GREGOR.

86—℞ Quininæ sulph. . . gr. xx.
Ferri sulph. exsiccat. . . . gr. xl.
Strychninæ sulph. . . gr. ss.—M.
Ft. massa et in pilulas no. xx div.
Sig. One pill thrice daily. BARTHOLOW.

87—℞ **Ferri sulph. exsiccat.,**
Potassii carbonat. . . . . āā ʒj.
Syrupi . . . . q. s. ut ft. massa.—M.
Ft. massa et in pil. no. xxiv div.
Sig. One pill after meals. **BLAUD.**

88—℞ Tincturæ ferri chloridi . f ʒiss.
Acidi phosphorici diluti . f ʒiiss.
Syrupi acidi citratis . . . . . q. s. ad f ʒiv.—M.
Sig. A dessertspoonful in water three times a day. GOODELL.

89—℞ Liquoris ferri dialyzati . . . . f ʒj.
Sig. A teaspoonful three times a day. **REED.**

90—℞ Pulveris ipecacuanhæ . . . . gr. vj.
Hydrargyri cum cretâ . . . . gr. xij.
Ferri subcarbonatis . . . . gr. xlviij.
Misce et divide in pulveres vi.
Sig. One powder twice a day. S. ASHWELL.

91—℞ Potass. bromidi . . . . gr. v-x.
Ferri et potass. **tart.** . . . . gr. v.
Infusi quassiæ . . . . ʒj.—M.
Sig. To be taken three times **daily.** (*Where headache is pro-
duced by ordinary tonics.*) FOTHERGILL.

92—℞ Emuls. amygdalæ **amar.** . . . . ʒx.
Pulpæ splenicæ . . . . ʒiv.
Spts. vini gallici . . . . ʒij.—M.
Sig. To be given in the twenty-four **hours.** MARAGLIANO.

ANEURISM.

93—℞ Potassii iodidi . . . . ʒj. (?)
Syrupi simplicis . . . . f ʒij.
Aquæ destillatæ . . . . q. s. ad f ʒiij.—M.
Sig. A teaspoonful three or four times a day, largely diluted.
BALFOUR.

94—℞ Antipyrin. . . . . 3iss.
      Syr. tolutan. . . . . 3iss.
      Aquæ . . . . ad 3ij.—M.
Sig. A tablespoonful at intervals of one to four hours until
  relieved. (*For cardiac pains.*)   GERMAIN SÉE.

95—℞ Tincturæ veratri viridis . . . . . .   f 3j.
      Tincturæ opii deodoratæ   f 3iss.
      Syrupi simplicis   . f 3vss.
      Aquæ destillatæ   . . . . f 3j.—M.
Sig. A teaspoonful every two, three, or four hours, cautiously.
                             DA COSTA.

96—℞ Tincturæ digitalis . . . . f 3ss.
      Extracti ergotæ fluidi . . . . f 3iiiss.—M.
Sig. A teaspoonful three times a day.   DA COSTA.

ANGINA PECTORIS.

97—℞ Amyli nitritis . . . . **f 3j.**
Sig. From two to five drops to be inhaled from a clean handkerchief.   BRUNTON.

98—℞ Methylal . . . .   3ix.
      Amyli nitritis . . . .   3j.—M.
Sig. Drop thirty or forty drops on a handkerchief and inhale. Repeat if necessary.   RICHARDSON.

99—℞ Antipyrin. .   . . . 3j.
      Syr. tolutan.   . 3j.
      Aquæ . . . . ad 3ij.—M.
Sig. A tablespoonful at intervals of one to four hours until
  relieved.   GERMAIN SÉE.

100—℞ Pyridin. . . . . 3ss.
Sig. Six to ten drops daily, increasing to twenty-five drops,
well diluted with water. Or five to ten drops may be inhaled.
                             DE RENZI.

101—℞ Zinci cyanidi . . . . gr. iv-v.
      Confect. rosæ . . . . q. s.—M.
In pilulas no. xl div.
Sig. One pill three times daily.   **LASHKEVITCH.**

102—℞ Sol. nitro-glycerin. (1 per cent.) . . . . **3ss.**
Sig. One to two drops internally. (*When pallor of face exists.*)
                          WM. PEPPER.

103—℞ Æther's chlorici . . . . .   f 3iss.
      Aquæ camphoræ . .   f 3ij.
      Syrupi amygdalæ   . .   f 3ss.—M.
Sig. A dessertspoonful in water every three hours.   EVANS.

104—℞ Tincturæ digitalis . . .   . f 3iiss.
      Spiritus chloroformi . . . . f 3vj.
      Extracti buchu fluidi . . . . f 3j.
      Spiritus juniperi compositi . . q. s. ad f 3iv.—M.
Sig. A dessertspoonful three times a day.   FOTHERGILL.

105—℞ Quiniæ muriatis . . . . **3j.**
In pilulas no. xx div.
Sig. Four pills daily.   J. C. WILSON.

ANTHRAX.

106—℞ Acidi **carbolici** . . . . ℳ xx-xxv.
      Aquæ . . . . 3j.—M.
Inject a few **drops into and around** the pustule.   USPENSKI.

107—℞ Quininæ . . . . 3j.
      Ol. terebinth. . . . . **q. s. ut** ft. pasta.—M.
Sig. Apply to pustule.   F. RIVAS.

APHTHÆ.

108—℞ Mel. boracis . . . . **3j.**
Apply to patches with a brush.   RINGER.

109—℞ Potassii chloratis . . . . 5j.
  Mellis despumati . . . . . . f3iss.
  Infusi herbæ salviæ . . f3viss.
 Misce et fiat gargarisma.
 Sig. Use as a mouth-wash frequently.   GOLDBERG.

110—℞ Potassii chloratis . . . . 3ij.
  Tincturæ ferri chloridi . . . . f5j.
  Syrupi simplicis . . . . f5vj.
  Aquæ cinnamomi . . . . . . q. s. ad f3ij.—M.
 Sig. A teaspoonful every two hours for a child two years old.
    STUBBS.

111—℞ Potassii **chloratis** . . . . gr. x.
  Aquæ . . . . f3j.—M.
 Sig. Apply locally several times daily.   BRUNTON.

112—℞ Zinci chloridi . . . . gr. iij-xv.
  Alcohol, diluti . . . . f3viij.—M.
 Sig. Gargle and mouth-wash. (*The weakest strength for infants ;
  the strongest for adults.*)   JULES SIMON.

113—℞ Sodii sulphitis . . . . **3ij.**
  Infusi coptis . . . . **f3vj.—M.**
 Sig. Use as a mouth-wash.   **NAGLE.**

114—℞ Acidi hydrochlorici diluti . . . . ℳxx.
  Syrupi simplicis . . . . f3ss.
  Aquæ destillatæ . . . . q. s. ad f3ij.—M.
 Sig. Two teaspoonfuls every two hours.   J. C. WILSON.

115—℞ Potassii **iodidi** . . . . gr. i-v.
  Aquæ . . . . f3j.—M.
 Sig. Apply locally.   BARTHOLOW.

116—℞ Papain. . . . . gr. xxx.
  Glycerini . . . . f3iss.
  Aquæ destillatæ . . . . ad f3v.—M.
 Sig. Apply four or five times daily with a brush on the white
  patches.   SCHMIDIGER.

117—℞ Sodii salicylat. . . . . 3iss.
  Aquæ destillatæ . . . . f3j.—M.
 Sig. Apply **five or six times daily.**   HIRTZ.

ASTHENIA.

118—℞ Quininæ sulphat. . . . . gr. xxx.
  Acidi sulphur. dil. . . . . q. s.
  Aquæ . . . . 3ij.
  Tinct. ferri mur. . . . . 3ss.
  Spts. chloroformi . . . . 3vj.
  Glycerini . . . . ad 3iv.—M.
 Sig. A teaspoonful three times daily.   LOOMIS.

119—℞ **Ext. quebracho alc.** . . . . 3j.
 Sig. **Twenty to thirty drops three** times daily. BOURDEAUX.

120—℞ Vini cocæ . . . . f3viij.
 Sig. A tablespoonful three times a day. J. C. WILSON.

121—℞ Tinct. nucis vomicæ . . . . f3j.
 Sig. Ten to fifteen drops in wine of coca three or four times
  a day.   J. C. WILSON.

ASTHMA.

122—℞ Syrupi hypophosphitum comp. . . . . f3iss.
  Syrupi acidi hydriodici . . . . f3vj.
  Extr. euphorbiæ piluliferæ **fluid.** . . . . f5vj.
  Extr. nucis vomicæ fluid. . . . . f5j.
  Syrupi simplicis . . . . f3j.
  Aquæ destillatæ . . . . f3ij.—M.
 Sig. A tablespoonful every three hours. Shake well.
    JOHNSON.

123—℞ Infusi quebracho . . . . 3ij-3iij.
    Potassii iodidi . . . . 9ij.
    Tinct. opii camphorati . . . . . . f3ij.—M.
Sig. A tablespoonful every two hours.   KRUTOVSKI.

124—℞ Ext. euphorbiæ piluliferæ fluid.   3j.
Sig. Thirty to sixty drops as required.   PAYNE.

125—℞ Tinct. sanguinariæ,
    Tinct. lobeliæ,
    Ammonii iodidi . . . . āā 3j.
    Syr. tolutani . . . . 3vj.—M.
Sig. A teaspoonful **every two** to four hours. (*In humid
asthma.*)   BARTHOLOW.

126—℞ Potassii iodidi . . . . 3ij.
    Potassii bromidi . . . . 3ss.
    Syrupi papaveris . . . . f3iss.
    Aquæ destillatæ . . . . q. s. ad f3iv.—M.
Sig. A dessertspoonful every half-hour or hour until relieved.
    PENDLETON TUTT.

127—℞ Potassii iodidi . . . . 3ij.
    Extracti belladonnæ fluidi . . . . f3j.
    Extracti lobeliæ fluidi . . . . . . f3ij.
    Extracti grindeliæ fluidi . . . . . f3ss.
    Glycerini,
    Aquæ destillatæ . . . . āā f3iss.—M.
Sig. A tablespoonful **every** two, three, or four hours, as
necessary.   BARTHOLOW.

128—℞ Potassii iodidi . . . . 3ss.
    Tinct. gentian. co. . . . . 3iij.—M.
Sig. One teaspoonful, gradually increased to two teaspoonfuls, three times daily for several months. ALONZO CLARK.

129—℞ Chloral. hydratis . . . . 3vj.
    Syrupi tolutani . . . . f3j.
    Aquæ fœniculi . . . . . . q. s. ad f3ij.—M.
Sig. A teaspoonful every half-hour or **hour, until** relieved.
    S. WEIR MITCHELL.

130—℞ Ammonii bromidi . . . . 3viij.
    Ammonii chloridi . . . . 3iss.
    Tinct. lobeliæ . . . . 3ij.
    Spts. ætheris co. . . . . 3j.
    Syr. acaciæ . . . . ad 3iv.—M.
Sig. A dessertspoonful **in** water every hour or two during
paroxysm.   PEPPER.

131—℞ Amyli nitritis . . . . 3j.
Sig. Inhale three to five drops from a handkerchief. **FRASER.**

132—℞ Pyridin. . . . . 3j.
Sig. Put on a hot plate in a small room, and send patient to
inhale the vapor several times.   GERMAIN SÉE.

133—℞ Potassii iodidi,
    Chloral. hydrat. . . . . āā 3j.
    Syr. aurantii cort. . . . . 3j.
    Aquæ aurantii flor. . . . . ad 3ij.—M.
Sig. A tablespoonful once or twice during the attack.
    LAZARUS.

134—℞ Foliorum belladonnæ,
    Foliorum hyoscyami . . . . āā **gr. iij.**
    Extracti opii aquosi . . . . **gr. ½.**
    Aquæ laurocerasi . . . . **q. s.**
Sig. Moisten the leaves with a solution of the opium extract in
the cherry-laurel water. Let them dry thoroughly and roll
into a cigarette. Two to four of these cigarettes may be
smoked every day.   TROUSSEAU.

135—℞ Potassii iodidi . . . . 3viiss.
    Tinct. lobeliæ . . . . 3viiss.
    Aquæ destillatæ . . . . 3xvss.—M.
Sig. From a teaspoonful to a tablespoonful in a glass of beer
before meals.   DUJARDIN-BEAUMETZ.

BERI-BERI.

136—℞ Pilocarpinæ **mur.** . . . . gr. iij.
  Aquæ font. . . . . ℥iv.—M.
 Sig. Ten to twenty minims hypodermically. **LODEWŸKS.**

BILIOUSNESS.

137—℞ Podophyllin.,
  Pulv. zingiberis . . . . āā gr. xlj.
  Mellis . . . . q. s. ut ft. massa.—M.
 Ft. massa et in pil. no. xxxvi div.   **C. PAUL.**

138—℞ Ammonii chloridi . . . . gr. xxiij.
 Sig. To be taken thrice daily in a glass of fresh milk.
        MURCHISON.

139—℞ Acidi nitromuriat. dil. . . . . f℥j.
 Sig. Ten or fifteen drops, well diluted, before meals.
        BARTHOLOW.

140—℞ Massæ hydrargyri,
  Ext. colocynth. co. . . . . āā ℈ij.
  Ext. hyoscyami . . . . ℈ss.—M.
 Ft. massa et in pil. no. xx div.
 Sig. Two pills at bedtime, followed **by a saline cathartic** be-
  fore breakfast.   **DARRACH.**

141—℞ Resinæ podophylli . . . . gr. ¼
  Resinæ jalapæ,
  Extracti colocynthidis compositi,
  Gambogiæ . . . . āā gr. iiss.
  Olei juniperi . . . . q. s.
 Misce et fiant pilulæ no. ii.
 Sig. One dose, at bedtime.   **GUY.**

142—℞ Pulveris ipecacuanhæ . . . . gr. iij.
  Massæ hydrargyri . . . . gr. viij.
  Extracti colocynthidis compositi . . . . gr. xvj.
 Misce et divide in pilulas no. viii.
 Sig. One pill night and morning. **PENDLETON TUTT.**

143—℞ Fellis bovini purificati . . . . ℥j.
  Manganesii sulphatis exsiccati . . . . . ℈ij.
  Resinæ podophylli . . . . gr. v.
 Misce et fiant pilulæ no. xx.
 Sig. One pill three times a day. (*In catarrhal jaundice.*)
        DA COSTA.

144—℞ Extracti hydrastis **fluidi** . . . . f℥ss.
  Tincturæ rhei . . . . f℥viss.
  Tincturæ cinchonæ compositæ . . . . . f℥iij.—M.
 Sig. A dessertspoonful **two** or three times a day. **NIEMEYER.**

145—℞ Sodii sulphat.,
  Potassii et sodii **tart.** . . . . āā ℥j.
  Infusi cascarillæ . . . . f℥viij.—M.
 Sig. Two tablespoonfuls three **times daily.** **FOTHERGILL.**

BITES OF SNAKES.

146—℞ Potassii permanganat. . . . . ℥j.
  Aquæ. . . . . f℥vi.—M.
 Sig. Apply freely to the wound, **and inject** hypodermically
  above the seat of the wound.   **HAWACK.**

147—℞ Strychninæ . . . . gr. j.
  Glycerini . . . . ℥xx.
  Aquæ. . . . . f℥ss.
 Sig. ℥xx hypodermically every **ten or** twenty minutes till
  slight muscular spasms result.   **MUELLER.**

148—℞ Aquæ ammoniæ . . . . ℥xxx.
  Aquæ. . . . . f℥iss.—M.
 To be injected into the vein with hypodermic syringe.
        HALFORD.

149—℞ Tinct. iodi . . . . f℥j.
 Sig. Apply freely to the wound. **S. WEIR MITCHELL.**

BLADDER, AFFECTIONS OF. (See Catarrh.)

BOILS. (See **Abscess.**)

BRIGHT'S **DISEASE.** (See Albuminuria.)

BROMIDROSIS.

150—℞ Ext. geranii **mac. fld.** . . . . ℨij.
Sig. For external use. PEPPER.

151—℞ Sodii biborat. . . . . ℨj.
Lanolini . . . . ℨx.—M.
Sig. For external use. WULFSBERG.

152—℞ Sodii biborat. . . . . ℨss.
Resorcin. . . . . ℨj.—M.
Sig. Use as a dusting-powder. J. C. WILSON.

153—℞ Tinct. belladonnæ . . . . f℥ss.
Sig. Three drops three times a day in water; gradually increase to six drops. J. C. WILSON.

BRONCHITIS.

154—℞ Terpin. hydrat. . . . . ℨj.
In pil. no. xxx div.
Sig. Two or three pills every three or four hours.
J. C. WILSON.

155—℞ Sol. hydrogen. dioxidi (10 vol.) . . . . . ℨij.
Sig. A teaspoonful in a glassful of water three times daily.
(*In chronic bronchitis with dyspnœa.*) DE BLEYER.

156—℞ Olei picis liquidæ . . . . f℥ij.
Magnesii carbonatis . . . . ℈ij.
Tere simul, et adde gradatim—
Aquæ . . . . f℥xiv.
Cola et adde—
Syrupi simplicis . . . . f℥ij.—M.
Sig. A wineglassful four times a day. B. J. CREW.

157—℞ Potassii cyanidi . . . . gr. j.
Syrupi limonis . . . . f℥ss.
Aquæ destillatæ . . . . f℥iiiss.—M.
Sig. A tablespoonful **every two hours.** (*In spasmodic cough with vomiting.*) DONOVAN.

158—℞ Syrupi lactucarii . . . . f℥ij.
Syrupi acaciæ . . . . f℥iss.
Syrupi aurantii florum . . f℥ss.—M.
Sig. A teaspoonful **every** three hours. (*In senile catarrh.*)
AUBERGIER.

159—℞ Pulveris scillæ,
Extracti conii . . . . āā ℨss.
Ammoniaci . . . . . . ℨj.
Fiat massa et divide in pilulas no. xxx.
Sig. One pill every four hours. PARISET.

160—℞ Pulveris ipecacuanhæ . . . . gr. vj.
Pulveris myrrhæ . . . . gr. xij.
Potassii nitratis . . . . . . ℨss.
Misce et divide in partes vi.
Sig. One every fourth hour. (*For elderly persons.*) PARIS.

161—℞ Tincturæ veratri viridis . . . ℳxv.
Syrupi ipecacuanhæ,
Spiritus ætheris nitrosi . . . . . āā f℥ss.—M.
Sig. Fifteen drops every three hours. (*For a child one to two years old.*) B. F. SCHNECK.

162—℞ Morphinæ acetatis . . . . gr. iij.
Tincturæ sanguinariæ . . . . f℥ij.
Vini antimonii,
Vini ipecacuanhæ . . . . āā f℥ij.
Syrupi pruni virginianæ . . . . f℥ij.—M.
Sig. A teaspoonful. J. C. AYER.

22

163—℞ Pulveris opii,
Pulveris ipecacuanhæ,
Hydrargyri chloridi mitis . . . . . āā gr. iij.
Potassii nitratis . . . . gr. xxx.
Misce et divide in chartulas vi.
Sig. One every three hours, in syrup.   CARSON.

164—℞ Aquæ laurocerasi . . . . f ʒij.
Extracti glycyrrhizæ fluidi . . . . . . f ʒj.
Syrupi althææ . . . . f ʒij.
Decocti althææ . . . . q. s. ad f ʒvj.—M.
Sig. A tablespoonful every two or three hours. LIEBREICH.

165—℞ Acidi hydrocyanici diluti . . . . gtt. j.
Tincturæ lobeliæ . . . . f ʒj.—M.
Sig. One dose. (*Complicated with asthmatic symptoms.*)
    LIVEZEY.

166—℞ Vini ipecac. . . . . f ʒij.
Vini antimonialis . . . . f ʒj.
Vini xerici . . . . f ʒiij.—M.
Sig. Three drops every hour to a child six months old.
(*Where larger tubes only are affected.*) DESSAU.

167—℞ Terebene . . . . f ʒss.
Sig. Two to five drops on sugar every four hours, according
to child's age. (*In chronic form.*) CARMICHAEL.

168—℞ Tinct. aconiti rad. . . . . f ʒss.
Sig. One or two drops every hour. (*In severe cases with fever,
where medium and small tubes are affected.*) DESSAU.

169—℞ Narceinæ . . . . gr. iv-vj.
In pil. no. x div.
Sig. A pill at bedtime. (*For persistent cough and insomnia.*)
    LABORDE.

170—℞ Ergotini . . . . ʒss-j.
Glycerini . . . . f ʒj.
Aquæ . . . . ad f ʒij.—M.
Sig. A teaspoonful at night. (*For violent and persistent cough.*)
    ALLAN.

171—℞ Capsulæ merrhuol. . . . . no. xxiv.
Sig. One capsule after meals and at bedtime. (*In chronic
form of adults.*) LAFARGUE.

172—℞ Vini ipecac. . . . . f ʒj.
Tinct. scillæ . . . . f ʒij.
Syr. tolutan . . . . f ʒv.
Aquæ . . . . f ʒj.—M.
Sig. A teaspoonful every three or four hours. DELAFIELD.

173—℞ Vini ipecac. . . . . f ʒij.
Liq. potass. citratis . . . . f ʒiv.
Tinct. opii camph.,
Syr. acaciæ . . . . āā f ʒj.—M.
Sig. A tablespoonful three times daily. (*In first stage of ordi-
nary acute bronchitis.*) DA COSTA.

174—℞ Acidi salicylici . . . . ʒij.
Ammonii carbonatis . . . . ʒvj.
Syrupi simplicis . . . . f ʒiij.
Aquæ . . . . ad f ʒviij.—M.
Sig. A dessertspoonful every hour or two to an adult.
    FLIESBURG.

175—℞ Liq. ammonii acetat. . . . . f ʒss.
Syr. ipecac. . . . . f ʒj.
Liq. morph. sulph. (U.S.P.) . . . . . . ℳxl.
Syr. acaciæ . . . . f ʒj.
Aquæ . . . . f ʒiss.—M.
Sig. A teaspoonful every two hours for a child two years old.
(*In capillary bronchitis.*) MEIGS AND PEPPER.

176—℞ Ammonii carb. . . . . ℈ij.
Spts. chloroformi . . . . f ʒss.
Inf. senegæ . . . . f ʒviij.—M.
Sig. Two tablespoonfuls every four or six hours. FOTHERGILL.

BRONCHITIS (Continued).

177—℞ Tinct. sanguinariæ............. f3j.
Tinct. lobeliæ .... f3j.
Vini ipecac. .... f3ij.
Syr. tolutan. .... f3ss.—M.
Sig. A teaspoonful **every three hours.** BARTHOLOW.

178—℞ Acidi hydrocyanici dil. .... ℳxvj.
Syr. pruni virginianæ,
Aquæ camphoræ .... āā f3j.—M.
Sig. A teaspoonful **every two or three hours.** (*In violent, troublesome cough.*) HARTSHORNE.

BUBO.

179—℞ Tinct. iodi .... f3j.
Sig. Apply with brush **every other day** till skin becomes tender. VAN BUREN.

180—℞ Iodi,
Terebinthinæ canadensis...... āā 3j.
Collodii .... f3iv.
Solve.
Sig. Apply with camel's-hair pencil **once a** day until rubefaction is produced. J. D. SHINN.

181—℞ Cadmii iodidi .... 3ss.
Ætheris .... ℳxl.
Tere simul, et adde—
Adipis .... 3j.
Misce et fiat unguentum.
Sig. Once or twice daily. A. B. GARROD.

182—℞ Hydrargyri **biniodidi** .... 3ij-iv.
Adipis .... 3ij.
Misce et fiat unguentum.
Sig. Apply twice daily. LUGOL.

183—℞ Unguenti **hydrargyri** .... 3ij.
Ammonii **chloridi** .... 3j.
Misce bene.
Sig. Apply twice daily. DUPUYTREN.

184—℞ Sol. hydrogen. peroxidi (10 vol.) .... f3viij.
Sig. Apply **after suppuration has begun.** RINGER.

BUNIONS.

185—℞ Tinct. iodi,
Tinct. belladonnæ .... āā f3ij.—M.
Sig. Apply twice daily. J. C. WILSON.

186—℞ Acidi tannici,
Cosmolini .... āā 3ss.—M.
Sig. Apply to joint after the skin has been removed by blister. GROSS.

BURNS AND SCALDS.

187—℞ Saloli .... 3ss.
Liq. calcis,
Olei olivæ .... āā f3ij.—M.
Sig. Use locally. NICOT.

188—℞ Acidi tannici .... 3j.
Spts. vini rectif. .... f3j.
Ætheris sulphur. .... f3viiss.—M.
Sig. Apply locally. (*In burns of the first degree.*) NIKOLSKI.

189—℞ Sodii bicarb. .... 3ij.
Aquæ................. Oj.—M.
Sig. Apply **freely on lint or linen.** LEVIS.

190—℞ Ol. lini.
Liq. calcis .... āā f3iv.
Acidi carbolici .... gtt. xxx.—M.
Sig. Apply freely. *Charity Hospital,* N. Y.

191—℞ Cocaini . . . . gr. x-xx.
      Boroglyceridi . . . . ℥ij.—M.
Sig. Apply locally on absorbent cotton.   Eller.

192—℞ Cocaini . . . . gr. v-xx.
      Lanolini . . . . ℥j.—M.
Sig. Apply locally.   -   Wende.

193—℞ Acidi borici . . . . ℥j.
      Aquæ . . . . . q. s. ut fiat solutio ad saturandum.
Sig. A piece of oiled silk dipped in the solution applied over
the burn first; over this a piece of lint, larger in size, steeped
in the boracic solution, the whole retained in position by a
bandage.   Lister.

194—℞ Acidi salicylici . . . . ℥j.
      Olei olivæ . . . . f℥viij.—M.
Sig. Apply to burn, covering with linen or lint. Bartholow.

195—℞ Cerati resinæ . . . . ℥ij.
      Olei terebinthinæ . . . . f℥ij.
Fiat ungentum.
Sig. Apply on linen or lint.   Kentish.

196—℞ Plumbi carbonatis . . . . ℥iv.
      Olei lini . . . . q. s.
Tere simul et fiat pinguentum.
Sig. Apply liberally on linen or lint.   Gross.

—C—

CALCULI, BILIARY.

197—℞ Sodii succinat. . . . . ℥j.
In pilulas (compressas) no. xcvj div.
Sig. One pill three times a day, fifteen minutes before food.
     J. C. Wilson.

198—℞ Sodii phosphatis . . . . ℥ss.
Divide in partes vi.
Sig. One before each meal, continued for several months.
     Bartholow.

199—℞ Olei olivæ optim. . . . . Oj.
Sig. To be taken in divided doses before breakfast.

200—℞ Sodii bicarb. . . . . ℥v.
In chartulas no. xx div.
Sig. One powder three times daily for several months. (Pro-
phylactic.)   Alonzo Clark.

201—℞ Chloroformi . . . . ℥iv.
Sig. To be inhaled, a small quantity at a time, until paroxysm
ceases.   Ringer.

202—℞ Morphinæ sulphat. . . . . gr. vj.
      Atropinæ sulphat. . . . . . . gr. ½.
      Aquæ destillatæ . . . . ℥ss.—M.
Sig. Ten minims to be injected hypodermically during paroxysm, and repeated if necessary.   Bartholow.

203—℞ Olei terebinthinæ,
      Ætheris . . . . āā f℥ss.—M.
Sig. A large teaspoonful on sugar every half-hour until relief is obtained.   Durand.

CALCULI, RENAL AND VESICAL, WITH ACID URINE.

204—℞ Sodii benzoatis,
      Lithii carbonatis,
      Ext. stigmat. maydis . . . . āā ℥j.
      Olei anisi . . . . gtt. iv.—M.
Ft. massa et in pil. no. lxxx div.
Sig. Four pills daily.   Huchard.

205—℞ Magnesii carbonatis . . . . ʒj.
    Sodii biboratis,
    Acidi citrici . . . . āā ʒij.
    Aquæ bullientis . . . . ad f ℥viij.—M.
Sig. A tablespoonful three or four times daily. BARTHOLOW.

206—℞ Magnesii carbonatis . . . . ʒj.
    Infusi gentianæ compositi . . . . . . f℥vj.
Fiat mistura.
Sig. A wineglassful to be taken three times daily. BRANDE.

207—℞ Liquoris potassæ . . . . f℥ij.
    Infusi buchu . . . . f℥viij.—M.
Sig. Three tablespoonfuls an hour after meals. REECE.

208—℞ Liquoris potassæ . . . . f℥ss.
    Tincturæ humuli . . . . f℥iss.
    Infusi calumbæ . . . . f℥iv.
    Syrupi aurantii corticis . . . . f℥ij.
Fiat mistura.
Sig. A tablespoonful three times daily. H. GREEN.

209—℞ Lithii citratis . . . . ʒss.
    Syrupi aurantii corticis . . . . f ʒj.
    Aquæ . . . . ad f ℥ij.—M.
Sig. A teaspoonful in a wineglassful of water three times
daily. GUY.

210—℞ Lithiæ carbonatis . . . . ʒj.
    Aquæ destillatæ . . . . Oj.
Solve.
Sig. To be injected into the bladder. URE.

211—℞ Pulveris uvæ ursi,
    Pulveris cinchonæ flavæ . . . . . . āā ʒij.
    Pulveris opii . . . . gr. iij.
Misce et divide in chartulas vi.
Sig. One powder three or four times a day. FERRIER.

CALCULI, RENAL AND VESICAL, WITH ALKALINE URINE.

212—℞ Acidi phosphorici diluti . . . . f℥ss.
    Tincturæ cardamomi compositæ . . . . f℥ss.
    Infusi calumbæ . . . . f℥vij.
Fiat mistura.
Sig. A tablespoonful in sweetened water every four hours.
NELIGAN.

213—℞ Acidi hydrochlorici diluti . . . . f℥j.
    Decocti hordei . . . . f℥viij.—M.
Sig. A tablespoonful, largely diluted, three times a day.
ELLIS.

214—℞ Acidi nitrici dil.,
    Acidi hydrochlor. dil. . . . . āā ♏xl.
    Infusi serpentariæ . . . . f℥viij.—M.
Sig. A half-wineglassful three times daily. GOLDING-BIRD.

215—℞ Acidi nitrici dil.,
    Acidi hydrochlor. dil. . . . . āā f℥ij.
    Syrupi aurantii corticis,
    Aquæ aurantii flor. . . . . āā f℥j.
    Aquæ destillatæ . . . . f℥xiiss.—M.
Sig. A wineglassful three or four times daily. DRUITT.

216—℞ Strychninæ . . . . gr. j.
    Acidi nitrici dil. . . . . f℥j.
    Aquæ . . . . f℥xij.—M.
Sig. Two tablespoonfuls three times daily. GOLDING-BIRD.

217—℞ Condurango corticis **contusæ** . . . . . . ℨiss.
    Syrupi simplicis . . . . f℥v.
    Aquæ bullientis . . . . ad f℥vj.—M.
Fiat infusio.
Sig. A tablespoonful every hour or two, the whole to be taken
  during the day. To be continued for several months. (*In
  gastric cancer.*)   L. Riess.

218—℞ Bismuthi subnitratis . . . . ℨij.
    Acidi hydrocyanici diluti . . . . . . f℥ss.
    Mucilaginis acaciæ,
    Aquæ menthæ piperitæ . . . . . . āā f℥ij.—M.
Sig. A tablespoonful three times a day in milk. (*In cancer of
  stomach.*)   BARTHOLOW.

219—℞ Bismuthi subnitratis . . . . ℨij.
    Morphinæ sulphatis . . . . gr. j.—M.
In pulveres no. vi div.
Sig. A powder three times daily in **milk when** gastric pain
  and vomiting. (*In gastric cancer.*)   BARTHOLOW.

220—℞ Ext. conii fructus fld. . . . . **f℥ss.**
Sig. Take ten minims every **half-hour** till sleep comes on.
  (*For pain and insomnia.*)   MADIGAN.

221—℞ Liquoris potassii arsenitis   f℥ss.
    Mucilaginis acaciæ .   f℥viiss.
    Aquæ cinnamomi   f℥j.—M.
Sig. A teaspoonful three times a day. (*In gastric and uterine
  cancer.*)   WASHINGTON ATLEE.

222—℞ Antifebrin. . . . . ℨj.
In capsules no. xii div.
Sig. Take a capsule, and repeat in twenty minutes if required.
  (*For lancinating pains and insomnia of cancer.*) DEMIÉVILLE.

223—℞ Zinci chloridi . . . . **ℨij.**
    Pulveris radicis althææ . . . . **ℨvj.**
    Aquæ destillatæ . . . . **q. s.**
Misce et fiat magma.
Sig. Apply to affected part. (*In epithelioma.*)   CANQUOIN.

224—℞ Acidi chromici .   . . . . **ℨij.**
    Aquæ destillatæ   q. s. **ut fiat magma.**
Sig. Apply to affected part as an escharotic.   **BUSCH.**

225—℞ Liquoris ferri subsulphatis   f℥j.
    Aquæ destillatæ . . . . f℥ij.—M.
Sig. **To** inject into the uterus, in hemorrhage from cancer.
                     BARNES.

226—℞ Terebene,
    Ol. olivæ   . . . . āā ℨij.
Sig. Use locally, saturating a piece of cotton and retaining
  with a large, dry tampon, having previously disinfected the
  vagina. (*In cancer of cervix uteri.*)   CORDES.

227—℞ Acidi arseniosi,
    Pulv. acaciæ . . . . āā ℨj.
    Aquæ . . . . f℥v.—M.
Sig. Paint over the tumor night and morning, not more than
  one square inch at a time. Aid sloughs by poulticing. (*For
  epithelioma.*)   MARSDEN.

228—℞ Iodoformi . . . . **gr. xv.**
    Ext. opii . . . . **gr. viij.**
    Essentiæ menthæ (vel bergamottæ) . . **gtt. x.**
    Butyr. cacao . . . . ℨiss.
Ft. supp. no. xli.
Sig. A suppository to be introduced into **the vagina** in cases
  of cancer of the cervix uteri.   SINÉTY.

229—℞ Iodoformi . . . . ℨj.
Sig. Use as a dusting-powder to **the broken surface** and cover
  with lint soaked in glycerin.   RINGER.

CARBUNCLE.

230—℞ Tinct. ferri mur. . . . . f ʒj.
Potassi chloratis . . . . ʒj.
Glycerini . . . . f ʒj.
Aquæ. . . . . ad f ʒiv.—M.

Sig. A teaspoonful in a wineglassful of water every two
hours.   RINGER.

231—℞ Calcii sulphidi . . . . gr. iij.
Ext. glycyrrhizæ . . . . . . q. s. ut ft. massa.—M.

In pil. no. xxx div.
Sig. One pill every hour or two.   RINGER.

232—℞ Quininæ hydrochloratis . . . . gr. xxiv.
Acidi hydrochlorici dil. . . . . ♏xl.
Tincturæ cardamomi . . . . f ʒiss.
Aquæ. . . . . q. s. ad f ʒvj.—M.

Sig. A tablespoonful three times a day after food.
                                   J. C. WILSON.

233—℞ Lini farinæ,
Aquæ bullentis . . . . āā q. s.

Misce et fiat cataplasma.
Sig. Apply as hot as bearable, cover with oil-silk, and renew
every four hours.   ELLIS.

234—℞ Argenti nitratis   ℈iv.
Aquæ destillatæ   f ʒiv.—M.

Sig. To be applied two or three times on the inflamed surface, and beyond it, on the healthy skin. HIGGINBOTTOM.

235—℞ Resorcin. . . . . ℈iss-ʒiss.
Lanolini . . . . ʒj.—M.

Ft. ungt.
Sig. Apply after making multiple parallel incisions into
carbuncle. (*Abortive.*)   L. WEISS.

236—℞ Pulveris opii,
Unguenti hydrargyri,
Saponis duræ. . . . . āā ʒss.—M.

Sig. Apply spread on thick leather.   BUXTON SHILLITOE.

237—℞ Extracti opii . . . . ʒss.
Glycerini . . . . q. s. ut fiat magma.—M.

Sig. Smear thickly over the swelling three or four times a
day; then apply—

238—℞ Tincturæ iodi . . . . f ʒj.

Sig. Apply so as to encircle the carbuncle until it produces
vesication.   FURNEAUX JORDAN.

CARIES.

239—℞ Syrupi phosphatum compositi cum oleo
morrhuæ. . . . . f ʒvj.

Sig. Dose, *pro ré nata.*   PARRISH.

240—℞ Syrupi calcii lactophosphatis (U.S.P.) . f ʒviij.

Sig. A dessertspoonful to a tablespoonful three times daily.
                                   BARTHOLOW.

241—℞ Cupri sulphatis,
Zinci sulphatis . . . . āā partes xv.
Liquoris plumbi subacetatis . . . . . . partes xxx.
Aceti . . . . partes cc.—M.

Sig. Inject thoroughly into sinus.   VILLATE.

CATARRH, BRONCHO-PULMONARY.

242—℞ Tinct. opii . . . . gtt. iij.
Spts. frumenti . . . . f ʒj.
Aquæ bullentis . . . . f ʒiv.
Sacchari albi . . . . q. s.—M.

Sig. Take at bedtime. (*Incipient catarrh.*)   RINGER.

243—℞ Morphinæ sulphatis . . . . gr. ss.
Quininæ sulphatis . . . . gr. xx.
Misce et fiant chartulæ no. ii.
Sig. At bedtime, *in incipient catarrh.*   BARTHOLOW.

244—℞ Morphinæ acetatis . . . . gr. ij.
Acidi acetici diluti . . . . f ʒj.
Syrupi pruni virginianæ,
Syrupi ipecacuanhæ,
Syrupi tolutani . . . . āā f ʒj.—M.
Sig. A teaspoonful every three hours.   ELLIS.

245—℞ Syr. tolutani,
Syr. pruni virgin.,
Tinct. hyoscyami,
Spts. ætheris co.,
Aquæ . . . . āā f ʒj.—M.
Sig. A teaspoonful three times daily. (*Chronic form.*)
                                                  JANEWAY.

246—℞ Ol. santal. . . . . ℳ v.
In capsules.
Sig. One every three hours. (*Chronic offensive bronchorrhœa.*)
                                                  J. C. WILSON.

247—℞ Ammonii carbonatis . . . . gr. xxxij.
Ext. senegæ fld.,
Ext. scillæ fld . . . . āā f ʒj.
Tinct. opii camph. . . . . f ʒvj.
Aquæ . . . . f ʒiv.
Syr. tolutani . . . . q. s. ad f ʒiv.—M.
Sig. A teaspoonful every three or four hours. (*Chronic form.*)
                                                  STOKES.

248—℞ Ammonii chloridi . . . . ʒiij.
Mucil. acaciæ . . . . f ʒiv.—M.
Sig. A tablespoonful four times daily. (*In chronic form.*)
                                                  HARTSHORNE.

249—℞ Tincture eucalypti,
Syrupi simplicis . . . . āā f ʒj.—M.
Sig. A teaspoonful every three hours. (*In the more chronic cases.*)
                                                  GUBLER.

CATARRH OF GALL-DUCTS.

250—℞ Sodii phosphatis . . . . ʒij.
In chartulas no. xvi div.
Sig. A powder every four hours. (**For** children, one-third to one-sixth the quantity.)
                                                  BARTHOLOW.

251—℞ Ammonii iodidi . . . . ʒj.
Liquoris potassii arsenitis . . . . f ʒss.
Tincture calumbæ . . . . f ʒss.
Aquæ destillatæ . . . . f ʒiss.—M.
Sig. A teaspoonful three times **a day,** before meals. (*With jaundice.*)
                                                  BARTHOLOW.

252—℞ Ext. hydrastis fld. . . . . f ʒj.
Sig. Five to fifteen drops before meals daily for some weeks.
                                                  BARTHOLOW.

253—℞ Ammonii chloridi . . . . ʒss.
Ext. taraxaci fld. . . . . f ʒiij.—M.
Sig. A teaspoonful three times daily.   BARTHOLOW.

254—℞ Potassii carbonatis . . . . ʒj.
Vini ipecacuanhæ . . . . f ʒj.
Extracti rhei fluidi . . . . f ʒj.
Aquæ destillatæ . . . . q. s. ad f ʒiij.—M.
Sig. One fluidrachm in boiling water before each meal.
                                                  WAUGH.

255—℞ Hydrargyri chloridi mitis . . . . gr. v.
Sodii bicarbonatis . . . . ʒij.
Misce et fiant chartulæ no. x.
Sig. One powder every three hours.   N. CHAPMAN.

CATARRH OF GALL-DUCTS (Continued).

256—℞ Ammonii chloridi . . . . ℨij.
    Extracti hydrastis fluidi . . . . f ℨss.
    Syrupi sarsaparillæ compositi . . . . . f ℨiss.
    Aquæ destillatæ . . . . f ℨij.—M.
Sig. A dessertspoonful every three hours.   NOTHNAGEL.

CATARRH, GASTRO-INTESTINAL.

257—℞ Liq. potass. arsenitis . . . . f ℨss.
Sig. One or two drops before meals. (*Vomiting of drunkards.*)
    BARTHOLOW.

258—℞ Tinct. capsici . . . . f ℨvj.
    Tinct. nucis vomicæ . . . . f ℨij.—M.
Sig. Twenty drops every four hours.   RINGER.

259—℞ Ext. hydrastis fld. . . . . f ℨss.
Sig. Five to fifteen drops before meals, in water.
    BARTHOLOW.

260—℞ Argenti nitratis . . . . gr. x.
    Ext. hyoscyami . . . . . . : . . . . ℈ii-iv.—M.
In pilulas no. xx div.
Sig. A pill every night for six or eight weeks.   SYMONDS.

261—℞ Liquoris potassii arsenitis . . . . f ℨss.
    Tincturæ nucis vomicæ . . . . f ℨiss.
    Tincturæ calumbæ . . . . f ℨxiv.—M.
Sig. A teaspoonful before each meal. (*With vomiting.*)
    F. G. SMITH.

262—℞ Acidi tannici . . . . ℈ss.
    Aquæ destillatæ . . . . f ℨij.
Fiat mistura.
Sig. A teaspoonful every two hours. (*In acute cases with purging.*)   NIEMEYER.

263—℞ Zinci oxidi . . . . ℨj.
    Sodii bicarbonatis . . . . ℈iiss.
    Piperinæ . . . . ℈j.
Misce et fiant chartulæ xx.
Sig. One powder three or four times a day. (*In drunkards.*)
    REVILLOUT.

264—℞ Caffeinæ citratis . . . . ℈ss.
    Syrupi aurantii florum . . . . f ℨiss.
    Aquæ destillatæ . . . . f ℨiiss.—M.
Sig. A dessertspoonful every two hours. (*With migraine.*)
    AUBERT.

265—℞ Argenti nitratis . . . . gr. xv.
    Aquæ destillatæ . . . . q. s.
    Extracti belladonnæ . . . . gr. x.
    Olei caryophylli . . . . gtt. x.
    Pulveris gentianæ radicis,
    Extracti gentianæ . . . . āā q. s.
Fiat massa in pilulas no. lx dividenda.
Sig. One pill three times a day. (*In chronic cases with jaundice.*)   FRERICHS.

266—℞ Carbonei bisulph. puri   gr. xxv.
    Essentiæ menthæ   gtt. xxx.
    Aquæ .   f ℨxv.—M.
The mixture is placed in a large bottle, shaken, and allowed to settle; eight to twelve tablespoonfuls are to be given daily in half a tumblerful of water and wine, or in milk.
    DUJARDIN-BEAUMETZ.

267—℞ Argenti nitratis . . . . gr. ¼.
    Aquæ destillatæ . . . . f ℨij.
    Gummi acaciæ . . . . ℈ij.
    Sacchari albi . . . . ℈ij.—M.
Sig. A teaspoonful every two hours. (*When evacuations are frequent. For child one year old.*)   HIRSCH.

268—℞ Bismuthi subnitratis . . . . ℈ij.
    Pulv. ipecac. co. . . . . gr. ix.—M.
In chartulas no. xii div.
Sig. One every three hours. (*For child one year old.*)
    J. LEWIS SMITH.

269 — ℞ Tinct. opii deodorat. . . . . gtt. xvj.
   Bismuth. subnitrat. . . . . ℨij.
   Syr. simplicis . . . . f℥iv.
   Aquæ cinnamomi . . . . f℥iss.—M.
 Sig. Shake bottle. Give one teaspoonful **every two to four**
  hours. (*For child one year old.*)   **J. Lewis Smith.**

270 — ℞ Hydrarg. chlorid. mit.   gr. iii-iv.
   Magnes. calc.   gr. xxxvj.
   Pulv. ipecac. . .   gr. ß-iij.
   Ext. hyoscyami.   gr. iv-vj.—M.
 Ft. chart. no. xii.
 Sig. One every three hours. (*In chronic forms in children.*)
                 Condie.

CATARRH, GENITO-URINARY.

271 — ℞ Fol. hyoscyami . . . . ℨss.
   Aquæ bullientis . . . . Oj.—M.
 Ft. infusio.
 Sig. A tablespoonful every half-hour for one forenoon, unless
  throat becomes dry or patient drowsy.   Diday.

272 — ℞ Ext. tritici fld.,
   Syr. amygdalæ   . . . . āā f℥ij.—M.
 Sig. A dessertspoonful in water, **five or six** times daily. (*In*
  chronic cystitis.)   Thompson.

273 — ℞ Atropinæ sulph. . . . . gr. j.
   Acidi acetici . . . . gtt. xx.
   Alcoholis,
   Aquæ . . . . āā f℥ss.—M.
 Sig. Four drops in a wineglassful of water before each meal.
  (*In acute cystitis.*)   Goodell.

274 — ℞ Copaibæ,
   Spts. lavand. co. . . . . āā f℥ij.
   Mucil. acaciæ. . . . . f℥ss.
   Syrupi simp. . . . . f℥ij.
   Aquæ . . . . f℥iv.—M.
 Sig. A tablespoonful **twice daily.**   Wood.

275 — ℞ Infusi buchu . . . . f℥vij.
   Potassii bicarb. . . . . ℨj.
   Tinct. hyoscyami. . . . . f℥iss.
   Ext. sarsæ fld. . . . . f℥iv.—M.
 Sig. Two tablespoonfuls three times daily. (*In irritable blad-*
  der, with acid urine.)   Coulson.

276 — ℞ Cubebæ . . . . ℨj.
   Sodii bicarbonatis,
   Potassii bitartratis . . . . āā ℨij.
 Misce et divide in partes æquales xii.
 Sig. One powder three times a day.   Druitt.

277 — ℞ Chimaphilæ . . . . ℨij.
   Aquæ bullientis . . . . Oj.
 Coque . . . . ad f℥vj.
 Cola et adde—
   Spiritus juniperi compositi . . . . . f℥ij.—M.
 Sig. A tablespoonful every two or three hours, with demul-
  cent drinks.   Proctor.

278 — ℞ Potassii citrat. . . . . ℨss.
   Spts. chloroformi . . . . f℥iss.
   Tinct. digitalis . . . . ℳ lxxx.
   Infusi buchu . . . . f℥viij.—M.
 Sig. Two tablespoonfuls three or four **times daily.**
                Fothergill.

279 — ℞ Pulveris uvæ ursi . . . . ℨiss.
   Sodii bicarbonatis . . . . ℨj.
 Misce et divide in chartulas xii.
 Sig. One powder three times a day, in sugar and water.
                 Ellis.

280—℞ Resinæ copalbœ . . . . ℨij.
 Alcoholis . . . . f℥v.
 Spiritus chloroformi . . . . fℨj.
 Mucilaginis acaciæ . . . . fℨij.
 Aquæ destillatæ . . . . q. s. ad f℥xij.—M.
 Sig. A tablespoonful three times a day.   WILKES.

281—℞ Extracti grindeliæ fluidi . . . . fℨj.
 Elixiris simplicis,
 Spiritus juniperi compositi . . . . . āā fℨiss.—M.
 Sig. A dessertspoonful every four hours.   C. J. RADEMAKER.

282—℞ Fol. uvæ ursi . . . . ℨj.
 Aquæ fervid. . . . . f℥xviij.—M.
 Sig. Macerate for two hours and boil down to one pint and
 strain. A wineglassful every two to four hours.   BRODIE.

283—℞ Extracti pareiræ fluidi . . . . f℥iij.
 Extracti buchu fluidi . . . . fℨiss.
 Decocti scoparii . . . . f℥viiss.—M.
 Sig. A tablespoonful three times a day.   CARSON.

284—℞ Olei terebinthinæ. . . . . f℥iss.
 Syrupi simplicis . . . . fℨj.
 Aquæ cinnamomi . . . . fℨij.
 Olei limonis . . . . ℳviij.—M.
 Sig. A teaspoonful every three hours.   MAUNSELL.

285—℞ Argenti nitratis . . . . gr. vij.
 Aquæ destillatæ. . . . . f℥iiiss.—M.
 Sig. Inject into the bladder, every third or fourth day, after
 washing it out with warm water.   RICORD.

286—℞ Iodoformi . . . . gr. xij.
 Ext. hyoscyami . . . . gr. vij.
 Olei theobromæ . . . . ℨvj.—M.
 In suppositoria no. viij div.
 Sig. Introduce one into the rectum twice daily, **one hour**
 after giving the patient a lukewarm-water enema.
    RELIQUET.

CATARRH, NASAL AND FAUCIAL.

287—℞ Iodoformi pulv.,
 Pulveris acaciæ . . . . āā gr. xxx.
 Cocaïnæ hydrochloratis . . . . gr. j.
 Sig. Use as a snuff.   GARAGEORGIADES.

288—℞ Resorcin. . . . . . gr. v-x.
 Aquæ destillatæ . . . . fℨij.—M.
 Sig. Use with atomizer twice daily, four minutes each time.
    MASINI AND MASSEI.

289—℞ Acidi boracici gr. lx.
 Glycerini . . . . ℳxx.
 Aquæ . f℥vj.—M.
 Dissolve with heat and saturate cotton-wool, a thin sheet
 (ℨj), with the solution, and dry. Pack the upper part of
 nose with the prepared cotton, leaving a space below for
 breathing. (*Rhinitis.*)   WOAKES.

290—℞ Acidi carbolici liq. . . . . ℳxxx.
 Sodii biborat.,
 Sodii bicarb. . . . . āā ℨj.
 Glycerini . . . . f℥iiss.
 Aquæ . . . . q. s. ad f℥iv.—M.
 Sig. To be used with atomizer. (*Simple chronic rhinitis.*)
    DOBELL.

291—℞ Chloroformi . . . . fℨij.
 Glycerini,
 Spts. vini gallici . . . . āā fℨj.—M.
 Sig. One teaspoonful in water every three hours. (*For acute
 coryza.*)   SAJOUS.

292—℞ Sodii salicylat. . . . . ℥ij.
　　Sodii biborat. . . . . ℥iij.
　　Glycerini . . . . f℥iv.
　　Aquæ. . . . . q. s. ad f℥vj.—M.
　Sig. A dessertspoonful in a pint of water, used with spray or
　　douche. 　　　　　　　　　　　　　　BEAN.

293—℞ Sodii bicarbonatis . . . . ℥j.
　Sig. Insufflate or apply with finger to the inflamed tonsil.
　　(Tonsillitis.) 　　　　　　　　　　　　GINÉ.

294—℞ Cocainæ muriatis . . . . gr. vj.
　　Bismuthi subcarb. . . . . ℥ss.
　　Talci . . . . ℥iss.—M.
　Sig. Enough to cover a silver five-cent piece insufflated into
　　each nostril every two hours. (For acute coryza.) SAJOUS.

295—℞ Tinct. aconiti radicis . . . . f℥j.
　　Tinct. belladonnæ . . . . f℥ij.—M.
　Sig. Three drops every hour. (Pharyngitis and acute tonsillitis.)
　　　　　　　　　　　　　　　　　　RINGER.

296—℞ Cocainæ hydrochloratis . 　　　　　partes ij.
　　Pulveris sacchari albi 　.　　　　　partes c.—M.
　Sig. Use as a snuff. 　　　　　　　　　WYETH.

297—℞ Pulveris cubebæ . . . . partem j.
　　Pulveris sacchari albi . . . . partes ij.—M.
　Sig. Use by insufflation. 　　　　　　J. C. WILSON.

298—℞ Tincturæ aconiti radicis 　. . . . . f℥j.
　　Tincturæ opii deodoratæ 　. . . f℥vj.—M.
　Sig. Eight drops in water every hour or two. BARTHOLOW.

CHANCRE.

299—℞ Iodoformi,
　　Lycopodii . . . . āā ℥ij.—M.
　Sig. Dust on and cover with dry lint. 　STURGIS.

300—℞ Iodoformi . . . . ℥ij.
　　Unguenti petrolei . . . . ℥j.
　　Olei cinnamomi . . . . gtt. v.
　Misce et fiat unguentum.
　Sig. Apply twice daily. 　　　　　　IZARD.

301—℞ Hydrargyri biniodidi . . . . ℈j.
　　Adipis . . . . ℥ss.—M.
　Sig. Apply on lint. (For inveterate chancres and indolent vene-
　　real ulcers.) 　　　　　　　　　　RATIER.

302—℞ Hydrarg. chlorid. mit. . . . . gr. xv.
　　Liq. calcis . . . . f℥ij.—M.
　Sig. Shake and apply as a wash. 　　BARTHOLOW.

303—℞ Hydrarg. chlorid. mit. . . . . ℥ss.
　Sig. Dust on and cover with dry lint.
　　　　　　　　　　　　VAN BUREN AND KEYES.

304—℞ Hydrarg. chlorid. corros. . . . . gr. j.
　　Liq. calcis . . . . f℥viij.—M.
　Sig. Shake and apply on lint. 　　JAS. L. LITTLE

305—℞ Cupri subacetatis,
　　Hydrargyri chloridi mitis . . . . . āā ℈j.
　Fiat pulvis subtilissimus.
　Sig. Dust over the sore. 　　　　　ELLIS.

306—℞ Hydrogen. peroxidi . . . . partem j.
　　Aquæ destillatæ . . . . part. ij.—M.
　Sig. Wash three times a day, and keep covered with lint
　　moistened with it. (Also for open buboes.) RINGER.

307—℞ Aristol. . . 　　　　　　　　　℥ss.
　Sig. Use as a dusting-powder. 　　J. C. WILSON.

CHANCROID.

308—℞ Acidi nitrici . . . . f3ss.

Sig. After cleaning the surface, apply with a match or glass rod, exposing the surface until nearly dry or painless; then dry the surface and reapply acid in same way. Dry-lint dressing. VAN BUREN AND KEYES.

309—℞ Acidi sulphurici,
Pulv. carbonis ligni . . . . . . āā q. s. ut ft. magma.

Sig. Dry the sore and apply evenly with wooden spatula.
RICORD.

310—℞ Pulv. acidi salicylici . . . . ʒij.

Sig. Dust on sore and cover with dry dressing. ANGLADA.

311—℞ Iodoformi . . . . ʒij.

Sig. Dust on sore and cover with lint dipped in glycerin.
RINGER.

312—℞ Hydrarg. chlorid. mit. . . . . ʒiij.

Sig. Use as a dusting-powder. J. C. WILSON.

313—℞ Bismuthi subiodidi . . . . ʒiv.

Sig. Dust on sore and use dry dressings. CHASSAIGNAC.

314—℞ Succi limonis . . . . ʒiss.
Vini opii . . . . ♏xlv.
Liq. plumbi subacet. . . . . ʒj.
Aquæ destillatæ . . . . ʒv.—M.

Ft. lotio.
Sig. Soak pledgets of lint in the solution and apply locally.
(In phagedæna.) RODET.

CHILBLAINS.

315—℞ Collod. flexil. . . . . ʒiv.
Olei ricini . . . . ʒiv.
Spts. tereb. . . . . ʒiv.—M.

Use two or three times daily. British Med. Journal.

316—℞ Lin. belladonnæ . . . . ʒij.
Lin. aconiti . . . . ʒj.
Acidi carbolici . . . . ♏vj.
Collod. flexil. . . . . ad ʒj.—M.

Sig. Apply every night with a camel's-hair pencil.
British Med. Journal.

317—℞ Bismuthi salicylat. ʒij.
Pulv. amyli . . . ʒxviij.—M.

Sig. First bathe the chilblains in a decoction of walnut-leaves, then rub with spirits of camphor and cover with the powder. To quiet the itching use the following:

318—℞ Glycerini,
Aquæ rosæ . . . . āā fʒj.
Acidi tannici . . . . gr. j.—M.

Sig. Use as a lotion, and then dust on the above powder.
E. BESNIER.

319—℞ Acidi carbolici . . . . gr. x.
Cosmolini,
Olei terebinthinæ . . . . āā ʒj.—M.

Sig. Apply to affected part. DAVIDSON.

320—℞ Camphoræ . . . . gr. lxxv.
Spts. vini rectif. . . . . fʒiij.
Glycerini . . . . fʒv.—M.

Ft. linimentum.
Use locally several times daily. FOY.

321—℞ Linimenti chloroformi fʒij.

Sig. Apply to part with gentle friction. (Early stage.)
DAVIDSON.

322—℞ Tinct. iodi . . . . fʒj.

Apply to parts with brush. DAVIDSON.

34

323—℞ Creolin................... ℳ xl.
    Aquæ................. f ℥viij.—M.
Sig. A dessertspoonful at **short intervals.**   GRONEMAN.

324—℞ Emplastri cantharidis   .. 2 in. × 4 in.
Sig. Apply from back of right ear downwards and forwards.
    HEGKIN.

325—℞ Magnesia sulphate........... ℨij.
    Sulphurous acid,
    Water .... of each ℥xvj.
    Tinct. capsicum........... ℨiv.—M.
Dissolve perfectly.
Sig. Teaspoonful night and morning. (*Prophylactic.*) **BEVAN.**

326—℞ Sulphurous acid,
    Water .... of each ℥xvj.
    Tinct. capsicum.......... ℨiv.
    Morphine sulphate........ gr. ij.—M.
Dissolve perfectly.
Sig. Teaspoonful every half-hour until relieved. (*Therapeutic.*)
    BEVAN.

327—℞ Tinct. opii,
    Tinct. capsici,
    Tinct. rhei arom.,
    Spts. menthæ pip.,
    Spts. camphoræ   .. .. āā p. æq.—M.
Sig. Twenty to forty minims, diluted.   RUSCHENBERGER.

328—℞ Tinct. opii,
    Tinct. capsici,
    Spts. camphoræ .... āā f ℨj.
    Chloroformi .... f ℨij.
    Alcoholis .... q. s. ad f ℥v.—M.
Sig. Twenty to forty minims, diluted.   **SQUIBB.**

329—℞ Tincturæ opii deodoratæ........ f ℨj.
    Acidi sulphurici aromatici........ f ℨij.—M.
Sig. Twenty drops every hour or two in ice-water.
    BARTHOLOW.

330—℞ Acidi nitrosi............... f ℨj.
    Tincturæ opii............ gtt. xl.
    Aquæ camphoræ.......... f ℥viij.—M.
Sig. One-fourth to be taken every three **or four hours. HOPE.**

331—℞ Strychninæ sulphatis.   gr. ¼.
    Acidi sulphurici diluti   f ℨss.
    Morphinæ sulphatis   gr. ij.
    Aquæ camphoræ   .... f ℨiiss.—M.
Sig. A teaspoonful every hour or two, well diluted. (*In threat-ened collapse. Also as a prophylactic, given less frequently.*)
    BARTHOLOW

332—℞ Acidi sulphurici .... ℨss.
    Morphinæ sulphatis .... gr. ⅛.
    Spiritus vini gallici .... f ℥iss.
    Aquæ destillatæ .... f ℥iij.—M.
Sig. Inject under the skin of the arms, legs, and over the stomach every hour until the symptoms are relieved. (*When rice-water discharges, vomiting, cramps, and shrinkage of the extremities supervene.*)   R. W. MITCHELL.

333—℞ Acidi sulphurici dilati .... f ℨj.
Sig. Fifteen to thirty drops in ice-water every fifteen to thirty minutes until vomiting and purging are arrested. (*This and ferri sulph. are prophylactic.*)   S. T. CHANDLER.

334—℞ Acidi phosphorici diluti .... f ℨj.
Sig. A half-fluidrachm in ice-water. (*In cholerine and early stage of confirmed cholera.*)   WILLIAM SEDGWICK.

335—℞ Tincturæ opii   . ℳ x–xv.
    Chloroformi   ℳ xv–xx.
    Spiritus vini.   f ℨj.
    Aquæ destillatæ   . f ℨj.
Misce et fiat haustus.   T. M. LOWNDES.

336—℞ Creasoti . . . . . . gt. j.
  Aquæ camphoræ,
  Iufusi gentianæ compositi . . . . . āā f℥vj.—M.
Sig. One dose every two hours.   J. T. JONES.

337—℞ Chloroformi . . . . ℳ vj.
  Aquæ destillatæ . . . . f℥j.—M.
Fiat haustus.
Sig. To be given after five grains of calomel **and** two grains
of opium, and to be repeated if necessary.   OATES.

338—℞ Morphinæ sulph. .   gr. ij.
  Spts. camphoræ   f℥j.—M.
Sig. Fifteen minims every three or four hours by mouth, or
hypodermically, in severe cases. *(In initial stage.)* Also—

339—℞ Morphinæ sulph. . . . . gr. x.
  Atropinæ sulph. . . . . gr. j.
  Aquæ destillatæ . . . . f℥x.—M.
Sig. Five to ten minims hypodermically, as required. *(In
stage of collapse.)*   NAKAMURA.

340—℞ Plumbi acetatis . . . . gr. xij.
  Liquoris morphinæ acetatis . . . . . . ℳ xij.
  Acidi acetici diluti . . . . f℥j.
  Aquæ destillatæ . . . . f℥ij.—M.
Sig. A teaspoonful every five, six, or eight hours **to a child**
one year old. *(Choleraic diarrhœa.)*   FLEMING.

CHOLERA INFANTUM.

341—℞ Argenti nitratis . . . . gr. j.
  Acidi nitrici diluti . . . . ℳ viij.
  Tincturæ opii deodoratæ . . . . . . ℳ viij.
  Mucilaginis acaciæ . . . . f℥ss.
  Syrupi simplicis . . . . f℥ss.
  Aquæ cinnamomi . . . . f℥j.—M.
Sig. A teaspoonful every three, four, or six hours. *(For a*
child one year old.)   BARTHOLOW.

341bis—℞ Creasoti . . . . ctt. viij.
  Aquæ chloroformi . . . . f℥ij.—M.
Sig. A teaspoonful every hour or two.   BUTTERFIELD.

342—℞ Potassii bromidi . . . . ℨij.
  Syrupi simplicis . . . . f℥ss.
  Aquæ menthæ piperitæ . . . . . . f℥iss.—M.
Sig. A teaspoonful every hour or two. *(With irritable nervous*
system.)   BARTHOLOW.

343—℞ Hydrarg. cum cretâ . . . . gr. j.
  Sacchari lactis . . . . gr. x.—M.
In pulv. no. xii div.
Sig. A powder every hour.   RINGER.

344—℞ Hydrarg. chlorid. mit. . . . . gr. j.
  Sodii bicarb. . . . . ℨj.
  Pulv. zingiberis . . . . gr. xij.—M.
In pulv. no. xii div.
Sig. One powder three **or four times daily.** *(In incipient*
stage.)   HARTSHORNE.

345—℞ Hydrarg. chlorid. mit. . . . . gr. j.
  Cretæ præp. . . . . gr. xxxvj.
  Plumbi acetat. . . . . gr. xij.
  Pulv. ipecac. . . . . gr. iij.—M.
In chart. no. xii div.
Sig. One every three hours.   CONDIE.

346—℞ Hydrargyri cum cretâ . . . . gr. ij.
  Bismuthi subnitratis . . . . gr. xxiv.
  Pulveris nucis myristicæ . . . . . . gr. ij.
Misce et divide in chartulas xii.
Sig. One powder every two hours.   R. A. F. PENROSE.

347—℞ Cupri sulphatis . . . . gr. ss.
Tincturæ opii deodoratæ . . . . gtt. iv.
Syrupi simplicis,
Aquæ fœniculi . . . . '. . āā f℥j.—M.

Sig. A teaspoonful every two, three, or four hours. (*For a child from one to two years old.*) TARDIEU.

348—℞ Plumbi acetatis . . . . gr. ij.
Acidi acetici diluti . . . . gtt. vj.
Tincturæ opii deodoratæ . . . . gtt. iv.
Syrupi simplicis,
Aquæ menthæ piperitæ . . . āā f℥ss.—M.

Sig. A teaspoonful every two or three hours. (*For a child two years old.*) DA COSTA.

349—℞ Acidi carbolici . . . . gr. ij.
Bismuthi subnitratis . . . . ℥j.
Syrupi acaciæ . . . . f℥ss.
Aquæ menthæ piperitæ . . . . f℥iss.—M.

Sig. A half-teaspoonful every two to **four hours**. (*For a child one to two years old.*) ROTTH.

350—℞ Hydrargyri chloridi mitis,
Plumbi acetatis . . . . āā gr. j.

Misce et fiant pulveres no. iv.
Sig. One powder every three hours. (*For a child from ten to twenty months old.*) T. D. MITCHELL.

351—℞ Ol. ricini . . . . f℥ij.
Pulv. acaciæ,
Sacch. albi . . . . āā ℥ij.
Tinct. opii . . . . ℔xxj.
Aq. cinnam. . . . . q. s. ad f℥iv.—M.

Sig. A teaspoonful every two or three hours. WEST.

352—℞ Tinct. opii deodoratæ . . . gtt. xvj.
Spts. ammon. aromat. . . . . f℥j.
Bismuthi subnitratis . . ℥j.
Syrupi simplicis . . . . f℥iv.
Mist. cretæ . . f℥iss.—M.

Sig. Shake well and give a teaspoonful every two or three hours to a child eight to twelve months old. (*Six months old, half the dose.*) J. LEWIS SMITH.

353—℞ Tinct. coccæ (1-8) . . . . f℥j.
Sig. **Four to six drops every two hours at three months of age. Fifteen to twenty drops in older children.**
DIEDERICHS.

354—℞ Resorcin . . . . gr. viij-xl.
Syr. aurantii cort. . . . . f℥j.
Aquæ aurantii flor. . . . . ad f℥ij.—M.

Sig. A teaspoonful every **two hours**. FLIESBURG.

355—℞ Naphthalini . . . . gr. xx-lxx.
Ol. bergamii . . . . gtt. j-ij.—M.

In pulv. no. xij div.
Sig. A powder every **two or three hours**. HOLT.

356—℞ Saloli . . . . gr. vj.
Sacchari lactis . . . . gr. x.—M.

In pulv. no. xij div.
Sig. A powder every two hours. (*For a child aged six months. Between five and ten years old, three grains of salol may be taken every two hours.*) GOELET.

356bis—℞ Pulv. opii . . . . gr. ss.
Bismuthi subnitratis . . . . gr. ix.
Iodoformi . . . . gr. iv.—M.

In chartulas no. xvi div.
Sig. One powder every two or three hours. SANDERS.

CHORDEE.

357—℞ Plumbi bromidi,
Lupulinæ,
Ext. belladonnæ . . . . āā gr. xv.—M.

Ft. massa et in pil. no. xxx div.
Sig. Two or three pills daily. VAN DEN CORPUT.

CHORDEE (Continued).

358—℞ Camphoræ,
    Ext. lactucarii . . . . āā 3j.
Misce et fiant pilulæ **no.** xxx.
Sig. One, two, or three pills at **bedtime.**   RICORD.

359—℞ Cannabis indicæ . . . . **gr. j.**
    Pulveres opii . . . . **gr. ss.**
    Camphoræ . . . . **gr. ij.**
Misce et fiat pilula.
Sig. At bedtime.   LOMBE ATTHILL.

360—℞ Ext. opii aquosi . . . . gr. ij.
    Pulv. camphoræ . . . . gr. iv.—M.
In pil. no. ij div.
Sig. One or both on retiring.   VAN BUREN AND KEYES.

361—℞ Liq. morph. sulph. (Magendii) . . . . f3iv.
    Atropinæ sulph. . . . . gr. j.
    Acidi acetici . . . . q. s.
    Aquæ destillatæ . . . . ad f3j.—M.
Sig. Five to eight minims at bedtime, hypodermically.
     STURGIS.

362—℞ Tincturæ cantharidis . . . . gtt. viij.
    Syrupi simplicis,
    Aquæ destillatæ . . . . āā f3ss.—M.
Sig. A **teaspoonful** three times a day, as a preventive.
     RINGER.

363—℞ Ext. opii . . . . **gr. iss.**
    Ol. theobromæ . . . . **gr. xxx.—M.**
Ft. suppositor. no. j.
Sig. Introduce into rectum on going to bed.
     VAN BUREN AND KEYES.

364—℞ Vini colchici seminis,
    Syrupi simplicis   . . . . . . āā f3ss.—M.
Sig. A teaspoonful at bedtime.   BRODIE.

CHOREA.

365—℞ Chloralamid . . . . **3ss.**
In chartulas no. xij div.
Sig. One powder twice a day.   J. C. WILSON.

366—℞ Chloral. hydratis   3iij.
    Syr. aurantii cort.   f3iij.—M.
Sig. A teaspoonful three times daily for one or two months.
    (*Child ten years old.*)   JOFFROY.

367—℞ Succi conii . . . . f3ij.
Sig. One teaspoonful, increased gradually to two or three,
    once daily before dinner.   J. HARLEY.

368—℞ Succi conii . . . . **f3vj.**
    Syrupi simplicis,
    Aquæ destillatæ   . . . . āā f3ix.—M.
Sig. A dessertspoonful three times a day.   JAMES ANDREW.

369—℞ Morphinæ sulphatis . . . . gr. j.
    Aquæ destillatæ . . . . f3j.
Solve.
Sig. A **teaspoonful or more,** *pro re nata.*   TROUSSEAU.

370—℞ Ext. cimicifugæ fld. .   . . . f3ij.
Sig. A half-teaspoonful, increased to one teaspoonful, three
    times daily. (*Six to ten years old.*)   JESSE YOUNG.

371—℞ **Extracti cimicifugæ fluidi,**
    Elixiris simplicis . . . . āā f3iss.—M.
Sig. A dessertspoonful four times a day.   BARTHOLOW.

372—℞ Lobeliæ hydrobrom. . . . . gr. j.
    Aquæ . . . . f3v.—M.
Sig. Three to fifteen minims hypodermically.   BARTHOLOW.

373—℞ Zinci valerianat.,
    Ext. hyoscyami,
    Bismuthi subnitrat. . . . . āā gr. xv.—M.
In pil. no. xxx div.
Sig. Three to six pills **daily**.   DESCROIZILLES.

374—℞ Ferri citratis . . . . ℨij.
    Syr. simplicis. . . . . f ℥iv.
    Aq. aurantii flor. . . . . f ℥iss.—M.
Sig. A teaspoonful before or after meals. (*In anæmic cases.*)
                    HARTSHORNE.

375—℞ Zinci sulphatis . . . . gr. ij.
    Extracti conii . . . . gr. iij.
Misce et fiat pilula.
Sig. To be taken every night.   JAMES ANDREW.

376—℞ Zinci valerianatis. . . . . gr. viij.
    Tincturæ valerianæ,
    Tincturæ calumbæ . . . . āā f ℨij.
    Aquæ aurantii florum . . . . f ℨij.—M.
Sig. A tablespoonful every six hours.   NELIGAN.

377—℞ Liq. potassii arsenitis . . . . f ℨss.
Sig. One to three minims hypodermically.   FRÜHWALD.

378—℞ Liquoris potassii arsenitis   f ℨij. (!)
    Syrupi simplicis   f ℨvj.
    Aquæ destillatæ   f ℨij.—M.
Sig. A dessertspoonful immediately after meals. (*For a child
five to twelve years of age.*)   EUSTACE SMITH.

379—℞ Eserinæ sulphatis   gr. j.
    Aquæ destillatæ . .   f ℨvj.—M.
Sig. Six minims hypodermically twice daily; with tonics.
                    RIESS.

380—℞ Strychninæ sulphatis   gr. j.
    Syr. simplicis   f ℨiiss.—M.
Sig. Fifty minims three times daily, increased to seventy-five
minims, or until itching of the scalp and muscular stiffness
are observed.   TROUSSEAU.

COLIC.

381—℞ Tinct. opii deodoratæ .   gtt. xij.
    Magnesii calcinat.   gr. xij-xxiv.
    Sacchari albi . . . .   ℨj.
    Aquæ anisi . . . .   f ℨiss.—M.
Sig. Shake **well**. One teaspoonful to a child one year old.
                    J. L. SMITH.

382—℞ Tincturæ asafœtidæ . . . . f ℨss.
    Tincturæ opii . . . . f ℨj.
    Decocti hordei . . . . Oss.
Misce et fiat enema.
Sig. One injection. (**For adults with flatulence.**)   HOOPER.

383—℞ Morphinæ sulphatis   gr. ij.
    Aquæ destillatæ   f ℨj.—M.
Sig. Five to ten minims hypodermically, repeated in fifteen
minutes.   RINGER.

384—℞ Spiritus chloroformi   f ℨvj.
    Aquæ camphoræ   q. s ad f ℨiv.—M.
Sig. A tablespoonful every hour or two.   **G. P. OLIVER.**

385—℞ Spts. chloroformi,
    Tinct. cardamomi co. . . . . . āā f ℨij.—M.
Sig. A teaspoonful every half-hour till relieved. BARTHOLOW.

386—℞ Tinct. stramonii   f ℨj.
    Tinct. hydrastis can.   f ℨj.
    Aquæ laurocerasi .   f ℨv.—M.
Sig. A teaspoonful in water every four hours for an adult.
                    DE MUSSY.

COLIC (Continued).

387—℞ Tinct. valerianæ . . . . f℥iss.
    Spts. ætheris sulph. (Ph. B.) . . . . . f℥j.
    Aquæ menthæ pip. . . . . f℥vss.
    Syr. aurantii flor. . . . . f℥iss.—M.
Ft. haustum.
Sig. For an adult.

388—℞ Aquæ camphoræ . . . . f℥j.
    Spiritus ætheris compositi . . . . . . f℥j.
    Tincturæ cardamomi compositæ. . . . f℥ss.
    Spiritus anisi . . . . f℥vj.
    Olei carui . . . . ℳxij.
    Syrupi zingiberis . . . . f℥ij.
    Aquæ menthæ piperitæ . . . . f℥vss.
Fiat mistura.
Sig. Two tablespoonfuls.   Joy.

389—℞ Asafœtidæ . . . . gr. vj-viij.
    Olei amygdalæ dulcis . . . . ℳiv.
  Tere simul, et adde—
    Pulveris acaciæ . . . . ℈ss.
    Infusi anthemidis . . . . f℥j.
Misce et fiat enema.
Sig. Inject as directed. (*In children with flatulent colic.*) Ure.

390—℞ Naphthalini . . . . gr. viiss.
    Iodoformi . . . . gr. iij.
    Acidi tannici,
    Antipyrin.   . . . . . āā gr. xv.—M.
Ft. massa et in pil. no. x div.
Sig. Three or four pills in succession until relieved. (*In violent colic.*)   Capitan.

391—℞ Atropinæ sulphatis . . . . gr. j.
    Zinci sulphatis . . . . gr. xxx.
    Aquæ destillatæ . . . . f℥j.—M.
Sig. Three to five drops two or three times daily. Bartholow.

392—℞ Magnesii carb. . . . . gr. xlv.
    Sacch. albi . . . . ℈iss.
    Tinct. asafœtidæ . . . . f℥iss.
    Tinct. opii . . . . f℈ss.
    Aquæ . . . . f℥iss.—M.
Sig. **Five to sixty drops, according to age.** (*In infantile colic.*)
                        Dewees.

393—℞ Spiritus ætheris compositi . . f℥j.
    Tincturæ cardamomi compositæ . f℥ij.
    Aquæ camphoræ . . . . f℥j.
Misce et fiat haustus.
Sig. At once, and repeat if necessary.   Neligan.

394—℞ Syr. rhei aromat.,
    Tinct. cardamomi co.,
    Tinct. opii camph.,
    Aquæ cinnamomi . . . . āā f℥j.—M.
Sig. Two to four teaspoonfuls.   Hartshorne.

COLICA PICTONUM.

395—℞ Olei tiglii . . . . gtt. vj.
    Micæ panis . . . . q. s. ut ft. massa.—M.
In pil. no. xii div.
Sig. A pill every three or **four hours until** free evacuations are produced.   Waring.

396—℞ Pulv. opii . . . . gr. xij.
    Ext. belladonnæ . . . . gr. ij.
    Olei tiglii . . . . gtt. xij.—M.
Ft. massa et in pil. no. xii div.
Sig. A pill every two hours until relieved.   Loomis.

397—℞ Magnesii sulphatis . . . . ℥j.
    Acidi sulphurici dil. . . . . f℥j.
    Aquæ . . . . f℥iv.—M.
Sig. A tablespoonful three times **daily, preceded by five to** ten grains of potassium iodide.   Brunton.

398—℞ Morphinæ sulphatis   gr. iv.
     Aquæ destillatæ   f3ij.—M.

Sig. Five to ten minims hypodermically, repeated every
    fifteen minutes till relieved.   BARTHOLOW.

399—℞ Aluminis . . . . 3ij.
     Magnesii sulphatis . . . . 3j.
     Syrupi simplicis . . . . f3ij.
     Aquæ rosarum . . . . f3v.—M.

Sig. Two tablespoonfuls in two wineglassfuls of water daily,
    early in the morning.   ALDRIDGE.

400—℞ Aluminis . . . . . . 3ij.
     Acidi sulphurici dil.   3j.
     Syr. limonis   f3j.
     Aquæ . . . . f3iij.—M.

Sig. Tablespoonful every hour or two.   BARTHOLOW.

401—℞ Acidi sulphurici . . . . f3j.
     Syrupi acidi citrici . . . . f3iv.
     Aquæ . . . . f3xxx.—M.

Sig. To be taken in small cupfuls twice or thrice daily. (As
    a preventive.)   MARTIN SOLON.

402—℞ Strychninæ sulphatis . . . . gr. j.
     Confectionis rosæ . . . . 3ss.

Misce et fiant pilulæ xx.
Sig. One pill three times a day. (In lead palsy.)

403—℞ Potassii iodidi . . . . 3j.
     Aquæ destillatæ . . . . f3iij.—M.

Sig. A teaspoonful three times a day. (In chronic poisoning.)

CONDYLOMATA, COMMON.

404—℞ Acidi nitrici . . . . f3ss.

Sig. Apply to wart with match or glass rod three or four
    times a week.   LEVIS.

405—℞ Acidi nitrici . . . . f3j.
     Aquæ . . . . Oj.—M.

Sig. Use frequently as a wash.   RINGER.

406—℞ Acidi acetici glacialis   f3j.
Sig. Apply locally.   J. C. WILSON.

407—℞ Acidi chromici . . . . 3v.
     Aquæ destillatæ . . . . f3j.—M.

Sig. Apply with a small stick of wood every other day.
    (Also for syphilitic warts.)   WOOSTER.

CONDYLOMATA, VENEREAL.

408—℞ Hydrargyri chloridi mitis . . . . 3ij.
Sig. First wash with solution of chlorinated soda, then dust
    with the calomel.   RICORD.

409—℞ Hydrarg. chlor. mit. . . . . 3vj.
     Acidi boracici . . . . 3ij.
     Acidi salicylici . . . . 3j.—M.

Sig. Dust over the vegetations.   GREGORY.

410—℞ Acidi carbolici . . . . 3j.
Sig. Apply locally once every day or two.   BARTHOLOW.

411—℞ Pulv. sabinæ,
     Pulv. aluminis . . . . ãã 3j.—M.

Sig. Dust on the parts every evening. (In condylomata of the
    vulva.)   BLACHEZ.

412—℞ Tinct. thujæ   f3ij.
Sig. Apply locally three times daily for one or two weeks,
    with five drops in a wineglassful of water, internally, night
    and morning.   PHILLIPS.

413—℞ Tinct. ferri mur.,
     Acidi muriatici dil. . . . . ãã f3ij.—M.

Sig. Apply night and morning.   BULKLEY.

414—℞ Acidi boracici . . . . 3ss.
    Aquæ destillatæ . . . . f3x.—M.
Sig. Use to cleanse the eyes after washing away all discharges,
and then use—

415—℞ Hydrargyri oxidi flavi . . . . gr. xvj.
    Acidi boracici . . . . gr. xx.
    Cocainæ muriatis . . . . gr. v-x.
    Vaselini . . . . 3j.—M.
Sig. **Apply to surface.**   HIGGINS.

416—℞ Acidi tannici   . . . . 3ss.
Sig. Evert the eyelids, and insufflate. (*In the granular form.*)
                     HAMILTON.

417—℞ Acidi borici . . . . **gr. x.**
    Pulver s aluminis . . . . **gr. xx.**
    Aquæ destillatæ . . . . 3j.—M.
Sig. Drop in the eye two or three **times daily.** (*For catarrhal
conjunctivitis.*)   KEYSER.

418—℞ Acidi boracici . . . . 3j.
    Aquæ rosæ . . . . f3iv.—M.
Sig. Bathe the **lids freely.** (*Early in measles as prophylactic.*)
                     TROUSSEAU.

419—℞ Hydrarg. chlorid. corr. . . . . gr. j.
    Aquæ . . . . f3viij.—M.
Sig. Bathe the eyelids freely inside and out several times
daily. (*Later in measles.*)   TROUSSEAU.

420—℞ Acidi boracici . . . . **gr. vj.**
    Aquæ camphoræ,
    Aquæ destillatæ   āā f3j.—M.
Sig. Bathe the eyelids and drop two drops in the eye three or
four times daily. (*In simple conjunctivitis.*)   L. W. FOX.

421—℞ Morphinæ   . . .   gr. iss.
    Hydrargyri oleatis   gr. v.
    Acidi oleici .   gr. xcv.—M.
Sig. Apply with camel's-hair pencil to outer surface of eyelids
only, twice daily.   RINGER.

422—℞ Hydrargyri oxidi flavi . . . . **gr. ¼-j.**
    Adipis benzoati . . . . 3j.
Misce et fiat unguentum exactum.
Sig. Apply in the eye daily. (*For phlyctenular conjunctivitis.*)
                     KEYSER.

423—℞ Hydrargyri oxidi flavi . . . . gr. j-iij.
    Vaselini . . . . 3j.—M.
Sig. A piece the size of a pin-head placed between the lids.
(*In the phlyctenular form.*)   PAGENSTECHER.

424—℞ Atropinæ sulphatis . .   . . gr. ss-j.
    Morphinæ sulphatis . .   gr. j-iv.
    Zinci sulphatis   . .   gr. j-viij.
    Aquæ rosæ .   f3j.
Misce et fiat collyrium.
Sig. For the eye.   **BARTHOLOW.**

425—℞ Cadmii sulphatis . . . . gr. iij.
    Vini opii . . . . f3j.
    Aquæ rosæ . . . . f3ij.—M.
Sig. Use twice daily. (*In the chronic form, and for opacities of
the cornea.*)   FRONMUELLER.

426—℞ Argenti nitratis   gr. ij-v.
    Aquæ destillatæ   . . . .   f3j.—M.
Sig. Two drops in the eye daily. (*In the granular form.*)
                     NOYES.

427—℞ Cupri sulphatis . . . . **gr. iij.**
    Aquæ camphoræ . . . . f3iv.
Solve.
Sig. To be dropped in the eye. (*In the purulent form.*) WARE.

428—℞ Sodii biboratis   gr. v.
    Acidi carbolici puri   . . . . gtt. j.
    Aquæ destillatæ . . . . f3j.—M.
Sig. Instil into the eye frequently, and then use—

CONJUNCTIVITIS (Continued).

429—℞ Acidi boracici . . . . gr. xv.
    Petrolati . . . . ʒij.—M.
Sig. Apply to lids. (*In purulent cases.*)   OLDHAM.

430—℞ Zinci sulphatis .   . gr. ij.
    Aquæ destillatæ . . . . f3j.—M.
Sig. Two drops in eye three or four times daily.   ROOSA.

CONSTIPATION.

431—℞ Mannæ . .   . . . ʒvj.
    Magnesiæ,
    Sulphur. loti . . . . .   āā ʒiss.
    Mellis . . . . f3vj.—M.
Sig. One or **two** teaspoonfuls diluted. (*For children.*)
                               FERRAUD.

432—℞ Mannæ . . . . gr. vj.
    Aquæ bullientis   . . . ʒx.—M.
Ft. infusum.
Sig. When cool, give a teaspoonful to a new-born child.
                               WIDERHOFER.

433—℞ Hydrargyri chloridi mitis . . .   . . gr. j.
    Sodii bicarbonatis . . . . .   gr. xij.
    Sacchari lactis   . .   gr. xx.
Misce et fiant chartulæ no. xii.
Sig. One every three hours until the bowels are freely
    moved. (*For infants.*)   WAUGH.

434—℞ Aloes purificatæ . .   . . gr. xx.
    Extracti belladonnæ . .   . gr. iv.
    Extracti nucis vomicæ   . gr. v.
    Oleoresinæ capsici .   gr. iv.
Misce et fiant pilulæ no. xx.
Sig. One pill daily at bedtime.   WAUGH.

435—℞ Ext. nucis vomicæ,
    Pulv. piper. nig. . . . . āā ʒj.
    Pil. colocynth. co. . . . . gr. L.—M.
In pil. no. xx div.
Sig. One every night or **second night.**   FOTHERGILL.

436—℞ Ext. cascaræ sagrad. fld.,
    Elixiris simplicis . . . . āā f3ij.—M.
Sig. Two teaspoonfuls at bedtime.   BARTHOLOW.

437—℞ Extracti stillingiæ fluidi . . . . f3v.
    Tincturæ belladonnæ,
    Tincturæ nucis vomicæ,
    Tincturæ physostigmatis . . . . . . āā f3j.—M.
Sig. Twenty drops in water, three times a day, **before meals.**
    (*In habitual constipation.*)   BARTHOLOW.

438—℞ Extracti hydrastis fluidi . . . . f3j.
    Syrupi simplicis,
    Elixiris simplicis . . . .   āā f3iss.—M.
Sig. A dessertspoonful three times a day. (*In deficient secre-*
tion with dry hard stools.)   PORCHER.

439—℞ Glycerini   . . . . ʒj.
Sig. Inject twenty to thirty minims into the rectum.
                               ANNACKER.

440—℞ Pulv. aloes socot. . . . . gr. xij.
    Ext. belladonnæ . . . . gr. iij.
    Saponis . . . . q. s. ut ft. massa.—M.
In pil. no. xxiv div.
Sig. One or two as **required.**   WALLACE.

441—℞ Pulv. aloes **socot.** . . . . gr. vij.
    Pulv. rhei. . . . . gr. xxiv.
    Ext. belladonnæ . . . . gr. j.—M.
In pil. no. xii div.
Sig. One or two pills as required.   DA COSTA.

442—℞ Resinæ podophylli   gr. ij.
     Quininæ sulphat.,
     Ext. aloes socot.   āā gr. vij.
     Fellis bovini   gr. xvj.—M.
In pil. no. xvi div.
Sig. One or two at bedtime.   GOODELL.

443—℞ Podophyllin. . . . . gr. j.
     Spts. vini rectif. . . . . ℨiss.
     Syr. althææ . . . . ad ℥iv.—M.
Sig. A half-teaspoonful daily. (For infants.)   BOUCHUT.

444—℞ Antimonii oxidi . . . . ℨss.
     Extracti colocynthidis compositi . . . ℨiss.
Misce et divide in pilulas xxx.
Sig. One or two pills at bedtime.   FOTHERGILL.

CONVULSIONS.

445—℞ Chloral. hydratis . . . . gr. xv-xxx.
     Syrupi acaciæ . . . . f℥j.
     Aquæ .   . . . . ad f℥iv.—M.
Sig. Inject a tablespoonful into the rectum, and repeat in fifteen or twenty minutes if required.   WIDERHOFER.

446—℞ Chloral. hydratis . .   gr. i-v.
     Syrupi simplicis . . . .   f℥j.—M.
Sig. One dose. (For infants and small children.)   WATERHOUSE.

447—℞ Ammonii bromidi . . . . ℨiv.
     Potassii bromidi . . . . ℨvj.
     Tincturæ calumbæ. . . . . f℥j.
     Aquæ destillatæ . . . . q. s. ad f℥iv.—M.
Sig. A dessertspoonful every hour or two.   ECHEVERRIA.

448—℞ Moschi . .   gr. iij.
     Camphoræ . . .   gr. xv.
     Chloral. hydratis   gr. vjss.
     Vitell. ovi . .   no. j.
     Aquæ destillatæ   . .   f℥iv ℨvj.—M.
Sig. Wash out the rectum with a simple enema, and then use above as an injection.   J. SIMON.

449—℞ Moschi   . gr. xij.
     Sacchari .   ℨij.
     Spiritus ammoniæ . . .   ℳxxx.
     Infusi lini compositi . .   f℥iv.
Fiat enema.
Sig. An injection for infantile convulsions.   ELLIS.

450—℞ Olei ricini . . . . f℥j.
Sig. A teaspoonful or two, according to age.
     MEIGS AND PEPPER.

451—℞ Mist. asafœtidæ . . . . f℥ij.
Sig. A tablespoonful as an enema.   WARING.

452—℞ Ætheris fort. . . .   . f℥iv.
Sig. As an inhalation until paroxysm is broken.   J. L. SMITH.

CORYZA. (See also Catarrh and Influenza.)

453—℞ Acidi carbolici . . . . ℨj.
     Sodii boratis,
     Sodii bicarbonatis . . . . āā ℨj.
     Glycerini,
     Aquæ rosæ . . . . āā f℥j.
     Aquæ . . . . q. s. ad Oj.—M.
Sig. Use as a spray.   LEFFERTS.

454—℞ Cocain. hydrochlor. . . . . gr. ivss.
     Antipyrin. . . . . gr. xviij.
     Sodii bicarb. . . . . gr. v.
     Aquæ . . . . f℥j.—M.
Sig. Nasal spray.   STOWELL.

455—℞ Cocain. hydrochlor. . . . . gr. ix.
    Aquæ . . . . f℥ss.
Ft. solutio et adde—
    Olei petrolei . . 3j.
    Olei eucalypti . . gtt. vj.
    Olei gaultheriæ . . . . gtt. iij.—M.
Sig. Nasal spray. Shake thoroughly before using. STOWELL.

456—℞ Cocain. hydrochlor. . . . gr. ix.
    Adipis anhydrat.,
    Vaselini . . . . āā ℥ss.—M.
Sig. Ointment for the nose. STOWELL.

457—℞ Sodii bicarb. . . . . gr. ij.
    Magnesiæ carb. (levis) . . . . . . gr. iij.
    Menthol . . . . gr. j.
    Cocain. hydrochlor. . . . . gr. iv.
    Sacch. lactis ; . . . . ℥jss.—M.
Sig. Use as snuff. STOWELL.

CROUP.

458—℞ Tinct. ferri chloridi . . . . ℥j-iss.
    Potassii chloratis . . . . ℥j.
    Glycerini . . . . ℥j.
    Aquæ cinnamomi . . . . ad ℥iv.—M.
Sig. A teaspoonful every two hours to a child four years old.
MEIGS AND PEPPER.

459—℞ Potassii chloratis,
    Ammonii muriatis . . . . āā ℈j-ij.
    Syrupi simplicis . . . . ℥j.
    Aquæ . . . . ℥iij.—M.
Sig. A teaspoonful hourly. J. LEWIS SMITH.

460—℞ Potassii chloratæ . . ℥j.
    Ammonii chloridi ℈ij
    Syrupi simplicis f℥j.
    Aquæ destillatæ . . . f℥ij.—M.
Sig. A teaspoonful every three hours. HAZARD.

461—℞ Acidi lactici ℥iiss.
    Aquæ destillatæ f℥x.—M.
Sig. Apply frequently by means of a spray-producer **or a**
simple mop. (*To dissolve false membrane.*)
MORELL MACKENZIE.

462—℞ Apomorphinæ . . . . gr. ½.
    Syr. simplicis,
    Aquæ . . . . āā ℥j.—M.
Sig. A teaspoonful or two every hour or two, according to
the urgency of the case. FLIESBURG.

463—℞ Hydrargyri sulphatis flavæ . . . . . . gr. iij-v.
Fiat pulvis.
Sig. As an emetic. FORDYCE BARKER.

464—℞ Pulv. aluminis . . . . ℥iiss.
    Mellis albi . . . . ℥x.—M.
Sig. A half-teaspoonful every hour ; and **powdered alum**
blown into the throat every four hours. TROUSSEAU.

465—℞ Pulv. aluminis . . ℥j.
    Syr. ipecac. . . ℥j.—M.
Sig. One teaspoonful every twenty minutes until vomiting
is produced. A hot mustard foot-bath should be given at
the same time. J. LEWIS SMITH.

466—℞ Syr. ipecacuanhæ . . . . ℥ij.
Sig. A teaspoonful every ten or fifteen minutes until vomiting is produced. Then five or ten minims every two or
three hours the next day. MEIGS AND PEPPER.

467—℞ Potassii bromidi,
    Chloral. hydratis . . . . āā ℈ij.
    Syr. acaciæ . . . . ℥ij.—M.
Sig. A teaspoonful or less, according to age. ELLIS.

468—℞ Tinct. belladonnæ . . . . gtt. iv.
    Tinct. opii camph. . . . . gtt. l.
    Pulv. aluminis . . . . gr. vj.
    Syr. acaciæ . . . . ʒss.
    Aquæ . . . . ʒiss.—M.

Sig. A **teaspoonful every two or three** hours at six months **of** age.   MEIGS AND PEPPER.

469—℞ **Tinct. aconiti radicis** . . . . ʒss.

Sig. One drop in a teaspoonful of water every hour till urgent symptoms abate; then every two or three hours.
       RINGER.

CYSTITIS. (See also Catarrh.)

470—℞ Iodoformi . . . . ʒxij.
    Glycerini . . . . ʒx.
    Tragacanthæ . . . . gr. xx.
    Aquæ destillatæ . . . . ʒiss.—M.
Ft. emulsio.
Sig. One tablespoonful in half a pint of water as an injection.
       FREY.

DEBILITY, GENERAL AND SENILE.

471—℞ Tinct. ferri chlor.,
    Syr. simplicis . . . . āā f ʒj.
    Aquæ cinnamomi . . . . f ʒij.—M.
Sig. A teaspoonful three times **daily.**   *Charity Hospital, N.Y.*

472—℞ Ferri et ammonii citratis,
    Ammonii chloridi . . . . āā gr. xxxij.
    Syrupi,
    Aquæ anisi . . . . āā f ʒij.—M.
Sig. A teaspoonful three **times daily.**   J. LEWIS SMITH.

473—℞ Quininæ sulphatis . . . . gr. xxx.
    Acidi sulphurici dil. . . . . q. s. ad ft. sol.
    Aquæ . . . . f ʒij.
    Tinct. ferri chlor. . . . . f ʒss.
    Spts. chloroformi . . . . f ʒvj.
    Glycerini . . . . f ʒiv.—M.
Sig. A teaspoonful three times daily.   LOOMIS.

474—℞ Ferri et potassii **tartratis** . . . . ʒss.
    Vini xerici . . . . Oj.
Solve et cola.
Sig. A tablespoonful three times a day.   BENNET.

475—℞ Infusi cocæ sacch. . . . . f ʒi.
    Glycerini . . . . f ʒv.
    Ext. cinchonæ fld. . . . . f ♏lxxv.
    Tinct. canellæ . . . . f ʒj.
    Tinct. vanillæ . . . . f ♏xlv.
    Tinct. casearillæ . . . . f ʒss.—M.
Sig. A tablespoonful thrice daily.   MONIN.

476—℞ Spiritus ferri chlorati ætherei (*Ph. Bo-*
    russ.) . . . . f ʒiij.
    Aquæ cinnamomi,
    Syrupi aurantii corticis . . . . āā f ʒj.
    Infusi valerianæ . . . . f ʒv.—M.
Sig. Shake well, **and** take a tablespoonful every two, four, or six hours. (*In nervous debility.*)
"Bestucheff's Nervine Tincture," or "Lamotte's Golden Drops," **a** great favorite in Germany.   SOBERNHEIM.

477—℞ Tincturæ cinchonæ,
    Tincturæ valerianæ . . . . āā f ʒj.
    Tincturæ cardamomi compositæ . . . f ʒij.
    Aquæ menthæ piperitæ . . . . f ʒiv.—M.
Sig. A tablespoonful three times a day.   ELLIS.

D

478—℞ Pulveris aloes socotrinæ . . . . 3j.
  Pulveris zedoariæ,
  Pulveris gentianæ,
  Croci,
  Pulveris rhei,
  Azarici . . . . āā 3j.
  Spiritus vini gallici . . . . Oij.
 Macera per dies septem, c da, et adde—
  Syrupi simplicis . . . . . . f3ij.—M.
 Sig. A tablespoonful three times a day in water. (This is the
  celebrated "Baume de Vie," or "Elixir of Life.")
               HOFFMANN.

479—℞ Sps. chloroformi . . . . f3v.
  Acidi hydrochlor. dil. . . . . . . f3iss.
  Inf. cinchonæ . . . . f3xv.—M.
 Sig. Two tablespoonfuls three times daily. FOTHERGILL.

DELIRIUM, TRAUMATIC.

480—℞ Chloral. hydratis . . . . 3ss.
  Syrupi aurantii corticis,
  Aquæ destillatæ . . . . . . āā f3ss.—M.
 Sig. One dose, to be repeated if necessary. (In maniacal
  delirium.)   LIEBREICH.

481—℞ Potassii bromidi . . . . 3ss.
  Syrupi simplicis . . . . f3j.
  Aquæ foeniculi . . . . q. s. ad f3iij.—M.
 Sig. A dessertspoonful every two hours. (In cases resembling
  delirium tremens.)   RINGER.

482—℞ Tincturæ belladonnæ . . . . f3iss.
  Syrupi simplicis . . . . f3viss.
  Aquæ cinnamomi . . . . f3j.—M.
 Sig. A teaspoonful every two or three hours. (In fevers.)
               S. G. MORTON.

DELIRIUM TREMENS.

483—℞ Infusi digitalis . . . . f3iij.
 Sig. A tablespoonful every four hours. (In anæmic cases with
  effusion and œdema.)   BARTHOLOW.

484—℞ Sodii bromidi . . . . gr. xv.
  Chloral. hydratis . . . . gr. x.
  Syrupi aurantii cort.,
  Aquæ . . . . . . āā q. s. ad ft. f3j. M.
 Sig. As required. Also to be taken, fluid extract of coca fif-
  teen minims, increased to tolerance. DA COSTA.

485—℞ Chloral. hydratis . . . . 3ss.
  Aquæ destillatæ . . . . f3ij.—M.
 Sig. One dose. (To enforce sleep.) LIEBREICH.

486—℞ Antimonii et potassii tartratis . . . gr. j
  Tincturæ aconiti radicis . . . . . f3ss.
  Tincturæ opii . . . . f3j.
  Aquæ destillatæ . . . . . q. s. ad f3iv.—M.
 Sig. A dessertspoonful in porter every two or three hours. (In
  strong and robust patients with boisterous delirium.) RINGER.

487—℞ Potassii bromidi . . . . 3j.
 In pulv. no. vij. div.
 Sig. A powder dissolved in one-half tumblerful of water,
  every four to six hours. (In the "horrors" preceding the delirium.)   BARTHOLOW.

488—℞ Liq. morph. sulph. (U. S. P.),
  Ext. valerian. fld. . . . . . . āā f3j.—M.
 Sig. One or two teaspoonfuls, as required. HARTSHORNE.

489—℞ Hyoscyami . . . . gr. j.
  Spts. vini rectif.,
  Aquæ destillatæ . . . . āā f3j.—M.
 Sig. Five to ten minims hypodermically. BRYCE.

490—℞ Amyli hydratis . . . . 3vj.
       Syr. aurantii cort. . . . . f 3ij.
       Aquæ . . . . ad f 3viij.—M.
   Sig. Two to three tablespoonfuls in a wineglassful of water.
                              VON MERING.

491—℞ Tinct. digitalis . . . . f 3ss.
   Sig. Thirty minims, repeated in four to six hours. RINGER.

492—℞ Ammonii carbonatis . . . . . . 3iss.
      Extracti glycyrrhizæ fluidi . f 3iss.
      Aquæ destillatæ . . . . f 3ivss.—M.
   Sig. A **tablespoonful every two** or three hours. ANSTIE.

493—℞ Tincturæ lupulinæ,
      Syrupi amygdalæ . . . . āā f 3j.
      Aquæ destillatæ . . . . f 3ij.—M.
   Sig. A tablespoonful every two hours. HAZARD.

494—℞ **Ext. cannabis indicæ** . . . . gr. vj–xij.
   In pil. no. xii div.
   Sig. One pill every two or three hours till drowsy. PHILLIPS.

495—℞ **Quininæ sulph.** . . . . gr. xij.
   In pil. no. xii div.
   Sig. One pill two or three **times daily, as a tonic.** ANSTIE.

DIABETES INSIPIDUS. (See also Polyuria.)

496—℞ Ext. ergotæ fld. . . . . f 3ij.
   Sig. A **teaspoonful three times** daily, increased to two tea-
    spoonfuls. DA COSTA.

497—℞ Pulv. opii . . . . gr. iv.
      Acidi galliei . . . . 3ij.—M.
   In chart. no. xii div.
   Sig. One three or four times daily. H. C. WOOD.

498—℞ Codeinæ . . . . gr. viij.
      Syrupi,
      Aquæ . . . . āā 3j.—M.
   Sig. A **half-teaspoonful thrice daily,** gradually increased to
    two teaspoonfuls. PAVY.

499—℞ Auri chloridi .   gr. j.
      Confect. rosæ .   gr. xx.—M.
   Ft. massa et in pilulas no. xx div.
   Sig. A pill after meals thrice daily. BARTHOLOW.

500—℞ Pulv. valerianæ radicis . . . . 3ij–iv.
   In chart. no. xii div.
   Sig. A powder three times daily. DEMANGE.

DIABETES MELLITUS.

501—℞ Morphinæ acetatis . . . . gr. viij.
      Aquæ . . . . f 3iv.—M.
   Sig. A teaspoonful four times daily, increasing rapidly, until
    in three months seven grains daily are taken. (*To be used*
    with restricted diet.) BRUCE.

502—℞ Ext. belladonnæ . . . . gr. xxx.
      Ext. opii . . . . gr. xv.—M.
   Ft. massa et in pil. no. xx **div.**
   Sig. One three times daily, gradually increased **to double the**
   quantity. (*To be used with restricted diet.*) VILLEMIN.

503—℞ **Iodoformi** . . . . gr. ij.
   In pil. no. xii div.
   Sig. One pill after meals, three times daily. (*With restricted*
   diet.) LEVI.

504—℞ Acidi arsenios. . . . . gr. iv.
Pulveris opii . . . . gr. viij.
Ammonii chloridi . . . . 3ss.

Misce et fiat massa in pilulas xxxii dividenda.
Sig. One pill after each meal. (*In thin subjects with faulty
assimilation.*)　　　　　　　　　　　　　　MARCUS.

505—℞ Pulveris opii . . . . gr. xij.
Fellis bovini inspissati . . . . 3iiss.

Fiat massa in pilulas no. xxiv dividenda.
Sig. One pill three times a day.　　　　BETHUNE.

506—℞ Codeinæ . . . . gr. vj.
Ext. nucis vom. . . . . gr. iij.—M.

In pil. no. xxiv div.
Sig. One pill three times a day; to be increased by degrees.
　　　　　　　　　　　　　　　　　J. C. WILSON.

507—℞ Pulv. jambul. sem. . . . . 3j.

Dispensa in capsulas no. xxiv.
Sig. One or two capsules thrice daily, after food.　FENWICK.

508—℞ Sodii salicylatis . . . . 3ss.
Extracti glycyrrhizæ fluidi . . . . . . f3iss.
Aquæ destillatæ . . . . f3ivss.—M.

Sig. A tablespoonful three times a **day.**　　EINSTEIN.

509—℞ Sodii salicylat. . . . . 3iv-vj.
Glycerini . . . . f3j.
Aquæ . . . . ad f3iij.—M.

Sig. Two teaspoonfuls three times daily.　　DA COSTA.

510—℞ Sodii salicylat. . . . . 3iij.
Liq. potassii arsenitis . . . . f3j.
Glycerini . . . . f3j.
Aquæ cinnamomi . . . . ad f3iij.—M.

Sig. A dessertspoonful three times daily.　　J. C. WILSON.

511—℞ Extracti jaborandi **fluidi,**
Elixiris simplicis . . . . āā f3j.—M.

Sig. A teaspoonful every four hours.　　LAYCOCK.

512—℞ Acidi lactici . . . . f3vj.
Syrupi simplicis . . . . f3x.
Aquæ destillatæ . . . . f3iij.—M.

Sig. A dessertspoonful three times a day.　　FOSTER.

513—℞ Aloes capensis . . . . 3v.
Sodii bicarbonatis . . . . 3iss.
Spiritus lavandulæ **compositi** . . . . . f3ss.
Aquæ destillatæ . . . . Oj.—M.

Macera per dies quatuordecim et cola.
Sig. A teaspoonful after each meal. (*In obese persons, and
when of hepatic origin.*)　　　　　　METTAUER.

514—℞ Lithii carbonat. . . . . gr. xxx.
Sodii arseniat. . . . . gr. j.
Ext. gentianæ . . . . gr. xv.—M.

Ft. massa et in pil. no. xx div.
Sig. One pill morning and evening.　　VIGIER.

515—℞ Potassii phosphat. . . . . gr. xvj.
Aquæ . . . . f3x.—M.

Sig. A teaspoonful in a little wine or hot tea three times
daily.　　　　　　　　　　　　　DUCHENNE.

516—℞ Pepsinæ cryst. . . . . 3j.

In pulv. no. xii div.
Sig. One three times daily, after meals. Gradually increased,
if necessary. (*Restricted diet at first.*)　　GARDNER.

517—℞ Sol. cocain. mur. (4 per cent.) . . . . . f3ss.

Sig. Two drops every three hours. (*With antidiabetic diet.*)
When polydipsia disappears, take with above—

518—℞ Tinct. opii . . . . f3j.
Tinct. ferri muriat. . . . . f3ix.—M.

Sig. Twenty drops three times daily.　　WELLER.

519—℞ Ergotinæ ... ℨj.
    Glycerini ... f℥j.
    Aquæ destillatæ ... f℥vij.—M.

Sig. Five or six drops daily, hypodermically. (*To diminish thirst.*)
                               CORNILLON.

DIARRHŒA, ADULTS.

520—℞ Acidi tannici . . . . gr. xxxvj.
    Pulv. opii . . . . gr. iv.—M.

In pil. no. xii div.

Sig. One pill every three or four hours.   HARTSHORNE.

521—℞ Cretæ præp. . . . . ℨij.
    Tinct. catechu . . ℨss.
    Tinct. opii . . . . ℳlxxx.
    Aquæ cinnamomi . ad ℥viij. M.

Sig. Two tablespoonfuls after each motion.   FOTHERGILL.

522—℞ Creasoti . . . . gtt. v.
    Pulveris opii . . . . gr. iij.
    Pulveris acaciæ . . . . gr. vij.

Tere simul, et divide in pilulas x.

Sig. One pill to be taken **every three hours.**   BLASIUS.

523—℞ Pulveris aromatici . . . . ℨij.
    Spiritus ammonii **aromatici** . . . . . . fℨij.
    Tincturæ catechu . . . . . . f℥x.
    Tincturæ cardamomi compositæ . . . . f℥vj.
    Tincturæ opii deodoratæ . . . . f℥j.
    Misturæ cretæ . . . . q. s. ad f℥xx.—M.

Sig. Eight drachms for an adult; four drachms for a child of twelve years; two drachms for one of seven years after each liquid motion. (*General cholera and diarrhœa mixture.*)
                           HENRY BEASLEY.

524—℞ Bismuthi subnitratis . . . . ℨij.
    Tinct. opii deodoratæ . . . . ℳxl.
    Elixiris guaranæ . . . . . . q. s. ad f℥iv.—M.

Sig. **Shake the** vial. A dessertspoonful every two hours.
                           J. C. WILSON.

525—℞ Ext. hæmatoxyli . . . . ℨss.
    Tinct. opii . . . . ℳij.
    Aquæ . . . . f℥ij.—M.

Sig. Three or four times daily.   PARIS.

526—℞ Tinct. opii camph.,
    Spts. ætheris co.,
    Ext. valerianæ fld. . . . . āā ℨss.
    Olei menthæ pip. . . . . gtt. xxx.
    Spts. lavandulæ co. . . . . q. s. ad ℥iv.—M.

Sig. A teaspoonful every two or three hours. WM. DARRACH.

527—℞ Extracti ergotæ aquosi (ergotinæ) . . . ℨj.
    Extracti nucis vomicæ . . . . gr. v.
    Extracti opii . . . . gr. x.

Misce et fiant pilulæ no. xx.

Sig. One every four to six hours. (*In chronic following acute attacks.*)
                           DA COSTA.

528—℞ Pilulæ massæ hydrargyri . . . . gr. x.
    Morphinæ sulphatis . . . . . . gr. j.
    Acidi tannici . . . . ℨj.
    Mucilaginis acaciæ . . . . q. s.—M.

Divide in pilulas x.

Sig. One to be given every two hours.   ELLIS.

529—℞ Morphinæ sulphat. . . . . . . gr. ss.
    Hydrarg. chlorid. mit. . . . . . . gr. j.
    Pulv. camphoræ . . . . . . ℨj.
    Mucil. acaciæ . . . . . q. s. ut ft. massa.—M.

Ft. massa et in pil. no. xii div.

Sig. A pill every two hours.   WM. DARRACH

530—℞ Liquoris iodi compositi . . . . f̃ ss.
    Syrupi papaveris f̃ 3viiss.
    Aquæ destillatæ . . . . f̃ ʒj.—M.

Sig. A teaspoonful every two hours. (*In attacks due to atony of the mucous membrane.*) SCHMIDT.

531—℞ Acidi tannici . . . . gr. xv.
    Ext. krameriæ . . . . ʒss.
    Syr. simplicis . . . . q. s. ut ft. massa.—M.

In pil. no. xx div.
Sig. One to ten pills **daily.** TROUSSEAU.

532—℞ Saloli . . . . **ʒj.**

In pulv. no. xii div.
Sig. A powder every two **hours,** followed by a draught of water. GOELET.

533—℞ Tincturæ krameriæ . . . . f̃ ʒj.
    Aquæ calcis . . . . f̃ ʒvj.—M.

Sig. A tablespoonful three times a day. **REECE.**

534—℞ Caffeinæ citratis . . . . ʒss.
    Aquæ destillatæ . . . . f̃ ʒij.—M.

Sig. A teaspoonful every four hours. (*In atonic cases.*) BARTHOLOW.

535—℞ Cupri sulphatis,
    Morphinæ sulphatis . . . . āā gr. j.
    Quininæ sulphatis . . . . gr. xxiv.

Misce et fiant pilulæ no. xii.
Sig. One pill three times a day. (**In chronic cases.**) BARTHOLOW.

536—℞ Spiritus lavandulæ comp. . . . . f̃ ʒij.
    Aquæ cinnamomi . . . . f̃ ʒvj.
    Syrupi rubi . . . . f̃ ʒij.
    Aquæ destillatæ . . . . f̃ ʒj.—M.

Sig. A tablespoonful every two or three hours. R. P. THOMAS.

537—℞ Aquæ camphoræ . . . . f̃ ʒiij.
    Spiritus lavandulæ comp. . . . . f̃ ʒj.
    Sacchari albi . . . . ʒj..

Fiat mistura.
Sig. A tablespoonful every **two hours.** PARRISH.

DIARRHŒA, **CHILDREN.**

538—℞ Tinct. opii deodoratæ . . . . gtt. xvj.
    Bismuthi subnitratis . . . . ʒij.
    Syr. simplicis . . . . f̃ ʒss.
    Mist. cretæ . f̃ ʒiss.—M.

Sig. Shake well and give one teaspoonful every three or four hours, to a child one year old. J. L. SMITH.

539—℞ Hydrargyri chloridi mitis . . . . . . gr. j.
    Pulveris nucis myristicæ . . gr. iij.
    Bismuthi subcarbonatis gr. x.
    Sacchari lactis . . . . ʒj.

Misce et divide in chartulas no. x.
Sig. One powder every two hours. (*For infants with green stools.*) R. A. F. PENROSE.

540—℞ Bismuthi subnitratis . . . . **gr. x.**
    Pulveris calcii phosphatis . . . . **gr. xij.**
    Sacchari lactis . . . . **ʒss.**

Misce et fiant chartulæ no. x.
Sig. One powder after each evacuation. (*In wasting diarrhœa of children.*) HAZARD.

541—℞ Argenti nitratis . . . . **gr. j.**
    Sacchari albi . . . . ʒij.
    Aquæ destillatæ . . . . f̃ ʒij.

Fiat mistura.
Sig. A teaspoonful every two hours. (*In newly-weaned infants.*) HIRSCH.

542—℞ Magnesii sulphatis . . . . ℥j.
    Tinct. rhei . . . . ℥j.
    Syr. zingiberis . . . . f℥j.
    Aquæ carui . . . . f℥ix.—M.
Sig. A teaspoonful three times daily to a child one year old.
WEST.

543—℞ Pulveris ipecacuanhæ compositi . . . . **gr. v.**
    Acidi tannici . . . . **gr. vj.**
    Sacchari albi . . . . **gr. xx.**
Misce et fiant **chartulæ no. x.**
Sig. One **every three hours.**
HAZARD.

544—℞ Pulv. ipecac. . . . . gr. ss.
    Pulv. rhei . . . . gr. ij.
    Sodii bicarb. . . . . gr. xij.—M.
In pulv. no. xii **div.**
Sig. One powder every four to **six hours** to an infant one
year old. (*In indigestion with* **acidity.**)   J. LEWIS SMITH.

545—℞ **Saloli** . . . . **gr. vj.**
In pulv. no. xii div.
Sig. A powder dry on the tongue, followed by a sip of water,
every two hours, to a child of six months.   GOELET.

546—℞ Sodii bromidi . . . . ℥ss.
    Mucilaginis acaciæ,
    Aquæ .   . . . āā f℥j.—M.
Sig. A teaspoonful every three hours for a child less than one
year old. (*Diarrhœa of dentition.*)   A. A. SMITH.

547—℞ Acidi nitrosi   ♏x–xv.
    Sacchari albi .   ℥ij.
    Ext. hyoscyami .   gr. vj.
    Aquæ cinnamomi . . . . f℥j.—M.
Sig. A **teaspoonful** every three hours. (*In protracted cases.*)
CONDIE.

548—℞ Olei ricini . . . . ℥j.
    Pulv. acaciæ,
    Pulv. sacchari . . . . āā ℥ij.
    Tinct. opii . . . . ♏xxj.
    Aquæ cinnamomi . . . . ad f℥iv.—M.
Sig. A teaspoonful every three or four hours.   WEST.

DIPHTHERIA.

549—℞ Papoid . .   . gr. x.
    Hydronaphthol .   . gr. iij.
    Hydrochloric acid   . gtt. xv.
    Distilled water   . f℥ij.
    Glycerin   f℥ss.—M.
Sig. To be used in atomizer every half-hour.   CALDWELL.

550—℞ Acidi salicylici .   gr. vij.
    Decocti eucalypti . .   ℥xv.
    Glycerini . . . .   ℥vij.
    Spts. vini rectif.   . . . ℥ij.—M.
Sig. To be applied locally every hour during the day and
every two hours during the night. Use lint wound around
a pencil or stick.   JULES SIMON.

551—℞ Trypsin. . . . . **gr. xxx.**
    Sodii bicarb. . . . . **gr. x.**
    Aquæ destillatæ . . . . ℥j.—M.
Sig. Apply locally to membrane.   FERNALD.

552—℞ Pulv. pepsinæ cryst. . . . . ℥jr.
    Sacchari lactis . . . . ℥j.—M.
Sig. To be insufflated locally.   RICHMOND.

553—℞ Papayotin . . . . ℥j.
    Aquæ . . . . ℥iv.
    Glycerini . . . . ℥viij.—M.
Sig. Apply locally to membranes.   A. JACOBI.

554—℞ Acidi carbolici . . . . gtt. x.
    Liq. ferri subsulphatis . . . . ℨiij.
    Glycerini . . . . ℨj.—M.
 Sig. To be applied **every three to six** hours with a camel's-hair brush.   J. LEWIS SMITH.

555—℞ Bromi pur.,
    Potassii bromidi . . . . āā gr. viij-xv.
    Aquæ destillatæ . . . . ℨl.—M.
 Sig. Apply locally every two or three hours.   LE GENDRE.

556—℞ Liq. ferri subsulphatis . . . . ℨij.
    Glycerini . . . . ℨij.—M.
 Sig. Apply locally with **brush twice daily.**   DRESCHER.

557—℞ Sodii sulphitis . . . . ℨj.
    Aquæ destillatæ . . . . f℥j.—M.
 Sig. Apply locally.   STILLÉ.

558—℞ Acidi lactici . . . . f℥iiss.
    Aquæ destillatæ . . . . f℥x.—M.
 Sig. Apply by means of a spray-producer or **a** mop. (*To dissolve the exudation.*)   MORELL MACKENZIE.

559—℞ Acidi carbolici . . . . gr. x.
    Acidi sulphurosa . . . . f℥iij.
    Glycerini,
    Tincturæ ferri chloridi . . . . . āā f℥ss.—M.
 Sig. Swab the throat frequently.   HAZARD.

560—℞ Aquæ chlori,
    Mellis despumati . . . . āā f℥ss.
    Aquæ destillatæ . . . . f℥iij.—M.
 Sig. As a gargle, or **by means of a swab.**   ROTHE.

561—℞ Carbolic acid . . . . ℨss.
    Alcohol . . . . ♏xx.
    Camphor . . . . ℨiss.
    Sweet almond oil . . . . f℥iij.—M.
 Sig. Apply locally.   SOULEZ.

562—℞ Carbolic acid . . . . ℨj.
    Camphor . . . . ℨiij.
    Alcohol . . . . ℨj.
    Sweet almond oil . . . . ℨiiss.—M.
 Sig. Apply locally.   SOULEZ.

563—℞ Tannic acid . . . . gr. xx.
    Mucilage . . . . f℥j.
    Alcohol . . . . f℥ss.—M.
 Sig. For nasal injection dilute with twice its weight of water.   COUSOT.

564—℞ Tincture of **rhatany** . . . . 150 grains.
    Tincture of **benzoin** . . . . 75 "
    Tincture of **aloes** . . . . 45 " –M.
 Sig. Apply with brush three times daily. OSIECKI.

565—℞ Iodi,
    Potassii iodidi . . . . āā gr. iv.
    Alcoholis . . . . f℥iv.
    Aquæ destillatæ . . . . f℥iv.—M.
 Sig. A teaspoonful to be added to hot water, kept hot by a spirit-lamp, and the steam to be inhaled many times a day, continued from eight to twelve minutes. As the patient becomes accustomed to the iodine, the quantity of the solution may be increased to half an ounce.
            WARING-CURRAN.

566—℞ Olei eucalypti . . . . ℨij.
    Olei terebinthinæ . . . . ℨviij.—M.
 Sig. Place in shallow vessels and keep boiling, or at least **simmering, over the stove.**   J. LEWIS SMITH.

567—℞ Coal tar . . . . ℨvij.
    Oil of turpentine . . . . ℨij ℨvj.—M.
 Sig. Light and keep burning in the sick-room.   DELTHIL.

568—℞ Olei terebinthinæ . . . . ℨiv.

Sig. Put in a cup and set it in a basin of water on the top of the stove, so that the vapor fills the room. Renew when necessary.　　　　　　　　　　　ELLIOTT.

569—℞ Tinct. ferri chloridi . . . . ℨss.

Sig. One drop every quarter of an hour. (*In the phlegmonous form.*)　　　　　　　　　　　LUNIN.

570—℞ Olei terebinthinæ . . . . ℨij.

Sig. Ten minims to one teaspoonful, one to three times daily, in milk, sugar-water, or gruel, with alcoholic stimulants.
　　　　　　　　　　　SCHENKER.

571—℞ Tinct. ferri chloridi . . . . ℨj.
　　　Syr. simplicis . . . . . ℨiij.—M.

Sig. A teaspoonful every hour to a child **ten** years old, or half a teaspoonful every half-hour.　　　　FERGUSON.

572—℞ Tinct. ferri chlor. . . . . ℨj.
　　　Glycerini,
　　　Aquæ . . . . āā ℨj.—M.

Sig. A teaspoonful every hour.　　　　BILLINGTON.

573—℞ Sodii phosphatis . . . . ℨiss.
　　　Aquæ ferventis . . . . f ℨij.
Solve, et adde—
　　　Acidi salicylici . . . . ℨiss.—M.

Sig. One to two teaspoonfuls every hour or two.　LETZERICH.

574—℞ Potassii chloratis . . . . ℨj.
　　　Acidi hydrochlorici dil. . . . . f ℨiss.
Misce, et adde—
　　　Tincturæ ferri chloridi . . . . f ℨij.
　　　Aquæ destillatæ . . . . q. s. ad f ℨiv.—M.

Sig. A teaspoonful every two hours.　　　　WAUGH.

575—℞ Potassii permanganatis . . . . gr. ij.
　　　Aquæ destillatæ . . . . f ℨij.
Solve.
Sig. A teaspoonful every three hours for a child eight or ten years old. (Keep in a glass-stoppered bottle.)　BARTHOLOW.

576—℞ Pilocarpinæ muriatis . . . . gr. ⅓-⅔.
　　　Pepsinæ cryst. . . . . gr. x-xij.
　　　Acidi hydrochlorici . . . . gtt. ij.
　　　Aquæ destillatæ . . . . ℨij ℨiss.—M.

Sig. A teaspoonful every hour, with a small amount of wine following it.　　　　　　　　　　　LAX.

577—℞ Tinct. iodi . . . . gtt. viij.
　　　Potassii iodidi . . . . gr. iss.
　　　Syr. simplicis,
　　　Aquæ . . . . āā ℨij.—M.

Sig. To be taken in one dose. (*Prevention for exposed children.*)
　　　　　　　　　　　DUMAS.

578—℞ Salinaphthol . . . . gr. xx-xxv.
　　　Spts. vini rectif. . . . . ℨj.—M.

Sig. A dessertspoonful in two-thirds of a tumbler of water as a gargle. Salinaphthol may also be used internally in doses of one or two drachms daily in children.　　GEORGI.

579—℞ Pilocarpinæ **muriatis** . . . . gr. iss.
　　　Pepsinæ cryst. . . . . gr. xxx.
　　　Acidi hydrochlorici . . . . gtt. ij.
　　　Aquæ destillatæ . . . . ℨviij.—M.

Sig. A tablespoonful every half-hour, in wine. (*For adults.*)
　　　　　　　　　　　GUTTMANN.

580—℞ Hydrarg. cyanidi . . . gr. ⅛.
　　　Tinct. aconiti radicis ℳxv.
　　　Aquæ destillatæ ℨxv.—M.

Sig. One teaspoonful hourly.　　　LE GENDRE.

581—℞ Tinct. ferri chloridi ℨij-iij.
　　　Potassii chloratis . ℨj.
　　　Acidi muriatici dil. . gtt. x.
　　　Syr. simplicis . ℨiv.—M.

Sig. A teaspoonful every hour or two.　J. LEWIS SMITH.

DIPHTHERIA (Continued).

582—℞ Hydrarg. bichloridi . . . . gr. ss.
Spts. frumenti . . . . ℨj.
Syr. simplicis . . . . ℨj.—M.

Sig. A teaspoonful **every three hours, night and day.**
DRESCHER.

583—℞ Hydrarg. chlor. cor. . . . . gr. j.
Spts. vini rectif. . . . . ℨij.
Elix. bismuthi et pepsinæ . . . . . . ad ℨiv.—M.

Sig. A teaspoonful every two hours for a child six years old.
J. LEWIS SMITH.

584—℞ Hydrarg. chlorid. mit. . . . . ℨj.
In pulv. no. xxiv div.
Sig. One or two powders every one, two, or three hours until
free catharsis follows, and then at longer intervals, so that
three or four evacuations are produced daily. W. C. RESTER.

585—℞ Acidi carbolici . . . . ℨx.
Acidi salicylici . . . . ℨij.
Acidi benzoici . . . . ℨiv.
Spts. vini rectif. . . . . . . q. s. ut ft. sol.—M.

Sig. To water constantly boiling add a spoonful of above
solution, using the whole quantity above in twenty-four
hours. The quantity may be increased if the size of the
room, age of the patient, or severity of the disease require
it. RENOU.

586—℞ Olei terebinthinæ . . . . ℨiv.
Sig. A tablespoonful twice daily, **or, in addition,** ten drops
every hour. (*In fibrinous forms.*) LANIN.

DIPSOMANIA. (See Alcoholism.)

DROPSY.

587—℞ Infusi digitalis . . . . f℥iv.
Sig. A tablespoonful **two or three times daily.** BARTHOLOW.

588—℞ Spts. chloroformi . . . . ℥xx.
Tinct. digitalis . . . . ℥x.
Infusi buchu . . . . f℥j.—M.
Sig. To be taken three or four times daily, and followed by a
good drink of water. (*In renal dropsy.*) FOTHERGILL.

589—℞ Potassii acetatis . . . . . ℨij.
Spiritus ætheris ni.rosi . f℥j.
Aquæ cinnamomi . f℥iss.
Infusi digitalis . . . . . f℥iv.—M.
Sig. A tablespoonful every four hours. (*In dropsy due to heart-
disease.*) KILGOUR.

590—℞ Pulv. digitalis . . . . gr. xxx.
Ferri sulph. exsiccat. . . . . gr. xv.
Pulv. capsici . . . . gr. xl.
Pil. aloë et myrrhæ . . . . ℨij.—M.
Ft. massa et in pilulas no. lx div.
Sig. One pill twice daily. (*In cardiac dropsy with flatulent
dyspepsia and constipation.*) FOTHERGILL.

591—℞ Potassii bicarb. . . . . gr. x.
Ferri et ammonii citratis . . . . gr. v.
Tinct. digitalis . . . . ℥x.
Infusi buchu . . . . f℥j.—M.
Sig. To be taken three times daily. (*In cardiac dropsy with
gouty tendency or debility.*) FOTHERGILL.

592—℞ Magnes. sulph. . . . . ℨj.
Aquæ . . . . f℥iiiss.
Syr. zingiberis . . . . f℥ss.—M.
Sig. Two teaspoonfuls **daily on waking.** SMITH.

593—℞ Antimonii et potassii **tartratis** . . . . . gr. ij.
Pulveris scillæ . . . . ℨj.
Potassii sulphatis . . . . ℥ss.
Potassii bitartratis . . . . ℥iss.—M.
Fiat pulvis et divide in partes æquales no. xx.
Sig. One powder four times daily. (*In general dropsy.*)
EBERLE.

55

594—℞ Potassii bicarbonatis . . . . ℨij.
Potassii acetatis . . . . ℨv.
Tincturæ scillæ . . . . f℥j.
Spiritus juniperi compositi . . . . f℥j.
Aquæ destillatæ . . . . f℥xij.
Fiat mistura.
Sig. Two tablespoonfuls three times a day. (*In local and general dropsy.*)   BROWN.

595—℞ Pil. scillæ co.,
Pil. colocynth. co. . . . . åå ℈ij.
Olei tiglii . . . . ♏[vj.—M.
Ft. massa et in pil. no. xviii div.
Sig. Three pills twice a week.   SELWYN.

596—℞ Pil. scillæ co. . . . . ℨj.
Hydrarg. chlorid. mit. . . . . gr. v.
Olei juniperi . . . . ♏j.—M.
Ft. massa et in pil. no. xx div.
Sig. One pill two or three times daily.   HOOPER.

597—℞ Pulveris jalapæ . . . . ℨj.
Potassii bitartratis . . . . ℨvj.
Misce et divide in chartulas vi.
Sig. One powder every three hours, in molasses. (*In general dropsy due to kidney-disease.*)   N. CHAPMAN.

598—℞ Pulveris opii . . . . gr. iv.
Hydrargyri chloridi mitis . . . . gr. vj.
Pulveris digitalis . . . . gr. xij.
Confectionis rosæ . . . . q. s.
Misce et fiant pilulæ no. xii.
Sig. One to be taken every eight hours. (*In hydrothorax and ascites.*)   ELLIS.

599—℞ Pulv. jalapæ . . . . gr. xv-xx.
Potass. bitart. . . . . ℨij.
Pulv. zingiberis . . . . gr. v.—M.
Sig. To be taken before breakfast, two or three times a week.   WARING.

600—℞ Potassii bitartratis . . . . ℨij.
Mucilaginis acaciæ . . . . f℥j.
Spiritus ætheris nitrosi,
Extracti taraxaci fluidi . . . . åå f℥ss.
Aquæ destillatæ . . . . f℥ij.—M.
Sig. A dessertspoonful every four hours. (*In cases associated with disease of the liver and portal system.*) HILDENBRAND.

601—℞ Resinæ podophylli . . . . gr. iv.
Potassii bitartratis . . . . ℨij.
Misce et divide in pulveres viii.
Sig. One powder every two hours. (*In anasarca.*)
                                      V. C. HOWE.

602—℞ Elaterii . . . . gr. iij-vj.
Hydrargyri chloridi mitis,
Pulveris capsici . . . . åå gr. xxiv.
Confectionis rosæ . . . . q. s.
Fiat massa in pilulas xii dividenda.
Sig. One pill daily, in the morning. (*In cardiac dropsy when diuretics fail.*)   GREGORY.

603—℞ Acidi arseniosi . . . . gr. j.
Sacchari albi . . . . gr. j.
Tere simul in pulverem subtilem, dein adde—
Micæ panis . . . . q. s.
Misce bene et divide in pilulas xx.
Sig. One pill twice daily. (*In swelling of the feet of old people.*)   WOOD.

604—℞ Vini colchici sem. . . . . f℥ss.
Liq. ammonii acetat. . . . . f℥iss.
Infusi petroselini . . . . f℥v.—M.
Sig. A teaspoonful every four hours. (*Especially adapted to scarlatinal dropsy.*)   BARTHOLOW.

605—℞ Mist. ferri et ammon. acetat. (U.S.P.) . . f℥vj.
Sig. One or two teaspoonfuls three or four times daily.
                                      BASHAM.

606—℞ Extracti jaborandi fluidi,
  Elixiris simplicis . . . .   āā f℥j.
  Aquæ destillatæ . . . . f℥j.—M.
Sig. A tablespoonful **every four** hours. *(In hydrothorax and ascites.)*
              GUBLER.

607—℞ Juniperi contusi,
  Sinapis,
  Zingiberis . . . āā ℥ss.
  Armoraciæ contusæ,
  Petroselini . āā ℥j.
  Succi fermenti pomorum   Oij.
Macera per diem unam et cola.
Sig. A wineglassful three or four times a day. *(In cases of general drossy which admit of stimulation.)* The cider should be old and sound.   JOSEPH PARRISH.

608—℞ Juniperi contusi . . . ℥iv.
  Aquæ bullientis . . . . f℥xij,
Macera per horas duodecim et exprime, dein adde—
  Spiritus juniperi compositi . . . . f℥iv.—M.
Sig. A wineglassful mixed with a teaspoonful of cream of tartar three times a day.   W. PROCTOR, JR.

609—℞ Potassii iodidi   ℈ss-℥j.
  Aquæ destillatæ . . . . f℥vj.—M.
Sig. A tablespoonful three times a day. *(In anasarca with scanty urine.)*   RINGER.

DYSENTERY.

610—℞ Hydrarg. chlorid mit. . . . . ℥j.
In pulv. no. viii div.
Sig. **A powder two** or three times daily. *(In the* **epidemic** *form.)*   HULL.

611—℞ Hydrargyri chloridi corrosivi . . . . . gr. j,
  Syrupi simplicis . . . . f℥j,
  Aquæ destillatæ . . . . f℥viij.—M.
Sig. A teaspoonful **every hour or** two. *(Where there is much mucus.)*   RINGER.

612—℞ Plumbi acetat. . . . . gr. xxiv.
  Pulv. ipecac. . . gr. iij.
  Pulv. opii . . . . gr. iij.—M.
Ft. massa et ir pil. no. xii div.
Sig. One pill every two hours until blood ceases; then at longer intervals.   DA COSTA.

613—℞ Tinct. opii . . . . ℥ss.
Sig. Twenty drops to be given after a mustard plaster has been put over the stomach, and one hour later give the following:

  ℞ Pulv. ipecac.   ℥ii-iiss,
In pulv. no. vi div.
Sig. One powder, stirred in a little water, to be taken every evening at bedtime.   McDOWELL.

614—℞ Cupri sulphatis .   . gr. j,
  Pulveris opii .   . gr. iij,
  Quininæ sulphatis . . . . . gr. xxiv.
Misce et fiant pilulæ no. zii.
Sig. One pill three times a day. *(In chronic dysentery.)* JOY.

615—℞ Cupri sulphatis . . . . gr. j,
  Morphinæ sulphatis . . . gr. j,
  Quininæ sulphatis   gr. xxiv.—M.
In pil. no. xii div.
Sig. One pill three times daily. *(In the chronic form.)*
      BARTHOLOW.

616—℞ Sol. hydrarg. bichlorid. (1–10,000) . . Oij.
*Sig. The whole quantity to be used as an irrigating enema, after the rectum has been washed out with water as hot as can be borne. To be repeated every twelve hours, and each time followed by—

617—℞ Suppositorium opii . . . . no. j.
  Sig. Introduce into the rectum.
  FORDYCE.

618—℞ Thymoli . . . . 3j.
  Ft. massa et in pil. no. xxiv. div.
  Sig. Two pills every six hours.
  MARTINI.

619—℞ Tinct. opii deodoratæ . . . . 3ss.
  Bismuthi subnitratis . . . . 3ij.
  Aquæ menthæ pip.,
  Syr. zingiberis . . . . āā f3j.—M.
  Sig. Shake bottle. Give one teaspoonful every two to four
  hours, to a child five years of age. Half dose for child one
  year of age.
  J. LEWIS SMITH.

620—℞ Vini ipecac. . . . . f3ss.
  Sig. One drop every hour. (*In the acute or chronic form of
  children, with slimy stools.*)
  RINGER.

621—℞ Sodii et potassii tartratis   3vj.
  Aquæ destillatæ . . .   f3viij.—M.
  Sig. A tablespoonful every two hours until a normal evacu-
  ation occurs, then treat with appropriate doses of Dover's
  powder.
  FRANCIS GURNEY SMITH.

622—℞ Tincturæ hamamelidis . . . . f3ss.
  Elixiris simplicis. . . . . f3iiss.
  Syrupi simplicis . . . . f3ss.
  Aquæ destillatæ . . . . f3j.—M.
  Sig. A teaspoonful **every two or three** hours. (*Where there is
  much blood.*)
  RINGER.

623—℞ Cupri sulphatis   gr. ss.
  Magnesii sulphatis . .   3j.
  Acidi sulphurici diluti .   f3j.
  Aquæ destillatæ   f3iv.—M.
  Sig. A tablespoonful every four hours. (*In acute dysentery.*)
  BARTHOLOW.

624—℞ Naphthalini . . . . 3iss.
  Dispensa in capsulas no. xviii.
  Sig. Two capsules every three hours. At least twelve to be
  taken during the twenty-four hours.
  HOLT.

625—℞ Ext. **quebracho ale.** . . . .   3ss.
  Sig. Twenty to thirty drops every two or four hours. (*In
  asthenic cases.*)
  BOURDEAUX.

DYSMENORRHŒA.

626—℞ Chloroform. (pur.),
  Spts. camphoræ . . . . āā f3ss.
  Spts. æther. nitrosi,
  Spts. æther. comp. . . . . . . āā f3iss.—M.
  Sig. f3ss-j in 3j of water containing 3j of spiritus frumenti
  every half-hour for three doses.
  J. C. DA COSTA.

627—℞ Alcohol of melissa,
  Tincture of saffron,
  Tincture of iodine, ... of each f3j.—M.
  Sig. Twelve drops daily, before each of the two principal
  meals.
  MONIN.

628—℞ Fluid extract of cimicifuga. . . . . . . 3ij.
  Fluid extract of gelseminum semper-
  virens (green root) . . . . 3j.—M.
  Sig. Ten drops every two or three hours. Begin treatment
  one day prior to expected menstruation.
  HOUSMAN

629—℞ Antipyrin. . . . . gr. ix.
  Ext. cannabis indicæ,
  Ext. digitalis,
  Camphoræ . . . . āā gr. 1/4.
  Sig. For one cachet. To be taken every two hours until the
  pain ceases, but not more than six to be taken. P. MÉNIÈRE.

630—℞ Antipyrin. . . . . ℨij.
    Syr. tolutani . . . . . fℨij.—M.

Sig. **Two** teaspoonfuls at first; one teaspoonful every hour or two afterwards until pain is relieved. DELLENBAUGH.

631—℞ Antipyrin. gr. xxviiiss.
    Cocaini. muriatis . gr. iss.
    Aquæ bullientis . fℨij.—M.

Sig. Ten to twenty minims hypodermically. (*In neuralgic and congestive forms.*) May also be taken by mouth.
P. MÉNIÈRE.

632—℞ Phenacetin. . . . ℨj.

In pil. (compressæs) no. xx div.
Sig. One pill every half-hour till relieved; no more than six in one series. J. C. WILSON.

633—℞ Liq. ammonii acetat. . . . . fℨiv.

Sig. A tablespoonful every two or three hours, with the **following**:

634—℞ **Pulv. ipecac.** . . . . gr. iv.

In pil. **no. xii div.**
Sig. One every two or three hours. EMMET.

635—℞ Extracti cannabis indicæ . . . . gr. iij.
    Sacchari lactis . . . . ℨss.

Misce et fiant chartulæ no. vi.
Sig. One powder **every** two or three hours. H. C. WOOD.

636—℞ Crotonis chloralis . . . . **gr. xxiv.**
    Pulveris tragacanthæ,
    Glycerini . . . . **āā q. s.**

Misce et fiant pilulæ no. xii.
Sig. Two pills every two hours. (*In neuralgic dysmenorrhœa.*)
LOUIS LEWIS.

637—℞ Tinct. pulsatillæ radicis . . . . fℨss.

Sig. Two or three drops every two hours for ten days preceding the period. BROWN.

638—℞ Tincturæ opii deodoratæ . . fℨij.
    Extracti cimicifugæ . . . fℨss.
    Syrupi simplicis . . . . . fℨx.—M.

Sig. A teaspoonful every three or four hours. (*To restore the menstrual flow after it has been suddenly checked.*) RINGER.

639—℞ Ext. opii . . . . **gr. v.**
    Ext. cannabis indicæ,
    Ext. hyoseyami . . . . . **āā gr. x.**
    Pulv. camphoræ . . . . gr. xxv.—M.

Ft. massa et in pil. no. x div.
Sig. A pill **two** or three times daily. **McLANE.**

640—℞ Potassii bromidi,
    Chloral. hydratis . . . . **āā ℨiv.**
    Syrupi simplicis,
    Aquæ . . . . **āā fℨij.—M.**

Sig. Two tablespoonfuls to be used **as an enema**, as required for pain. MÉNIÈRE.

641—℞ Tinct. guaiaci ammoniatæ . . . . fℨij.

Sig. One-half to one teaspoonful **in** milk every two or three hours until pain is relieved. SIR JAMES SAWYER.

642—℞ Apiolis . . . . fℨj.
    Alcoholis . . . . fℨij.
    Syrupi simplicis . . . . fℨss.
    Aquæ destillatæ . . . . fℨij.—M.

Sig. A teaspoonful **every** two hours. (*In anæmic cases.*)
JORET ET HOMOLLE.

643—℞ Extracti gelsemii fluidi . . . . fℨiss.
    Elixiris simplicis . . . . fℨvss.
    Syrupi aurantii corticis . . . . fℨj.—M.

Sig. A teaspoonful every two **hours.** PORCHER.

DYSMENORRHŒA (Continued).

644—℞ Gossypii radicis contusi . . . . 3ii.
       Aquæ bullientis Oij.
    Misce, coque ad Oj, et cola.
    Sig. A wineglassful every hour. **T. J. SHAW.**

645—℞ Tincturæ arnicæ,
       Tincturæ guaiaci ammoniatæ . . āā f3iij.—M.
    Sig. Sixty drops four times daily, in sweetened water.
                                            SCHUBARTH.

646—℞ Camphoræ . . . 3j.
       Alcoholis q. s. ut fiat pulvis.
    Dein adde—
       Pulveris acaciæ,
       Sacchari albi . . . . āā 3j.
       Aquæ cinnamomi . . f3j.
    Fiat mistura.
    Sig. The one-half the instant pain is felt; if not relieved in
      an hour or two, give the remainder. DEWEES

DYSPEPSIA.

647—℞ Salicylate of bismuth,
       Magnesia,
       Bicarbonate of sodium . . . of each 10 grammes.
    Divide into thirty powders.
    Sig. One powder after each meal. SONNEBERG.

648—℞ Salicylate of bismuth,
       Naphthol,
       Magnesia . . . . of each 10 grammes.
    Divide into thirty powders.
    Sig. One powder after each meal. SONNEBERG.

649—℞ Extracti quassiæ 3ij
       Extracti conii . . . . gr. x.
       Ferri subcarbonatis . . . . gr. x.
       Liquoris potassii arsenitis . . . . . . gtt. x.
    Misce et fiant pilulæ no. xl.
    Sig. One pill three times daily. J. K. **MITCHELL.**

650—℞ Pulveris radicis rhei . . . . . . 3j.
       Pulveris aloes . . . . . . 3ij.
       Sodii bicarbonatis . . . 3ij.
       Valerianæ contusæ,
       Serpentariæ contusæ,
       Gentianæ contusæ,
       Quassiæ contusæ . . . . āā 3ss.
       Spiritus frumenti . . . . Oij.
    Macera in vaso **leviter clauso** per horas bis quatuor et
      viginta, et cola.
    Sig. A wineglassful three times a day. LIEBREICH.

651—℞ Tinct. opii deodoratæ . . . . gtt. xij.
       Magnesii calcinati . . . . gr. xij-xxiv.
       Sacchari albi . . . . 3j.
       Aquæ anisi . . . . f3ss.—M.
    Sig. Shake bottle. One teaspoonful every two hours to a
      child one year old, until relieved. If much pain, add a
      little chloroform or Hoffmann's Anodyne to the mixture.
                                            J. LEWIS SMITH.

652—℞ Bismuthi subcarb. . . . . 3ij.
       Morphinæ sulph. . . . . gr. j-ij.
       Pulv. aromat. . . . . 3j.—M.
    In chartulas no. xij div.
    Sig. A powder in **milk before each meal.** (In the irritative
      form.) BARTHOLOW.

653—℞ Bismuthi subnitratis,
       Sodii bicarbonatis,
       Pulv. cubebæ . . āā 3j.
       Pulv. zingiberis . . . . 3j.—M.
    In pulv. no. xij div.
    Sig. A powder in a wineglassful of water before each meal.
                                            ALONZO CLARK.

DYSPEPSIA (Continued).

654—℞ Bismuthi subnitratis . . . . ℨiv.
    Muci. acaciæ . . . . ℨj.
    Sodii bicarb. . . . . ℨiv.
    Infus. calumbæ. . . . . ad f℥viij.—M.
    Sig. Two tablespoonfuls before meals. (*In irritative dyspepsia,
    with mal-nutrition and raw tongue.*)   FOTHERGILL.

655—℞ Naphthalini . . . . 5ᵏˢ.
    Dispensa in capsulas no. xviii.
    Sig. One or two capsules every three to six hours. (*In flatu-
    lent dyspepsia and intestinal indigestion.*)   HOLT.

656—℞ Ammonii salicylatis . . . . ℨij.
    Syr. aurantii cort. . . . . f℥j.
    Aquæ menthæ pip. . . . . ad f℥iv.—M.
    Sig. A tablespoonful half an **hour** before meals. (*In fermenta-
    tive dyspepsia.*)   SULLIVAN.

657—℞ Sodii sulpho-carbolat. . . . . ℨiv.
    Glycerini . . . . . . ℨij.
    Infusi quassiæ . . . . . . f℥vj.—M.
    Sig. A tablespoonful before meals. (*In flatulent dyspepsia.*)
                                               DELAFIELD.

658—℞ Carbonis ligni . . . . ℨj.
    Bismuthi subnitratis . . ℈ij.
    Misce et fiant chartulæ iv.
    Sig. One powder three times a day. (*With flatulence.*)
                                               RINGER.

659—℞ Pulveris zingiberis . . . . ℨj.
    Magnesii carbonatis . . . . ℈ij.
    Carbonis ligni . . . ℨj.
    Misce et divide in chartulas iv.
    Sig. One powder three times a day. (*With acidity.*)
                                               DUNGLISON.

660—℞ Potassii iodidi,
    Manganesii sulphatis exsiccati . . . āā **ℨj.**
    Mellis despumati . . . . q. s.
    Fiat massa, in pilulas no. xxx dividenda.
    Sig. One pill morning and night. (*Keep in well-stoppered
    bottle.*)   HANNON.

661—℞ Sol. iodi trichlor. (1-1500) . . . . f℥iv.—M.
    Sig. A teaspoonful every two hours. (*When due to presence of
    bacteria.*)   LANGENBUCH.

662—℞ Tinct. capsici . . . . ℳ xvj.
    Tinct. nucis vomicæ . . . . f℥ij.
    Tinct. gentianæ co. . . . . ad f℥ij.—M.
    Sig. A teaspoonful in water three times daily, with gr. ½ aloin
    at bedtime, avoiding starchy diet.   DA COSTA.

EARACHE. (See Otitis.)

ECTHYMA. (See Skin Diseases.)

ECZEMA. (See Skin Diseases.)

EMISSIONS. (See Spermatorrhœa.)

EMPHYSEMA. (See Asthma and Bronchitis.)

EMPYEMA.

663—℞ Mist. ferri et ammonii acetatis . . . . . f℥iv.
    Sig. One to two teaspoonfuls three or four times daily, with
    quinine and stimulants. (*In chronic cases.*)   DA COSTA.

664—℞ Aquæ chlori . . . . f℥j.
    Aquæ destillatæ . . . . f℥ix.—M.
    Sig. To wash out the pleural cavity after the evacuation of
    the pus.   RINGER.

61

665—℞ Quininæ sulphatis . . . . ℈ij.
Aquæ . . . . f℥xij.—M.
Sig. Inject after evacuating the pus. RINGER.

666—℞ Liquor iodi co. . . . . f℥j.
Aquæ destillatæ . . . . f℥xv.—M.
Sig. Inject after aspirating the pus. BARTHOLOW.

667—℞ Ext. belladonnæ . . . . gr. ij.
Strychninæ sulph. . . . . gr. j.—M.
In pil. no. xxx div.
Sig. One pill four times daily, as a respiratory stimulant.
J. C. WILSON.

ENDOCARDITIS.

668—℞ **Tinct.** veratri viridis . . . . f℥j.
Sig. Two **drops** every two or three hours. J. C. WILSON.

669—℞ Tinct. digitalis . . . . f℥j.
Sig. Ten **or** fifteen drops **every four** hours. (*When heart's action is irregular.*) DA COSTA.

670—℞ Tinct. aconiti radicis . . . . f℥ss.
Sig. One drop every hour or two. RINGER.

671—℞ Lini farinæ,
Aquæ bullientis . . . . ā̄ā q. s.—M.
Ft. cataplasma.
Sig. Apply over **heart as hot as can be borne, and renew** frequently. DA COSTA.

672—℞ Emplastri cantharidis . . 3 in. × 3 in.
Sig. Apply over heart. When drawn, poultice blister till full, then cut and dress with simple cerate. (*To promote absorption of effusion.*) WARING.

ENTERITIS.

673—℞ Pulv. opii . . . . **gr. v.**
Bismuthi subnitratis . . . . **℈ij.—M.**
Divide in pulveres no. xx.
Sig. A powder every two to four hours, for a child of five years. J. LEWIS SMITH.

674—℞ Hydrargyri chloridi mitis . . . . gr. vj.
Pulveris opii . . . . gr. iij.
Quininæ sulphatis . . . . gr. xij.
Syrupi simplicis . . . . q. s.
Fiat massa, in pilulas xii dividenda.
Sig. One pill night and morning. CHANNING.

675—℞ Olei ricini . . . . ℥j.
Pulv. acaciæ,
Sacch. albi . . . . ā̄ā ℈iss.
Tinct. opii . . . . ♏iij.
Aquæ cinnamomi . . . . f℥xj.—M.
Sig. A teaspoonful every four hours, for a child of one year. TANNER.

676—℞ **Liq. potassii** arsenitis . . . . gtt. l.
Tinct. opii . . . . gtt. cxx.
Aquæ . . . . ad f℥iij.—M.
Sig. A teaspoonful before meals thrice daily. (*In the chronic form.*) BARTHOLOW.

677—℞ Tinct. **opii deodoratæ** . . . . f℥j.
Sig. Ten drops every second or third hour, according to age, to the point of tolerance. DA COSTA.

678—℞ Liquoris potassii arsenitis . . . . . f℥ss.
Tincturæ opii deodoratæ . . . . f℥j.
Tincturæ calumbæ . . . . f℥iv.—M.
Sig. A dessertspoonful every **two** or three hours. MARTIN.

679—℞ Hydrargyri chloridi corrosivi . . . . . gr. j.
    Tincturæ rhei,
    Tincturæ cinchonæ . . . . ââ f3j.—M.

Sig. A teaspoonful twice a day. (*In chronic cases.*)
                                         ASTLEY COOPER.

680—℞ Extracti chrysophylli . . . . 3ss.
    Aquæ destillatæ . . . . f3ij.
Tere simul, cola, et adde—
    Syrupi acaciæ . . . . f3j.—M.

Sig. A teaspoonful every four hours.   TROUSSEAU.

681—℞ Hydrarg. chlor. mit.,
    Pulv. ipecac. . . . . ââ gr. ij.
    Ext. hyoscyami . . . . gr. iv–vj.
    Plumbi acetatis . . . . . . gr. viij–xij.—M.

Ft. massa et in pil. no. xij div.
Sig. One pill every three hours. For children.   CONDIE.

682—℞ Pulv. ipecac. co. . . . . 3j.
    Bismuthi subnitratis . . . . . . 3ij.—M.

In pulv. no. xxiv div.
Sig. A powder every two to four hours, for a child five years
old.   J. LEWIS SMITH.

683—℞ Lini farinæ,
    Hordei farinæ . . . . ââ partes æquales.
    Aquæ . . . . q. s. ut fiat cataplasma.
Sig. Sprinkle surface coming next to skin lightly with dry
ground mustard, and apply to abdomen.   *Hôtel-Dieu.*

EPILEPSY.

684—℞ Nickel. bromidi . . . . gr. xvj.
    Aquæ destillatæ . . . . 3ij.—M.
Sig. A teaspoonful several times daily, according to tolerance.
                                     DA COSTA.

685—℞ Ammonii bromidi,
    Potassii iodidi . . . . ââ 3viij.
    Potassii bromidi . . . . 3vj.
    Sodii bicarbonatis . . . . 3ij.
    Tincturæ calumbæ . . . . f3ij.
    Aquæ destillatæ . . . . fXvj.—M.
Sig. A dessertspoonful after each meal, and a tablespoonful
at bedtime.   BROWN-SÉQUARD.

686—℞ Ferri bromidi . . . . gr. iv.
    Potassii bromidi . . . . 3j.
    Aquæ destillatæ . . . . f3ij.
    Syrupi simplicis . . . . f3vj.—M.

Sig. A tablespoonful twice daily. (*In anæmic subjects.*)
                                      BARTHOLOW.

687—℞ Potassii bromidi,
    Ammonii bromidi . . . . . ââ 3j.
    Ext. ergotæ fld. . . . . 3ss.
    Aquæ . . . . q. s. ad 3ij.—M.
Sig. One teaspoonful thrice daily. (*When maniacal excitement follows the attack, or cerebral congestion or hemorrhage is
feared.*)   CHARLES R. SMITH.

688—℞ Acetanilid. (antifebrin) . . . . 3j.
    Spts. vini gallici . . . . 3j.
    Syr. simplicis . . . . ad 3iss.—M.
Sig. A teaspoonful two or three times daily.   **LEIDY, JR.**

689—℞ Chloralis hydratis . . . . 3ss.
    Syrupi simplicis,
    Aquæ destillatæ . . . . ââ f3ij.
Misce et fiat haustus.
Sig. At bedtime. (*To prevent nocturnal fits.*)   DA COSTA.

690—℞ Iodi . . . . gr. ij.
    Potassii iodidi . . . . 3iv.
    Aquæ menthæ **piperitæ** . . . . f3vj.
Fiat solutio.
Sig. A teaspoonful thrice daily.   MAGENDIE.

EPILEPSY (Continued).

691—℞ Cupri ammoniati,
  Extracti cannabis indicæ . . . . . ãã ʒj. (!)
Misce et divide in pilulas no. xxiv.
Sig. One pill morning and evening. (*As a palliative in hopeless cases.*)
              GRIEVE.

692—℞ Lobeliniæ hydrobromatis . . . . gr. ¼-½.
  Aquæ destillatæ . . . . Ʒiss.—M.
Sig. A teaspoonful three or four times daily. BARTHOLOW.

693—℞ Ext. conii fld. (Squibb) . Ʒij.
Sig. Fifteen to sixty minims, not over three times daily.
              SPITZKA.

EPISTAXIS.

694—℞ Ext. hamamelidis fld. . . . . . . fʒij.
Sig. A teaspoonful every one to three hours. If pulse is
rapid and bounding, add veratrum viride and morphine.
          J. V. SHOEMAKER.

695—℞ Ext. geranii mac. fld. . . . . fʒj.
  Aquæ . . . . fʒiij.—M.
Sig. Syringe the nostrils, or plug with cotton saturated with
the fluid.   J. V. SHOEMAKER.

696—℞ Olei erigerontis (canad.) . . . . fʒj.
Sig. Five to fifteen drops on sugar every hour, or repeated as
required.   ELLWOOD WILSON.

697—℞ Tincturæ aconiti radicis . ♏︎viij.
  Liquoris ammonii acetatis . . fʒj.—M.
Sig. A teaspoonful every half-hour. (*In plethoric cases.*)
          THOMAS.

698—℞ Pulv. ipecac. . . . . gr. xx.
  Olei theobromæ . . . . Ʒss.—M.
Ft. suppositor. no. i.
Sig. Introduce into the rectum, and when vomiting ceases
give—

699—℞ Pulv. ipecac.,
  Ext. glycyrrhizæ . . . . ãã Ʒss.—M.
Sig. A powder every three hours. PEPPER.

700—℞ Pulv. aluminis,
  Pulv. acidi tannici . . ãã partes æquales.—M.
Sig. To be insufflated into the nares anteriorly and posteriorly.
          SAJOUS.

701—℞ Strychninæ sulphatis .   gr. ¼.
  Tincturæ ferri chloridi   fʒij.
  Vini ergotæ . . . . fʒss.
  Elixiris simplicis . . . . fʒiss.
  Aquæ destillatæ . q. s. ad fʒvj.—M.
Sig. A tablespoonful three times a day. (*In anæmic cases.*)
         LOMBE ATTHILL.

702—℞ Liquoris ferri persulphatis . . . . fʒj.
  Aquæ destillatæ . . . . fʒij.—M.
Sig. Inject into the nostril.   R. J. LEVIS.

703—℞ Antipyrin. . . . . Ʒij.
In capsulas no. xxiv div.
Sig. One, two, or three to be taken as required. To be used
with local treatment.   BEVERLEY ROBINSON.

704—℞ Pulveris aluminis,
  Pulveris acaciæ . . . . ãã partes æquales.—M.
Sig. To be blown into the nostrils. LECLUYSE.

705—℞ Pulv. acidi tannici . . . . Ʒij.
Sig. To be insufflated after a small quantity of cocaine has
been applied.   FLETCHER INGALS.

706—R Ichthyol,
   Ætheris . . . . āā f℥v.
   Collodii . . . . f℥x.—M.
 Sig. Paint on.   UNNA.

707—R Ichthyol, ... ℨss.
   Ætheris,
   Glycerini . . . . āā ℨij.—M.
 Sig. Apply locally.   LORENZ.

708—R Ichthyol . . . . ℨj.
   Vaselini   ℨix.—M.
 Sig. Apply locally.   NUSSBAUM.

709—R Creolin . . . . 1 part.
   Iodoform . . . . 4 parts.
   Lanolin . . . . 10 "
 Sig. Paint on.   KOCH.

710—R Acidi carbolici puri,
   Alcoholis absoluti . . . . āā ♏xlv.
   Aquæ destillatæ . . . . f℥iij.—M.
 Sig. For hypodermic injection.   HUNTER.

711—R Acetanilid. (antifebrin.) . . . . ℨj.
 Dispense in capsulas no. xv.
 Sig. Two capsules as required. (To reduce the temperature.)
             OSLER.

712—R Acidi sulphurosi,
   Glycerini . . . . āā f℥iss.—M.
 Sig. Apply locally to inflamed part.   DEWAR.

713—R Tincturæ digitalis . . . . f℥ij.
   Aquæ bullientis . . . . Oj.—M.
 Sig. Apply locally by means of flannels wrung out of this
 decoction.   ROYSTON FAIRBANK.

714—R Sol. hydrarg. bichlor. (3-1000) . . . . . q. s.
 Sig. Bathe the parts and irrigate the wounds, and cover with
 iodoform gauze wet with the solution. Apply tar to the
 red portions of the skin and a little beyond. Then cover
 with a wet dressing made with "Burow's Fluid" (No. 717,
 infra).

715—R Plumb. acetatis   ℨj.
   Tinct. opii   ℨj.
   Aquæ .   ad Oj.—M.
 Sig. Shake the bottle well, and wet cloths or lint thoroughly
 with the lotion and apply to affected parts.
         Charity Hospital, N. Y.

716—R Cretæ præparatæ,
   Adipis . . . . āā ℨj.
   Acidi carbolici . . . . ℨj.—M.
 Ft. unguentum.
 Sig. Apply externally and cover with lint.
         SIR DYCE DUCKWORTH.

717—R Aluminis crudi .   ℨj.
   Plumbi acetatis cryst. . . . . ℨv.
   Aquæ destillatæ . . . . ℨxiiss.—M.
 Sig. "Burow's Fluid."   FRAIPONT.

718—R Tinct. ferri chloridi,
   Syr. simplicis . . . . āā ℨj.
   Aquæ . . . . ℨij.—M.
 Sig. A teaspoonful every two or three hours, well diluted.
         Charity Hospital, N. Y.

719—R Tincturæ ferri chloridi . . . . f℥vj-f℥iss.
   Syrupi simplicis . . . . f℥ij.
   Aquæ destillatæ . . . . q. s. ad f℥vj.—M.
 Sig. A tablespoonful every two hours.   GOLDBERG.

720—R Potassii permanganatis   gr. vj.
   Aquæ destillatæ . . .   f℥vj.—M.
 Sig. A tablespoonful three times a day. (Keep in glass-stop-
 pered bottle.)   BARTHOLOW.

ERYSIPELAS (Continued).

721—℞ Ammonii carbonatis . . . . ℨij.
    Extracti glycyrrhizæ fluidi . . . . . . f ℨj.
    Liquoris ammonii acetatis . . . . . . f ℨiij.—M.
  Sig. A dessertspoonful every three hours,   BRANDE.

ERYTHEMA. (See Skin Diseases.)

FAVUS. (See Skin Diseases.)

FETOR OF AXILLÆ, BREATH, AND FEET.

722—℞ Sodii bicarbonatis . . . . ℨiij.
    Aquæ . . . . f ℨviij.—M.
  Sig. Apply as a lotion frequently.   BARTHOLOW.

723—℞ Potassii permanganatis . . . . gr. x-xxx.
    Aquæ . . . . f ℨviij.—M.
  Sig. Apply locally frequently.   BARTHOLOW.

724—℞ Atropinæ sulphatis . . . . gr. iv-viij.
    Aquæ rosæ . . . . f ℨij.—M.
  Sig. Apply to the part with a brush.   BARTHOLOW.

725—℞ Aluminii chloridi . . . . ℨss.
    Aquæ . . . . Oj.—M.
  Sig. Apply locally.   GOLDBERG.

726—℞ Sodii bicarbonatis . . . . ℨss.
    Aquæ . . . . Oj.—M.
  Sig. Apply locally.   GOLDBERG.

727—℞ Sodii biboratis . . . . gr. xv.
    Thymoli . . . . gr. viiss.
    Aquæ destillatæ . . . . f ℨlxxv.—M.
  Ft. sol.
  Sig. Mouth-wash. (*For fetor of breath due to carious teeth.*)
      MAGITOT.

728—℞ Glycerini . . . . f ℨiiss.
    Liq. ferri perchlor. . . . . f ℨviiss.
    Ess bergamii . . . . gtt. xx.—M.
  Ft. lotio.
  Bathe the feet morning and evening with a brush wet with
    the lotion. (*For fetid feet.*)   LEGROUX.

729—℞ Acidi salicylici . . . . gr. xxx.
    Pulv. amyli . . . . ℨv.
    Pulv. talci . . . . ℨxxij.—M.
  Sig. Dust in socks.   J. C. WILSON.

FEVERS, ERUPTIVE AND SIMPLE.

730—℞ Antipyrin . . . . ℨj.
    Syr. simplicis . . . . f ℨss.
    Aquæ cinnamomi . . . . ad f ℨij.—M.
  Sig. One-half to one teaspoonful every hour or two for chil-
    dren.   PENZOLDT.

731—℞ Antifebrin . . . . ℨj-ij.
    Spts. vini gallici . . . . f ℨss.
    Syr. simplicis . . . . ad f ℨij.—M.
  Sig. A teaspoonful every four hours, or as required. (*To
reduce the temperature.*)   HEINZELMANN.

732—℞ Amyli hydratis . . . . ℨiij.
    Syr. simplicis . . . . f ℨj.
    Aquæ . . . . ad f ℨiv.—M.
  Sig. Two tablespoonfuls at bedtime, in water, for adult. (*For
insomnia of fevers.*)   VON MERING.

733—℞ Ammonii salicylatis . . . . ℨj.
    Syr. simplicis . . . . f ℨss.
    Aquæ menthæ pip. . . . . f ℨiiss.—M.
  Sig. A teaspoonful every four hours to a child three years
    old. To adults, two or three teaspoonfuls may be given
    every four hours.   SULLIVAN.

F

734—℞ Tincturæ aconiti folii . . . . f℥v.
    Extracti veratri viridis fluidi . . . . . . fℨj.—M.
Sig. Twelve drops every two hours, watching effects.
                                   WEBER.

735—℞ Tincturæ aconiti **radicis** . . . . ℳxxx.
    Syrupi limonis . . . . f℥ss.
    Liquoris ammonii **acetatis** . . . . . . fℨij.—M.
Sig. A dessertspoonful every three hours.   R. P. THOMAS.

736—℞ Sodii bromidi . . . . **gr. x-xx.**
    Syr. aurantii cort.. . . . . f℥ss.
    Aquæ . . . . ad f℥iiss.—M.
Sig. A teaspoonful every quarter of an hour for children.
                                    A. A. SMITH.

737—℞ Liq. ammonii acetatis . . . . f℥iiss.
    Spts. ætheris nitrosi . . . . ad f℥iv.—M.
Sig. A teaspoonful to a tablespoonful, according to age.
                                    HARTSHORNE.

738—℞ Antimonii et potassii tartratis . . . . . gr. viij.
    Aquæ destillatæ . . . . f℥viij.—M.
Sig. Sponge the scalp frequently. (*For loss of hair after fever.*)
                                    POULAIN.

739—℞ Antimonii et potassi, tartratis,
    Morphinæ sulphatis . . . . āā gr. j.
    Hydrargyri chloridi mitis . . . . gr. iij.
    Potassii nitratis . . . . ℨj.
Misce et fiant chartulæ no. xij.
Sig. One powder every two or three hours. **PENDLETON TUTT.**

740—℞ Vini antimonii . . . . fℨj.
    Potassii vel sodii nitratis . . . . ℨj.
    Spiritus ætheris nitrosi . . . . fℨij.
    Liquoris morphinæ sulphatis . . . . fℨj.
    Syrupi acidi citrici . . . . f℥ss.
    Liquoris potassii citratis . . . . f℥iv.—M.
Sig. A tablespoonful **every two hours.**   CARSON.

741—℞ Cocain. hydrochloratis . . . . gr iv.
    Aquæ destillatæ . . . . fℨj.
Sig. Seven to fifteen minims hypodermically every two hours.
  (*In low forms with weak circulation.*)   DA COSTA.

742—℞ Tincturæ opii deodoratæ . . . . gtt. xlv.
    Vini antimonii . . . . f℥iss.
    Spiritus ætheris nitrosi . . . . f℥ij.
    Syrupi limonis . . . . f℥j.
    Liquoris ammonii acetatis . . . . f℥vj.
Fiat mistura.
Sig. A tablespoonful every two hours.   EBERLE.

743—℞ **Glycerini** . . . . f℥viiss.
    Acidi citrici vel tartarici . . . . ℨss.
    Aquæ . . . . f℥xix.—M.
Sig. One **to** two tablespoonfuls every hour as a beverage.
  (*When used freely, the excretion of urea is diminished.*)
                                    SEMMOLA.

FEVER, HECTIC.

744—℞ Antipyrin. . . . . ℨij.
    Aquæ . . . . f℥viij.—M.
Sig. Two tablespoonfuls, followed by **one** tablespoonful
  every hour till temperature is normal.   PRIBRAM.

745—℞ Quininæ sulphatis . . . . ℨj.
In pulv. no. xij div.
Sig. A powder, in water, three or four times daily. PHILLIPS.

746—℞ Quininæ hydrochloratis . . . . gr. xxxij.
    Acidi hydrochlorici diluti . . . . f℥j.
    Syrupi aurantii rubri . . . . f℥vij.
    Aquæ . . . . f℥iij.—M.
Sig. A dessertspoonful every **four hours.** ELLWOOD WILSON.

747—℞ Syr. calcis lactophosphatis . . . . f ℥iv.
Sig. A teaspoonful three or four times daily. BENEKÉ.

748—℞ Syrupi phosphatum compositi . . . . . f ℥iij.
Sig. A teaspoonful every four hours. PARRISH.

749—℞ Tinct. digitalis . . . . f ℥iij.
Tinct. ferri chlor. . . . . f ℥v.—M.
Sig. Fifteen drops three or four times daily, well diluted.
BARTHOLOW.

FEVER, INTERMITTENT AND REMITTENT.

750—℞ Quininæ sulphatis . . ℈ij.
Acidi sulphurici diluti f ℥j.
Syrupi zingiberis . f ℥j.
Aquæ destillatæ . . . . . q. s. ad f ℥iv.—M.
Sig. A dessertspoonful every two hours during the intermission. DA COSTA.

751—℞ Quininæ sulphatis . . . . gr. vj.
Acidi tartarici . . . . gr. iij.
Syrupi simplicis . . . . f ℥j.—M.
Sig. A teaspoonful. CASOVATI.

752—℞ Quininæ ferrocyanatis . . . . gr. iv.
Alcoholis . . . . f ℥j.
Solve, et adde—
Aquæ camphoræ . . . . f ℥vij.—M.
Sig. A teaspoonful every hour or two. ELLIS.

753—℞ Quininæ sulphatis . . . . ℈ij.
Acidi salicylici . . . . ℨiiiss.
Misce et divide in chartulas xvi.
Sig. One powder **every** three hours. SARZANCE.

754—℞ Extracti nucis vomicæ . . . . gr. iv.
Quininæ sulphatis . . . . ℨss.
Glycerini . . . . q. s. ut fiat massa in
pilulas xvi dividenda.
Sig. One pill three times a day. DA COSTA.

755—℞ Quininæ sulphatis . . . . gr. xlv.
Ferri et potassii tartratis . . . . gr. cv.
Aquæ destillatæ . . . . f ℥x.
Liquoris potassii arsenitis . . . . . . gtt. xxv.—M.
Sig. One to three tablespoonfuls daily. BACCELLI.

756—℞ Quininæ hydrochloratis . . . . gr. xv.
Sodii chloridi . . . . gr. xij.
Aquæ destillatæ . . . . ℥iij ℥ij.—M.
Sig. For hypodermic injection. BACCELLI

757—℞ Cinchoninæ sulphatis . . . . ℨss.
Liquoris potassii arsenitis . . . . . . f ℥iss.
Tincturæ ferri chloridi . . . . f ℨss.
Syrupi zingiberis . . . . f ℨiss.
Aquæ destillatæ . . . . q. s. ad f ℥iv.—M.
Sig.—A dessertspoonful after meals. (*In chronic cases.*)
PENDLETON TUTT.

758—℞ Antimonii et potassii tartratis gr. iij.
Quininæ sulphatis gr. x.
Misce et divide in partes æquales vi.
Sig. One powder every two hours during intermission. GOLA.

759—℞ Salicini . . . . gr. xxiv.
Sacchari albi. . . . . ℈iv.
Misce et divide in partes æquales viii.
Sig. One powder three times a day. KROMBHOLZ.

760—℞ Ferri ferrocyanidi,
Pulveris guaiaci resinæ . . . . . . āā ℨj.
Misce et divide in chartulas xii.
Sig. One powder three times a day. (*In obstinate intermittents.*)
ELLIS.

FEVER, INTERMITTENT AND REMITTENT (Continued).

761—℞ Cupri sulphatis . . . . gr. iv.
    Extracti cinchonæ . . . . gr. xxxij.
    Syrupi simplicis . . . . q. s. ut fiat massa in
        pilulas xvi dividenda.
Sig. One to be taken three times a day. (*In obstinate cases.*)
                        CHAPMAN.

762—℞ Narcotinæ . . . . gr. xxx.
    Acidi sulphurici diluti . . . . f ʒj.
    Syrupi simplicis . . . . f ʒss.
    Aquæ destillatæ . . . . f ʒiiiss.—M.
Sig. A teaspoonful every three hours. W. O'SHAUGHNESSY.

763—℞ Extracti hydrastis fluidi,
    Tincturæ eucalypti . . . . āā f ʒiss.
    Elixiris simplicis . . . . f ʒj.
    Vini xerensis . . . . f ʒij.—M.
Sig. A tablespoonful three times a day. (*In convalescents with hepatic and splenic enlargement.*) BARTHOLOW.

764—℞ Quiniæ muriatis . . . . gr. vj.
    Aquæ bullientis . . . . ℳxij.—M.
Sig. Inject deeply into the tissues four to six minims of the hot solution. PULAWSKI.

765—℞ Quininæ sulphatis . . . . ℨiv.
    Acidi sulphurici diluti . . . . q. s. ut ft. sol.
    Spts. ætheris nitrosi . . . . f ʒss.
    Syr. tolutani,
    Aquæ . . . . āā q. s. ad f ʒij.—M.
Sig. A teaspoonful three or four times daily. DA COSTA.

766—℞ Quininæ sulphatis . . . . gr. xvj.
    Ext. glycyrrhizæ . . . . ʒj.
    Syr. rubi idæi (raspberry) . . . . ʒj.—M.
Sig. A teaspoonful three to five times daily for a child three years old. J. LEWIS SMITH.

767—℞ Chinoidini . . . . ℨij.
    Resinæ podophylli . . . . gr. iv.
    Ferri sulph. exsic. . . . . ℨj.—M.
Ft. massa et in pil. no. xx div.
Sig. One three times daily. BARTHOLOW.

768—℞ Cupri arsenit. (tablet triturate) . . . . . gr. 1/10.
    Aquæ destillatæ . . . . f ʒij.—M.
Sig. Shake well. A tablespoonful **every three** hours. (*For the anæmia of ague.*) JOHNSON.

769—℞ Acidi carbolici . . . . ʒj.
    Tinct. Iodi comp. . . . . f ʒiij.—M.
Sig. Four drops every four hours, well diluted. BARTHOLOW.

770—℞ Acidi carbolici . . . . gr. xlviij.
    Syrupi acaciæ . . . . f ʒiss.
    Aquæ cinnamomi . . . . ad f ʒiv.—M.
Sig. A teaspoonful **every three** hours until five **doses are** taken daily. LUZZATO.

771—℞ Acidi arseniosi . . . . gr. j.
    Extracti taraxaci . . . . ℨj.—M.
Ft. massa et in pil. no. xl div.
Sig. One to four pills every three or four hours until twenty or thirty pills are taken. (*In hemorrhagic malarial fever.*)
                    RIGGS.

772—℞ Pulv. opii . . . . gr. xij.
    Pulv. capsici . . . . gr. xxxvj.
    Quininæ sulph. . . . . ʒj.—M.
In pulveres no. xij div.
Sig. One powder three times daily. (*In tubercule forms.*)
          ALONZO CLARK.

773—℞ Ext. ergotæ aquosi (Bonjean) . . . . gr. xxx.
    Aquæ destillatæ,
    Glycerini . . . . āā f ʒiiss.—M.
Sig. Inject a hypodermic syringeful into the spleen once or twice, at intervals of a few days. ROUQUETTE.

774—℞ Olei phosphorati . . . . f℈ss.
Sig. Five drops, well diluted, three times daily.   SOZINSKY.

775—℞ Potassii permanganatis . . . . gr. xij.
Aquæ destillatæ . . . . f℥iij.—M.
Sig. One or two teaspoonfuls three times daily.   (*In chronic malarial cases.*)   JOS. LEVI.

776—℞ Antipyrin. . . . . ℨiv.
Syr. tolutani . . . . f℥ss.
Aquæ . . . . ad f℥iij.—M.
Sig. One or two teaspoonfuls thrice daily.   ANTONY.

777—℞ Tinct. iodi . . . . f℥vj.
Potassii iodidi . . . . ℨij.
Aquæ cinnamomi . . . . ad f℥iij.—M.
Sig. A teaspoonful three times daily.   *Charity Hospital, N.Y.*

778—℞ Potassii nitratis . . . . ℨiij.
Aquæ destillatæ . . . . f℥iv.
Syrupi simplicis . . . . f℥j.—M.
Sig. Shake well and take a tablespoonful every three hours.   JOHNSON.

779—℞ Ammonii picratis . . . . ℈j.
Ft. massa et in pilulas no. xl div.
Sig. One to three pills four or five times daily.   H. M. CLARK.

FEVER, TYPHOID.

780—℞ Acidi carbolici . . . . ℳxxiv.
Glycerini . . . . f℥j.
Liquid. pepsin. aromat. . . . . . . f℥j.
Aquæ menthæ pip. . . . . f℥ij.—M.
Sig. A teaspoonful one hour after food.   McCOCKLE.

781—℞ Hydrarg. chlorid. mit. . . . . gr. xxij.
In pulv. no. iii div.
Sig. One powder every half-hour till three are taken.   (*Only during the first week.*)   VON ZIEMSSEN.

782—℞ Hydrargyri chloridi mitis . . . . gr. vj.
Sacchari albi . . . . ℈ij.
Misce et fiant chartulæ xii.
Sig. One every three hours.   (*During first nine days, carefully avoiding ptyalism.*)   PARKES.

783—℞ Hydrarg. chlorid. mit. . . gr. x.
Sodii bicarb. . . gr. xv.—M.
In chartulas no. ii div.
Sig. One at night. To be given the first and third night of treatment, if before the tenth day.   J. C. WILSON.

784—℞ Antipyrin. . . . . ℈viij.
Syr. tolutani . . . . f℥j.
Aquæ . . . . ad f℥ij.—M.
Sig. Two or three teaspoonfuls at first, and one teaspoonful hourly thereafter, until temperature is reduced.   MINOT.

785—℞ Thallin. sulphat. . gr. xxxij.
Aquæ menthæ pip. . . f℥j.—M.
Sig. A teaspoonful when required.   (*For pyrexia of typhoid.*)   MINOT.

786 ℞ Antifebrin. . . . . ℨss-j.
Elixiris simplicis . . . . f℥j.—M.
Sig. A teaspoonful when required.   (*For pyrexia.*)   BEREZOVSKY.

787—℞ Sodii salicylatis ℨss.
Syrupi simplicis f℥ss.
Aquæ destillatæ q. s. ad f℥ij.—M.
Sig. A tablespoonful every other night.   (*To lower temperature.*)   MOELI.

788—℞ Acidi hydrochlorici diluti . . . . f3j.
    Syrupi . . . . f3vij.
    Aquæ destillatæ . . . . f3ij.—M.
Sig. A dessertspoonful every two or three hours. (*In uncomplicated cases.*)
                                   DA COSTA.

789—℞ Olei terebinthinæ . . . . f3iss.
    Pulv. acaciæ,
    Syrupi simplicis,
    Aquæ destillatæ . . . . āā q. s.
Fiat emulsio, secundum artem, ad f3ij.
Sig. A teaspoonful every two or three hours. (*With diarrhœa and tympanitis.*)
                                   G. B. WOOD.

790—℞ Pulveris ipecacuanhæ compositi . . . . gr. x.
Divide in chartulas iv.
Sig. One every hour or two. (*Used at night in wakeful delirium.*)
                                   RINGER.

791—℞ Strychninæ . . . . gr. $\frac{1}{10}$.
    Aquæ . . . . q. s.—M.
Sig. Use hypodermically in cardiac asthenia.   J. C. WILSON.

792—℞ Bismuthi subnitratis,
    Pepsinæ . . . . āā 3ij.—M.
In pulv. no. xii div.
Sig. Four powders daily, at suitable intervals, in milk.
                             Roosevelt Hospital.

793—℞ Thymoli . . . . 3j.
    Ext. gentianæ . . . . q. s.
Ft. massa et in pil. no. xxiv div.
Sig. Two pills every six hours. (*For diarrhœa and dry tongue of typhoid.*)
                                   HENRY.

794—℞ Pulv. pepsinæ cryst. . . . . 3ij.
    Acidi muriatici dil. . . . . 3ss.
    Syr. simplicis . . . . 3j.
    Aquæ . . . . q. s. ad 3ij.—M.
Sig. A teaspoonful after food **three times daily.**
                                   PORCHER.

795—℞ Tinct. strophanth. hisp. (1-20) . . . . . f3ss.
Sig. Four to eight minims three or four **times daily.** (*For weak heart of typhoid.*)
                                   QUINLAN.

796—℞ Acidi sclerotici . . . . 3j.
    Aquæ destillatæ . . . . f3v.—M.
Sig. A hypodermic syringeful every half-hour as a styptic. (*In typhoid intestinal hemorrhage.*)
                              VON ZIEMSSEN.

797—℞ Extracti ergotæ aquosi (ergotinæ) . . . gr. xv.
    Syrupi aurantii corticis . . . . f3j.
    Aquæ destillatæ . . . . f3ij.—M.
Sig. A tablespoonful every hour or two. (*In alarming intestinal hemorrhage.*)
                                  BONJEAN.

798—℞ Caffeine . . . . 6 gr.
    Salicylate of sodium . . . . 4½ gr.
    Distilled water . . . . up to 16 minims.—M.
Dissolve with the aid of heat. Sixteen minims of the solution contain six grains of caffeine. (*For hypodermic injections for heart-failure in enteric fever.*)
                                   TANRET.

FEVER, TYPHUS.

799—℞ Ext. opii . . . . gr. vj.
In pil. no. xii div.
Sig. One pill every three hours, until quiet. (*For restlessness, when there is no lung-complication present.*)
                                   TANNER.

800—℞ Tinct. digitalis,
    Spts. chloroformi . . . . āā f3ss.
    Syr. aurantii cort. . . . . f3ij.—M.
Sig. A teaspoonful every two hours. (*In cardiac asthenia.*)
                                  J. C. WILSON.

801—℞ Moschi . . . . gr. x.
  Ætheris,
  Tinct. opii . . . . āā ♏xx.
  Aquæ cinnamomi . . . . f℥j.—M.

Fiat haustus.
To be taken at one draught. (*In last stages of typhus.*) HOOPER.

802—℞ Antimonii et potassii tartratis . . . . . gr. iv.
  Tincturæ opii . . . . f℥j.
  Aquæ camphoræ . . . . f℥viij.—M.

Sig. A tablespoonful every two hours. (*With sleeplessness and extreme nervous excitement.*) GRAVES.

803—℞ Moschi optimi . . . . gr. x-aj.
  Tincturæ castorei . . . . f℥ij.
  Syrupi zingiberis . . . . f℥j.
  Aquæ destillatæ . . . . f℥j.

Misce et fiat haustus.
Sig. One dose, given in coma and last stage of typhus.
E. J. CLARK.

804—℞ Quininæ sulphatis . . . . ℈iv.
  Acidi sulphurici dil. . . . . . q. s. ut ft. sol.
  Syr. simplicis . . . . f℥ss.
  Aquæ . . . . ad f℥j.—M.

Sig. A teaspoonful every two hours until fever is lessened.
GOOLDEN.

805—℞ Acidi phosphorici dil. . . . . f℥j.

Sig. Twenty to thirty minims, well diluted, every four or six hours. TANNER.

806—℞ Tinct. belladonnæ . . . . ℥ss.
  Tinct. aconiti radicis . . . . ℥ss.—M.

Sig. Ten drops every two hours. HARLEY.

FEVER, YELLOW.

807—℞ Hydrargyri chloridi mitis . . . . gr. xx.
  Quininæ sulphatis . . . . gr. xxiv.

Misce et fiat chartula.
Sig. One dose, given in simple syrup, to be repeated every four to six hours until four doses are taken. (*Given at the very onset to abort the disease.*) BLAIR.

808—℞ Morphinæ sulphatis . gr. j-ij.(!!)

Fiat chartula.
Sig. One dose. (To be given at the *very commencement after* a free mercurial purge followed by a saline cathartic.)
EDWARD FOWLER.

809—℞ Hydrarg. chloridi mitis,
  Pulv. jalapæ . . . . āā gr. x.—M.

Ft. pulv. no. i.
Sig. To be given early in the disease. RUSH.

810—℞ Hydrargyri chloridi mitis,
  Quininæ sulphatis,
  Pulveris opii et ipecacuanhæ . . . āā gr. xij.

Misce et fiant chartulæ no. iv.
Sig. One every three hours: if pyrexia is intense, it may be reduced by—

811—℞ Tincturæ aconiti foliorum gtt. x.
  Spiritus ætheris nitrosi . . . . f℥j.—M.

In water every three or four hours. In forty or fifty hours the fever subsides and the stage of calm comes on. When much exhaustion during this stage, stimulants; when much restlessness, valerianate of zinc, gr. v-x, or morphine, gr. ¼, repeated as necessary. When retching and vomiting supervene, give—

812—℞ Morphinæ sulphatis . . . . gr. iv.
  Creasoti . . . . ℥j.
  Spiritus vini gallici . . . . f℥iv.—M.

Sig. A tablespoonful every three hours as needed.
DOWELL.

813—℞ Chloroformi . . . . f ʒj.
Syr. acaciæ . . . . f ʒij.—M.
Sig. A teaspoonful before nourishment.   MacDonald.

814—℞ Sodii chloridi . . . . ʒss,
Olei olivæ . . . . f ʒss,
Olei terebinthinæ . . . . f ʒj.
Aquæ ferventis . . . . Oiss.—M.
Sig. Use as an enema.   Lawson.

815—℞ Potassii chloratis . . . . ʒiij.
Syrupi papaveris . . . . f ʒss.
Aquæ destillatæ . . . . f ʒivss.—M.
Sig. A tablespoonful every two or three hours with lime-water. (*To allay irritability of the stomach.*)   Frost.

816—℞ Olei terebinthinæ . . . . f ʒlss.
Mucilaginis acaciæ . . . . f ʒxlvss.—M.
Sig. A teaspoonful every hour or **two.** (*To allay retching and vomiting.*)   La Roche.

817—℞ Chloroformi . . . . f ʒj.
Syrupi acaciæ . . . . f ʒxv.—M.
Sig. A teaspoonful every **hour or two.** (*With pain, retching, and vomiting.*)   Condie.

818—℞ Pilocarpinæ muriatis . . . . gr. iij.
Aquæ destillatæ . . . . f ʒij.—M.
Sig. Ten minims hypodermically. (**To favor diaphoresis.**)   Hebersmith.

819—℞ Potassii iodidi . . . . gr. ij.
Liquoris potassii arsenitis . . . . gtt. ij.—M.
Sig. One dose every two or three hours. (This should be **given** throughout the entire course of the disease, beginning with the second day.)   Edward Fowler.

820—℞ Tincturæ ferri chloridi . . . . f ʒiij.
Syrupi acidi citrici . . . . f ʒxiij.—M.
Sig. A teaspoonful in ice-water every three or four hours.   Bailey.

821—℞ Creasoti . . . . ʒj-iss.
Alcoholis . . . . q. s. ut ft. sol.
Liq. ammonii acetatis . . . . ad f ʒiv.—M.
Sig. A teaspoonful every three or four hours.   Lewis.

FISSURE OF ANUS AND NIPPLES.

822—℞ Extracti hydrastis fluidi . . . . f ʒss.
Sig. Apply to the affected part.   Bartholow.

823—℞ Iodoformi,
Acidi tannici . . . . āā ʒij.
Misce et fiat chartula.
Sig. Expose the fissure and dust over.   **Bartholow.**

824—℞ Liquoris ferri subsulphatis . f ʒij.
Glycerini . . . . . . f ʒvj.—M.
Sig. Apply **with** camel's-hair brush to affected parts. (*For nipple.*)   Bartholow.

825—℞ Plumbi nitratis . . . . . . gr. x.
Glycerini . . f ʒj.—M.
Sig. Apply after each nursing, carefully washing before next nursing. (*For excoriated and fissured nipple.*)   Bartholow.

826—℞ Acidi carbolici . . . . gr. xxiv.
Aquæ . . . . f ʒj.—M.
Ft. lotio.
Sig. Apply several **times daily** to the nipples.   Parvin.

827—℞ Cocainæ muriatis . . . . gr. x.
Aquæ destillatæ . . . . f ʒij.—M.
Sig. Apply with a brush to the fissure half an hour before nursing, and wash well with warm water just before nursing. (*For fissure of nipple.*)   Starr.

828—℞ Acidi boracici . . . . gr. xx.
Mucilag. acaciæ . . . . ʒj.—M.

Sig. Use a nipple-shield, and, after nursing, dry the nipple
well with absorbent cotton and apply the lotion with a
camel's-hair brush. Should this fail, touch the fissure with
a point of argenti nitras every other day. STARR.

829—℞ Argenti oxidi . . . . ʒj.
Unguenti adipis . . . . ʒj.

Fiat unguentum.
Sig. Apply locally. (*For nipples.*) ELLIS.

830—℞ Acidi tannici . . . . ʒj.
Glycerini . . . . fʒij.—M.

Sig. Introduce into the rectum night and morning on a tent.
(*For fissure of anus.*) WARING.

831—℞ Potassii bromidi . . . . ʒj.
Glycerini . . . . fʒv.—M.

Sig. Apply locally. (*For anus.*) RINGER.

FISTULÆ.

832—℞ Camphor . . . . ʒj.
Salol . . . . ʒss.
Ether . . . . fʒj.—M.

Sig. Use as an injection. *St. Louis Hospital, Paris.*

833—℞ Argenti nitratis . . . . gr. xij.
Aquæ destillatæ . . . . fʒviij.

Solve.
Sig. Inject once daily. (*Fistula in ano.*) DRUITT.

834—℞ Tinct. iodi . . . . fʒj.
Sig. Inject once daily. WARING.

835—℞ Ext. sanguinariæ fld. . . . . fʒij.
Sig. Inject a quantity sufficient to fill and distend the fistula.
PHILLIPS.

836—℞ Hydrargyri chloridi corrosivi . . . . . gr. ij.
Aquæ destillatæ . . . . fʒviij.

Misce et fiat collyrium.
Sig. Apply to inner canthus of the eye twice daily. (*In lach-
rymal fistula.*) DRUITT.

837—℞ Cupri sulphatis . . . . gr. ij-iv.
Aquæ destillatæ . . . . fʒiv.—M.

Sig. Inject once daily. (*Fistula in ano.*) ASTLEY COOPER.

838—℞ Methyl violet (blue pyoktanin) . . . . . ʒj.
Water . . . . fʒiij.—M.

Sig. Inject every two or three days. (*Sinus communicating
with carious cartilage after enteric fever.*) J. C. WILSON.

FLATULENCE. (See also Acidity, Colic, and Dyspepsia.)

839—℞ Pulv. carbonis ligni . . . . ʒi-ij.

In pulv. no. xii div.
Sig. A powder at the time the flatulence usually appears.
RINGER.

840—℞ Tinct. asafœtidæ . . . . fʒj.
Aquæ . . . . fʒviij.—M.

Sig.—A teaspoonful three or four times daily. (*For children.*)
RINGER.

841—℞ Spiritus armoraciæ,
Elixiris simplicis . . . . āā fʒss.—M.

Sig. A teaspoonful. RINGER.

842—℞ Olei caryophylli . . . . gtt. iij.
Camphoræ monobromatis . . . . . . gr. xij.—M.

In pil. no. xii div.
Sig. One pill an hour after meals. J. C. WILSON.

843—℞ Tinct. nucis vomicæ,
    Tinct. physostigmatis,
    Tinct. belladonnæ . . . . āā f3j.—M.
Sig. Fifteen drops, in a little water, two or three times daily.
                                     BARTHOLOW.

844—℞ Pulv. calumbæ,
    Pulv. zingiberis . . . . āā 3ss.
    Sennæ fol. . . . . 3j.
    Aquæ bullientis . . . . Oj.—M.
Ft. infusum.
Sig. A wineglassful three times daily.   BARTHOLOW.

845—℞ Olei terebinthinæ . . . . f3j.
Sig. Three to five drops on sugar.   BARTHOLOW.

846—℞ Magnesiæ . . . . 3j.
    Spiritus ammoniæ aromatici . . . . . . f3j.
    Spiritus cinnamomi . . . . f3iij.
    Aquæ destillatæ . . . . f3vj.—M.
Sig. A tablespoonful every two hours. *(In sour eructations.)*
                                       ELLIS.

847—℞ Sodii sulpho-carbonatis . . . . 3iij.
    Syrupi zingiberis . . . . f3ss.
    Aquæ destillatæ . . . . q. s. ad f3iv.—M.
Sig. A dessertspoonful before meals. *(In extreme flatulence.)*
                                       SANSOM.

848—℞ Olei cajuputi . . . . f3j.
    Mucilaginis acaciæ . . . . f3ss.
    Syrupi simplicis . . . . f3j.
    Aquæ destillatæ . . . . q. s. ad f3vj.—M.
Sig. A tablespoonful.   SWEDIAUR.

849—℞ Acidi sulphurosi . . . . f3iss.
    Syrupi zingiberis . . . . f3viss.
    Aquæ destillatæ . . . . f3j.—M.
Sig. A teaspoonful.   POLLI.

850—℞ Olei cajuputi . . . . 3ss.
    Spts. lavandulæ co . . . . f3ss.
    Syr. zingiberis . . . . f3ij.
    Mucil. acaciæ . . . . ad f3ij.—M.
Sig. A dessertspoonful, as required.   HARTSHORNE.

851—℞ Aquæ anisi,
    Liq. calcis . . . . āā f3ss.
    Syr. acaciæ . . . . f3j.—M.
Sig. Add from ten to thirty drops of chloroform, according to age of child, and give a teaspoonful every two hours.
                                       CONDIE.

FRECKLES, SUNBURN, AND TAN. (See Skin Diseases.)

FROST-BITE. (See also Chilblains.)

852—℞ Acidi carbolici . . . . 3j.
    Tinct. iodi . . . . 3j.
    Acidi tannici . . . . 3j.
    Cerati simplicis . . . . 3iv.—M.
Ft. ungt.
Sig. Apply locally.   BARTHOLOW.

853—℞ Acidi sulphurosi . . . . f3iij.
    Glycerini,
    Aquæ . . . . āā f3j.—M.
Sig. Apply to affected part.   BARTHOLOW.

854—℞ Fellis bovini recentis . . . . Oss.
Sig. Warm and rub in well daily.   HUGH SMITH.

855—℞ Fellis bovini recentis . . . . f3iij.
    Balsami peruviani . . . . f3j.—M.
Sig. Apply two or three times a day. *(With broken or unbroken skin.)*
                                       HUGH SMITH.

FROST-BITE (Continued).

856—℞ Olei caryophylli,
Olei succini rectificati . . . . āā f℥ss.
Olei olivarum . . . . f℥j.—M.
Sig. Apply twice daily. ROCHE.

857—℞ Tinct. capsici . . . . f℥ss.
Sig. Paint over the unbroken surfaces. RINGER.

858—℞ Tinct. benzoini . . . . ℥ij.
Olei lini . . . . ℥iv.
Ceræ flavæ . . . . ℥ij.
Glycerini . . . . q. s.—M.
Ft. ungt.
Sig. Apply locally. REVEIL.

859—℞ Iodi . . . . ℈j.
Potassii iodidi . . . . gr. iv.
Aquæ destillatæ . . . . ♏vj.
Adipis . . . . ℥j.—M.
Sig. Apply once daily. (*With unbroken skin.*) HEBRA.

860—℞ Olei cajuputi . . . . f℥vij.
Olei amygdalæ dulcis . . . . f℥xvij.—M.
Sig. Apply three times a day on lint. (*With broken skin.*)
RADIUS.

861—℞ Camphoræ . . . . ℥j.
Olei cajuputi . . . . f℥ij.
Ætheris . . . . f℥j.—M.
Ft. linimentum.
Sig. Apply locally to the unbroken skin. TORTUAL.

862—℞ Linimenti camphoræ,
Linimenti saponis comp.,
Olei cajuputi . . . . āā f℥j.—M.
Ft. linimentum.
Sig. Apply locally to the unbroken skin. BRANDE.

FURUNCLE. (See Carbuncle.)

GALACTORRHŒA.

863—℞ Atropinæ sulph. . . . . gr. iv.
Aquæ rose . . . . f℥j.—M.
Sig. Apply on lint around **the breast,** and remove when the
throat becomes dry. BARTHOLOW.

864—℞ Olei camphorati . . . . f℥vj.
Sig. Apply **externally to breasts.** WARING.

865—℞ Potassii iodidi . . . . ℥j.
Aquæ . . . . f℥j.—M.
Sig. Twenty-five to thirty drops in water once or twice daily.
ROUSSEL.

GALL-STONES. (See Calculi.)

GANGRENE.

866—℞ Creasoti . . . . f℥ss.
Tincturæ gentianæ . . . . f℥j.
Spiritus vini (95°) . . . . f℥j.
Vini xerici . . . . f℥vj.—M.
Sig. From three to five tablespoonfuls a day, with milk.
ROMANOVSKY.

867—℞ Pulveris ligni **carbonis,**
Micæ panis,
Lactis . . . . āā q. s.
Fiat cataplasma.
Sig. Apply to correct fetor. GROSS.

868—℞ Acidi **chromici** . . . . ℥v.
Aquæ . . . . f℥iij.—M.
Sig. Apply to slough. BARTHOLOW.

G

GANGRENE (Continued).

869—℞ Pulv. acidi salicylici . . . . ℨj.
Ft. chart. no. j.
Sig. Use locally as a dusting powder. (*To destroy fetor and change morbid action.*) BARTHOLOW.

870—℞ Acidi carbolici . . . . ℨij.
Glycerini . . . . f℥viij.—M.
Sig. Apply on lint. LISTER.

871—℞ Potassii bromidi . . . . ℨij ℈ij. ·
Aquæ destillatæ . . . . f℥ij.
Solve. Dein adjice—
Bromi . . . . ℨj (by weight).
Aquæ destillatæ . . . . q. s. ad f℥iv.—M.
Sig. Apply to slough. (*In hospital gangrene.*)
J. LAWRENCE SMITH.

872—℞ Sodii sulphitis . . ℨj–ij.
Aquæ . f℥x.—M.
Ft. lotio.
Sig. Use as a lotion, or apply on compresses. WARING.

873—℞ Liquor. hydrogenii peroxidi (10 vol.) . **f℥iv.**
Sig. Apply locally, pure or diluted.

874—℞ Acidi nitrici . . . . fℨj.
Sig. Apply to the ulcer with a glass rod until it is **converted** into a firm, dry mass. WARING.

875—℞ Bromini . . . ℨj.
Sig. Apply to the slough with a glass rod. (*Hospital gangrene.*)
BARTHOLOW.

GASTRALGIA. (See Neuralgia, Catarrh, Colic, and Dyspepsia.)

GASTRIC ULCER. (See Ulcer.)

GLANDS, ENLARGED LYMPHATIC.

876—℞ Tinct. Iodi . . . . f℥ss.
Sig. Apply with a brush to the part. T. M. MARKOE.

877—℞ Iodi,
Terebinthinæ canadensis . . . . . āā ℨj.
Collodii . . . . f℥iv.—M.
Sig. Paint over diseased part. J. T. SHINN.

878—℞ Ungt. plumbi iodidi . . . . ℨj.
Sig. Apply locally. BARTHOLOW.

878bis.—℞ Ungt. iodi comp. . . . . ℨj.
Sig. Apply locally. H. B. SANDS.

879—℞ Potassii iodidi . ℈j.
Cerati simplicis ℨj.—M.
Sig. Apply to tumor. GOLDBERG.

880—℞ Zinci iodidi . . . . ℨj.
Adipis . . . . ℨj.—M.
Sig. Apply to swelling. URE.

881—℞ Barii iodidi . . . . gr. iv.
Adipis . . . . ℨj.—M.
Sig. Apply to scrofulous tumors. BIETT.

882—℞ Hydrargyri biniodidi . . . . gr. vij.
Potassii iodidi . . . . ℈j.
Adipis . . . . ℨj.—M.
Sig. Apply to enlargement. C. C. HILDRETH.

883—℞ Hydrargyri protiodidi . . . . gr. vj.
Morphinæ acetatis . . . . gr. vij.
Adipis . . . . ℨj.—M.
Sig. Apply to swelling. PELLETAN.

884—℞ Syr. ferri iodidi . . . . f ℨj.
Sig. Five to forty minims, according to age, well diluted, after meals, internally. BARTHOLOW.

885—℞ Potassii iodidi . . . . ℨj-iv.
Syr. aurantii cort. . . . . f ℨj.
Aquæ cinnamomi . . . . ad f ℨiij.—M.
Sig. A teaspoonful in water three times daily. RINGER.

886—℞ Calcii sulphidi . . . . gr. vj.
In pil. no. xxiv **div.**
Sig. One pill every four to six hours. RINGER.

887—℞ Hydrarg. cum **cretâ** . . . . gr. iv.
Sacch. lactis . . . . ℨj.—M.
In pulv. no. xx div.
Sig. One every two hours. (*In acute stage, tonsillitis, parotiditis, etc.*) BARTHOLOW.

GLEET. (See Gonorrhœa.)

GOITRE.

888—℞ Iodi . . . . . gr. lxiv.
Potassii iodidi gr. xxx.
Alcoholis . f ℨj.
Fiat solutio.
Sig. Paint once every other day. *King's College Hospital.*

889—℞ Unguenti iodi compositi,
Unguenti belladonnæ . . . . āā ℨj.—M.
Sig. Rub in well once daily. DA COSTA.

890—℞ Ungt. hydrarg. iodi rubri. . . . . ℨj.
Sig. Rub in a piece the size of a pea, and expose to sun's rays. RINGER.

891—℞ Tinct. iodi comp. . . . . f ℨj.
Sig. Apply locally with a brush. Also five to fifteen minims in water three times daily, internally. BARTHOLOW.

892—℞ Iodoformi . . . . ℨj.
Adipis . . . . ℨj.—M.
Ft. unguentum.
Sig. Apply locally. WARING.

893—℞ Ichthyol. . . . . ℨij.
Ext. belladonnæ . . . . ℨj.
Adipis . . . . ℨv.—M.
Sig. Apply twice a day. J. C. WILSON.

894—℞ Tincturæ **iodi** . . . . f ℨj.
Sig. Inject ℳxxx into the substance of the gland once a week for the first two or three weeks, and, after, once a fortnight as long as necessary. Give iodide of potassium internally. MORELL MACKENZIE.

895—℞ Iodi . . . . gr. ij.
Potassii iodidi . . . . ℨiv.
Aquæ menthæ piperitæ . . . . f ℨvj.
Fiat solutio.
Sig. A teaspoonful thrice daily. MAGENDIE.

896—℞ Potassii bromidi . . . . ℨss.
In pulv. no. xii div.
Sig. A powder in a half-tumblerful of water three times daily. (*In exophthalmic goitre.*) JON. HUTCHINSON.

GONORRHŒA.

897—℞ Creolin. . . . . gtt. xxx.
Extr. fluid. hydrast. canad. . . . . f ℨiss.—M.
Sig. Two teaspoonfuls in a pint of **warm water** to be used at one injection. (*Vaginal.*) LUTAUD.

898—℞ Extr. fluid. hydrast. canad. . . . . gtt. xxx.
  Creolin. . . . . gtt. x.
  Aquæ. . . . . f ʒviij.—M.
Sig. Use pure as a urethral injection.   LUTAUD.

899—℞ Potassii permanganatis . . . . gr. j–iij.
  Aquæ destillatæ . . . . f ʒj.—M.
Sig. Use as injection. (*In gleet.*)   VAN BUREN AND KEYES.

900—℞ Liq. plumbi subacet. dil. . . . . f ʒj.
  Ext. opii aquosi. . . . . gr. vj.—M.
Sig. Use as injection two **to** four times daily.
        VAN BUREN AND KEYES.

901—℞ Zinci sulpho-carbolatis . . . . gr. xx.
  Aquæ destillatæ . . . . f ʒviij.—M.
Sig. Inject a half-ounce two or three times a day.   RINGER.

902—℞ Zinci sulphatis . . . . gr. j–iij.
  Liq. plumbi subacet, dil. . . . . āā.—M.
Sig. Shake, and inject three or four times daily, **or**

903—℞ Zinci sulphatis . . . . ʒj.
  Aluminis . . . . ʒiij.—M.
Sig. Dissolve **a** teaspoonful in one pint of water, and inject
 three times a day. (*In females.*)   RINGER.

904—℞ Balsami copaibæ,
  Spts. ætheris nitrosi . . . . āā f ʒj.
  Liq. potassæ . . . . f ʒij.
  Ext. glycyrrhizæ . . . . f ʒss.
 Misce et adde—
  Olei gaultheriæ . . . . gtt. xvj.
  Syr. acaciæ. . . . . f ʒvj.—M.
Sig. A tablespoonful **three times daily.**   BUMSTEAD.

905—℞ Potassii citratis .   ʒss–j.
  Spts. limonis   f ʒss.
  Syr. simplicis   f ʒiij.
  Aquæ   f ʒj.—M.
Sig. A dessertspoonful, well diluted, three or four times daily,
 fasting. (*In first stage.*)   VAN BUREN AND KEYES.

906—℞ Tincturæ opii .   f ʒij.
  Vini colchici seminis   f ʒss.
  Liquoris potassii citratis . . . . f ʒviss.—M.
Sig. A tablespoonful three or four times a day.   BRODIE.

907—℞ Olei copaibæ,
  Olei cubebæ,
  Olei santali flavi . . . . āā ʒj.
  Magnesiæ. . . . . ʒij.
 Misce et fiant pilulæ no. lx.
Sig. Two pills every four hours.   BARTHOLOW.

908—℞ Methyl violet (blue pyoktanin) . . . . . ʒj.
  Water   f ʒvj.—M.
Sig. Use three times a day as an injection.   J. C. WILSON.

909—℞ Zinci sulphatis,
  Acidi tannici , ... āā gr. xv.
  Aquæ rosæ . . . . f ʒvj.—M.
Sig. A half-ounce as an injection two or three times daily.
 (*In gleet.*)   RICORD.

910—℞ Zinci chloridi . . . . gr. j–ij.
  Aquæ destillatæ . . . . f ʒvj.
Solve.
Sig. Inject once or twice daily.   R. J. LEWIS.

911—℞ Bismuthi **subnitratis,**
  Glycerini . . . . āā ʒss.
  Aquæ destillatæ . . . . f ʒiij.—M.
Sig. Inject twice **daily.** (*In chronic cases and gleet.*)   RINGER.

912—℞ Morphinæ acetatis . . . . gr. vj.
Plumbi acetatis,
Zinci sulphatis . . . . āā gr. viij.
Creasoti . . . . gtt. viij.
Aquæ destillatæ . . . . f℥vj.—M.
Sig. As an injection twice daily. H. H. SMITH.

913—℞ Hydrastinæ . . . . 3j.
Mucilaginis **acaciæ** . . . . f℥iv.—M.
Sig. A half-ounce as an injection. (*In chronic gonorrhœa and gleet.*)
BARTHOLOW.

914—℞ Liquoris potassæ f℥j.
Balsami copaibæ . f℥ss.
Tincturæ cubebæ . f℥vj.
Liquoris morphinæ sulphatis . f℥j.
Aquæ camphoræ . . . . q. s. ad f℥vj.—M.
Sig. A tablespoonful four times a day. D. HAYES AGNEW.

915—℞ **Ferri persulph.** . . . . ℥ss.
Aquæ . . . . f℥vj.—M.
Sig. Use as injection. (*In gleet.*) BUMSTEAD.

916—℞ Balsami copaibæ . . . . ℥ss.
Tinct. ferri mur.,
Tinct. cantharidis . . . . āā f℥ij.
Glycerini . . . . f℥ss.
Syrupi . . . . q. s. ad f℥iv.—M.
Sig. A tablespoonful after meals. BUMSTEAD.

917—℞ Balsami copaibæ,
Spts. ætheris nitrosi,
Spts. lavandulæ comp. . . . . āā f℥ss.
Liq. potassæ . . . . f℥j.
Mucil. acaciæ . . . . q. s. ad f℥iv.—M.
Sig. Shake, and take **one** tablespoonful. ("*Lafayette Mixture.*")
Charity Hospital, N. Y.

918—℞ Aquæ rosæ f℥ij.
Vini rubri . . f℥j.—M.
Sig. Use as injection. (*In gleet.*) Gradually increase the red wine until pure wine can be used. RICORD.

919—℞ Thallin. sulphatis Әj.
Aquæ destillatæ f℥ij.—M.
Ft. injectio.
Sig. Use as an injection three or four times daily.
KREIS AND GOLL.

920—℞ Quininæ sulphatis . . . . gr. x.
Glycerini . . . . f℥ss.
Aquæ . . . . ad f℥ij.—M.
Sig. Use as injection. LEDESON.

921—℞ Liq. hydrarg. chlor. corros. (1-1000) . Oj.
Sig. Distend the vagina with a speculum and cleanse thoroughly with the above solution. Then dust over and rub in iodoform, and tampon the vagina with iodoform gauze.
SCHWARZ.

922—℞ Argenti nitratis . 3j.
Aquæ destillatæ . . f℥ij.—M.
Sig. Wipe the vagina and cervix, and apply thoroughly by means of a tubular speculum. GRANDIN.

923—℞ Olei gaultheriæ . . . . f℥ij.
Mucil. acaciæ . . . . . . q. s. ut ft. emulsio.
Syr. simplicis . . . . f℥j.
Aquæ . . . . ad f℥ij.—M.
Sig. A teaspoonful three times daily. (*In gonorrhœal rheumatism.*)
R. W. TAYLOR.

924—℞ Olei santali . . . . 3j.
Sig. Fifteen or twenty drops **on sugar, or in** capsules (five-drop), after meals. LATZEL.

925—℞ Ext. colchici acetici,
    Ext. aloes,
    Pulv. ipecac.,
    Hydrarg. chlor. mit. . . . . āā gr. j.
    Ext. nucis vomicæ . . . . gr. ¼–ss.—M.
Ft. pil. no. i.
Sig. To be taken every four hours until it purges.   **LOOMIS.**

926—℞ Vini colchici seminis . . . . f℥iij.
    Spiritus ammoniæ aromatici . . f℥xij.—M.
Sig. A teaspoonful every three hours until some physiological effect is produced.   BARTHOLOW.

927—℞ Colchicinæ . . . . gr. j.
    Extracti colocynthidis compositi . . . ℈ss.
    Quininæ sulphatis . . . . ℈j.
Misce et divide in pilulas no. lx.
Sig. One pill every four hours.   BARTHOLOW.

928—℞ Extracti colchici acetici,
    Extracti rhei,
    Extracti aloes socotrinæ . . . āā gr. vj.
    Extracti belladonnæ . . . . gr. j.
Misce et fiant pilulæ no. vi.
Sig. One pill at bedtime twice a week.   A. B. GARROD.

929—℞ Pulveris colchici seminis . . . . ℈ss.
    Hydrargyri chloridi mitis,
    Extracti colocynthidis . . . . āā gr. viij.
    Pulveris digitalis,
    Quininæ sulphatis . . . . āā gr. xv.
Misce et fiat massa, in pilulas no. xx dividenda.
Sig. From **one to** four pills a day.   TROUSSEAU **ET REVEIL.**

930—℞ Aceti colchici . . . . f℥j-ij.
    Magnesiæ . . . . gr. **xv-xx.**
    Magnesii sulphatis . . . . ℥j-ij.
    Syrupi simplicis . . . . f℥j.
    Aquæ cinnamomi . . . . f℥ix.
Fiat haustus.
Sig. Repeat in **three hours if necessary.**   **SCUDAMORE.**

931—℞ Extracti colchici acetici . . . . gr. x.
    Pulveris ipecacuanhæ **compositi,**
    Pulveris digitalis,
    Extracti colocynthidis compositi . . āā gr. xij.
Misce et fiant pilulæ no. xii.
Sig. One pill twice or thrice a **day.**   HENRY HALFORD.

932—℞ Tincturæ colchici seminis . . . . ℥xv.
    Magnesii carbonatis . . . . gr. vj.
    Magnesii sulphatis . . . . gr. xxx.
    Aquæ menthæ piperitæ . . . . q. s. ad f℥j.
Fiat haustus.
Sig. Repeat *pro ne rata.*   *University Hospital.*

933—℞ Tincturæ colchici seminis . . . . ℥xx.
    Potassii bicarbonatis . . . . gr. x.
    Aquæ pimentæ . . . . f℥j.
Misce et fiat haustus.
Sig. Three or four times a day   *London Hospital.*

934—℞ Chloroformi,
    Spts. ammoniæ aromatici . . . . . āā f℥j.
    Spts. ætheris comp.,
    Tinct. opii camph. . . . . āā f℥ss.
    Mucil. acaciæ . . . . f℥ss.—M.
Sig. A teaspoonful at once.   HARTSHORNE.

935—℞ Magnesii sulphatis . . . . ℥j.
    Magnesiæ optimæ . . . . ℈j.
    Vini colchici radicis . . . . f℥j.
    Aquæ menthæ pip. . . . . f℥x.—M.
Sig. A **tablespoonful every hour until it operates.**
    SCUDAMORE.

f   81

936—℞ Potassii iodidi . . . . gr. v.
    Potassii bicarb. . . . . gr. x.
    Mist. ammoniaci . . . . f℥j.—M.
Ft. haustus.
Sig. To be taken thrice daily.   FOTHERGILL.

937—℞ Potassii bromidi . . . . gr. xx.
    Tinct. hyoscyami . . . . f℥ss.
    Tinct. lupuli . . . . f℥j.
    Aquæ camphoræ . . . . f℥j.—M.
Ft. haustus.
Sig. Take at bedtime. *(For gouty insomnia.)*   FOTHERGILL.

938—℞ Sodii salicylatis . .   ℨij.
    Syr. aurantii cort. . . . . . .   f℥j.
    Aquæ   . . . . ad f℥iv.—M.
Sig. A tablespoonful three times daily, in conjunction with
   rest. Joints involved are wrapped in cotton wool.
                 JACCOUD.

939—℞ Lithii **benzoatis** . . . . ℨij.
    Aquæ **cinnamomi** . . . . f℥iss.—M.
Sig. A teaspoonful in a wineglassful of water **every four or**
   six hours. *(During intervals.)*   JACCOUD.

940—℞ Gran. efferv. lithii benzoatis . . . . . . ℥iv.
Sig. A teaspoonful in water two or three times daily.
                 R. V. MATTISON.

941—℞ Gran. efferv. lithii citratis . . . . ℥iv.
Sig. One or two teaspoonfuls in water **three times daily.**
            R. V. MATTISON.

942—℞ Tinct. iodi . . . . ℳclx.
    Glycerini . . . . f℥ij.—M.
Sig. A teaspoonful thrice daily.   J. M. GRANVILLE.

943—℞ Lithii carbonatis vel citratis . . . . . . ℈v.
    Aquæ destillatæ . . . . f℥xx.—M.
Sig. Apply by means of lint, especially if the skin is broken.
                 GARROD.

944—℞ Veratrinæ . . . . ℈j.
    Adipis . . . . ℥j.—M.
Sig. Apply to painful joint *at onset. (Not when the skin is*
broken.)   TURNBULL.

GRAVES' DISEASE. (Exophthalmic **Goitre**.)

945—℞ Ext. belladonnæ . . . . gr. v.
In pil. no. xxx div.
Sig. One pill three or four times a day.   J. C. WILSON.

946—℞ Antipyrin. . . . . ℨj.
In chartulas no. xx div.
Sig. One powder three or four times a day.   J. C. WILSON.

947—℞ Spartein. sulphatis . . . . gr. iij.
In pil. no. xv div.
Sig. One pill three or four times a day.   CLARK.

948—℞ Cannabin. . . . . gr. ivss.
    Sacchari lactis . . . . q. s.—M.
Ft. pil. no. v.
Sig. To be taken in twenty-four hours.   VALIERI.

949—℞ Cannabin. . . . . gr. ivss.
    Aquæ destillatæ . . . . ℥iij.
    Syr. aurantii flor. . . . . ℥j.—M
Sig. To be taken in teaspoonful doses in twenty-four hours.
                 VALIERI.

GUMS, INFLAMED OR BLEEDING.

950—℞ Glyceriti acidi tannici . . . . ℥j.
Sig. Apply with a camel's-hair brush. *(For spongy or bleeding*
gums.)   BARTHOLOW.

951—℞ Tinct. myrrhæ . . . . fℨij-iv.
Aquæ vel infusi cinchonæ . . . . fℨiv.—M.

Ft. gargarisma.
(*For spongy or ulcerated gums.*)   **PHILLIPS.**

952—℞ Chloral. hydratis,
Tinct. cochleariæ (Ph. P.) . . . . āā ℨiss.—M.

Sig. Apply to the gums, by means of a pledget of cotton, every
day or two. (*For the gingivitis of pregnancy.*)   **PINARD.**

953—℞ Acidi carbolici . . . . gr. xv.
Tinct. iodi . . . . ♏xiv.
Glycerini . . . . ♏lxxv.—M.

Sig. Paint the gums morning and evening with a camel's-
hair brush dipped in the solution. (*For painful gingivitis.*)
      BARATOUX.

HÆMATEMESIS.

954—℞ Tinct. hamamelidis . . . . fℨss.

Sig. Two to four drops every two or three hours.   **RINGER.**

955—℞ Ergotini (Bonjean) . . . . gr. xij.
Aquæ destillatæ . . . . fℨj.—M.

Sig. Five to ten minims hypodermically every three or four
hours.   **RINGER.**

956—℞ Liquoris ferri subsulphatis . . . gtt. xx.
Aquæ destillatæ . . . . fℨij.—M.

Sig. A teaspoonful every half-hour or hour, in ice-water,
allowing the patient to swallow cracked ice. **BARTHOLOW.**

957—℞ Plumbi acetatis . . . . ℨss.
Hydrargyri chloridi mitis . . . . gr. v.
Confectionis rosæ . . . . q. s.

Misce et fiant pilulæ no. x.
Sig. One pill every two to four hours. (*From ulcer.*) **ELLIS.**

958—℞ Acidi tannici . . . . gr. xx.
Pulveris opii . . . . gr. v.
Glycerini . . . . q. s.

Fiat massa, in pilulas no. x dividenda.
Sig. One pill every hour or two.   **ELLIS.**

959—℞ Acidi gallici . . . . gr. x.
Acidi sulphurici dil. . . . . ♏x.
Aquæ . . . . fℨj.—M.

Ft. haustus.
Sig. To be repeated in **four or six** hours if necessary.
      BRINTON.

960—℞ Ferri et ammonii sulphatis . . . . ℨij.
Aquæ cinnamomi . . . . fℨiv.—M.

Sig. A tablespoonful every two **or three hours.** BARTHOLOW.

961—℞ Aluminis . . . . . ℨiss.
Syrupi krameriæ . . . . fℨij.
Aquæ destillatæ . . . . fℨvj.—M.

Sig. The one-fourth part to be given every half hour.
      TROUSSEAU ET REVEIL.

HÆMATURIA.

962—℞ Acidi gallici . . . . ℨss.
Acidi sulphurici dil. . fℨj.
Tinct. opii deodoratæ . . fℨj.
Infusi digitalis . . fℨiv.—M.

Sig. A tablespoonful every four hours.   DRUITT.

963—℞ Olei terebinthinæ . fℨx.
Magnesii sulphatis ℨj.
Pulveris uvæ ursi . ℨj.
Aquæ camphoræ . fℨvlij.—M.

Sig. Shake well. Two tablespoonfuls every two hours.
      SMITH.

964—℞ Olei terebinthinæ . . . . f 3ss.
Mucil. acaciæ . . . . q. s.
Syr. simplicis . . . . ad f 3iij.
Olei gaultheriæ . . . . gtt. vilj.—M.
Ft. emulsio.
Sig. One to three teaspoonfuls every two to four hours.
JOHN HUNTER.

965—℞ Tinct. ferri muriatis . . . . . . ♏︎xxx.
Tinct. digitalis . . . . ♏︎xv.
Aquæ menthæ pip. . f 3iss.—M.
Ft. haustus.
Sig. To be repeated every four hours. AITKEN.

HÆMOPTYSIS.

966—℞ Ext. ergotæ fld. . . . . . . f 3j.
Tinct. opii deodoratæ f 3ij.—M.
Sig. Twenty drops in half an ounce of cold water every half-
hour, watching the effect. J. C. WILSON.

967—℞ Ferri acetatis . 3ij.
Aquæ . . . . q. s.
Sig. Make the solution distinctly but not disagreeably sour,
and let the patient constantly sip. RINGER.

968—℞ Sodii chloridi . . . . 3ij.
Sig. Take a half-teaspoonful dry. Repeat till nausea occurs.
RINGER.

969—℞ Ext. ergotæ fld. . . . . f 3j.
Olei gaultheriæ . . . . gtt. iv.—M.
Sig. A teaspoonful **every hour** at first, then every four to six
hours. RINGER.

970—℞ Plumbi acetatis . . . . gr. xx.
Pulv. digitalis . . . . gr. x.
Pulv. opii . . . . gr. v.—M.
Ft. massa et in pil. no. x div.
Sig. One pill every four hours. BARTHOLOW.

971—℞ Infusi digitalis . . . . f 3iv.
Sig. A tablespoonful every hour until the pulse is reduced.
BRINTON.

972—℞ Pulv. aluminis . . . . 3j.
Saechari albi . . . . 3ss.
Pulv. ipecac. comp. . . . . 3j.—M.
In pulv. no. vi div.
Sig. One powder every two hours. SKODA.

973—℞ Morphinæ sulphatis . . . . gr. ⅙
Sig. Use hypodermically and repeat *pro re nata*. J. C. WILSON.

HAIR, FALLING OF THE. (See also Alopecia.)

974—℞ Chloral. hydratis . . . . 3j.
Aquæ coloniensis . . . . f 3vj.
Glyeerini . . . . f 3iss.—M.
Sig. Hair-tonic. W. A. JAMIESON.

975—℞ Sodii biboratis . . . . 3iv.
Aquæ ammoniæ . . . . f 3j.
Spts. myreiæ . . . . f 3ij.
Aquæ rosæ . . . . f 3xiij.—M.
Sig. Shampoo hair-wash. POTTER.

976—℞ Ext. jaborandi fld.,
Tinct. cantharidis . . . . ā ā f 3ss.
Glyeerini,
Olei vaselini ā ā f 3j.—M.
Sig. Hair-tonic. For use after continued fevers. Apply lo-
cally with a sponge at night. BARTHOLOW.

977—℞ Tinct. cantharidis . . . . f℥j.
Aceti destillati . . . . f℥iss.
Glycerini . . . . f℥ss.
Spts. rosmarini, ... f℥iss.
Aquæ rosæ . . . . ad f℥viij.—M.

Sig. Hair-tonic. **To be well sponged on** to the scalp night
and morning. TILBURY FOX.

978—℞ Liquor. hydrogenii peroxidi (10 vol.) . . f℥iv.

Sig. Apply locally with a sponge or a soft brush. (*To bleach
the hair.*) ERASMUS WILSON.

HAY FEVER.

979—℞ Pulveris ipecacuanhæ compositi . . . . gr. xv–xx.

Fiat chartula.
Sig. One dose. (*For temporary relief in attacks of dyspnœa.*)
HYDE SALTER.

980—℞ Antipyrin. . . 3ss.
Syr. aurantii cort. . . . . f℥j.
Aquæ . . . . ad f℥iij.—M.

Sig. A teaspoonful one to three times daily. CHEATHAM.

981—℞ Cocain. muriatis . . . . gr. v.
Aquæ destillatæ . . . . f℥ij.

Sig. Apply with a camel's-hair brush to the nasal passages.
SAJOUS.

982—℞ Cocain. muriatis . . gr. vj.
Aquæ destillatæ . . f℥ij.—M.

Sig. Instil a few drops into the nares while the head is
lowered. DA COSTA.

983—℞ Quininæ hydrochloratis . gr. iv–viij.
Aquæ destillatæ . . . . . f℥j.—M.

Sig. Apply with large camel's-hair brush, or spray-producer,
to nares and fauces. BARTHOLOW.

984—℞ Tincturæ iodi . . . . 3j.
Acidi carbolici . . . . gr. x.
Aquæ destillatæ . . . . f℥iv.—M.

Sig. Apply to fauces and nares. BARTHOLOW.

985—℞ Tincturæ aconiti radicis . . . . f℥ss.
Glycerini . . . . f℥iss.—M.

Sig. Apply to outside **of nose.** RINGER.

986—℞ Liquoris hydrogenii peroxidi (10 vol.) . f℥j.
Aquæ ferventis . . . . ad f℥iv.—M.

Sig. Inject into the naso-pharynx with a post-nasal syringe.
S. W. INGRAHAM.

987—℞ Atropinæ sulphatis . . gr. ¼.
Morphinæ sulphatis . . gr. viiss.
Aquæ destillatæ . . . . f℥v.—M.

Sig. Five to fifteen minims hypodermically two or three
times daily (five minims = atropine gr. 1/80 and morphine
gr. ¼). S. N. BISHOP.

988—℞ Hydrarg. chlor. corros. . gr. j.
Quininæ muriatis . . 3j.
Acidi carbolici . . 3iss.
Glycerini . . . . f℥viss.—M.

Sig. Use a tepid douche of boro-glyceride (3j ad Oj); then
apply the solution with a brush to the nasal and pharyn-
geal walls. ANDREW CLARKE.

989—℞ Syr. acidi hydriodici . . . . f℥iv.

Sig. A teaspoonful every two hours. JUDKINS.

990—℞ Potassii arsenitis gr. xv.
Aquæ destillatæ . f℥j.

Solve.
Sig. Unsized white paper to be thoroughly moistened with this
solution, cut into twenty equal parts, and each part rolled
into a cigarette, two or three of which may be smoked
daily. TROUSSEAU.

HAY FEVER (Continued).

991—℞ Potassii iodidi . . . . 3j.
    Liquoris potassii arsenitis . . . . f5j.
    Aquæ destillatæ . . . . f3iv.—M.
Sig. A teaspoonful every four or six hours.   SMITH.

HEADACHE.

992—℞ Tinct. belladonnæ . . .   f3ss.
Sig. Six drops every three hours. *(In congestive headache.)*
         RINGER.

993—℞ Atropinæ sulphatis   gr. ss.
    Chinoidinæ .   . . 3j.
Misce et fiant pilulæ no. lx.
Sig. One pill twice or thrice daily. *(In sick headache.)*
         BARTHOLOW.

994—℞ Tinct. nucis vomicæ . . . . . . '. . . . f3ss.
Sig. One drop frequently. *(In bilious headache with nausea.)*
         RINGER.

995—℞ Caffeinæ . . . . .   gr. vij.
    Acidi hydrochlorici . .   ♏ij.
    Syrupi aurantii florum   f3ss
    Aquæ destillatæ .   f3iij.—M.
Sig. A tablespoonful every hour or two, as required. *(In hemicrania.)*   BEASLEY.

996—℞ Pulveris guaranæ   gr. x–xv.
    Sacchari albi   q. s.
Misce et fiat pulvis.
Sig. To be taken once or oftener in the day. *(In migraine or periodical headache.)*   S. WILKS.

997—℞ Pulveris valerianæ .   3j.
    Pulveris cinnamomi compositi . . . . gr. x.
Misce et fiat pulvis.
Sig. Repeat every fourth hour.   JOY.

998—℞ Sodii chloridi . . .   3j.
    Spiritus camphoræ . .   f3j.
    Aquæ ammoniæ   f3ss.
    Aquæ   Oj.
Misce et fiat lotio.
Sig. "*Eau sédatif.*" For external use.   RASPAIL.

999—℞ Ammonii carbonatis   gr. x.
    Olei valerianæ . . . . . .   gtt. iij.
    Syrupi simplicis   f3ss.
    Aquæ cinnamomi . . . .   f3iss.—M.
Sig. One-fourth part every four hours.   HAZARD.

1000—℞ Ætheris,
    Spiritus ammoniæ aromatici . . . ãã f3j.
    Aquæ camphoræ   f3x.
    Tincturæ cardamomi compositæ . f3j.
Misce pro haustu.
Sig. Two to three times a day. *(In nervous headache.)*
         BRANDE.

1001—℞ Pulv. capsici . . .   gr. xij.
    Ext. colocynth. comp.   gr. iv.
    Ext. gentianæ   gr. xxiv.–M.
Ft. massa et in pil. no. xii div.
Sig. One pill three times daily. Twenty-five grains of sodium bromide to be taken at night. *(In congestive headache.)*
         DA COSTA.

1002—℞ Potassii citratis . . . . 3j.
    Spts. juniperi . . . . 3j.
    Spts. ætheris nitrosi . . . . ♏xx.
    Inf. scoparii . . . . f3j.—M.
Sig. To be taken thrice daily. *(In uræmic form.)* W. H. DAY.

1003—℞ Ext. belladonnæ . .   gr. v.
Sig. To be rubbed into the affected temple every night. *(In nervous form, migraine, clavus, etc.)*   W. H. DAY.

HEADACHE (Continued).

1004—℞ Ext. aconiti alc.. . . . . 3j.
      Adipis . . . . 3ij.—M.
Ft. ungt.
Sig. Rub into the affected **temple every night.** (*In nervous form, migraine, etc.*)
                                    W. H. DAY.

1005—℞ Gran. efferv. bromo-caffeini . . . . . . 3iv.
Sig. A teaspoonful in a half-glassful of cold water. **Repeat** in half an hour if necessary (*In nervous form.*)
                         R. V. MATTISON.

1006—℞ Ethoxycaffeini . . . . gr. xij.
      Sodii salicylatis . . . . gr. xv.
      Aquae destillatae . . . . f3j.—M.
Sig. From a teaspoonful to a tablespoonful, as required
                    DUJARDIN-BEAUMETZ.

1007—℞ Ammonii chloridi . . . . 3iij.
      Morphinæ acetatis . . . . gr. j.
      Caffeinæ citratis . . . . 3ss.
      Spts. ammoniæ aromatici . . . . f3j.
      Elix. guaranæ . . . . f3iv.
      Aquæ **rosæ** . . . . f3iv.—M.
Sig. A dessertspoonful every quarter-hour **until relieved.** (*In bilious form.*)
                         CARPENTER.

1008—℞ Zinci phosphidi . . . . gr. iij.
      Ext. nucis vomicæ . . . . gr. x.
      Confect. rosæ . . . . q. s.—M.
Ft. massa et in pil. no. xxx **div.**
Sig. One after each meal. (**In** *nervous form.*)
                    FORDYCE **BARKER.**

1009—℞ Potassii acetatis . . . . 3vj.
      Infusi digitalis . . . . f3vj.—M.
Sig. A **tablespoonful** every third hour. (*In uræmic headache.*)
                       A. A. SMITH.

1010—℞ Chloroformi . . . . f3j.
Sig. Ten drops, stirred in a wineglassful of cold water, four or **five times** a day. (*For habitual headache.*) J. C. WILSON.

HEART-BURN. (See Acidity.)

HEART-DISEASE.

1011—℞ Tincturæ digitalis . . . . f3j.
Sig. Ten minims three **times daily.** (*In irritable heart, with palpitation.*)
                        DA COSTA.

1012—℞ Tincturæ digitalis . . . f3iss.
      Extracti ergotæ fluidi . . . . . f3ij.—M.
Sig. A teaspoonful three times a day. (*In simple enlargement.*)
                    BARTHOLOW.

1013—℞ Pulveris scillæ . . . . **gr. x.**
      Pulveris ferri,
      Pulveris digitalis (English),
      Quininæ sulphatis . . . . . . āā ǝj.
Misce et fiant pilulæ no. xx.
Sig. One pill three or four times a day. (*In fatty degeneration; dilatation of cavities, especially the right; mitral regurgitation, with anæmia.*) BARTHOLOW.

1014—℞ Pulveris digitalis . . . . gr. ss-j.
      Ferri sulphatis . . . . gr. j.
      Pulveris capsici . . . . gr. ¼.
      Extracti gentianæ . . . . gr. ij.
Misce et fiat pilula.
Sig. One to be taken **thrice daily.** (*In chronic heart-disease.*)
                    FOTHERGILL.

1015—℞ Tincturæ digitalis . . . . ♏x.
      Spiritus chloroformi . . . . ♏xxv.
      Infusi buchu . . . . f3j.
Fiat haustus.
Sig. To be taken three times a day. (*In simple cardiac debility.*)
                    FOTHERGILL.

1016—℞ Pulv. digitalis . . . . gr. xxx.
Ferri sulph. exsiccati . . . . gr. xv.
Pulv. capsici . . . . gr. xl.
Pil. aloe et myrrhæ . . . . ʒij.—M.

Fiat massa et in pil. no. lx div.
Sig. One pill morning and night. (*Chronic heart-disease, with gastric catarrh and constipation.*)   FOTHERGILL.

1017—℞ Potassii iodidi . . . . ʒj.
Potassii bicarb. . . . . ʒiij.
Infusi buchu . . . . ad fℨxij.—M.

Sig. Two tablespoonfuls three or four times daily. (*Cardiac hypertrophy and increased arterial tension.*)   FOTHERGILL.

1018—℞ Pulv. fol. digitalis . . . . ʒj.

In pulv. no. x div.
Sig. A powder every three hours. (*In great dilatation and hypertrophy.*)   RINGER.

1019—℞ Pulveris digitalis . . . . gr. ij.
Aquæ . . . . fℨj.—M.

Sig. One tablespoonful *twice only*. (*In cardiac dropsy.*)
NIEMEYER.

1020—℞ Tincturæ digitalis . . . . ♏x-xx.
Tincturæ calumbæ . . . . fʒj.
Aquæ camphoræ . . . . fℨx.

Fiat haustus.
Sig. One dose, twice daily. (*In nervous palpitation.*)   PARIS.

1021—℞ Infusi digitalis . . . . fℨiv.
Potassii acetatis . . . . ʒij.
Spiritus ætheris nitrosi . . . . fʒij.
Aquæ cassiæ . . . . fℨiss.—M.

Sig. A tablespoonful **every fourth hour.** (*With pericardiac effusion.*)   KILGOUR.

1022—℞ Infusi digitalis   fℨviiss.
Potassii nitratis . . . . .   ʒij.
Acidi hydrocyanici diluti   ♏xiv.
Syrupi aurantii corticis   fʒij.—M.

Sig. A tablespoonful every two hours. (*In hypertrophy.*)
COPLAND.

1023—℞ Pulveris digitalis . . . . gr. v.
Pulveris scillæ . . . . gr. x.
Pilulæ hydrargyri . . . . ʒss.

Fiat massa et divide in pilulas **x.**
Sig. One pill three times daily. (*In palpitation with anasarca.*)
BAILLIE.

1024—℞ Cocain. hydrochloratis . . . . gr. vj.
Aquæ destillate . . . . fℨiij.—M.

Sig. A teaspoonful three times daily. (*In nervous cardiac debility.*)   ROSENBACH.

1025—℞ Iodi carbolati   fʒss.
Sig. Fifteen or twenty drops on cotton, or in an inhaler. **To** be inhaled several times daily. (*In endocarditis.*) McCLUN.

1026—℞ Gran. efferv. caffeini **citratis** . . . . . ℨiv.
Sig. Three to five teaspoonfuls several times daily, gradually increased. (*In intermittent heart.*)   NOTHNAGEL.

1027—℞ Sodii iodidi,
Potassii iodidi . . . . āā ʒss.
Aquæ . . . . ad fʒj.—M.

Sig. One drop three times daily for fifteen days; then sub-stitute—

1028—℞ Sol. nitro-glycerin. (1 per cent.) . . . . fʒj.
Sig. Take two to four drops three times daily for fifteen days, and then revert to iodides. Alternate for one, two, or three years. (*For atheromatous condition of the heart.*)
HUCHARD.

1029—℞ Strychninæ sulphatis . . . . gr. j.
      Aquæ fontanæ . . . . ℥ij.—M.

Ft. sol.
Sig. Eight to fifteen minims hypodermically. (*For exhausted
heart-muscle and its nerves.*)   HABERSHON.

1030—℞ Vini cocæ .   . . . Oj.
Sig. A wineglassful three or four times daily. (*In overstrain
of heart.*)   BEVERLEY ROBINSON.

1031—℞ Infusi digitalis . . . . ℥ij.
      Liq. potassii citratis . . . . ℥iss.
      Aceti scillæ . . . . ℥ss.—M.
Sig. A tablespoonful every four hours. (*In cardiac complications of acute rheumatism.*)   OPPOLZER.

1032—℞ Tinct. strophanthi (1-20) . . . .   ℥j.
Sig. Five to fifteen drops three times daily. (*In fatty heart
and valvular disease.*)   FRASER.

1033—℞ Extracti aconiti **radicis fluidi** . . . . . ℥ss.
      Vini antimonii . . . . ℥ss.—M.
Sig. From ten to fifteen **drops three times a day.** (*In pericarditis with great pain*)   KUST.

1034—℞ Pulveris opii . . . . gr. ij.
      Hydrargyri chloridi mitis . . . . gr. xvj.

Misce et fiant chartulæ no. viij.
Sig. **One powder three times a day.** (*In endocarditis.*)
    BUDD.

1035—℞ Potassii citratis .   ℨij.
      Tincturæ stramonii   . . . . ℥j.
      Tincturæ colchici seminis . . . . . . ℥j.
      Infusi digitalis . . . . ℥iij.
      Aquæ menthæ piperitæ . . . . ℥viij.—M.
Sig. Two tablespoonfuls **three times a day.** (*In violent palpitation.*)   HAZARD.

1036—℞ Tincturæ veratri viridis . . . . ℥ss.
Sig. Five drops. (*To reduce heart's action.*)   HAZARD.

1037—℞ Extracti cimicifugæ fluidi,
      Syrupi acaciæ . . . . āā ℥ss.
      Aquæ amygdalæ amaræ . . . . . ℥iiij.—M.
Sig. A teaspoonful every three hours. (*In fatty degeneration.*)
    ELLIS.

HEMICRANIA. (See Headache.)

HEMIPLEGIA. (See Paralysis.)

HEMORRHAGE.

1038—℞ Ergotæ,
      Ferri subcarb. . . . . āā ℨiss.
      Quininæ sulph. . . . . ℈ss.
      Ext. digitalis . . . . gr. xv.
Misce et in pil. no. c div.
Sig. Two to be taken at **each** meal. Intermit the medicine
every three days.   GALLARD.

1039—℞ Infusi digitalis . . . . ℥ij.
      Ext. ergotæ fld..
      Tinct. krameriæ . . . . āā ℥j.—M.
Sig. A tablespoonful as required.   BARTHOLOW.

1040—℞ Ext. ipecac. fld. . . . . ℥ij.
      Ext. ergotæ fld. . . . . ℥iv.
      Ext. digitalis fld. . . . . ad ℥j.—M.
Sig. One-half to one teaspoonful, repeated as required. (*Ex-
cellent anti-hemorrhagic combination.*)   BARTHOLOW.

HEMORRHAGE (Continued).

1041—℞ Olei terebinthinæ . . . . f ʒij.
    Extracti digitalis fluidi . . . . f ʒj.
    Mucilaginis acaciæ . . . . f ʒss.
    Aquæ menthæ piperitæ . . . . f ʒj.—M.
Sig. A teaspoonful every **three hours.** (*In passive hemor-rhage.*)
                        BARTHOLOW.

1042—℞ Argenti nitratis fusæ . . . . . . q. s.
Sig. Wipe the wound dry and apply locally. (*In leech-bites.*)
                        RINGER.

1043—℞ Acidi acetici **diluti** . . . . f ʒvj.
Sig. Apply locally. (*For leech-bites, piles, cuts, etc.*) RINGER.

1044—℞ Tinct. **hamamelidis** . . . . f ʒiv.
Sig. Use pure or diluted (1 to 8). (*In cuts, leech-bites, oozing from wounds, etc.*) Also, internally, one to three minims every two or three hours. RINGER.

1045—℞ Tinct. opii . . . . f ʒj.
    Spts. vini gallici . . . . f ʒj.—M.
Fiat haustus.
Sig. To be taken at **once.** (*In flooding after delivery, with uterine exhaustion.*) RINGER.

1046—℞ Ammonii carbonatis . . . . ʒij.
    Tincturæ opii deodoratæ . . . . . . f ʒiss.(!)
    Extracti glycyrrhizæ fluidi . . . . f ʒvj.
    Aquæ destillatæ . . . . q. s. ad f ʒvj.—M.
Sig. A tablespoonful every two hours. (**After hemorrhage ad deliquium.**) CARSON.

1047—℞ Acidi carbolici . . . . ʒj.
    Aquæ destillatæ . . . . f ʒiij.—M.
Sig. **Apply to bleeding** part. (*Does not prevent union by first intention.*)

1048—℞ Potassii **carbonatis** . . . . ʒij.
    Saponis . . . . ʒi–ij.
    Alcoholis . . . . f ʒiij.—M.
Sig. ("Pancoast's Styptic.") Use as a styptic, especially for operations about the face. JOS. PANCOAST.

1049—℞ Ergotini . . . . 10.00 grammes.
    Aquæ destillatæ . . . . 70.00   "
    Glycerini . . . . 20.00   "
    Acidi salicylici . . . . 0.20   " M.
Sig. One teaspoonful in three teaspoonfuls of water, for rectal injection. (*Uterine hemorrhage.*) REINSTADLER.

HEMORRHAGE, POST-PARTUM, AND UTERINE.
(See Menorrhagia.)

HEMORRHOIDS.

1050—℞ Cocain. **hydrochloratis** . . . . gr. iv.
    Aquæ . . . . f ʒj.—M.
Sig. Apply locally. (*In ulcerated piles.*) J. C. WILSON.

1051—℞ Ext. belladonnæ . . . . ʒj.
    Cerati simplicis . . . . ʒj.—M.
Ft. ungt.
Sig. Use as an ointment. (**In painful piles.**) HARTSHORNE.

1052—℞ Acidi **tannici** . . . . gr. xx–xxx.
    Aquæ . . . . f ʒvj.—M.
Sig. To be injected, after being cooled with ice, into the rectum. (*In bleeding piles.*) HARTSHORNE.

1053—℞ Acidi **nitrici** . . . . f ʒss–j.
    Aquæ . . . . f ʒvij.—M.
Ft. lotio.
Sig. Apply as a wash. (*In bleeding piles.*) RINGER.

1054—℞ Tincturæ hamamelidis . . . . f℥iv.
Sig. Inject into the rectum one-half to one teaspoonful in an
ounce of cold water daily before rising. Also take internally two to five minims three times daily. RINGER.

1055—℞ Potassii bromidi 5j.
Glycerini . f℥v.—M.
Sig. Apply to ease pain. RINGER.

1056—℞ Extracti ergotæ fluidi f℥j.
Tincturæ nucis vomicæ . f℥j.—M.
Sig. A teaspoonful every four hours. *(In bleeding piles.)*
BARTHOLOW.

1057—℞ Iodoformi . . . . 5j-ij.
Adipis benzoatis . . . . 5j.—M.
Ft. unguentum.
Sig. Apply locally, after washing with cold water.
BARTHOLOW.

1058—℞ Pulv. gallæ . . . . . . gr. xx.
Pulv. opii . gr. x.
Ungt. plumbi subacetatis . gr. xl.
Ungt. simplicis . . . . 5j.—M.
Ft. unguentum.
Sig. Use locally. OESTERLEN.

1059—℞ Ext. opii . . . . **gr. x.**
Pulv. stramonii . . . . **5j.**
Pulv. tabaci . . . . **5ss.**
Ungt. simplicis . . . . **5ss.—M.**
Ft. unguentum.
Sig. Use locally. SHOEMAKER.

1060—℞ Sulphuris loti . . . . 5iss.
Confectionis sennæ . . . . 5ij.
Potassii nitratis . . . . 5j.
Syrupi aurantii **corticis** . . . . q. s.
Misce et fiat confectio.
Sig. One or two drachms twice a day. **ELLIS.**

1061—℞ Pulveris jalapæ,
Potassii bitartratis,
Potassii nitratis . . . . āā 5ss.
Confectionis sennæ . . . . 5j.
Syrupi simplicis . . . . q. s.
Misce et fiat electuarium.
Sig. A bolus the size of **a hazel-nut three times a day.** ELLIS.

1062—℞ Potassii sulphatis . . . . **5ss.**
Sulphuris sublimati . . . . **5ij.**
Confectionis sennæ . . . . **5ij.**
Syrupi simplicis . . . . **q. s.**
Misce et fiat electuarium.
Sig. A dessertspoonful at night. AINSLIE.

1063—℞ Pulveris opii . . . . **5ij.**
Unguenti picis liquidæ . . . . **5j.**
Fiat unguentum.
Sig. Apply once or twice daily. ELLIS.

1064—℞ Pulveris tenerii scordii . . . . 5ij.
Unguenti petrolei . . . . 5j.—M.
Sig. Apply after each action of the bowels. R. R. CRUICE.

1065—℞ Plumbi tannatis . 5j.
Unguenti simplicis 5j.—M.
Sig. Apply twice daily. MACDONALD.

1066—℞ Hydrargyri chloridi mitis . . . . . . 5ij.
Unguenti petrolei . . . . 5j.—M.
Sig. Apply twice daily. I. BARTLETT.

1067—℞ Iodoformi . . . . 5ij.
Unguenti simplicis . . . . 5j.—M.
Sig. Apply twice daily. BARTHOLOW.

1068--℞ Olei theobromæ .   ᴣss.
        Extracti krameriæ   ᴣij.
        Pulveris opii   gr. **v**.
Misce secundum artem, et fiant suppositoria no. x.
Sig. Use one morning and night.   J. PANCOAST.

1069--℞ Unguenti belladonnæ . . . . **ᴣij.**
        Camphoræ . . . . **ᴣj.**
        Tincturæ **camphoræ composita** . . . . **fᴣj.**
Misce et fiat unguentum.
Sig. Apply to painful piles.   NELIGAN.

1070--℞ Morphinæ sulphatis . . . . **gr. ij.**
        Vitell. unius ovi,
        Olei anthemidis,
        Olei papaveris . . . . āā **fᴣj.**
Misce et fiat injectio.
Sig. Inject, in painful piles.   BRERA.

1071--℞ Chrysarobin . . . . gr. xvj.
        Iodoform . . . . gr. vj.
        Extract **of belladonna** . . . . gr. xij.
        Vaseline . . . . ᴣvj.—M.
Sig. A small quantity to be applied to the tumor several times
   a day, the parts having previously been washed with a
   solution of carbolic acid 1 to 50, or of creolin 1 to 100.
   (*External piles.*)   KOSSOBUDSKI.

1072--℞ Chrysarobin,
        Iodoform . . . . āā gr. iss.
        Extract of belladonna . . . . gr. ¼.
        Cacao butter . . . . gr. xxx.—M.
Make one suppository.
Sig. Use at bedtime. (*Internal piles.*)   KOSSOBUDSKI.

1073--℞ Acidi carbolici . . . . **ᴣij.**
        Acidi tannici . . . . **ᴣj.**
        Alcoholis . . . . fᴣiv.
        Glycerini . . . . fᴣj.—M.
Sig. Hypodermic injection for piles.   GIRARD.

1074--℞ Ceræ flavæ   ᴣviij.
        Resinæ   ᴣiv.
        Adipis . . .   ᴣss.
        Olei sassafras   ♏xl.—M.
Sig. Melt wax, resin, and lard together; when the mixture
   shows signs of stiffening, add the oil of sassafras and stir
   until cold. Apply locally.   *Charity Hospital, N. Y.*

1075--℞ Ext. colocynth. comp. . . . . **ᴣss.**
        Ext. nucis vomicæ . . . . **gr. vj.**
        Hydrarg. chlor. mit.,
        Ext. hyoscyami . . . . āā **gr. xij.**
Ft. massa et in pil. no. xii div.
Sig. One as required. (*For sluggish bowels.*)   BARKER.

1076--℞ Ferri subsulphatis   ᴣss.
        Adipis .   ᴣj.—M.
Ft. unguentum.
Sig. Apply every morning locally.   ELLIS.

1077--℞ Creolin. . . . .   ♏xxiv.
        Olei theobromæ .   q. s.—M.
Ft. suppositoria no. xii.
Sig. One at night.   J. C. WILSON.

1078--℞ Ext. opii . . . . gr. viij.
        Ext. belladonnæ . . . . gr. ij.
        Olei theobromæ . . . . q. s.—M.
Ft. massa et in suppositoria no. viii div.
Sig. One to be introduced into the bowel every four or six
hours.   LEVIS.

1079--℞ Ext. hydrastis fld. . . . . fᴣiv.
Sig. Use as a lotion externally; also take internally the following:

1080--℞ Tinct. hydrastis can. . . . . .   fᴣj.
Sig. Five minims three times daily, internally.   PHILLIPS.

HEPATITIS. (See Catarrh and Biliousness.)

HERPES. (See Skin Diseases.)

HICCOUGH.

1081—R Apomorphinæ muriatis .   gr. ⅒.
      Aquæ destillatæ . .   ℳx.—M.
Sig. Inject hypodermically.   RINGER.

1082—R Seminis sinapis . . . .   ʒj.
      Aquæ bullientis . . . .   f ʒiv.
Fiat infusum pro haustu.
Sig. One dose.   RINGER.

1083—R Pulv. sinapis . . . .   ʒj.
      Aquæ bullientis . . . .   f ʒiv.—M.
Ft. infusum.
Sig. Take at one draught.   RINGER.

1084—R Extracti valerianæ fluidi . .   . . f ʒij.
      Olei cajuputi   . ℳxvj.
Tere simul et adjice—
      Syrupi acaciæ . . . .   f ʒvj.
      Aquæ aurantii florum . . .   f ʒj.—M.
Sig. A teaspoonful.   HAZARD.

1085—R Pilocarpinæ muriatis   . gr. ⅒.
      Aquæ destillatæ   . ℳx.—M.
Sig. Inject hypodermically.   ORTILLE.

1086—R Zinci valerianatis   gr. ix.
      Ext. belladonnæ . .   gr. iij.—M.
Ft. massa et **in** pil. no. xii div.
Sig. One every six hours as required.   DANET.

HOOPING-COUGH. (See Whooping-Cough.)

HYDROCEPHALUS.

1087—R Potassii iodidi . . . .   ʒss-j.
      Syr. aurantii cort. . . . .   ʒj.
      Aquæ . . . . ad   f ʒiv.—M.
Sig. A teaspoonful every two hours **to an** infant of **six** months.   J. LEWIS SMITH.

1088—R Potassii iodidi . . . .   gr. xvj.
      Iodi . . . .   gr. iv.
      Aquæ . . . .   ʒj.—M.
Sig. A teaspoonful every four hours. Used in connection **with—**

1089—R Unguenti hydrargyri biniodidi   ʒj-iv.
      Cerati simplicis   ʒj.—M.
Ft. unguentum.
Sig. Rub into scalp every four hours.   CHRISTIE.

1090—R Unguenti hydrargyri . . . .   ʒj.
Sig. Rub on head, and take—

     R Potassii iodidi .   . gr. xij.
        Aquæ destillatæ .   f ʒss.—M.
Sig. A teaspoonful three times a day.   HAZARD.

1091—R Olei tiglii   . .   . .   ℳij.
      Mucilaginis acaciæ . . . .   f ʒij.
      Aquæ destillatæ . . . .   f ʒj.—M.
Sig. The fourth part every four hours. (*To remove fluid from ventricles.*)   DUNGLISON.

1092—R Pulv. digitalis,
      Hydrargyri chloridi mitis,
      Pulv. ipecac.   . . . . āā gr. ij.
      Sacchari albi   . . . . gr. x.—M.
In pulv. no. **xii div.**
Sig. A powder every three or four hours. (*In subacute form.*)   CONDIE.

HYDROCEPHALUS (Continued).

1093—℞ Pulveris digitalis . . . . gr. vj.
   Hydrargyri chloridi mitis . . . . . . gr. xij.
   Sacchari albi . . . . gr. xviij.
Misce et fiant chartulæ no. xii.
Sig. One powder every six hours.   HAZARD.

1094—℞ Collodii cum cantharide . . . . . . f ʒiv.
Sig. Paint back of neck every few days.   HARTSHORNE.

HYDROPS PERICARDII. (See Dropsy and Heart-Disease.)

HYDROTHORAX. (See Dropsy.)

HYPOCHONDRIA.

1095—℞ Morphinæ sulphatis . . . . gr. j–ij.
   Sacchari lactis . . . . gr. x.—M.
In pulv. no. xii div.
Sig. A powder three times daily for at least two months. The dose should never be large enough to induce sleep.
            W. A. HAMMOND.

1096—℞ Liq. potassii arsenitis . . . . ℳxl.
   Tinct. opii . . . . f ʒss–j.
   Aquæ menthæ pip. . . . . ad f ʒiiss.—M.
Sig. A teaspoonful three times daily. (In the aged.)
           LEMARE-PICQUOT.

1097—℞ Liquoris potassii arsenitis . . . . . . f ʒss.
   Tincturæ opii deodoratæ . . . . . . f ʒj.
   Aquæ cinnamomi . . . . f ʒxivss.—M.
Sig. A teaspoonful three times a day.   LEMARE-PICQUOT.

1098—℞ Tincturæ opii deodoratæ . . . . . . f ʒss.
Sig. Five to ten drops three times a day.   KRAFFT-EBING.

1099—℞ Potassii bromidi . . . . ʒss.
   Syrupi simplicis . . . . f ʒj.
   Aquæ destillatæ . . . . q. s. ad f ʒiij.—M.
Sig. A dessertspoonful three times a day.   RINGER.

1100—℞ Auri chloridi . . . . gr. j–iss.
   Ext. gentianæ . . . . gr. xv.—M.
Ft. massa et in pil. no. xxx div.
Sig. One pill thrice daily. (In anæmic subjects.) BARTHOLOW.

1101—℞ Mist. asafœtidæ . . . . f ʒiv.
Sig. One to two tablespoonfuls three or four times daily.
            BARTHOLOW.

1102—℞ Spiritus lavandulæ compositi . . . . f ʒss.
   Spiritus ammonii aromatici . . . . . f ʒj.
   Misturæ asafœtidæ . . . . f ʒvss.—M.
Sig. From one to three tablespoonfuls three times a day.
            AINSLIE.

HYSTERIA.

1103—℞ Liq. potassii arsenitis . . . . f ʒss.
Sig. Three to five drops thrice daily, after meals.
            BARTHOLOW.

1104—℞ Spts. ætheris comp.,
   Tinct. valerianæ ammon. . . . . . āā f ʒj.—M.
Sig. A teaspoonful in water every fifteen minutes until relieved.
            BARTHOLOW.

1105—℞ Pulveris camphoræ,
   Extracti eucalypti . . . . āā gr. xij.
Misce et fiant pilulæ no. xii.
Sig. One pill every three hours. (In debilitated subjects.)
            BARTHOLOW.

1106—℞ Ammonii bromidi . . . . ℨij.
    Spts. ammoniæ aromat. . . . . ꜰℨj.
    Aquæ . . . . ꜰℨiv.—M.

Sig. A dessertspoonful thrice daily.   HARTSHORNE.

1107—℞ Ferri citratis . . . . ℨj.
    Syr. simplicis . . . . ꜰℨss.
    Aquæ aurantii florum . . . . ad ꜰℨvj.—M.

Sig. A tablespoonful three times **daily.** *(In anæmic cases.)*
                HARTSHORNE.

1108—℞ Ammonii valerianatis   ℨj.
    Elixiris curaçoæ,
    Syrupi simplicis . . . . āā ꜰℨj.
    Aquæ aurantii florum . . . . ꜰℨij.—M.

Sig. A teaspoonful every three hours.   HAZARD.

1109—℞ Camphoræ.
    Asafœtidæ . . . . āā ℨj.
    Extracti belladonnæ . . . . ℨss.
    Extracti opii aquosi . . . . gr. x.

Misce et fiant pilulæ no. xl.
Sig. One pill night and morning.   HAZARD.

1110—℞ Castorei . . . . .   ℨj.
    Acidi succinici . .   ℨss.
    Extracti gentianæ . . . . q. s.

Fiant pilulæ no. xxiv.
Sig. Three pills night and morning.   HAZARD.

1111—℞ Zinci valerianatis . . . . gr. ix.
    Pulveris tragacanthæ . . . . ℨss.

Misce et divide in pilulas no. xii.
Sig. One pill night and morning. *(With headache.)*
                DEVAY.

1112—℞ Zinci valerianatis,
    Quininæ valerianatis . . . . āā gr. xv.
    Extracti gentianæ . . . . q. s.

Fiant pilulæ no. xv.
Sig. One pill every hour. *(In the epileptoid form.)*   MARTINI.

1113—℞ Tincturæ opii deodoratæ   ꜰℨj.
    Tincturæ nucis vomicæ   . .   ꜰℨij.—M.

Sig. Three drops three or four times a day. *(In middle-aged
people with flatulence, flushings, weight on head, etc.)*
                RINGER.

1114—℞ **Tincturæ** avenæ concentratæ . . . . . ꜰℨss.

Sig. Fifteen drops in a **fluidounce of hot water at** bedtime.
(Nervous tonic.)   WAUGH.

1115—℞ Ext. conii fd.,
    Ext. hyoscyami fld. . . . . āā ♏vij.
    Chloral. hydratis . . . . gr. x.
    Aquæ . . . . ad ꜰℨj.—M.

Ft. haustus.
Sig. To be taken at a single dose and repeated as required.
                MADIGAN.

1116—℞ Ext. salicis nigræ,
    Elixiris simplicis   . . .   . . āā ꜰℨj.—M.

Sig. A teaspoonful three times daily.   HUTCHINSON.

1117—℞ Paraldehyd. . . . . ♏xxx-l.
    Syr. simplicis . . . . ꜰℨss.
    Aquæ menthæ pip. . . . . ꜰℨj.—M.

Fiat haustus.
Sig. To be taken **at a draught.** *(To produce sleep.)*

1118—℞ Apomorphinæ muriatis . . . . gr. j.
    Syr. simplicis . . . . ꜰℨiv.
    Aquæ . . . . ad ꜰℨx.

Sig. A teaspoonful as required. Repeat in a few hours if
necessary.   RINGER.

1119—℞ Ergotini . . . . gr. lx.
    Extracti cannabis ind. . . . . gr. iv.
    Strychninæ . . . . gr. ⅓.—M.
In pil. no. xlviii div.
Sig. Two pills three times a day, after meals.   J. C. WILSON.

ICHTHYOSIS. (See Skin Diseases.)

IMPETIGO. (See Skin Diseases.)

IMPOTENCE.

1120—℞ Zinci phosphidi . . . . gr. ij.
    Confectionis rosæ . . . . ʒj.—M.
Ft. massa et in pil. no. xxiv div.
Sig. One to three pills three times daily.   BARTHOLOW.

1121—℞ Ferri arseniatis . . . . gr. v.
    Extracti ergotæ aquosi . . . . ʒss.
Misce et fiant pilulæ no. xxx.
Sig. One pill night and morning. (*With spermatorrhœa.*)
                              BARTHOLOW.

1122—℞ Tincturæ sanguinariæ . . . . f ʒiij.
    Extracti stillingiæ fluidi . . . . f ʒv.—M.
Sig. Fifteen to twenty drops in water three times a day.
                              BARTHOLOW.

1123—℞ Pulveris cantharidis . . . . gr. xviij.
    Pulveris opii,
    Pulveris camphoræ . . . . āā gr. xxxvj.
    Confectionis rosæ . . . . q. s.
Misce et fiant pilulæ no. xxxvi.
Sig. One pill at night. (*From general debility.*)   HAZARD.

1124—℞ Phosphori . . . . gr. ss.
    Ætheris . . . . f ʒss.
Solve, et adde—
    Tincturæ cantharidis,
    Tincturæ nucis vomicæ . . . . . . āā f ʒss.—M.
Sig. Thirty drops three or four times a day.
                               VOGT.

1125—℞ Extracti cannabis indicæ,
    Extracti nucis vomicæ . . . . . āā gr. xv.
    Extracti ergotæ aquosi . . . . ʒj.
Misce et divide in pilulas no. xxx.
Sig. One pill morning and evening.   DA COSTA.

1126—℞ Tinct. phosphori . . . . f ʒiss.
    Tinct. cantharidis . . . . f ʒiiiss.
    Elixiris simplicis . . . . ad f ʒv.—M.
Sig. One teaspoonful three or four hours before retiring. Increase the dose carefully.   VAN BUREN AND KEYES.

1127—℞ Pulv. sanguinariæ . . . . gr. ij.
    Ext. ergotæ . . . . ʒj.—M.
Ft. massa et in pil. no. xx div.
Sig. One pill thrice daily.   S. O. POTTER.

1128—℞ Phosphori . . . . gr. j.
    Alcoholis absoluti . . . . f ʒv.
    Glycerini . . . . f ʒiss.
    Alcoholis . . . . f ʒij.
    Spts. menthæ pip. . . . . f ʒj.—M.
Sig. One-half to one teaspoonful three times daily. (*For old people.*)   J. A. THOMSON.

INCONTINENCE OF URINE.

1129—℞ Syrupi belladonnæ . . . . f ʒij.
    Syrupi tolutani,
    Syrupi althææ . . . . āā f ʒj.—M.
Sig. A half-teaspoonful two to eight times a day.
                              DESCROIZILLES.

I

1130—℞ Ext. belladonnæ . . . . gr. vj.
    Pulv. acaciæ,
    Pulv. althææ . . . . āā q. s.—M.
Fiant pilulæ no. xl.
Sig. One to fifteen to be taken daily, according to the severity
    of the case.   DESCROIZILLES.

1131—℞ Atropini . . . . gr. l.
    Sacchari albi . . . . ӡiij.—M.
Fiant pulveres no. xl.
Sig. Two to four to be taken daily.   DESCROIZILLES.

1132—℞ Potassii bromidi . . . . ӡiss.
    Aquæ cinnamomi . . . . f ӡij.
    Syrupi,
    Syrupi aurantii amari-cort. . . . . āā f ӡj.—M.
Sig. A half-teaspoonful one to four times a day.
                                    DESCROIZILLES.

1133—℞ Strychninæ sulphatis . . . . gr. ij.
    Syrupi . . . . f ӡvj.
    Aquæ . . . . f ӡij.—M.
Sig. A half-teaspoonful one to twenty times a day.
                                    DESCROIZILLES.

1134—℞ Syrupi ferri iodidi . . . . .   f ӡss.
Sig. Fifteen to twenty drops, well diluted, three times a day.
    (In pale, delicate, and strumous children.)   BARTHOLOW.

1135—℞ Atropinæ sulphatis . . . . gr. j.
    Aquæ destillatæ . . . . f ӡj.—M.
Sig. Four to eight drops in water.   (For children.)
                                      BARTHOLOW.

1136—℞ Tinct. belladonnæ . . . . f ӡj.
Sig. Ten to twenty drops thrice daily.   RINGER.

1137—℞ Santonini . . . . gr. xvj.
    Olei ricini . . . . f ӡj.—M.
Sig. One or two teaspoonfuls before breakfast, for two or three
    mornings.   RINGER.

1138—℞ Strychninæ . . . . gr. j.
    Acidi acetici . . . . gtt. ij.
    Sacchari albi . . . . ӡij.
    Aquæ destillatæ . . . . f ӡij.
Fiat solutio.
Sig. Fifteen to thirty drops for a child six to twelve years of
    age.   MAGENDIE.

1139—℞ Acidi benzoici . . . . ӡij.
    Aquæ cinnamomi . . . . f ӡvj.—M.
Sig. A tablespoonful thrice daily.   HARTSHORNE.

1140—℞ Syrupi ferri bromidi
    Syrupi simplicis . . . . āā f ӡss.—M.
Sig. A half-teaspoonful three times a day. (Child six to ten
    years old.)   DA COSTA.

1141—℞ Tinct. ferri muriatis . . . . f ӡj.
    Decocti uvæ ursi . . . . f ӡvj.—M.
Sig. A tablespoonful two or three times daily.   WILLIS.

1142—℞ Collodii . . . . f ӡj.
Sig. Pull forward the prepuce and smear over to form a cap.
    Continue for a fortnight. Is easily picked off with finger-
    nail.   D. CORRIGAN.

1143—℞ Strychninæ sulph. . . . . gr. j.
    Pulv. cantharidis . . . . gr. ij.
    Morphinæ sulph. . . . . gr. lss.
    Ferri redacti . . . . gr. xx.—M.
Ft. pil. no. xl.
Sig. One pill thrice daily to a child ten years old.   GROSS

1144—℞ Ext. rhois aromaticæ fld. . .   f ӡj.
Sig. Five minims at two years of age; ten minims at age of
    two to six years; fifteen minims for older children. To be
    given in sweetened water.   UNNA.

1145—℞ Tincturæ cantharidis . . . . ♏ij.
      Tincturæ hyoscyami . . . . ♏v.
      Aquæ destillatæ . . . . f ʒx.
Fiat haustus.
Sig. Repeat the dose four times a day. (*For middle-aged and old women.*)
                          GREGORY.

1146—℞ Chloral. hydratis . . . . gr. vijss.
      Aquæ destillatæ . . . . f ʒss.
Fiat haustus.
Sig. Take at bedtime.
                          VECCHIZETTI.

1147—℞ Tinct. ferri chlor. . . . . f ʒij.
      Ext. ergotæ fld. . . . . f ʒv.
      Spts. chloroformi . . . . f ʒij.
      Tinct. quassiæ . . . . ad f ʒiv.—M.
Sig. A teaspoonful in a wineglassful of water thrice daily. (*For children.*)
                          S. O. POTTER.

1148—℞ Linimenti cantharidis . . . . f ʒss.
Sig. Paint, high up, over the nape of the neck, a space three inches by two inches, till blistered.
                          HARKIN.

1149—℞ Chloral hydratis . . . . ʒj.
      Syr. tolutani . . . . f ʒiss.—M.
Sig. A teaspoonful thrice daily. (*For infantile incontinence.*)
                          DA COSTA.

INDIGESTION. (See Dyspepsia.)

INFLAMMATION. (See the names as applied to the particular organs inflamed, Heart-Disease, Pleurisy, Synovitis, etc.)

INFLUENZA. (See Catarrh and Hay Fever.)

INGROWING TOE-NAIL.

1150—℞ Liquoris potassæ . . . . f ʒij.
      Aquæ . . . . f ʒj.—M.
Sig. Apply on cotton to the margin of the nail at the ulcerated surface, to soften the nail.
                          BARTHOLOW.

1151—℞ Liquoris potassæ . . . . f ʒij.
      Aquæ destillatæ . . . . f ʒj.—M.
Sig. Apply with pledgets of cotton-wool.
                          NORTON.

1152—℞ Acidi tannici . . . . ʒj.
      Aquæ destillatæ . . . . f ʒvj.—M.
Sig. Paint the soft parts twice daily.
                          MIALL.

1153—℞ Pulv. plumbi acetatis . . ʒj.
      Tinct. opii . . . . f ʒj.
      Aquæ . . . . ad f ʒviij.—M.
Sig. Shake well, and apply constantly until the inflammation is reduced and pain alleviated ; then separate the granulating surface from the nail and insert a small pledget of cotton ; then use—

1154—℞ Argenti nitratis . . . . gr. xxx.
      Aquæ destillatæ . . . . f ʒj.—M.
Ft. lotio.
Sig. Apply two or three times daily with a brush.
                          DAVIDSON.

INSOMNIA.

1155—℞ Antimonii et potassii tartratis   gr j-ij.
      Morphinæ sulphatis   gr. iss.
      Aquæ laurocerasi . .   f ʒj.—M.
Sig. A teaspoonful every two, three, or four hours. (*In the delirium and wakefulness of fevers.*)
                          BARTHOLOW.

1156—℞ Amyl. hydratis . . . . gr. xlv.
  " Syr. aurantii cort. . . . . f℥ss.
  Aquæ . . . . f℥j.—M.
Ft. haustus.
Sig. To be taken **at bedtime**. Half as much more may be
  given when by **enema**. VON MERING.

1157—℞ Tincturæ hyoscyami f℥ij.
Sig. From one to four drachms. (*Where opium is not borne.*)
  CAMPBELL.

1158—℞ Antipyrin. . . . ℈j–ij.
  Syr. aurantii cort. . . f℥j.
  Aquæ cinnamomi . . . . ad f℥ij.—M.
Sig. One tablespoonful every hour or two till effective.
  WILLIAMS.

1159—℞ Chloral. hydratis . . . . ℈j.
  Potassii bromidi . . . . ℈ij.
  Syrupi aurantii corticis . . . . f℥ss.
  Aquæ caryophylli . . . . . . q. s. ad f℥vj.—M.
Sig. A tablespoonful three **times a day in** a wineglassful **of**
  water. QUAIN.

1160—℞ Ext. piscidiæ erythrinæ fld. . . . . . . **f℥j.**
  Syr. simplicis . . . . **f℥j.**
  Aquæ aurantii flor. . . . . ad **f℥iv.—M.**
Sig. A teaspoonful to a tablespoonful **at bedtime**. (*For ner-
vous cases that do not bear opiates well.*) **PAYNE.**

1161—℞ Antimonii et potass. tart. gr. ⅓j–iv.
  Tinct. opii . . . ♏xxxvj–l.
  Syr. simplicis . . . . . . f℥ss.
  Aquæ ad f℥ij.—M.
Sig. A teaspoonful every two hours till tranquil or asleep.
  (*In wakefulness or delirium of fevers.*) GRAVES.

1162—℞ Codeinæ . . . . gr. iss.
  Aquæ laurocerasi . . f℥iss.
  Syrupi simplicis . . f℥j.
  Aquæ florum tiliæ f℥ij.—M.
Sig. A tablespoonful every half-hour. (*For sleeplessness due
  to pain.*) TROUSSEAU ET REVEIL.

1163—℞ Pulv. opii . . gr. iv–viij.
  Pulv. camphoræ . . . gr. xij.
  Ext. hyoscyami . . . ℈j.—M.
Ft. massa et in pil. no. xij div.
Sig. One or two pills at night. (*A good calmative.*)
  HARTSHORNE.

1164—℞ Chloral. hydratis . . . . gr. xxv.
  Tincturæ cardamomi compositæ . . . f℥ss.
  Syrupi simplicis . . . . f℥j.
  Infusi caryophylli . . . . . . q. s. ad f℥ss.
Fiat haustus.
Sig. Use pro re nata. (*When due to mental overwork, anxiety, or
  physical fatigue.*) PRIESTLEY.

1165—℞ Pulveris opii . . . . gr. iv.
  Extracti hyoscyami,
  Extracti conii . . . . āā gr. xv.
Misce et divide in pilulas **x.**
Sig. One pill at bedtime. ELLIS.

1166—℞ Potassii bromidi . ℈iv.
  Chloral. hydratis . ℈ij.
  Syr. pruni virgin. . f℥j.
  Aquæ . . ad f℥ij.—M.
Sig. A dessertspoonful in a wineglassful of water at bedtime.

1167—℞ Paraldehyd . . . . f℥iss.
  Alcoholis (90 per cent.) . . . . f℥ss.
  Tinct. vanillæ . . . . f℥ss.
  Aquæ . . . . f℥j.
  Syr. simplicis . . . . ad f℥iv.—M.
Sig. A teaspoonful or two every hour till sleep is obtained.
  YVON.

1168—℞ Methylal . . . . ℨj.
       Syr. aurantii flor. . . . . ad f℥iv.—M.
Sig. A tablespoonful at bedtime. May be increased to four
tablespoonfuls.   RICHARDSON.

1169—℞ Urethan. . .   . ℨss.
       Aquæ aurantii flor. . . . . f℥ij.—M.
Sig. One to four teaspoonfuls at bedtime. (*In nervous cases
not bearing opiates.*)   ANDREWS.

1170—℞ Narceinæ . . . . gr. viij.
       Confect. rosæ . . . . gr. xv.—M.
Ft. massa et in pil. no. xxiv div.
Sig. One to three pills at bedtime.   LABORDE.

1171—℞ Morphinæ sulph.   . . . . . . gr. j.
       Ext. valerianæ fld.   . . . . . . f℥j.
       Elix. humuli   . . . . f℥j.—M.
Sig. One or two teaspoonfuls, as required. (*In insomnia of
delirium tremens.*)

1172—℞ Morphinæ sulph. . . . . gr. ij.
       Aquæ camphoræ . . . . f℥ij.—M.
Sig. One to two teaspoonfuls at bedtime.   SMITH.

INTERMITTENT FEVER. (See Fever.)

INTERTRIGO. (See Skin Diseases.)

INTESTINAL CATARRH. (See Catarrh.)

INTESTINAL PARASITES. (See Worms.)

INTUSSUSCEPTION.

1173—℞ Lobeliæ . . . . ℨss.
       Aquæ bullientis . . . . Oj.
Fiat infuso.
Sig. Inject one-fourth or one-half, and repeat if permissible.
         BARTHOLOW.

1174—℞ Sodii bicarbonatis . . . . ℈ij-iij.
       Aquæ . . . . f℥vj.
Solve et fiat enema.
Sig. Inject, and follow immediately with—

1175—℞ Acidi tartarici pulverizati   . gr. xxxv-xlvij.
       Aquæ   f℥iv.
Solve et fiat enema.
Sig. Inject immediately after the foregoing. (*The effervescence
will cause the bowel suddenly to distend.*) BARTHOLOW.

1176—℞ Fellis bovini .   gr. x-xxx.
       Aquæ ferventis   . Oj-iv.—M.
Sig. Inject slowly into the bowel until it is fully distended.
  (*Knee-chest position is the best.*)   HAWKINS.

1177—℞ Ext. belladonnæ. . . . . gr. iv.
       Aquæ ferventis . . . . Oj.—M.
Ft. solutio.
Sig. Inject into the rectum.   WARING.

1178—℞ Tabaci . . . . ℨj.
       Aquæ bullientis . . . . Oj.
Macera per sextam horæ partem, et cola.
Sig. Inject one-quarter or one-half, and repeat in half an hour
  if necessary, *carefully watching its effects.* *Guy's Hospital.*

IRITIS.

1179—℞ Atropinæ sulphatis . . . . gr. iv.
    Aquæ destillatæ . . . . ƒ ʒj.—M.

Sig. A drop or two in the eye two or three times daily. Use with hot water, bathing for fifteen minutes every hour till pain is relieved.   CHILTON.

1180—℞ Atropinæ sulphatis . . . . gr. ij.
    Aquæ destillatæ . . . . ƒ ʒss.—M.

Sig. Drop into the eye twice daily, continuing for a week.
      KEYSER.

1181—℞ Extracti belladonnæ . . . . ʒj.
    Ungt. hydrargyri . . . . ʒvj.—M.

Sig. For inunction to the brow.   LEVIS.

1182—℞ Emplastri cantharidis . . . . 1 in. × 1 in.

Sig. Apply behind the ear, and poultice when blistered.
      HARTSHORNE.

1183—℞ Atropinæ sulphatis . . . . gr. j-iij.
    Morphinæ sulphatis . . . . gr. iv.
    Zinci sulphatis . . . . gr. ij-viij.
    Aquæ destillatæ . . . . ƒ ʒj.—M.

Sig. Apply as a lotion.   BARTHOLOW.

1184—℞ Hydrarg. chlor. corros. . . . . gr. j.
    Potassii iodidi . . . . ʒj.
    Tinct. calumbæ . . . . ƒ ʒij.
    Aquæ destillatæ . . . . ad ƒ ʒvj.—M.

Sig. A dessertspoonful in a wineglassful of water two or three times daily.   LAWSON.

1185—℞ Hydrargyri chloridi mitis . . . . . . gr. x.
    Extracti glycyrrhizæ . . . . q. s.

Misce et fiant pilulæ no. xx.
Sig. Two pills twice a day.   NIEMEYER.

1186—℞ Hydrargyri chloridi corrosivi . . . . . gr. iv.
    Opii purificati . . . . gr. viij.
    Extracti guaiaci . . . . ʒss.

Misce et fiant pilulæ no. xxiv.
Sig. One pill three times a day with sarsaparilla.
      DUPUYTREN.

1187—℞ Hydrargyri biniodidi . . . . gr. ij.
    Potassii iodidi . . . . ʒiij.

Solve in—
    Aquæ destillatæ . . . . ƒ ʒss.
Dein adde—
    Syrupi stillingiæ compositi . . . . ƒ ʒiss.—M.

Sig. A teaspoonful after each meal.   KEYSER.

1188—℞ Scopolinæ . . . . gr. j.
    Aquæ destillatæ . . . . ƒ ʒj.—M.

Ft. collyrium.
Sig. One to three drops into the eye two or three times daily.
      DUNN.

1189—℞ Duboisiæ sulphatis . . . . gr. j.
    Aquæ destillatæ . . . . ƒ ʒj.—M.

Ft. collyrium.
Sig. One drop into the eye once or twice daily.   TWEEDY.

1190—℞ Olei terebinthinæ . . . . ƒ ʒj.
    Mucil. acaciæ . . . . q. s. ut ft. emulsio.
    Syr. simplicis . . . . ƒ ʒj.
    Aquæ menthæ pip. . . . . ad ƒ ʒiv.—M.

Sig. A dessertspoonful three times daily.   HOGG.

ITCH. (See Skin Diseases and Lice.)

JAUNDICE. (See Biliousness, Catarrh, and Calculi.)

JOINTS, DISEASES OF. (See Synovitis.)

KERATITIS, PHLYCTENULAR.

1191—℞ Hydrarg. chloridi corrosivi . . . . . . gr. j.
Aquæ destillatæ . . . . f 3iv.—M.
Ft. collyrium.
Sig. Apply as a bath to the eye by means of a reservoir eye-cup. GRANDMONT.

1192—℞ Hydrarg. chloridi corrosivi gr. j.
Ammonii chloridi gr. vj.
Tinct. belladonnæ f 3ij.
Aquæ destillatæ . f 3viij.—M.
Ft. collyrium.
Sig. A teaspoonful in a wineglassful of tepid water, to be applied frequently with a pledget of lint on the closed lids.
TURNBULL.

1193—℞ Atropinæ sulphatis gr. ij–iv.
Aquæ destillatæ . . . . f 3j.—M.
Ft. collyrium.
Sig. One or two drops in the eye two or three times daily.
BARTHOLOW.

1194—℞ Duboisiæ sulphatis . . . . gr. j.
Aquæ destillatæ . . . . f 3j.—M.
Ft. collyrium.
Sig. One or two drops in the eye two or three times daily.
THOMPSON.

1195—℞ Acidi carbolici . . . . gr. xl.
Aquæ . . . . f 3viij.—M.
Ft. collyrium.
Sig. Any trace of ulceration or granulation on the cornea, or any pustule on the conjunctiva, is scraped bare by a delicate eye-scraper. The cornea, lids, and conjunctival sac are washed with the above solution, and the cornea and conjunctival sac are dredged with—

1196—℞ Pulv. iodoformi . . . . 3ss.
Sig. Use as a dredge; then moisten and paint the skin of the eyelids and eyebrows with solid nitrate of silver. Dredge with iodoform, and bandage. TEALE.

KIDNEYS, DISEASES OF. (See Albuminuria, Nephritis, and Uræmia.)

LABOR.

1197—℞ Morphinæ sulphatis . . . . gr. ij.
Aquæ destillatæ . . . . 3j.—M.
Sig. Five to ten minims hypodermically, repeated if necessary. (In protracted labor due to rigid os.) RINGER.

1198—℞ Morphinæ sulphatis . . . . gr. j–ij.
Olei theobromæ . . . . 3ij.—M.
Ft. massa et in suppositoria no. iv div.
Sig. One as required. (In precipitate labor.) LEISHMAN.

1199—℞ Antimonii et potassii tartratis . . . . . gr. ij.
Tincturæ opii deodoratæ . . . . ♏xx.
Aquæ destillatæ . . . . f 3vj.—M.
Sig. A tablespoonful every hour, until nausea or vomiting supervenes. (In rigid os.) HARDY.

1200—℞ Tincturæ opii deodoratæ gtt. xlv.
Tincturæ lactucarii,
Syrupi papaveris ãã f 3ij.
Aquæ aurantii florum f 3ss.—M.
Sig. The one-third part. (In protracted labor due to irregular tetanic pains.) VELPEAU.

1201—℞ Vini opii . . . . gtt. xl–lx.
Sig. Inject with a little starch-water, in two or three doses, in the course of a couple of hours. (To prevent premature labor.) CAZEAUX.

1202—℞ Ext. ergotæ fld. . . . . 3j.
Olei gaultheriæ . . . . gtt. iv.—M.
Sig. A teaspoonful every four hours, only if os is dilated and soft parts not rigid. (In protracted labor from atony of uterus.) LEISHMAN.

$^-K, L^-$

LABOR (Continued).

1203—℞ Pulveris ergotæ . . . . ʒij.
    Aquæ . . . . f℥xij.
Coque, et cola, ut fiat **enema.**
Sig. Inject into rectum. (*To accelerate delivery.*)   FOY.

1204—℞ Tincturæ nucis vomicæ . . . . ♏v.
    Extracti ergotæ fluidi . . . . ♏xxx.
    Elixiris simplicis . . . . f℥iij.
Fiat haustus.
Sig. Repeat every three hours. (*In retained placenta.*)
                        LOMBE ATTHILL.

1205—℞ Pulveris ergotæ . . . . . ʒss.
    Syrupi simplicis . . . . . . f℥ss.
    Aquæ menthæ piperitæ . . . f℥j.—M.
Sig. One-third part every twenty minutes. (*In lingering labor.*)
                        SOUBEIRAN.

1206—℞ Antimonii et potassii tartratis . . gr. iij.
    Magnesii sulphatis . . . . . ʒj.
    Syrupi zingiberis . . . . . f℥ss.
    Infusi sennæ . . . . . . f℥viiss.—M.
Sig. Two tablespoonfuls every hour or half-hour. (*In rigid os.*)
                        HULL.

1207—℞ Chloral. hydratis . . . . . ʒij.
    Syr. aurantii cort. . . f℥j.
    Aquæ aurantii flor. . . . . . f℥iv.—M.
Sig. A tablespoonful every twenty minutes for three doses; perhaps a fourth, after an hour's interval.   PLAYFAIR.

1208—℞ Chloroformi . . . . f℥iv.
Sig. Let the patient inhale, but not to complete anæsthesia, lest uterine action be interrupted.   SIMPSON.

1209—℞ Quininæ sulphatis . . . . ʒij.
    Acidi sulph. aromat. . . . . . q. s. ut ft. sol.
    Syr. zingiberis . . . . f℥j.
    Aquæ . . . . ad f℥ij.—M.
Sig. A tablespoonful at once, and a dessertspoonful every **four hours afterwards.** (*In atony of the uterus.*)   RINGER.

1210—℞ Amyl. nitritis . . . . ʒj.
Sig. Three to five drops to be inhaled from **a handkerchief.** (*In hour-glass contraction of the uterus.*)   **BARNES.**

LARYNGISMUS STRIDULUS.

1211—℞ Antipyrin. . . . . gr. xxx.
    Syrupi acaciæ . . . . f℥ss.
    Aquæ . . . . f℥iiss.—M.
Sig. A teaspoonful every hour or two.   J. C. WILSON.

1212—℞ Potassii bromidi . . . . ʒij.
    Chloral. hydratis . . . . ʒss.
    Syr. tolutani . . . . f℥ss.
    Aquæ . . . . f℥iss.—M.
Sig. A teaspoonful every half-hour.   **BARTHOLOW.**

1213—℞ Chloroformi . . . . f℥j.
Sig. A few drops inhaled from a handkerchief. BARTHOLOW.

1214—℞ Syr. ipecacuanhæ . . . . f℥ij.
Sig. A teaspoonful every ten or **fifteen minutes until free** emesis occurs.   **BARTHOLOW.**

1215—℞ Chloral. hydratis . . . . ʒss.
    Potassii bromidi . . . . ʒij.
    Syrupi tolutani . . . . f℥ss.
    Aquæ destillatæ . . . . f℥iss.—M.
Sig. A teaspoonful **every half-hour.**   BARTHOLOW.

1216—℞ Chloral. hydratis . . . . gr. v–xv.
    Syrupi simplicis . . . .
    Aquæ destillatæ . . . . āā f℥ss.—M.
Sig. One dose. (*To arrest impending attack.*)   BARTHOLOW.

1217—℞ Quininæ sulphatis . . . . gr. vj.
    Acidi sulphurici diluti . . . . ℳvj.
    Tincturæ aurantii,
    Syrupi zingiberis . . . . āā f℥ij.
    Aquæ destillatæ . . . . f℥iij.—M.
    Sig. A teaspoonful three times a day. (*In rickety, cachectic
    children.*)   OKE.

1218—℞ Syrupi scillæ compositi . . f℥j.
    Sig. Thirty drops every quarter- or half-hour as an emetic, or
    ten drops every three hours as an expectorant. (*For a child
    two years old.*)   COXE.

1219—℞ Syrupi ipecacuanhæ . . . . f℥j.
    Sig. A teaspoonful every fifteen minutes.   **MEIGS.**

1220—℞ Potassii citratis . . . . ʒj.
    Syr. ipecac. . . . . f℥ij.
    Tinct. opii deod. . . . . gtt. xij.
    Syr. simplicis . . . . f℥ij.
    Aquæ . . . . f℥ss.—M.
    Sig. A teaspoonful every two hours at two years of age. (*In
    severe form.*)   MEIGS AND **PEPPER.**

1221—℞ Atropinæ sulphatis . . . . gr. ₁ss.
    Aquæ destillatæ . . . . f℥j.—M.
    Sig. Mix in a gobletful of water (*sixty doses*), of which give a
    teaspoonful every hour or half-hour.   A. A. SMITH.

1222—℞ Tinct. aconiti radicis   f℥ss.
    Sig. One drop in a teaspoonful of water every hour for three
    or four doses; then every two hours.   RINGER.

1223—℞ Ferri citratis . . . . ʒij.
    Aquæ aurantii flor. . . . . f℥vss.
    Syr. simplicis . . . . f℥ss.—M.
    Sig. From a teaspoonful to a tablespoonful thrice daily be-
    tween the paroxysms. (*For the anæmic condition.*)
          HARTSHORNE.

LARYNGITIS.

1224—℞ Potassii iodidi . . . . ʒj-ʒiij (!).
    Aquæ destillatæ . . . . f℥vj.
    Solve.
    Sig. A dessertspoonful every four hours. (*In rapidly destruc-
    tive syphilitic form.*)   BARTHOLOW.

1225—℞ Sol. cocain. muriatis (15-20 per cent.) . f℥ss.
    Sig. Apply locally to the larynx before and, if much pain,
    after the following:

1226—℞ Acidi lactici   . . .   ʒss.
    Sig. Apply locally to all infiltrations and ulcerations in the
    larynx. (*In tuberculous laryngitis.*)   HERING.

1227—℞ Argenti nitratis . . . . gr. ss-v.
    Aquæ destillatæ . . . . f℥j.—M.
    Sig. Apply by means of atomizer. (*In chronic form.*) RINGER.

1228—℞ Hydrargyri biniodidi . . . . gr. ij.
    Potassii iodidi . . . . ʒij.
    Extracti sarsaparillæ fluidi . . . . . . f℥ij.—M.
    Sig. A teaspoonful three times a day. Follow in five or six
    days with—

1229—℞ Potassii iodidi . . . . ʒss.
    Aquæ destillatæ . . . . f℥ij.—M.
    Sig. A teaspoonful three times a day. (*In syphilitic form.*)
          HAZARD.

1230—℞ Potassii permanganatis . . . . gr. ij.
    Aquæ destillatæ . . . . f℥ij.—M.
    Sig. Use with atomizer several times daily. (*In fetid variety
    of chronic laryngitis.*)   SAJOUS.

1231—℞ Sodii biboratis . . . . gr. viij.
Aquæ . . . . f℥ij.
Aquæ coloniensis . . . . gtt. x.—M.
Sig. Use frequently as a spray with atomizer. (*Chronic form.*)
SAJOUS.

1232—℞ **Tinct. aconiti radicis** . . . . f℥ss.
Sig. One drop every hour in water. Best results when following a dose of castor oil. When it has existed some days,
then give—

1233—℞ Vini cocæ . . . . Oj.
Sig. A wineglassful every three hours, with absolute rest of
voice. (*In acute laryngitis.*)
SAJOUS.

1234—℞ Tincturæ aconiti radicis . . . ℥xxx.
Syrupi limonis . . . . f℥ss.
Liquoris ammonii acetatis . . f℥ij.—M.
Sig. A dessertspoonful every three hours. (*In acute form.*)
R. P. THOMAS.

1235—℞ Acidi sulphurosi . . . . partem j.
Aquæ destillatæ . . . . partes ij.—M.
Sig. Apply twice **daily by** means of atomizer. (*In chronic form.*)
BIETT.

1236—℞ Acidi benzoici . . . . gr. ss.
Sodii biboratis . . . . gr. iss.
Acaciæ, sugar, or currant-paste . . q. s.—M.
Ft. trochiscum no. j.
Sig. One every hour. (*In acute laryngitis.*)
SAJOUS.

1237—℞ Hydrargyri protiodidi . . . . **gr. ij.**
Potassii iodidi . . . . **℥ij.**
Tincturæ gentianæ comp.,
Syrupi sarsaparillæ comp. . . . . . . āā f℥ij.—M.
Sig. A teaspoonful three times daily. (*In follicular laryngitis and ulcerations of the epiglottis.*)
HORACE GREEN.

1238—℞ **Argenti nitratis** . . . . gr. lx.
Aquæ destillatæ . . . . f℥j.—M.
Sig. Apply locally on cotton after using—

1239—℞ **Sol. cocain. muriatis** (10 per cent.) f℥j.
Sig. Apply locally to the larynx. (*In chronic form.*) SEILER.

1240—℞ Menthol . . . . gr. xxv-c.
Olei olivæ . . . . f℥j.—M.
Sig. Apply locally **to the ulcerations.** (*In tuberculous laryngitis.*)
M. A. ROSENBERG.

1241—℞ Iodol . . . . ℥j.
Sig. Apply a small portion to the larynx by insufflation once **daily, or two or three times a** week. (*In tuberculous laryngitis.*)
LUBLINSKI.

1242—℞ Hydrarg. cyanidi . . . . gr. ij.
Sacch. lactis . . . . gr. xv.
Mucil. acaciæ . . . . q. s. ut ft. massa.—M.
Ft. massa et in pil. no. xx div.
Sig. One pill twice daily. (*In syphilitic laryngitis.*)
MORELL MACKENZIE.

1243—℞ Hydrarg. chloridi **corrosivi** . . . . . . gr. j.
Potassii iodidi . . . . ℥ij.
Aquæ cinnamomi . . . . ℥ij.—M.
Sig. A teaspoonful three times daily. (*In syphilitic laryngitis.*)
L. ELSBERG.

1244—℞ Hydrarg. chloridi corrosivi . gr. j-ij.
Aquæ destillatæ . . ℥ij.—M.
Sig. Inhale from an atomizer several times daily. (*In syphilitic laryngitis.*)
DEMARQUAY.

LEAD POISONING. (See Colic.)

LEPRA. (See Skin Diseases.)

LEUCOCYTHÆMIA.

1245—℞ Quininæ sulphatis . . . . 3j.
Ferri sulphatis exsiccatæ . . . . 3iss.
Fiat massa, in pilulas no. xxx dividenda.
Sig. Four or five pills during the day. (*Ague cake.*)
BARTHOLOW.

1246—℞ Chinoidinæ . . . . ℈ij.
Resinæ podophylli . . . . gr. iv.
Ferri sulphatis exsiccatæ . . . . ℈j.
Misce et fiant pilulæ no. xx.
Sig. One pill three times a day. BARTHOLOW.

1247—℞ Acidi arseniosi . . . . gr. j.
Pilulæ ferri carbonatis . . . . 3j.
Quinidinæ sulphatis . . . . 3j.
Misce et divide in pilulas xl.
Sig. Two pills three times a day. DA COSTA.

1248—℞ Acidi nitro-muriatici dil. . . . . f3j.
Sig. Ten to twenty drops in a wineglassful of water thrice
daily. HARTSHORNE.

1249—℞ Olei eucalypti . . . . gtt. c.
Piperini,
Ceræ albæ . . . . āā 3j.
Pulv. althœæ . . . . 3ij.—M.
Ft. massa et in pil. no. c div.
Sig. Three to five pills thrice daily., MOSLER.

1250—℞ Pulveris aloes socotrinæ,
Ferri sulphatis exsiccatæ . . . . . āā ℈j.
Mastiches . . . . gr. x.
Pulveris capsici . . . . ℈j.
Syrupi simplicis . . . . q. s.
Fiat massa, in pilulas xx dividenda.
Sig. One pill every four hours. COPLAND.

LEUCORRHŒA.

1251—℞ Sodii biboratis . . . . 3ij.
Sig. A teaspoonful in a pint of water as a vaginal wash. (*For
leucorrhœa of pregnancy.*) PARVIN.

1252—℞ Potassii chloratis . . . . 3ij.
Sig. A teaspoonful to a pint of water as a vaginal injection.
(*In simple cases.*) PARVIN.

1253—℞ Potassii permanganatis . . . . . . 3ss.
Aquæ . . . . f3xv.
Sig. For vaginal injection. (*In fetid discharges.*)
BARTHOLOW.

1254—℞ Iodoformi . . . . 3j.
Acidi tannici . . . . 3j.—M.
Sig. Pack a sufficient quantity in the dry state around the
cervix uteri. BARTHOLOW.

1255—℞ Extracti hydrastis fluidi . . . . f3j.
Sig. Apply topically to cervix uteri. (*When due to ulcerations
and erosions.*) BARTHOLOW.

1256—℞ Zinci sulphatis,
Aluminis . . . . āā 3iss.
Glycerini . . . . f3vj.—M.
Sig. Add a tablespoonful to a pint of water, and inject night
and morning. HAZARD.

1257—℞ Pulveris catechu,
Aluminis . . . . āā 3j.
Olei theobromæ . . . . q. s.
Fiant suppositoria vaginalia no. vi.
Sig. Use one night and morning. HAZARD.

1258—℞ Creolini . . . . f3j.
Sig. Half a teaspoonful in two quarts of hot water as a
douche. J. C. WILSON.

1259—℞ Creasoti . . . . ♏xij.
Mucilaginis tragacanthæ . . . . ℨij.
Aquæ ferventis . . . . f ℨxiv.

Fiat mistura.
Sig. After washing out the vagina with warm water, use **the**
injection. (*In ribbated discharges from puerperal fever.*)

MACKENZIE.

1260—℞ Acidi tannici . . ℥iv.
Glycerini . . f ℨxvj.—M.

Sig. A tablespoonful to a quart of tepid water, used as a
vaginal injection for five minutes, night and morning, by
means of a Davidson's or a fountain syringe.

T. GAILLARD THOMAS.

1261—℞ Zinci sulphatis . ℨiss.
Aluminis sulphatis . ℨiss.
Glycerini . . . f ℨvj.—M.

Sig. A tablespoonful to a quart of water, as a vaginal injection. T. GAILLARD THOMAS.

1262—℞ Liquoris sodæ chlorinatæ . . . . f ℨj.
Aquæ . . . . f ℨx.—M.

Sig. Inject **once or twice daily.** TROUSSEAU.

1263—℞ Aristol. . . . . ℨj.

Sig. Apply freely as a dusting-powder, **by means of a spec-**
ulum, every second or third day J. C. WILSON.

1264—℞ Acidi boracici . . . . ℥vj.
Aquæ ferventis . . . . Oj.—M.

Ft. lotio.
Sig. To be used as a vaginal injection. RINGER.

1265—℞ Sodii **bicarbonatis** . . . . ℨj.
Tinct. **belladonnæ** . . . . ℨij.
Aquæ . . . . Oj.—M.

Sig. Use as a vaginal wash. (*In over-secretion of the glands*
about the os uteri, with pain.) RINGER.

1266—℞ Ext. belladonnæ gr. x-xx.
Acidi tannici ℨij-iv.
Olei theobromæ ℨx.—M.

Ft. massa et in suppositoria no. x div.
Sig. Introduce one into the vagina, place in contact with the
os, and retain with a small tampon. Renew as required.
(*In ulcerated and painful os, and leucorrhœa.*) TROUSSEAU.

LICE.

1267—℞ Vinegar . . . . 500 parts.
Sublimate . . . . 1 part.—M.

Sig. Apply night and morning. (*For pediculi pubis.*) BROCQ.

1268—℞ Hydrarg. chloridi corrosivi . . . . ℨj.
Aquæ rosæ . . . . ℥iv.—M.

Ft. lotio.
Sig. Use as a wash.

1269—℞ Pulv. cocculi indici . . . . ℨiv.
Adipis . . . . ℨj.—M.

Ft. ungt.
Sig. Apply locally, **rubbing in well.** HARTSHORNE.

1270—℞ Acidi carbolici . . . . ℨj-ij.
Glycerini . . . . ℨj.
Aquæ . . . . ad f ℨviij.—M.

Ft. lotio.
Sig. Apply as a wash. (*To destroy lice or relieve pruritus.*)

HARTSHORNE.

1271—℞ Hydrargyri chloridi corrosivi . . gr. iv.
Alcoholis f ℨvj.
Ammonii chloridi . f ℨss.
Aquæ rosæ . q. s. ad f ℨvj.—M.

Sig. Apply once daily. (*In scabies and head lice.*)

TILBURY FOX.

107

LICE (Continued).

1272—℞ Acidi carbolici . . . . ℨj.
    Potass. caustic. . . . . ℨss.
    Aquæ . . . . f℥vj.—M.
Sig. Dilute with two parts of water and apply locally.
                                J. C. WILSON.

1273—℞ Storacis . . . . f℥j.
    Spiritus vini rectificati . . . . f℥ij.
Misce, et adde—
    Olei olivæ . . . . f℥j.
Sig. Rub the whole body carefully except the head; repeat
in twenty-four hours. (*In scabies.*) McCALL ANDERSON.

1274—℞ Pulveris seminis staphisagriæ   ℨss.
    Adipis .   ℨij.—M.
Sig. Digest the powder in melted lard for an hour or two,
and strain while hot. Apply once daily. (*In head and
body lice.*)   SQUIRE.

1275—℞ Hydrargyri oleatis . . . . gr. v.
    Acidi oleici . . . . gr. xcv.
    Ætheris . . . . gtt. xij.—M.
Sig. **Make two** applications twenty-four hours apart. (*In crab
lice.*)   MARSHALL.

1276—℞ Olei rosmarini . . . . f℥ss.
    Olei olivæ . . . . f℥iss.—M.
Sig. **Apply once daily.** (*In head and body lice.*)   RINGER.

1277—℞ Manganesii oxidi nigri . . . . ℨij.
    Adipis . . . . ℨj.
Misce et fiat unguentum.
Sig. Apply once or twice daily. (*In scabies.*) BARTHOLOW.

1278—℞ Sodii hyposulphitis . . . . ℨij.
    Acidi sulphurosi diluti . . . . . . f℥iv.
    Aquæ . . . . q. s. ad f℥xxvj.—M.
Sig. **Apply once daily.** (*In scabies and head lice.*) STARTIN.

1279—℞ Tinct. delphinii,
    Aquæ coloniensis . . . . āā f℥ij.—M.
Sig. Apply night and **morning.** (*For pediculi pubis.*)
                            J. C. WILSON.

LICHEN. (See Skin Diseases.)

LIVER, DISEASES OF. (See Biliousness, Colic, and Catarrh.)

LOCOMOTOR ATAXIA. (See also Sclerosis.)

1280—℞ Strychninæ sulphatis   gr. iss.
    Syr. hypophosphiti   f℥xij.—M.
Sig. A teaspoonful thrice daily. (*When the system is saturated
with silver.*)   DA COSTA.

1281—℞ Argenti nitratis . . . . gr. x.
    Confect. rosæ . . . . ℨj.—M.
Ft. massa et in pil. no. xl div.
Sig. One or two pills thrice daily. Cease giving after a few
weeks, to prevent argyria.   DA COSTA.

1282—℞ Extracti physostigmatis . . . . gr. x.
    Pulveris zingiberis . . . . ℨj.
Misce et fiant pilulæ no. xx.
Sig. One pill three times a day.   RINGER.

1283—℞ Antipyrin. . . . . ℨj.
    Syr. zingiberis . . . . f℥j.
    Aquæ cinnamomi . . . . ad f℥iv.—M.
Sig. A teaspoonful every one to four hours for three to six
doses. (*In lightning-pain of locomotor ataxia.*) GERMAIN SÉE.

1284—℞ Ext. physostigmatis . . . . gr. x.
    Ext. gentianæ . . . . ℨij.—M.
Ft. massa et in pil. no. c div.
Sig. One pill every three hours.   MURRELL.

1285—℞ Antifebrin. . . . . 3j.

Dispensa in capsulas no. xv.
Sig. One or two capsules every half-hour for two doses, if
necessary; then one every four or six hours if required.
(*For pains of locomotor ataxia.*)　　　DUJARDIN-BEAUMETZ.

LUMBAGO.

1286—℞ Aquæ destillatæ . . . . f3j.
Sig. Thirty to sixty minims hypodermically.　BARTHOLOW.

1287—℞ Tinct. actææ racemosæ (1–i) . . . . f3ss.
Sig. Five minims every hour, or fifteen to thirty minims
thrice daily.　　　　　RINGER.

1288—℞ Empl. belladonnæ (6 in. × 4 in.).
Sig. Apply locally. (*For persistent remains, affecting a small
spot.*)　　　　　　　**RINGER.**

1289—℞ Pulv. potassii nitratis . . . . **3ij.**
In pulv. no. xii div.
Sig. A powder in a half-tumblerful of water every hour or
two. (*When urine is scanty and high-colored.*)　RINGER.

1290—℞ Atropinæ sulphatis　　　　　　gr. jl.
Morphinæ sulphatis　　　　　gr. xvj.
Aquæ destillatæ　　. . . . f3j.—M.
Sig. Five minims injected deep into the muscular tissues.
　　　　　　　　DA COSTA.

1291—℞ Extracti cimicifugæ fluidi.
Syrupi acaciæ . . . . āā f3ss.
Aquæ amygdalæ amaræ . . . . . . f3iij.—M.
Sig. A teaspoonful every three hours.　BARTLETT.

1292—℞ Potassii iodidi,
Potassii carbonatis . . . . āā 3j.
Tincturæ aconiti radicis . . . . f3ij.
Aquæ destillatæ . . . . f3x.—M.
Sig. Apply locally every few hours.　ERICHSEN.

1293—℞ Potassii iodidi . . . . 3ss.
Tincturæ opii deodoratæ . . f3ij.
Spiritus lavandulæ compositi　f3j.
Spiritus ætheris nitrosi　　　f3ss.
Aquæ destillatæ . 　　　f3xij.—M.
Sig. Two tablespoonfuls twice daily.　B. BRODIE.

1294—℞ Olei terebinthinæ . . 　　　f3ij–iij.
Mucilag. acaciæ　　 . . . q. s. ut ft. emulsio.
Syr. zingiberis　　　　　 . . f3j.
Aquæ　　　　　 . . . . . ad f3iij.—M.
Sig. A tablespoonful every four to six hours, carefully, lest
strangury and nephritis intervene. (*When urine is clear
and abundant, and bowels regular.*)　WARING.

1295—℞ Antipyrin. . . . . 3j.
Syr. tolutani . . . . f3j.
Aquæ menthæ pip. . . . . ad f3iv.—M.
Sig. A **teaspoonful** every one to **four hours** for three to six
doses.　　　　　　GERMAIN SÉE.

1296—℞ Methyl. chloridi　 . . . . 3ss.
Sig. Use locally, applying carefully.　　　**DEBOVE.**

1297—℞ Potassii iodidi . . . . 3iv.
Vini colchici sem. . . . . f3j.
Syr. sarsaparillæ comp. . . . . f3j.
Aquæ . . . . q. s. ad f3iij.—M.
Sig. A teaspoonful in a wineglassful of water every four
hours.　　　　　J. M. LEEDOM.

1298—℞ Tinct. iodi . . . . f3ij.
Tinct. aconiti rad. . . . . . f3ij.
Chloroformi . . . . . . f3iv.
Linimenti saponis comp. . . ad f3iij.—M.
Sig. Apply every **few** hours locally.　*Bellevue Hospital, N.Y.*

1299—℞ Resorcin. . . . . ȝiss.
  Vaselini . . . . ȝv.—M.
Ft. ungt.
Sig. Apply locally. (*In all forms of lupus.*) BERTARELLI.

1300—℞ Phosphori concisi . . . . gr. ij.
  Glycerini . . . . ȝj.
Solve cum leni calore.
Sig. Ten minims three times a day.   CREWCOUR.

1301—℞ Iodi . . . . gr. ss.
  Olei olivæ . . . . ȝij.
  Olei amygdalæ dulcis . . . . ȝss.—M.
Sig. The one-third part three times a day. DUNCAN.

1302—℞ Arsenici iodidi . . . . gr. ½.
  Hydrargyri biniodidi . . . . gr. ½.
  Confectionis rosæ . . . . q. s.
Fiat pilula.
Sig. Two pills daily after meals. (*In lupus exedens.*)
           A. T. THOMPSON.

1303—℞ Acidi pyrogallici . . . . ȝj.
  Adipis . . . . ȝj.—M.
Sig. Apply thickly twice a day, watching effect. J. C. WILSON.

1304—℞ Zinci chloridi,
  Antimonii chloridi . . . . āā ȝj.
  Pulv. iridis florentinæ radicis. . . . gr. x.
  Acidi hydrochlorici puri . . . . ♏x.—M.
Sig. Use as a caustic, spread on linen strips a quarter-inch wide. Lay the strips on the spot, cover with lint, and leave for twenty-four hours. KAPOSI.

1305—℞ Iodi,
  Potassii iodidi . . . . āā gr. xv.
  Glycerini . . . . ♏xxx.—M.
Sig. Apply locally. (*To flatten remaining scars.*) KAPOSI.

1306—℞ Sol. acidi lactici (80 per cent.) . . . . ȝss.
Sig. To be applied locally, after poulticing to detach scabs. (*In lupus of nasal cavities.*) MOSETIG.

1307—℞ Vitelli ovi,
  Acidi acetici dil. . . . . . āā partes æquales.—M.
Sig. Apply over the affected surface. (*In erythematous lupus.*)
           BROCQ.

1308—℞ Zinci sulphatis exsiccatæ . . . . ȝj.
Sig. Dust over diseased part.   BARTHOLOW.

1309—℞ Acidi chromici . . . . ȝv.
  Aquæ destillatæ . . . . ȝiij.—M.
Sig. Apply to diseased part.   WOOSTER.

1310—℞ Liquoris potassii arsenitis . . . . ȝj.
  Aquæ destillatæ . . . . ȝj.
Fiat lotio. (*In mild cases.*)   HOOPER.

1311—℞ Acidi arseniosi . . . . gr. j-ij.
  Hydrargyri chloridi mitis . . . . . . gr. c.
Fiat pulvis. (*As a caustic.*)   BURGESS.

1312—℞ Acidi pyrogallici . . . . ȝj.
  Cerati simplicis . . . . ȝx.—M.
Sig. Apply locally. (*In lupus of eyelids and skin.*) KAPOSI.

1313—℞ Acidi lactici puri . . . . ȝj.
Sig. Soak moderately a pledget of absorbent cotton, and apply to the ulcer. Cover with oiled silk and bandage. If the surrounding tissue be quite normal, protect it with grease or collodion. WICHMANN.

1314—℞ Sat. sol. cocain. muriatis . . . . . . ȝj.
Sig. Apply locally.   FOWLER.

LUPUS (Continued).

1315—℞ Acidi arseniosi . . . . ℈j.
Hydrarg. sulphureti rubri . . . . . . ℥j.
Ungt. simplicis . . . . ℥j.—M.
Ft. ungt.
Sig. Spread thickly on cloth, and apply to the patch for two
or three days, until the lupus nodules and points **are**
blackish and destroyed. "Cosmes' Paste" modified by
HEBRA.

MALARIA. (See Fever.)

MAMMARY INFLAMMATION. (See also Abscess.)

1316—℞ Ext. gelsem.l fld. . . . . f℥vj–viij.
Syr. limonis. . . . . f℥j.
Aquæ . . . . ad f℥ij.—M.
Sig. A teaspoonful two or three times daily. Increase the
dose until the patient has dilated pupil, drooping eyelids,
and a feeling of languor. BARTHOLOW.

1317—℞ Atropinæ sulphatis . . . . gr. viij.
Aquæ rosæ . . . . f℥ij.—M.
Ft. lotio.
Sig. Apply locally, but discontinue **in case of** dilatation of
pupils or dryness of throat. L. STARR.

1318—℞ Ammonii carbonatis . . . . ℥j.
Aquæ . . . . Oj.—M.
Ft. lotio.
Sig. Apply locally. L. STARR.

1319—℞ Ammonii chloridi. . . . . ℥j.
Aquæ . . . . Oj.—M.
Sig. Apply locally by means of compresses frequently re-
newed. J. C. WILSON.

1320—℞ Extracti belladonnæ . . . . ℈j.
Aquæ. . . . . f℥iv.
Ft. lotio. DRUITT.

1321—℞ Extracti belladonnæ,
Syrupi fusci . . . . āā ℥ij.
Pulveris opii . . . . ℈ss.
Misce accuratissime.
Sig. Rub in three times **a day**. DEBREYNE.

1322—℞ Ext. phytolaccæ decandræ fld. . . f℥j.
Sig. Ten drops in water every hour for three or four doses,
then gradually lengthen the intervals. The breast may be
bandaged, but not poulticed or rubbed. Give a brisk purgative. (*In threatened mastitis.*) TODD.

1323—℞ Ungt. belladonnæ . . . . ℥j.
Pulv. camphoræ . . . . ℈ss.—M.
Sig. Apply locally, supporting the breast with a bandage.
NELIGAN.

1324—℞ Linimenti camphoræ . . . . . . f℥viij.
Sig. Apply locally, rubbing gently from the circumference
toward the nipple. (*In incipient mastitis.*) PARRY.

1325—℞ Hydrarg. chloridi mitis,
Pulv. jalapæ . . . . āā gr. x.—M.
Ft. pulv. no. i.
Sig. Take at once. (*Brisk purge for incipient mastitis.*) RUSH.

1326—℞ Morphinæ . . . . gr. x.
Hydrargyri oleatis . . . . ℈ss.
Acidi oleici . . . . ℥ixss.—M.
Sig. Anoint three times a day. MARSHALL.

1327—℞ Tincturæ belladonnæ. . . . . f℥ij.
Linimenti saponis camphorati . . . . f℥viij.
Fiat linimentum. NELIGAN.

1328—℞ Extracti belladonnæ . . . . ℥j.
Liquoris plumbi subacetatis diluti . . Oj.
Misce et fiat lotio. GRAEFE.

1329—℞ Tinct. digitalis,
    Aquæ cinnamomi . . . . āā f ʒj.—M.
Sig. One to two teaspoonfuls three times daily. (*Watch pulse.*)
                               MAUDSLEY.

1330—℞ Hyoscyaminæ sulphatis . . . . gr. j.
    Aquæ destillatæ . . . . f ʒxij.—M.
Sig. Five to twelve minims hypodermically.
                Ward's Island Insane Asylum, N.Y.

MANIA, ACUTE.

1331—℞ Extracti gelsemii fluidi   f ʒiij.
    Syrupi acidi citrici   f ʒij.
    Aquæ destillatæ   . .   f ʒxj.—M.
Sig. A teaspoonful every two hours until physiological effects
are produced. (*With great motor excitement.*) BARTHOLOW.

1332—℞ Potassii bromidi . . . . ʒj.
    Tincturæ cannabis indicæ . . . . . . f ʒj.(!)
    Mucilaginis acaciæ . . . . f ʒij.
    Aquæ cinnamomi . . . . f ʒj.
Misce et fiat haustus.
Sig. Immediately after mixing.   CLOUSDEN.

1333—℞ Methylal. . . . . f ʒiij.
    Syr. aurantii corticis . . . . f ʒij.
    Aquæ . . . . ad f ʒiv.—M.
Sig. From a teaspoonful to a tablespoonful, repeated if necessary, to produce quietness or sleep.
             MAIRET AND COMBEMALE.

1334—℞ Potassii bromidi . . . . ʒj.
    Tinct. cannabis indicæ . . . . f ʒj.
    Syr. simplicis . . . . f ʒij.
    Aquæ . . . . q. s. ad f ʒiv.—M.
Sig. A tablespoonful thrice daily. (*In periodical mania and
senile mania.*)   CLOUSTON.

1335—℞ Potassii bromidi . . . . gr. xxv.
    Tincturæ hyoscyami . . . . f ʒss.
    Spiritus chloroformi . . . . ♏x.
    Aquæ destillatæ . . . . q. s. ad f ʒiss.
Fiat haustus.
Sig. At once.   TYLER SMITH.

1336—℞ Chloral. hydratis . . . . gr. xxv.
    Tincturæ cardamomi compositæ . . . . f ʒss.
    Syrupi simplicis . . . . f ʒij.
    Infusi caryophylli . . . . . . q. s. ad f ʒiss.
Misce et fiat haustus.
Sig. To be repeated in an hour if necessary.   PRIESTLEY.

1337—℞ Amyl. hydratis . . . . ʒj.
Sig. Forty to seventy-five minims, in sweetened water, as
required.   VON MERING.

1338—℞ Coninæ . . . . gr. ij.
    Spiritus rectificati . . . . f ʒss.
    Aquæ destillatæ . . . . q. s. ad f ʒss.—M.
Sig. A teaspoonful.   FRONMUELLER.

1339—℞ Ext. conii fld.,
    Ext. hyoscyami fld. . . . . āā ♏vij.
    Chloral. hydratis . . . . gr. x.
    Aquæ . . . . f ʒij.—M.
Ft. haustus.
Sig. To be taken at a draught, and repeated if required.
                MADIGAN.

1340—℞ Paraldehyd. . . . . f ʒss.
Sig. Thirty to fifty minims in an ounce or two of water, by
the rectum.   RINGER.

1341—℞ Pulv. tragacanthæ comp. . . . . ʒj.
    Syr. aurantii corticis . . . . f ʒiv.
    Paraldehyd. . . . . f ʒj.
    Spts. chloroformi . . . . ♏xv.
    Aquæ . . . . ad f ʒiij.—M.
Ft. haustus.
Sig. To be taken at one draught.   HODGSON.

MANIA, ACUTE (Continued).

1342—℞ Tinct. digitalis,
    Aquæ cinnamomi . . . . āā f ℨj.—M.
Sig. One or two teaspoonfuls three **times daily.** (*Watch pulse for intermittence.*)
              MAUDSLEY.

1343—℞ Hyoscin. hydrobromatis   gr. 1⁄20.
Sig. This dose in pill or hypodermically cautiously repeated at intervals of four or six hours.   J. C. WILSON.

MANIA, CHRONIC.

1344—℞ Tincturæ ferri chloridi   f ℨij.
    Syrupi zingiberis   f ℨj.
    Aquæ destillatæ . . . . f ℨvj.—M.
Sig. A tablespoonful three or four times a day. (*In anæmic cases.*)
              BUCKNILL.

1345—℞ Tinct. ferri chloridi,
    Tinct. nucis vomicæ . . . . āā ℨj.
    Aquæ . . . . q. s. ad ℨvj.—M.
Sig. A teaspoonful **thrice** daily, after meals.
     Ward's Island Insane Asylum, N.Y.

1346—℞ Tincturæ ferri chloridi   f ℨij.
    Spiritus ætheris nitrosi . . . . f ℨss.
    Infusi quassiæ . . . . q. s. ad f ℨvj.—M.
Sig. A tablespoonful three times a day. (*In debilitated cases.*)
             TUKE.

1347—℞ Ergotini . . . .   gr. lx.
    Ext. cannabis indicæ   gr. lj.
    Strychninæ   gr. ½.—M.
In pil. no. xx div.
Sig. One pill after each meal, and at bedtime.   J. C. WILSON.

1348—℞ Extracti ergotæ fluidi . . . . **f ℨiss.**
    Syrupi aurantii corticis . . . . **f ℨj.**
    Aquæ destillatæ . . . . **f ℨiliss.—M.**
Sig. A tablespoonful three **or four times a day.**
           CRICHTON BROWNE.

1349—℞ Caffeinæ citratis . . . . ℨss.
    Syrupi acidi citrici . . . . f ℨss.
    Aquæ destillatæ . . . . f ℨss.—M.
Sig. A teaspoonful three or four times a day.   BARTHOLOW.

MANIA, PUERPERAL.

1350—℞ Olei tiglii   . . . . gtt. vj.
    Micæ panis   . q. s. ut ft. massa.
Ft. massa et in pil. no. vi div.
Sig. One or two pills, as a purge. (*When cerebral congestion is present.*)
             LEISHMAN.

1351—℞ Extracti cimicifugæ fluidi   f ℨss.
    Mucilaginis acaciæ .   f ℨj.
    Aquæ dest'llatæ .   f ℨiliss.—M.
Sig. A tablespoonful every three hours.   RINGER.

1352—℞ Potassii bromidi . . . . ℨij.
    Chloral. hydratis . . . . ℨss.
    Syrupi aurantii corticis . . . . , f ℨj.
    Aquæ fœniculi . . . . q. s. ad f ℨvj.—M.
Sig. A tablespoonful every two hours.   QUAIN.

MARASMUS.

1353—℞ Syr. ferri iodidi . . . . . .   f ℨj.
Sig. Three **to** five drops, in water, thrice daily after eating.
            EUSTACE SMITH.

1354—℞ Quininæ . . . . gr. viij.
    Alcoholis . . . . f ℨj.
Fiat solutio. Dein adde—
    Olei morrhuæ . . . . **f ℨiv.**
Solve cum leni calore.
Sig. From a half to **one** teaspoonful, according to age of child.   LYMAN.

1355—℞ Tinct. cinchonæ comp.,
 Tinct. gentianæ comp. . . . . . . ãã f3j.—M.
 Sig. Fifteen drops to a teaspoonful, in sweetened water, thrice
 daily. J. L. SMITH.

1356—℞ Olei morrhuæ . . . . f3ij.
 Aquæ calcis . . . . f3iv.
 Syr. calcis lactophosphatis . . . . ad f3iv.—M.
 Sig. A teaspoonful two or three times daily. BOSLEY.

1357—℞ Pepsini saccharati . . . . ʒj-iss.
 In pulv. no. xx div.
 Sig. A powder after each feeding. BARTHEZ.

1358—℞ Quininæ sulphatis . . . . gr. ij-vj.
 Acidi sulphurici diluti . . . . gtt. ij-vj.
 Syrupi aurantii corticis . . . . f3j.
 Aquæ destillatæ . . . . f3ij.—M.
 Sig. A teaspoonful three or four times a day. COULSON.

1359—℞ Iodi . . . . gr. iss.
 Olei morrhuæ . . . . f3v.
 Tere simul.
 Sig. A half to one teaspoonful for a child. FLEISCHMANN.

1360—℞ Syrupi ferri iodidi . . . . f3j.
 Syrupi acaciæ . . . . f3vij.
 Aquæ fœniculi . . . . f3j.—M.
 Sig.—A teaspoonful three times a day. DUPASQUIER.

MEASLES. (See Fever.)

MELANCHOLIA. (See also Hypochondria.)

1361—℞ Tinct. ferri chloridi,
 Syr. simplicis . . . . ãã f3j.
 Sig. Twenty or thirty drops, well diluted, thrice daily.
 BARTHOLOW.

1362—℞ Camphoræ,
 Extracti hyoscyami . . . . ãã ʒiss.
 Misce et fiant pil. no. xl.
 Sig. Two pills three times a day. GOOCH.

1363—℞ Zinci valerianatis,
 Ferri valerianatis,
 Quininæ valerianatis . . . . ãã ʒss.—M.
 Ft. massa et in pil. no. xxx div.
 Sig. One pill three times daily. J. C. WILSON.

1364—℞ Moschi optimi,
 Pulveris camphoræ . . . . ãã ʒss.
 Olei cajuputi . . . . ℳv.
 Misce et divide in pilulas xii.
 Sig. One pill every two or three hours. HOOPER.

1365—℞ Moschi optimi . . . . ʒiij.
 Tincturæ castorei . . . . f3ss.
 Syrupi zingiberis . . . . f3j.
 Aquæ destillatæ . . . . . q. s. ad f3vj.—M.
 Sig. A dessertspoonful three or four times a day.
 E. J. CLARK.

1366—℞ Potassii bromidi . . . . ʒij.
 Tinct. calumbæ . . . . f3iij.
 Spts. ammoniæ aromatici . . . . . . f3j.
 Aquæ cinnamomi . . . . f3iij.
 Aquæ . . . . q. s. ad f3viij.—M.
 Sig. A wineglassful two or three times daily. LAWRENCE.

MENINGITIS.

1367—℞ Sodii bromidi . . . . ʒij.
 Chloral. hydratis . . . . ʒj.
 Syr. aurantii corticis . . . . f3j.
 Aquæ . . . . q. s. ad f3iij.—M.
 Sig. A dessertspoonful every hour or two until excitement
 abates. HERRMANN.

MENINGITIS (Continued).

1368—℞ Potassii bromidi . . ʒss.
　Syrupi simplicis . f ʒss.
　Aquæ destillatæ . . f ʒj.
Sig. A teaspoonful every two hours. (*In after-remaining convulsions.*) RINGER.

1369—℞ Morphinæ sulphatis gr. ij.
　Aquæ destillatæ . . . . . f ʒj.—M.
Sig. Five minims hypodermically every three to five hours, **or oftener.** (*In the cerebro-spinal form.*) LEYDEN.

1370—℞ Olei tiglii . . . . ℳv.
　Saponis,
　Pulveris acaciæ . . . . āā ℈j.
Misce et fiant pilulæ no. xx.
Sig. One to three pills. (*After effusion and in hydrocephalus.*) SUNDELIN.

1371—℞ Iodoformi . . . . gr. xv.
　Vaselini . . . . gr. lxxv.-M.
Ft. ungt.
Sig. Shave the scalp, and rub **in** night and morning the above quantity of ointment. Keep the head covered with an oiled-silk cap. (*In the tubercular variety.*) WARFVINGE.

1372—℞ Tincturæ opii deodoratæ,
　Extracti gelsemii fluidi . . . . . . āā f ʒj.
　Syrupi limonis . . . . f ʒij.
　Aquæ fœniculi . . . . f ʒiss.—M.
Sig.—A teaspoonful every two hours. BARTHOLOW.

1373—℞ Hydrarg. chloridi mitis,
　Pulv. jalapæ,
　Sacchari albi . . . . āā ℈j.—M.
In pulv. no. x. **div.**
Sig. A powder every hour until free purgation occurs. (*In cerebro-spinal meningitis.*) KOBERT.

1374—℞ Antimonii et potassii tartratis . . . . . ℈j-ij.
　Adipis . . . . ℥j.
Tere simul.
Sig. Apply to the shaved scalp. (*Also in the tubercular form.*) HANNAY.

1375—℞ Acidi tannici . . . . ℈j.
In capsulas no. xx div.
Sig. A capsule every three hours. **With ice** to the head. (*In simple meningitis.*) LARDIER.

1376—℞ Morphinæ sulphatis . . . . . . gr. ss.
　Acidi sulphurici aromatici . . . . f ʒj.
　Elixiris cinchonæ . . . . . . q. s. ad f ʒij.—M.
Sig. A teaspoonful every two hours for a child twelve years old. (*In the cerebro-spinal form.*) MEIGS AND PEPPER.

1377—℞ Tinct. ferri chloridi . . . . f ʒij.
Sig. Twenty to thirty minims every two hours. KLAPP.

1378—℞ Tinct. aconiti radicis f ʒj.
　Tinct. opii deodoratæ . . . . f ʒv.—M.
Sig. Seven drops in water, every two hours, during the stage of excitement. (*In cerebral meningitis.*) BARTHOLOW.

1379—℞ Acidi hydrocyanici dil. . . ℳxx-xl.
　Sodii bicarbonatis ℈ij-v.
　Syr. simplicis,
　Aquæ . . . . q. s. ad f ʒiss.—M
Sig. A teaspoonful every three or four hours for severe vomiting. (*In the cerebro-spinal form.*) DELAFIELD.

MENINGITIS, CEREBRO-SPINAL. (See Meningitis.)

MENORRHAGIA.

1380—℞ Ext. ergotæ fld. . . . . f ʒij.
Sig. A half to one teaspoonful thrice daily. MEIGS.

1381—℞ Liq. ferri perchloridi . . . . f ʒiv.
  Aquæ . . . . f ʒxij.—M.
Sig. Inject slowly and carefully into the uterus with a Davidson's syringe fitted with a long uterine tube. Avoid introducing air. Allow **a** free outlet for the fluid. (*In postpartum hemorrhage.*) R. BARNES.

1382—℞ Tinct. hamamelidis . . . . f ʒij.
Sig. One-half to one teaspoonful thrice daily. RINGER.

1383—℞ Pulv. potassii bromidi . . . . ʒij.
In pulv. no. xii div.
Sig. A powder in a wineglassful of water three times daily. Begin before the period, and continue till it is over.
  RINGER.

1384—℞ Tinct. sabinæ . . . . f ʒss.
Sig. Five to ten drops in cold water every half-hour to every three hours. PHILLIPS.

1385—℞ Olei erigerontis . . . . f ʒj.
Sig. Five drops on a lump of sugar every three or four hours.
  ELLWOOD WILSON.

1386—℞ Tincturæ capsici,
  Tincturæ cubebæ . . . . ãã f ʒj.
  Tincturæ cantharidis . . . . f ʒss.
  Mucilaginis acaciæ . . . . . . q. s. ad f ʒiv.—M.
Sig. A tablespoonful twice a day. (*When from debility.*)
  HAZARD.

1387—℞ Acidi gallici . . . . gr. xv.
  Acidi sulphurici aromatici . . . . . . ᴹxv.
  Tincturæ cinnamomi . . . . f ʒij.
  Aquæ destillatæ . . . . f ʒij.—M.
Sig. One dose, to be taken every four hours until **bleeding ceases.** (*In profuse bleeding.*) HAZARD.

1388—℞ Acidi arseniosi . . . . gr. j.
  Mastiches . . . . gr. x.
  Ferri sulphatis exsiccati,
  Pulveris capsici,
  Pulveris aloes socotrinæ . . . . . . ãã ʒj.
  Syrupi simplicis . . . . q. s.
Fiat massa, in pilulas xx dividenda.
Sig. One pill three or four times a day. (*In relaxed and debilitated cases.*) COPLAND.

1389—℞ Potassii bromidi . . . . gr. x.
  Tincturæ cannabis indicæ . . . . . . ᴹx.
  Infusi gentianæ compositi . . . q. s. ad f ʒj.
Fiat haustus.
Sig. To be taken three times a day. (*At climacteric and with uterine fibroid.*) GREENHALGH.

1390—℞ Ext. gossypii fld.,
  Syr. simplicis . . . . . ãã f ʒj.—M.
Sig. A teaspoonful every four hours. PARVIN.

1391—℞ Ext. geranii fld. . . . . f ʒiv.
Sig. A teaspoonful every hour for a few doses, then every three to four hours. May be used with advantage locally.
  SHOEMAKER.

1392—℞ Ext. rhois aromat. fld. . . . . f ʒj.
Sig. Fifteen to sixty minims thrice daily. UNNA.

1393—℞ Ext. hydrastis can. fld. . . . . f ʒj.
Sig. Twenty drops four times daily. R. W. WILCOX.

1394—℞ Acidi gallici . . . . ʒss.
  Acidi sulphurici dil. . . . . f ʒj.
  Tinct. opii deod. . . . . f ʒj.
  Inf. rosæ comp. . . . . f ʒiv.—M.
Sig. A tablespoonful every four hours or oftener.
  BARTHOLOW.

1395—℞ Tincturæ krameriæ,
  Extracti ergotæ fluidi   ãã f℥j.
  Infusi digitalis   f℥ij.—M.
 Sig. A tablespoonful *pro re nata.* (*In plethoric cases, and when
 due to mitral regurgitation.*)   BARTHOLOW.

1396—℞ Extracti ipecacuanhæ fluidi,
  Extracti digitalis fluidi,   ãã f℥ij.
  Extracti ergotæ fluidi   f℥ss.—M.
 Sig. One-half to one teaspoonful at a dose, as required.
             BARTHOLOW.

1397—℞ **Ext.** viburni fld...   f℥iij.
 Sig. A teaspoonful in water every three or four hours in
 connection with local treatment.   J. C. WILSON.

1398—℞ Pulveris ergotæ,
  Pulveris sabinæ   ãã ℈j.
 Misce et fiant chartulæ no. iv.
 Sig. One powder morning and night. (*In atony of uterus.*)
             RINGER.

MERCURIALISM. (See Ptyalism.)

METRITIS.

1399—℞ Tincturæ aconiti radicis gtt. xvj.
  Extracti gelsemii fluidi   f℥j.
  Extracti ergotæ fluidi   f℥vij.—M.
 Sig. A teaspoonful **every** two to six hours. (*Also in uterine
 tumor.*)   BARTHOLOW.

1400—℞ Potassæ   ℥v.
  Calcis   ℥vj.
  Alcoholis   q. s. ut fiat magma.
 Sig. Apply locally with extreme caution. (*In induration of
 cervix and chronic metritis.*)   BENNETT.

1401—℞ Tinct. iodi comp.   f℥j.
 Sig. Use locally on a probe wrapped with absorbent cotton,
 once or twice weekly. Two applications are made, and a
 glycerin tampon is left against the cervix. In the intervals
 let the patient use a gallon of hot water as a vaginal injection twice or thrice daily.   T. G. THOMAS.

MIGRAINE. (See also **Headache.**)

1402—℞ Caffeinæ citratis,
  Ammonii carbonatis   ãã ℈j.
  Elixiris guaranæ   f℥j.—M.
 Sig. A tablespoonful every hour till the pain is relieved.
             BEARD.

1403—℞ Caffeinæ citratis   gr. xv.
  Phenacetin   gr. xxx.
  Sacchari albi   gr. xv.
 Fiat pulv. Div. in capsulas no. x.
 Sig. One capsule to be taken, in the intervals of the attacks,
 every two or three hours.   HAMMERSCHLAG.

MITRAL DISEASE. (See Heart-Disease.)

MORNING SICKNESS. (See also **Vomiting.**)

1404—℞ Cerii oxalatis   gr. xxiv.
  Ext. hyoscyami   gr. xxxvj.
 Misce et fiat massa, in pil. no. **xii div.**
 Sig. One pill twice daily.   GOODELL.

1405—℞ Cupri sulphatis   gr. ij.
  Aquæ destillatæ   f℥ss.—M.
 Sig. Six drops three times a **day.** BARTHOLOW.

1406—℞ Liquoris potassii arsenitis f℥ss.
 Sig. One drop before meals. (*In bloody vomit.*) **BARTHOLOW.**

1407—℞ Tincturæ iodi . . . . f ʒss.
      Mucilaginis acaciæ . . . . f ʒj.
      Aquæ destillatæ . . . . q. s. ad f ʒiv.—M.
Sig. A dessertspoonful every hour or two.   ELLIS.

1408—℞ Tinct. cantharidis,
      Tinct. ferri muriatis . . . . āā f ʒj.—M.
Sig. Twenty-five drops, well diluted, three times daily.
                        HIGGINS.

1409—℞ Sodii bicarbonatis . . . . gr. iv.
      Acidi hydrocyanici dil. . . . . gt. j.
      Syr. lactopeptini . . . . f ʒj.—M.
Sig. To be given half an hour before meals.   J. FREE.

1410—℞ Creasoti . . . . ♏ iij.
      Pulveris hyoscyami . . . . gr. xij.
      Confectionis rosæ . . . . q. s.
Misce et fiant pilulæ no. xii.
Sig. One pill three times a day.   HAZARD.

1411—℞ Cerii oxalatis . . . . gr. xv.
      Extracti gentianæ . . . . gr. v.
Fiat massa, in pilulas x dividenda.
Sig. One pill an hour after each meal.   J. Y. SIMPSON.

1412—℞ Cerii valerianatis . . . . gr. xv.
In pil. no. xx div.
Sig. Two to four pills daily.   MUNDÉ.

1413—℞ Cocain. hydrochloratis . . . . gr. j.
      Aquæ . . . . f ʒj.—M.
Sig. A teaspoonful three **times daily before meals.** (*May be
given hypodermically.*)   PARVIN.

1414—℞ Extracti opii aquosi . . . . gr. x.
      Fellis bovini inspissati . . . . ʒij.
Misce et fiant pilulæ no. xl.
Sig. Two pills an hour before **meals.**   CAZEAUX.

1415—℞ Acidi hydrocyanici diluti .   ♏ xij.
      Syrupi papaveris . . .   f ʒj.
      Aquæ destillatæ . .   f ʒv.—M.
Sig. A tablespoonful two or three times a day.
               WALTER AND BLUNDELL.

1416—℞ Cocain. muriatis .   gr. j.
      Ext. belladonnæ.   ʒvj.—M.
Sig. **Apply locally to the** cervix uteri morning and evening.
               FENN.

1417—℞ Acidi phenici deliquesc. . . . . f ʒj.
      Aceti opii . . . . f ʒiij.—M.
Sig. Four drops in a little **sweetened water five minutes**
before meals thrice daily.

1418—℞ Tinct. nucis vomicæ . . . . f ʒss.
Sig. One drop every hour or two, in water.   RINGER.

1419—℞ Atropinæ sulphatis . . . . gr. j.
      Morphinæ sulphatis . . . . gr. iv.
      Acidi sulphurici **aromatici** . . . . . . f ʒiij.
      Aquæ . . . . f ʒv.—M.
Sig. Ten to twenty drops, in water, thrice daily.   BOYS.

1420—℞ Bismuthi subnitratis . . . . ʒij.
In pulv. no. xii div.
Sig. A powder thrice daily before **meals.**   CAZEAUX.

MUMPS. (See also Fever.)

1421—℞ Magnesii sulphatis   ʒiv.
      Aquæ puræ . . . . . .   ʒiv.
      Antimonii et potassii tartratis   gr. j.
      Spts. ætheris nitrosi   f ʒiij.
      Sacchari albi   f ʒvj.—M.
Sig. A teaspoonful every three hours, after the bowels have
been well moved. With flaxseed poultices locally.
               CONDIE.

MUMPS (Continued).

1422—℞ Hydrargyri cum cretà . . . . gr. ij.
Sacchari lactis . . . . gr. xx.
Misce et fiant chartulæ no. vi.
Sig. One powder three or four times a day. RINGER.

1423—℞ Tincturæ belladonnæ,
Tincturæ opii,
Ætheris . . . . āā f℥j.
Linimenti saponis camphorati . . . . f℥ij.—M.
Sig. Rub frequently. HAZARD.

MYALGIA.

1424—℞ Linimenti belladonnæ . . . . ℨiv.
Sig. Rub in well, several times daily. BARTHOLOW.

1425—℞ Extracti xanthoxyli fluidi . . . . . . f℥j.
Sig. From fifteen minims to two drachms. (In torticollis, lumbago, etc.) BARTHOLOW.

1426—℞ Unguenti iodi . . . . ℨj.
Sig. Rub in a small portion two or three times daily. RINGER.

1427—℞ Ammonii chloridi . . . . ℨj.
Extracti cimicifugæ . . . . f℥ij.
Syrupi acaciæ,
Aquæ laurocerasi . . . . āā f℥j.—M.
Sig. A teaspoonful three or four times a day. ANSTIE.

NÆVUS.

1428—℞ Acidi chromici . . . . gr. c.
Aquæ destillatæ . . . . f℥j.—M.
Sig. Apply locally with care. BARTHOLOW.

1429—℞ Hydrarg. chloridi corrosivi . . . . . gr. xvj.
Collodii . . . . f℥ss.—M.
Sig. Apply with a brush locally. (For small, superficial birthmarks.) S. D. GROSS.

1430—℞ Creasoti . . . . f℥ss.
Sig. Paint the spots daily. WARING.

NECROSIS. (See Caries.)

NEPHRITIS. (See also Albuminuria.)

1431—℞ Ext. jaborandi fld. . . . . f℥j.
Sig. Five to ten minims every hour or half-hour, until free diaphoresis is established. May be combined with digitalis. (In acute nephritis.) DA COSTA.

1432—℞ Pilocarpinæ muriatis . . . . gr. vj.
Aquæ destillatæ . . . . f℥ij.—M.
Sig. Five to ten minims by the stomach, or hypodermically if uræmia is present. (In acute nephritis.) RINGER.

1433—℞ Potassii nitratis . . . . gr. xv.
Pulveris scillæ,
Pulveris pimentæ . . . . āā gr. x.
Misce et fiant chartulæ no. iii.
Sig. One three times a day. SWEDIAUR.

1434—℞ Tincturæ ferri chloridi . . . . f℥ij.
Acidi acetici diluti . . . . f℥ss.
Syrupi simplicis . . . . f℥ss.
Liquoris ammonii acetatis . . **q. s. ad** f℥iv.—M.
Sig.—A dessertspoonful every three or four hours. BASHAM.

119

1435—℞ Potassii acetatis . . . . ℨss.
  Infusi digitalis . . . . f ℨvj.—M.
Sig. One teaspoonful every fourth hour to a child five years
  old. Used with the following:

1436—℞ Resinæ podophylli . . . . gr. j.
  Saechari albi . . . . ℨj.—M.
In pulv. no. viii-xii div.
Sig. Take one powder. Repeat if necessary. (To produce
  catharsis.) J. LEWIS SMITH.

1437—℞ Potassii bitartratis . . . . ℨij.
  Aquæ ferventis . . . . Oij.
  Corticis limonis,
  Saechari . . . . āā q. s. ad conciliandum
  gustum.
Sig. Use ad libitum. JOY.

1438—℞ Extracti jaborandi fluidi . . . . f ℨj.
  Elixiris simplicis,
  Syrupi simplicis . . . . āā f ℨss.—M.
Sig. One to two teaspoonfuls. (With uræmia.) BARTHOLOW.

1439—℞ Stigmatæ maidis (corn-silk) . . . . . ℨliss.
  Aquæ bullientis . . . . Oij.—M.
Ft. infusum.
Sig. A wineglassful several times daily; or the following:

1440—℞ Scoparii flor . . . . ℨviiss.
  Juniperi . . . . ℨiiss.
  Aquæ bullientis . . . . f ℨxxxj.—M.
Ft. infusum et adde—
  Syr. e quinque radicibus (Edinb., 1744) f ℨiss.—M.
Sig. A wineglassful several times daily. DUBIEF.

1441—℞ Potassii tartratis . . . . ℨj.
  Potassii nitratis . . . . ℨss.
  Mannæ . . . . ℨj.
  Decocti taraxaci . . . . f ℨvj.—M.
Sig. A tablespoonful every hour or two. (After scarlet fever.)
  PHŒBUS.

1442—℞ Potassii acetatis . . . . ℨj.
  Oxymellis scillæ . . . . f ℨj.
  Vini opii . . . . ♏Lxv.
  Aquæ florum tiliæ . . . . f ℨss.
  Syrupi althææ . . . . f ℨj.—M.
Sig. A tablespoonful. PIERQUIN.

1443—Pulv. jalapæ comp. . . . . ℨj.
In pulv. no. xii. div.
Sig. A powder every four hours until free catharsis occurs.
  To be given after the patient has been rolled in blankets
  wrung out of hot water. (In acute nephritis.) FOTHERGILL.

1444—℞ Sodii iodidi . . . . gr. xv.
  Sodii phosphatis . . . . gr. xxx.
  Sodii chloridi . . . . gr. xc.—M.
Sig. Dissolve in water, and give in the course of the twenty-
  four hours, either alone or in milk. SEMMOLA.

1445—℞ Sodii phosphatis,
  Sodii chloridi,
  Sodii iodidi . . . . āā ℨij.
  Sodii bromidi . . . . ℨj.
  Aquæ destillatæ . . . . f ℨxiiss.—M.
Sig. A tablespoonful four times daily, in a cupful of milk.
  Used with the following:

1446—℞ Acidi tannici,
  Ext. cinchonæ . . . . āā gr. xxx.
  Fuchsin . . . . gr. xv.—M.
Ft. massa et in pil. no. xx div.
Sig. One pill morning and evening. (In chronic cases.)
  MONIN.

NEPHRITIS (Continued).

1447—℞ Camphoræ . . . . gr. v.
   Lanolini,
   Ungt. belladonnæ . . . . āā 3ss.—M.
Ft. unguentum.
Sig. Apply to the abdomen. (*Per tympany occurring in chronic Bright's disease and due to peritoneal congestion.*) DA COSTA.

NERVOUSNESS. (See Hysteria.)

NETTLERASH. (See Urticaria.)

NEURALGIA. (See also Sciatica.)

1448—℞ Butyl. chloral. . . . . gr. xl-lxxv.
   Alcohol. rect. . . . . f3iiss.
   Glycerini . . . . f3v.
   Aquæ destillatæ . . . . f3iv.—M.
Sig. Two to four spoonfuls at once. LEIDREICH.

1449—℞ Sol. nitro-glycerin. (1 per cent.) . . . . f3ss.
Sig. One or two drops on the tongue every four to six hours, as required. (*When pallor of face is present.*) TRESSEWITSCH.

1450—℞ Antipyrin . . . . 3iss.
   Aquæ destillatæ . . . . f3v.—M.
Sig. Twenty-five minims hypodermically every three or four hours till relieved. DUJARDIN-BEAUMETZ.

1451—℞ Antipyrin . . . . gr. lxxv.
   Aquæ destillatæ . . . . f3iss.
   Spts. jamaicensis . . . . f3v.
   Syr. limonis . . . . f3viiss.—M.
Sig. To be taken in teaspoonful doses in the twenty-four hours. DUJARDIN-BEAUMETZ.

1452—℞ Ethoxycaffeini,
   Sodii salicylatis . . . . āā gr. iiiⱼ.
   Cocainæ muriatis . . . . gr. iss.
   Aquæ aurantii flor. . . . . f3xv.
   Syr. simplicis . . . . f3v.—M.
Sig. To be taken at one dose at the commencement of the attack. (*For migraine.*) DUJARDIN-BEAUMETZ.

1453—℞ Ext. cocæ fld. . . . . 3ⱼ.
   Syr. aurantii flor. . . . . f3v.
   Aquæ . . . . ad f3ij.—M.
Sig. A teaspoonful every hour till relieved. (*In gastralgia.*)
      D'ARDENNE.

1454—℞ Liq. chloroformi aq. sat. . . . . f3xv.
   Aquæ aurantii flor. . . . . f3xiv.
   Tinct. anisi stellati . . . . f3j.—M.
Sig. A teaspoonful every quarter of an hour. (*In gastralgia.*)
      DUJARDIN-BEAUMETZ.

1455—℞ Olei amygdalæ amari . . . . ♏xx.
   Alcoholis . . . . f3iij.—M.
Sig. Ten drops three times a day. HAZARD.

1456—℞ Liquoris potassii arsenitis . . . . . . f3iij.
   Tincturæ opii deodoratæ,
   Alcoholis . . . . āā f3iss.—M.
Sig. Ten drops three times a day. HAZARD.

1457—℞ Quininæ valerianatis . . . . gr. x.
   Tincturæ sumbuli . . . . f3ij.
   Extracti taraxaci fluidi . . . . . . f3vj.
   Infusi cascarillæ . . . . f3v.—M.
Sig. A dessertspoonful three times a day. HAZARD.

1458—℞ Tincturæ aconiti (Fleming) . . . . . f3j.
   Sodii carbonatis . . . . 3iss.
   Magnesii sulphatis . . . . 3iss.
   Aquæ destillatæ . . . . f3vj.
Fiat mistura.
Sig. A tablespoonful when pain is urgent. (*In gastralgia.*)
      FLEMING.

1459—℞ Tincturæ cannabis indicæ . . . . . . f℥vj.
    Syrupi acaciæ . . . . f℥iss.
    Aquæ destillatæ . . . . q. s. ad f℥vj.—M.)
Sig. A tablespoonful every four to six hours. (*In sciatica.*)
                               NELIGAN.

1460—℞ Conii hydrobromatis . . . . gr. iss.
    Aquæ aurantii flor. . . . . f℥iss.—M.
Sig. Three to five drops three times daily.

1461—℞ Thein.,
    Sodii benzoatis . . . . āā ℨj.
    Sodii chloridi . . . . gr. x.
    Aquæ destillatæ . . . . f℥j.—M.
Sig. Three to twenty drops, as required.   MAYS.

1462—℞ Ferri carbonatis . . . . ℨij.
    Quininæ sulphatis . . . . gr. vj.
    Ext. opii . . . . gr. ⅓.
    Syr. simplicis . . . . q. s. ut ft. massa.—M.
Ft. massa et in pil. no. xvi div.
Sig. Eight pills during the day.   JOLLY.

1463—℞ Aconitinæ nitratis cryst. . . . . gr. ¼.
    Quininæ hydrobromatis . . . . gr. lxxv.
    Syrupi . . . . q. s. ut ft. massa.—M.
Ft. massa et in pil. no. l div.
Sig. One pill every four hours until five or six are taken.
The following day take at longer intervals if there be any
disturbance of digestion or formication in the extremities.
                               LABORDE.

1464—℞ Delphinii (alkaloid of staphisagria) . . gr. xv.
    Ext. tritici repentis . . . . ℨss.
    Pulv. althææ . . . . q. s.—M.
Ft. massa et in pil. no. l div.
Sig. Four to six pills daily.   TURNBULL.

1465—℞ Tinct. conii . . . . ℨj.
    Tinct. valerianæ.
    Tinct. opii camphoratæ,
    Aquæ laurocerasi . . . . āā f℥ij.—M.
Sig. Seven drops in a little milk when the pain appears. (*In gastralgia.*)   MONIN.

1466—℞ Sulphonal. . . . . ℨj.
In chart. no. xii div.
Sig. One powder after each meal, and at bedtime. (*In neuralgic headaches of elderly people, with restlessness.*)
                           J. C. WILSON.

1467—℞ Ferri sulphatis exsiccati,
    Potassii carbonatis . . . . āā gr. ccl.
Misce et fiant pilulæ no. c.
Sig. Begin with three a day, and increase to six: take several
hundred.   J. E. GARRETSON.

1468—℞ Extracti stramonii . . . . gr. lij-vj.
    Extracti conii,
    Extracti papaveris . . . . āā gr. xxiv.
Misce et divide in pilulas no. xii.
Sig. One pill twice a day. (*In mastodynia.*)   ROMBERG.

1469—℞ Strychninæ sulphatis . . . . gr. j.
    Morphinæ sulphatis,
    Acidi arseniosi . . . . āā gr. iss.
    Extracti aconiti . . . . gr. xv.
    Quininæ sulphatis . . . . ℨj.
Misce et fiant pilulæ no. xxx.
Sig. One pill three times a day.   S. D. GROSS.

1470—℞ Chloroformi . . . . f℥j.
    Liq. vaselini . . . . f℥iv.—M.
Sig. Fifteen to thirty minims hypodermically at the seat of
pain.   MEUNIER.

1471—℞ Extracti belladonnæ . . . . ℨiss.
    Tincturæ opii . . . . ℳxl.
    Chloroformi . . . . f℥j.—M.
Sig. Apply locally.   HAZARD.

1472—℞ Atropinæ sulphatis . . . . gr. ss.
   Aconitinæ . . . . gr. iss.
   Olei tiglii . . . . gtt. ij.
   Unguenti petrolei . . . . 3ij.
Misce accuratissime.
Sig. Apply to the affected part.   J. R. LUDLOW.

1473—℞ Tinct. momordicæ (balsam-apple) . . . 3v.
   Tinct. aconiti . . . . f3j.
   Chloroformi . . . . f3ss.—M.
Sig. Soak a piece of flannel, lay it on the painful part, and
 cover with oiled silk.   GUÉNEAU DE MUSSY.

1474—℞ Aconiti . . . . gr. iss.
   Spts. vini rectificati . . . . q. s.
   Adipis præparatæ . . . . 3ij.—M.
Ft. unguentum.
Sig. To be rubbed in three times daily.   BROCKES.

1475—℞ Carbonis bisulphidi . . . . 3iv.
   Pulv. camphoræ . . . . q. s.—M.
Ft. sol. saturat.
Sig. Apply with a brush to the painful region. (For lumbo-
abdominal neuralgia.)   CHÉRON.

1476—℞ Chloroformi . . . . ℳxx.
   Tincturæ aconiti radicis,
   Tincturæ opii . . . . āā f3j.
   Linimenti saponis camphorati . . . . f3ss.—M.
Sig. Apply to the painful part.   NELIGAN.

1477—℞ Veratrinæ,
   Morphinæ sulphatis . . . . āā gr. x.
   Adipis . . . . 3j.—M.
Sig. Rub in three times daily. .   T. KENNARD.

1478—℞ Camphoræ,
   Chloral. hydratis . . . . āā 3ss.—M.
Sig. Apply frequently. (In pleurodynia, toothache, and neu-
ralgia about the head.)   GEORGE BIRD.

1479—℞ Menthol . . . . gr. xxiiss.
   Cocain. muriatis . . . . gr. viiss.
   Chloral. hydratis . . . . gr. ivss.
   Vaselini . . . . 3iiss.—M.
Ft. unguentum.
Sig. Apply to the painful part and cover with a strip of court-
plaster. (For supraorbital neuralgia.)   GALEZOWSKI.

1480—℞ Methyl. chloridi pur. . . . . 3j.
Sig. Apply with a brush or an atomizer, or on pledgets of lint,
to the painful parts.   DEBOVE.

1481—℞ Camphoræ . . . . 3iss.
   Chloroformi . . . . f3ss.
   Olei olivæ . . . . f3ij.—M.
Sig. Apply frequently.   HAZARD.

NIPPLES, SORE. (See Fissure.)

NYMPHOMANIA.

1482—℞ Potassii bromidi . . . . 3ss.
In pulv. no. xii div.
Sig. A powder in half a tumblerful of cold water thrice daily.
    BEGBIE.

1483—℞ Potassii bromidi   3vj.
   Aquæ destillatæ .   f3v.—M.
Sig. Three teaspoonfuls before dinner and four at bedtime.
    BROWN-SÉQUARD.

1484—℞ Pulveris camphoræ,
   Extracti lactucarii . . . . āā 9iiss.
Misce et fiant pilulæ no. xx.
Sig. From four to six pills to be taken daily.   RICORD.

OBESITY.

1485—℞ Potassii permanganatis . . . . gr. iv-xℨj.
  Aquæ destillatæ . . . . ƒℨiv.—M.
Sig. A dessertspoonful three times a day.   BARTHOLOW.

1486—℞ Liq. potassæ . . . . ƒℨij.
Sig. A half-teaspoonful in milk thrice daily.   WARING.

1487—℞ Ammonii bromidi . . . . ℨij.
  Aquæ destillatæ . . . . ƒℨiij.
Solve.
Sig. A dessertspoonful three times a day. (*Strict dietetic regimen.*)
                                              TANNER.

ŒDEMA. (See Dropsy.)

ONYCHIA.

1488—℞ Olei terebinthinæ . . . . ƒℨiv.
Sig. Apply on a pledget of lint wet with the above solution.
                                              RINGER.

1489—℞ Unguenti hydrargyri   ℨss.
Sig. Apply for ten minutes every hour, applying poultices at other times.
                                              RINGER.

1490—℞ Pulveris plumbi nitratis . . . . ℨss.
Detur in scatula.
Sig. Dust on the diseased tissue night and morning.
                                    SCOTT AND McCORMAC.

1491—℞ Acidi boracici,
  Ceræ albæ . . . . āā ℈iv.
  Paraffini,
  Olei amygdalæ dulcis . . . . . . āā ℈viij.—M.
Ft. ceratum.
Sig. To be used as a dressing, after the pus has been evacuated. (*For whitlow.*)   SELLDÉN.

OPHTHALMIA.

1492—℞ Distilled water . . . . grammes 100.
  Naphthol-α . . . . grammes 0.50.
  Alcohol . . . . grammes 25.—M.
Sig. Instil in the eyes.   BUDIN.

1493—℞ Hydrarg. chloridi corrosivi . . . . . . gr. j.
  Aquæ . . . . ƒℨxij.—M.
Sig. Irrigate the eye frequently with the solution.   CREDÉ.

1494—℞ Argenti nitratis . . . . gr. x.
  Aquæ destillatæ . . . . ƒℨj.—M.
Ft. collyrium.
Sig. Bathe the eyes frequently, removing all the pus, and apply the above locally, followed by a solution of sodium chloride.   CREDÉ.

1495—℞ Hydrargyri chloridi corrosivi . . . . . gr. j.
  Aquæ destillatæ . . . . ƒℨiv.—M.
Fiat collyrium. (*In gonorrhœal ophthalmia.*)   ELLIS.

1496—℞ Ferri sulphatis . . . . gr. ij.
  Aquæ destillatæ . . . . ƒℨj.—M.
Fiat solutio. (*In the chronic form.*)   HAZARD.

1497—℞ Acidi boracici . . . . gr. xvj.
  Acidi salicylici . . . . gr. ij.
  Glycerini . . . . ℳxl.
  Aquæ bullientis . . . . ad ƒℨj.—M.
Sig. Instil into the eye, after cauterizing trachoma follicles with the thermo-cautery. (*In trachoma.*)   ARMAIGNAC.

1498—℞ Hydrarg. chloridi corrosivi . . . . . . gr. j
  Aquæ . . . . ƒℨj.—M.
Sig. Apply once daily to the lids with a brush. Use 1-7000 solution several times daily.   QUAITA.

1499—℞ Argenti nitratis . . . . ℈ss.
Aquæ destillatæ . . . . f℥j.

Fiat collyrium.
Sig. One or two drops into the eye every second day. (*In Egyptian ophthalmia.*) RIDGEWAY.

1500—℞ Argenti nitratis . . . . gr. iv.
Aquæ destillatæ . . . . f℥j.
Fiat collyrium.
Sig. One drop to the eye every five or six **hours.** (*In catarrhal ophthalmia and superficial ulceration.*) MACKENZIE.

1501—℞ Coniine . . partes ij.
Alcoholis . . . partes xlj.
Aquæ destillatæ partes cc.
Fiat solutio.
Sig. Drop in the eye **and** rub around the orbits several **times** a day. (*In scrofulous ophthalmia with photophobia.*)
FRONMUELLER.

1502—℞ Pulv. acidi tannici . . . . ℈j.
Pulv. acidi borcici . . . . ℈ij.—M.
Sig. Dust the **lids.** Cautery **may precede** it. (*In trachoma.*)
WICHERKIEWICZ.

1503—℞ Pulveris aluminis . . . . gr. x.
Aquæ rosæ . . . . f℥iij.
Misce et fiat collyrium.
Sig. Apply thrice daily. (*After the acute stage.*) BRANDE.

1504—℞ Cocain. sulphatis . . . . gr. iv.
Atropinæ sulphatis . . . . gr. ss.
Vaselini . . . . ℈v.—M.
Sig. To be applied with **a camel's-hair brush. The chemosis** and pain **are** relieved **instantly.** (*In catarrhal ophthalmia.*)
LEAHY.

1505—℞ Hydrarg. oxidi rubri . . . . gr. vj.
Plumbi subacetatis cryst. . . . . gr. iij.
Vaselini . . . . ℈v.—M.
Ft. ungt.
Sig. Apply to the free **border of the** eyelids once daily, after bathing the eyelids **in hot water.** (*In chronic blepharitis.*)
PARINAUD.

1506—℞ Acidi tannici pulverizati . . . . ℈ij.
Detur in scatula.
Sig. Evert the lid and dust over. (*In the granular, phlyctenular, pustular, and chronic forms, and in pannus.*) HAMILTON.

1507—℞ Argenti nitratis . . . . ℈ss.
Potassii nitratis . . . . ℈j.
Funde.
Sig. For cauterization. (*In infantile purulent ophthalmia.*)
LIEBREICH.

1508—℞ Sodii biboratis . . . . gr. xx.
Aquæ camphoræ . . . . ℥iss.
Mucil. cydonii semiris,
Aquæ laurocerasi . . . . āā f℥ss.—M.
Sig. Apply to the lids and drop into the **eyes** three times daily. (*In catarrhal blepharitis.*) PARINAUD.

1509—℞ Iodoformi . . . ℈ss.
Sacchari lactis ℈ij.—M.
Sig. Evert the lids and dust over. (*In the granular form.*)

1510—℞ Hydrargyri **chloridi mitis (lævigati)** . ℈ij.
Detur in scatula.
Sig. Evert the lid and dust over once or twice daily. (*In the phlyctenular form.*) BARTHOLOW.

1511—℞ Argenti nitratis . . . . gr. ij-x.
Liquoris plumbi subacetatis . . . . . . ℥x-xx.
Cerati cetacei . . . . ℈j.—M.
Sig. The size of a pin's head to be put within the eyelids and repeated according to the degree of inflammation produced. (*In opacity of the cornea.*) GUTHRIE.

OPHTHALMIA (Continued).

1512—℞ Glyceriti Iodoformi (10 per cent.) . . . ʒss.
Sig. Instil into the eyes. (*In non-specific conjunctivitis in infants.*)
HOGNER.

1513—℞ Iodi . . . . gr. j.
Potassii iodidi . . . . gr. iv.
Aquæ destillatæ . . . . ʒss.
Sig. Use as a spray. (*In chronic conjunctivitis*). BEDOIN.

1514—℞ Hydrargyri oxidi flavi . . . . gr. v.
Zinci sulphatis . . . . gr. x.
Adipis . . . . ʒj.—M.
Ft. ungt.
Sig. Smear on the everted eyelids, and on the free border of the lids. (*In the chronic scrofulous form.*) DUPUYTREN.

OPIUM HABIT.

1515—℞ Spartein. sulphatis gr. j.
Aquæ destillatæ . fʒj.—M.
Sig. Ten minims hypodermically, to tide the patient over the period of collapse produced by withdrawing the drug.
BALL.

1516—℞ Zinci oxidi . . . . ʒss.
Syr. simplicis . . . . q. s. ut ft. massa.
In pil. no. xxx div.
Sig. One pill once daily, increasing to tolerance. (*For vomiting and diarrhœa.*) DA COSTA.

1517—℞ Ext. cannabis indicæ (Squibb) . . . fʒij.
Sig. A teaspoonful every hour or two, as required. (*For restlessness.*)

1518—℞ Tinct. nucis vomicæ . . . . gtt. xij.
Acidi phosphorici dil. . . . . gtt. xx.
Syr. pruni virginianæ . . . . fʒss.—M.
Sig. To be taken twice daily. MATTISON.

ORCHITIS.

1519—℞ Tinct. aconiti . . . . ♏j.
Morphinæ sulph. . . . . gr. ¼.
Antimonii tart. . . . . gr. ¼.
Magnesii sulph. . . . . gr. xlj.—M.
Sig. One dose. Repeat thrice daily. HORWITZ.

1520—℞ Tinct. iodi . . . . fʒj.
Sig. Apply locally to the swollen testicle after the acute symptoms are over. BARTHOLOW.

1521—℞ Ammonii chloridi . . . . ʒij.
Spiritus vini rectificati,
Aquæ destillatæ . . . . āā fʒij.—M.
Sig. Apply with moistened cloths frequently. BARTHOLOW.

1522—℞ Antimonii et potassii tartratis . . . . . gr. j.
Potassii nitratis . . . . ʒj.
Magnesii sulphatis . . . . ʒiss.
Aquæ destillatæ . . . . q. s. ad fʒvj.—M.
Sig. A tablespoonful every four to six hours. (*In the acute form.*) ERICHSEN.

1523—℞ Antimonii et potassii tartratis . . . . . gr. j.
Aquæ . . . . fʒviij.—M.
Sig. One or two teaspoonfuls every hour or two. RINGER.

1524—℞ Sodii salicylatis . . . . ʒss.
Syrupi simplicis . . . . fʒij.
Aquæ menthæ piperitæ . . . . . . ad fʒvj.—M.
Sig. A tablespoonful every hour till the pain is relieved; then every four to six hours. PIGORNET.

1525—℞ Iodi . . . . gr. ij.
Potassii iodidi . . . . ʒj.
Aquæ destillatæ . . . . fʒiv.—M.
Fiat lotio.
Sig. Apply with a camel's-hair pencil. (*After the acute symptoms have subsided.*) NIEMEYER.

1526—℞ Morphinæ sulphatis . . . . gr. viij.
Hydrargyri oleatis (10 per cent.). . . . ʒj.—M.
Sig. Apply twice daily. (*For the subsequent induration.*)
MARSHALL.

1527—℞ Tincturæ pulsatillæ . . . . f ʒss.
Sig. One to three drops every hour or two, in water.
BROWN.

1528—℞ Tincturæ phytolaccæ (1-10) . . . . . . f ʒj.
Sig. Ten drops every three or four hours. J. C. WILSON.

OTITIS AND OTORRHŒA.

1529—℞ Creolin. . . . . gtt. x.
Aquæ tepidæ . . . . Oj.—M.
Sig. Inject into the ear. EITELBERG.

1530—℞ Acidi carbolici,
Zinci sulphatis,
Plumbi acetatis. . . . . āā gr. x.
Aquæ destillatæ . . . . f ʒviij.—M.
Sig. Inject twice a day. (*When discharge is offensive.*)
HAZARD.

1531—℞ Lactis recentis,
Aquæ calcis . . . . āā f ʒj.
Pulveris myrrhæ . . . . gr. xlj.—M.
Sig. As an injection. (*In the acute form.*) HAZARD.

1532—℞ Liquor. hydrogenii peroxidi (10 vol.) f ʒiv.
Sig. Syringe the ear carefully with one part of solution to two
parts of water, and when cleansed instil a few drops of the
above solution. C. H. BURNETT.

1533—℞ Sol. boroglycerid. (50 per cent.) . . . . ʒj.
Sig. Instil a few drops into the ear, after cleansing it, twice
or thrice daily. L. W. FOX.

1534—℞ Pulv. iodol. . . . ʒss.
Spts. vini rectif. . f ʒiiiss.
Glycerini . . f ʒviiiss.—M.
Sig. Use once or twice daily by instillation, after cleansing
the canal. (*In purulent otitis.*) MAZZONI.

1535—℞ Tincturæ aconiti radicis . . . . f ʒiss.
Glycerini . . . . f ʒiiiss.—M.
Sig. To be dropped into the ear. SMITH.

1536—℞ Atropinæ sulphatis . . . . gr. ss-iss.
Morphinæ muriatis . . . . gr. iss.
Glycerini . . . . f ʒj.—M.
Ft. sol.
Sig. Instil into the ear, morning and evening, one or two
drops. Also saturate a piece of absorbent cotton and intro-
duce it well into the auditory canal. MOURE.

1537—℞ Morphinæ muriatis . gr. v.
Atropinæ sulphatis gr. j.
Olei olivæ f ʒj.
Glycerini . . f ʒiss.—M.
Sig. Three to five drops in the ear. Repeat every hour until
the pain is relieved. Place a small pledget of cotton in the
ear after introducing the drops. (*For otalgia.*)

1538—℞ Acidi carbolici . . . . ʒj.
Glycerini . . . . f ʒix.—M.
Sig. Instil a few **drops into the ear two or three times daily,**
after cleansing. HARTMANN.

1539—℞ Sodii carbonatis . . . . ʒij.
Infusi picis liquidæ . . . . Oj.—M.
Sig. Inject and instil into the ear twice daily, using the
following after each cleansing :

1540—℞ Picis liquidæ . . . . ʒj.
Vaselini . . . . ʒv.
Sulphuris loti . . . . gr. vj.
Spts. camphoræ . . . . gr. iv.
Chloral. hydratis . . . . gr. ij.—M.
Ft. ungt.
Sig. Anoint the external ear and auditory canal, morning
and evening, after cleansing. Then twice weekly use—

1541—℞ Tinct. iodi . . . . ♏xxiv.
Glycerini,
Aquæ . . . . āā fʒj.
Potassii iodidi . . . . gr. vj.
Vini opii . . . . gr. xxiv.—M.
Sig. Bathe the whole surface of the auditory canal and the
external ear two or three times weekly. (*For eczematous
inflammation of the external ear.*) MIOT.

1542—℞ Unguenti hydrargyri nitratis rubri . . ʒss.
Sig. Apply a small quantity to the integument. (*In chronic inflammation of the external meatus.*) BARTHOLOW.

1543—℞ Glyceriti acidi tannici . . . . ʒss.
Sig. Fill the meatus and plug with cotton-wool. (*In the
chronic form.*) RINGER.

1544—℞ Pulv. iodol. . . . . ʒss.
Sig. To be insufflated once or twice daily after thorough
cleansing and drying. (*In acute purulent cases.*) STETTER.

1545—℞ Pulv. iodoformi . . . . ʒij.
Sig. Insufflate into the ear, after thoroughly cleansing and
drying it. (*For chronic cases, when discharge is slight.*)
BEZOLD.

OXALURIA.

1546—℞ Glyceriti pepsinæ . . . . ʒiss.
Acidi lactici . . . . ad fʒij.—M.
Sig. A teaspoonful after meals thrice daily. BARTHOLOW.

1547—℞ Acidi nitro-muriatici dil. . . . . ʒij-iij.
Tinct. gentianæ comp.,
Tinct. cinchonæ comp. . . . . āā fʒj.
Elixir. curaçoæ . . . . ad fʒiij.—M.
Sig. A dessertspoonful in a wineglassful of water thrice daily.
RINGER.

1548—℞ Acidi hydrochlorici diluti . . . . fʒss.
Tincturæ ferri chloridi . . . . fʒij.
Syrupi simplicis . . . . fʒiiss.
Aquæ destillatæ . . . . fʒiij.—M.
Sig. A tablespoonful three times a day through a glass tube.
(*With anæmia and nervous atony.*) HAZARD.

1549—℞ Tincturæ aconiti foliorum . . . . ♏xxx.
Acidi nitro-hydrochlorici diluti . . . . fʒij.
Tincturæ gentianæ . . . . fʒiij.
Syrupi aurantii corticis . . . . fʒj.
Infusi aurantii . . . . fʒviij.—M.
Sig. A tablespoonful three times a day. HAZARD.

OZÆNA.

1550—℞ Creolin . . . . gtt. iij-v.
Aquæ destillatæ . . . . Oj.
Sig. Use as a nasal douche. LICHTWITZ.

1551—℞ Acidi carbolici . . . . f℥iv.
Glycerini . . . . f℥iss.
Alcoholis (90°) . . . . ℥x.
Aquæ . . . . f℥ix.—M.

Sig. A tablespoonful to a pint of tepid water, as a douche or
spray. MOURE.

1552—℞ Creolin. . . . . gr. xv.
Alcoholis . . . . f℥iiiss.—M.

Sig. A coffeespoonful to a quart of tepid water, as a douche
or spray. MOURE.

1553—℞ Alum. acet. tart. . . . . ℈v-x.
Acidi borici . . . . ℈iss-iij.—M.

Sig. A coffeespoonful of this mixture to a quart of water.
MOURE.

1554—℞ Acidi carbolici . . . . gr. xxx.
Resorcin. crystal. . . . . gr. xlv.
Glycerini . . . . f℥iss.
Aquæ . . . . f℥xss.—M.

Sig. Use as a spray. MOURE.

1555—℞ Salol. . . . . gr. lxxv.
Olei petrolei . . . . f℥v.—M.

Sig. Apply locally. MOURE.

1556—℞ Sodii biboratis.
Ammonii chloridi . . . . āā ℈j.
Potassii permanganatis . . . . gr. x.

Sig. To be dissolved in one pint of tepid water, and used
thrice daily with a syringe or douche. SAJOUS.

1557—℞ Syr. ferri iodidi . . . . ℥j.

Sig. Five drops, increased to thirty drops, thrice daily after
meals. SAJOUS.

1558—℞ Hydrargyri chloridi mitis . . . . gr. xv.
Sacchari albi . . . . ℥iv.—M.

Sig. For insufflation. TROUSSEAU.

1559—℞ Hydrargyri ammoniati . . . . gr. ivss.
Sacchari albi . . . . ℥ss.

Misce et fiat pulvis et detur in scatula.
Sig. After clearing the nose, snuff up twice or thrice daily.
TROUSSEAU.

1560—℞ Potassii permanganatis . . . . ℈ss.
Tincturæ myrrhæ . . . . f℥ij.
Aquæ destillatæ . . . . Oj.—M.

Sig. Use with a douche three times a day. HAZARD.

1561—℞ Sodii hyposulphitis . . . . ℥iij.
Aquæ . . . . Oj.—M.

Sig. Use with a douche three times a day. HAZARD.

1562—℞ Ungt. hydrargyri nitratis . . . . ℥ss.

Sig. Warm slightly and apply twice a day, after clearing the
nose. (In syphilitic ozæna of children.) RINGER.

1563—℞ Glyceriti acidi tannici . . . . ℥ss.

Sig. Apply with a camel's-hair brush two or three times daily,
after clearing the nose. RINGER.

1564—℞ Extracti hydrastis fluid.,
Aquæ destillatæ . . . . āā f℥j.—M.

Sig.—Ten to twenty drops three times a day; also as injection
into the nares. BARTHOLOW.

1565—℞ Bromi . . . . ℥ss.
Alcoholis . . . . f℥iv.—M.

Sig. Warm the wide mouthed bottle in the hand, and snuff
the vapor well into the nose. BARTHOLOW.

1566—℞ Pulv. carbonis ligni.
Pulv. quininæ sulphatis.
Pulv. myrrhæ . . . . āā partes æquales.

Sig. To be insufflated into the nares once or twice daily.
MEYER.

OZÆNA (Continued).

1567—℞ Plumbi nitratis . . . . ℈ij.
Aquæ destillatæ . . . . f℥v.
Solve.
Sig. Inject into the nostril night and morning.　　STILLÉ.

1568—℞ Iodi . . . . gr. ij-iv.
Potassii iodidi . . . . gr. iv-vilj.
Aquæ destillatæ . . . . f℥vj.
Fiat injectio.
Sig. Use twice daily.　　NIEMEYER.

1569—℞ Iodol . . . . ℈j.
Ætheris . . . . ℈j.—M.
Sig. Use with an atomizer.　　WOLFENDEN.

1570—℞ Pulv. saloli,
Pulv. talci . . . . āā ℈ij.—M.
Sig. Insufflate the nose every two hours.　　GEORGI.

PAIN. (See Neuralgia, Myalgia, Colic, etc.)

PALPITATION. (See Heart-Disease.)

PARALYSIS.

1571—℞ Ammonii iodidi . . . . ℈j.
Ammonii carbonatis . . . . ℈ij.
Liquoris ammonii acetatis . . . . . . ℥vj.—M.
Sig. A tablespoonful thrice daily. (*To absorb thrombi in incipient hemiplegic paralysis, due to endarteritis deformans.*)
　　BARTHOLOW.

1572—℞ Strychninæ sulphatis . . . . gr. j.
Aquæ destillatæ . . . . f℥x.
Fiat solutio.
Sig. For hypodermic use. Ten minims contain ⅒ gr. of strychnine sulphate. Inject in substance of paralyzed muscle. (*In diphtheritic paralysis; in local paralyses, such as facial, of the vocal cords, in lead palsy, paralysis of the sphincters ani and vesicæ; also in paraplegia when no structural alteration of cord, and in long-standing cases of hemiplegia.*)
　　BARTHOLOW.

1573—℞ Phosphori . . . . gr. j.
Ætheris . . . . ℳc.
Glycerini . . . . f℥v.
Aquæ destillatæ . . . . q. s. ad f℥xiiss.—M.
Sig. A teaspoonful three times a day. (*In paralysis agitans.*)
　　S. M. BRADLEY.

1574—℞ Phosphori . . . . gr. ij.
Alcoholis absoluti . . . . ℥xxiij.
Tinct. vanillæ . . . . ℥ss.
Olei aurantii cort. . . . . ℳxj.
Alcoholis absoluti . . . . . . q. s. ad ℥iij.—M.
Sig. Twenty to forty minims two or three times daily. (*In cerebral softening and hysterical paralysis.*)　　HAMMOND.

1575—℞ Strychninæ sulphatis . . . . gr. j.
Acidi arseniosi . . . . gr. ij.
Extracti belladonnæ . . . . gr. v.
Quininiæ sulphatis,
Pilulæ ferri carbonatis . . . . . . āā ℈ij.
Extracti taraxaci . . . . ℈j.
Misce et fiant pilulæ no. xl.
Sig. One pill three times a day. (*In paralysis agitans.*)
　　S. W. GROSS.

1576—℞ Coninæ,
Acidi acetici fortioris . . . . āā f℥iij ℳxij.
Misce gradatim ad neutralizandum. Dein adde—
Spiritus vini rectificati . . . . f℈j.
Aquæ destillatæ . . . . q. s. ad f℥ij.—M.
Sig. For hypodermic use. Begin with one minim and gradually increase as necessary.　　EULENBURG.

- P -

PARALYSIS (Continued).

1577—℞ Ext. physostigmatis. . . . . gr. j.
   Ext. gentianæ . . . . ℈j.—M.
Ft. massa et in pil. no. xxx div.
Sig. A pill every two hours. (*In general paralysis of the insane.*)
             CRICHTON BROWNE.

1578—℞ Ext. physostigmatis . . . . gr. iij.
   Ext. taraxaci . . . . gr. xxiv.-M.
Ft. massa et in pil. no. xxx div.
Sig. A pill every three hours. (*In paraplegia, locomotor ataxia, writer's cramp, and progressive muscular atrophy.*) MURRELL.

1579—℞ Extracti ergotæ aquos. . . . . gr. xv.
   Syrupi aurantii corticis . . . . ℨj.
   Aquæ destillatæ . . . . f℥iij.—M.
Sig. A tablespoonful three or four times a **day.** (*In paralysis of sphincter ani and sphincter vesicæ.*) BONJEAN.

1580—℞ Extracti buchu fluidi,
   Extracti uvæ ursi . . . . āā f℥ij.
   Syrupi rosæ cæ . . . . f℥ss.
   Aquæ menthæ viridis . . . . f℥j.—M.
Sig. A dessertspoonful every three **hours.** HAZARD.

1581—℞ **Hyoscyaminæ sulphatis** . . . . gr. ss.
   Aquæ destillatæ . . . . ℥vj.—M.
Sig. Five minims hypodermically once daily, **or by the stomach** twice daily. (*In paralysis agitans.*) SÉGUIN.

PARTURITION. (See Labor.)

PEDICULI. (See Lice.)

PEMPHIGUS. (See Skin Diseases.)

PERICARDITIS. (See also Heart-Disease.)

1582—℞ Hydrarg. chloridi mitis,
   Pulv. ipecac. . . . . āā gr. vj.
   Potassii nitratis . . . . ℨss-j.—M.
In pulv. no. xii div.
Sig. A powder every **three hours.** HARTSHORNE.

1583—℞ Antimonii et potassii tart. . . . . . . gr. iv.
   Tinct. opii . . . . f℥j.
   Aquæ camphoræ . . . . f℥vij.—M.
Sig. A tablespoonful every two hours. (**In** *the acute form.*) GRAVES.

1584—℞ **Tinct. aconiti radicis** . . . . f℥ss.
Sig. Half a drop **to a** drop **in a** teaspoonful of **water every** ten minutes or quarter **of an** hour for two hours; then every hour or two. RINGER.

1585—℞ Empl. **cantharidis** . . . . 2 in. × 3 in.
Sig. Apply over the præcordial space. Repeat at intervals after the skin is healed. (*In the chronic stage.*) TANNER.

PERIOSTITIS (NODES).

1586—℞ Potassii iodidi . . . . gr. ij-x.
   Potassii bromidi . . . . gr. v-xx.
   Ammonii carbonatis . . . . gr. v.
   Spts. chloroformi . . . . ℳxv.
   Aquæ . . . . q. s. ad f℥j.—M.
Sig. Take three times daily. BERKELEY HILL.

1587—℞ Iodi . . . . . gr. ss.
   Potassii iodidi . . . . ℨss.
   Syr. papaveris . . . . f℥ss.
   Infusi gentianæ comp. . . f℥x.—M.
Sig. Take two tablespoonfuls thrice daily. Take a half-grain of morphine acetate at night. (*In weakly constitutions.*) BRANSBY COOPER.

131

1588—℞ Iodi . . . . gr. ss.
Potassii iodidi . . . . ℈ss.
Syrupi papaveris . . . . f℥ss.
Aquæ destillatæ . . . . f℥viij.—M.
Sig. Take two tablespoonfuls three times a day.   TYRELL.

1589—℞ Potassii iodidi . . . . ℈j.
Syrupi aurantii corticis . . . . f℥j.
Aquæ aurantii florum . . . . f℥v.—M.
Sig. Take a tablespoonful morning and night in hop-tea.
LISFRANC.

1590—℞ Potassii iodidi . . . . gr. xv.
Spiritus vini rectificati . . . . f℥ij.
Extracti dulcamaræ . . . . ℈ij.
Pulveris glycyrrhizæ,
Aquæ destillatæ . . . . āā q. s.
Fiat massa in pilulas clxxx dividenda.
Sig. Take six pills two or three times a day.   VOGT.

1591—℞ Potassii iodidi . . . . ℥ij.
Ammonii iodidi . . . . ℥j.
Tinct. cinchonæ comp. . . . . f℥iij.—M.
Sig. A teaspoonful, largely diluted with water, after eating.
VAN BUREN AND KEYES.

1592—℞ Hydrargyri biniodidi . . . . gr. vij.
Potassii iodidi . . . . ℈j.
Adipis . . . . ℥j.
Fiat unguentum.   C. C. HILDRETH.

1593—℞ Iodi,
Terebinthinæ canadensis . . . . . āā ℥j.
Collodii . . . . f℥iv.
Solve.
Sig. Paint over with a brush.   J. T. SHINN.

1594—℞ Potassii iodidi,
Potassii carbonatis . . . . āā ℥ij.
Spts. vini rectificati . . . . f℥j.
Aquæ . . . . f℥xj.—M.
Fiat lotio.
Sig. Apply twice daily *(in the early stage)*, with the following
internally :

1595—℞ Potassii iodidi,
Potassii chloratis . . . . āā ℥j.
Potassii bicarbonatis . . . . ℥ij.—M.
In chartulas no. xii div.
Sig. One powder morning and evening in half a pint of milk.
ERICHSEN.

1596—℞ Barii iodidi . . . . gr. iv.
Adipis . . . . ℥j.
Fiat unguentum.   BIETT.

1597—℞ Zinci iodidi . . . . ℥j.
Adipis . . . . ℥j.
Fiat unguentum.
Sig. Apply twice a day.   URE.

1598—℞ Sodii iodidi . . . . ℥j.
Decocti sarsaparillæ comp. . . . . . . f℥viij.—M.
Sig. One-sixth part three times daily.   TANNER.

1599—℞ Cadmii iodidi . . . . ℈ss.
Ætheris . . . . ℳxl.
Tere simul et adde—
Adipis . . . . ℥j.
Misce et fiat unguentum.   A. B. GARROD.

1600—℞ Cadmii iodidi . . . . ℈j.
Adipis præparatæ . . . . ℥j.
Linimenti aconiti . . . . f℥ij.—M.
Fiat unguentum.   TANNER.

1601—℞ Unguenti plumbi iodidi. . . . . . . ℥j.
Sig. Apply twice daily. (*In chronic periosteal thickening*)
HOOPER.

PERIOSTITIS (Continued).

1602—℞ Potassii iodidi . . . . ℥j.
Aquæ bullientis . . . . f℥j.
Vaselini . . . . ℥vij.—M.
Fiat unguentum.
Sig. Apply twice daily, and use the following:

1603—℞ Potassii iodidi . . . . ℥j-ij.
In pulv. no. xii div.
Sig. One powder, morning and evening, in a glassful of milk.
RINGER.

1604—℞ Morphinæ . . . . gr. viij.
Hydrargyri oleatis (10-20 per cent.) . . ℥j.—M.
Sig. Apply with a brush.
MARSHALL.

PERITONITIS.

1605—℞ Hydrargyri chloridi mitis . . . . . . gr. ij.
Pulv. ipecacuanhæ et opii . . . . . . gr. xvj.—M.
In pil. no. xvi div.
Sig. One every hour, watching the effect. **J. C. WILSON.**

1606—℞ Antimonii et potassii tartratis . . . . . gr. j.
Tincturæ opii . . . . f℥j.
Aquæ camphoræ . . . . f℥viij.—M.
Sig. A tablespoonful every **two hours.** GRAVES.

1607—℞ Tincturæ aconiti radicis . . f℥ij.
Tincturæ opii deodoratæ . . . f℥vj.—M.
Sig. Eight drops in water every hour or two. BARTHOLOW.

1608—℞ Pulveris opii . . . . **gr. j.**
Pulveris antimonialis . . . . **gr. viij.**
Hydrargyri chloridi mitis . . . . **gr. iv.**
Misce et divide in chartulas iv
Sig. One powder every six hours with a saline effervescent
draught. (*At the commencement of the attack.*) GREGORY.

1609—℞ Morphinæ sulphatis . gr. iv.
Aquæ destillatæ f℥j.—M.
Sig. Ten or fifteen minims as required, hypodermically, **to**
control the vomiting. Give no food for twenty-four or
forty-eight hours. (*Especially in peritonitis following surgical
operations.*) TAIT.

1610—℞ Morphinæ sulphatis . . . . **gr. viij.**
Aquæ destillatæ . . . . **f℥iv.—M.**
Sig. Begin with a dessertspoonful and wait two hours. If no
effect, give three teaspoonfuls and wait two hours. If still
no effect, give four teaspoonfuls and wait two hours. The
medicine should be increased gradually to produce these
effects : to allay pain, to produce gentle sleep, to reduce the
respirations to twelve per minute when aroused (may get
as low as eight, but should go no lower). Continue these
effects for two days, and then gradually diminish the dose ;
but if the symptoms return, increase again.
ALONZO **CLARK.**

1611—℞ Olei terebinthinæ . . . . f℥ij.
Lactis asafœtidæ . . . . f℥iij.
Aquæ ferventis . . . . f℥iv.—M.
Sig. Use as an injection. LEVIS.

1612—℞ Tinct. aconiti folii . . f℥v.
Ext. veratri viridis fld. . . . f℥j.—M.
Sig. Twelve drops **every two** hours. (*Where opium is inad-
missible.*) ELLIS.

1613—℞ Magnesii sulphatis . . . . **℥iss.**
In pulv. no. xii div.
Sig. A powder in hot peppermint-water every hour until the
bowels are freely opened. (*In acute peritonitis, at the beginning of the attack.*) MUNDÉ.

1614—℞ Camphoræ, redactæ in pulverem . : . gr. v.
Pulveris ipecacuanhæ compositi . . . gr. x.
Potassii nitratis . . . . gr. xx.
Misce et fiant chartulæ ii.
Sig. One powder at bedtime.   SIMPSON.

1615—℞ Pulveris piperis,
Pulveris zingiberis . . . . āā ℨj.
Sinapis nigræ contusæ . . . . ℔ss.
Aquæ bullientis . . . . q. s.
Misce et fiat cataplasma. (*As a rubefacient.*)   ELLIS.

1616—℞ Acetphenetidin. . . . . ℨij.
In pulv. no. xii div.
Sig. A powder stirred in a little water, **as required.** One-
third to one-half the dose for children. (*For febrile condition.*)   KOBLER.

1617—℞ Acidi tannici . . . . gr. clxxx.
Glycerini . . . . q. s. ad ℥ ft. sol.—M.
Sig. To be taken in divided doses during the **day.** (*In local-
ized peritonitis.*)   DEBOUÉ.

PERTUSSIS. (See Whooping-Cough.)

PHAGEDÆNA.

1618—℞ Potassii permanganatis . . . . ℨss.
Aquæ . . . . Oj.—M.
Sig. Apply locally.   LEVIS.

1619—℞ Hydrargyri chloridi corrosivi . . . . . gr. j.
Iodoformi,
Ferri redacti . . . . āā ℨj.
Misce et fiant pilulæ xx.
Sig. One pill three times a day. (*In sloughing phagedæna.*)
                                        BARTHOLOW.

1620—℞ Acidi salicylici . . . . ℨss.
Sig. Dust over the slough.   BARTHOLOW.

1621—℞ Ferri et potassii tartratis . . . . ℨj-ij.
Aquæ . . . . f℥j.—M.
Ft. lotio.
Sig. Apply freely locally. (*When caustics cannot be used, as
where large vessels are exposed, large surface, weak condition of
patient, etc.*)   RICORD.

1622—℞ Acidi pyrogallici . . . . ℨij.
Pulv. amyli . . . . ℨj.—M.
Ft. pulv.
Sig. Dust over or insufflate the sores twice daily. The pow-
der should be fresh, and kept in a tightly-corked bottle.
                                        TERRILLON.

1623—℞ Saloli . . . . gr. v-l.
Amyli . . . . ℨj.—M.
Ft. pulv.
Sig. Dust **over** locally.   SEIFERT.

1624—℞ Acidi nitrici diluti . . . . ♏x.
Extracti opii . . . . gr. v.
Aquæ . . . . f℥j.
Ft. lotio. (*In sloughing incised wounds.*)   ERICHSEN.

1625—℞ Iodoformi . . . . ℨijss.
Thymoli . . . . ℨv.
Sacchari lactis . . . . gr. ij.—M.
Ft. pulv.
Sig. Dust over the sores.   HOWARD.

1626—℞ Acidi nitrici fort. . . . . f℥j.
Sig. Apply thoroughly but carefully **to** the whole secreting
surface, after drying it. Give the patient an anæsthetic if
necessary, **and a** hypodermic of morphine later.
                                VAN BUREN AND KEYES.

1627—℞ Aristol. . . . . ℨj.
Sig. Apply lightly and cover with **a** poultice.   J. C. WILSON.

1628—℞ Pilocarpinæ muriatis . . . . gr. ij.
Aquæ,
Glycerini . . . . āā f 3j.—M.
Sig. A teaspoonful thrice daily. (*In atrophic or dry pharyngitis.*)
SAJOUS.

1629—℞ Tinct. guaiaci **ammoniatæ** . . . . . . f 3j.
Sig. A teaspoonful in a half-glassful of milk, used as a gargle and swallowed every three hours. (*In rheumatic subjects.*)
SAJOUS.

1630—℞ Argenti nitratis . . . . gr. xl.
Aquæ destillatæ . . . . f 3j.—M.
Sig. Apply to the throat after cleansing **it.** (*In chronic pharyngitis.*)
SAJOUS.

1631—℞ Olei vaselini . . . . 3ij.
Sig. Apply with **a** brush or an atomizer three or four times daily. (*Where astringents are not tolerated, in chronic pharyngitis.*)
SAJOUS.

1632—℞ **Liq. potassii arsenitis** . . . . f 3j.
Sig. One or two drops in water, thrice daily. (*To remove the tendency to attacks of pharyngitis.*)
SAJOUS.

1633—℞ Extracti ergotæ aquosi . gr. xx.
Tincturæ iodi . f 3j.
Glycerini . f 3j.—M.
Sig. Apply frequently to pharynx with a camel's-hair brush.
HAZARD.

1634—℞ Corticis granati fructus,
Aluminis . . . . āā 3ss.
Potassii chloratis . . . . 3ij.
Quercus albæ contusæ . . . . . . 3j.
Aquæ bullientis . . . . Oij.
Fiat infusum.
Sig. Gargle frequently.
HAZARD.

1635—℞ Quininæ sulphatis . . . . gr. xij.
Cupri sulphatis . . . . gr. xvj.
Acidi sulphurici **aromatici** . . . . . . f 3j.
Aquæ . . . . f 3viij.
Fiat mistura.
Sig. Use as a gargle three or four times **a day.** HARTSHORNE.

1636—℞ Ammonii chloridi . . . . 3j.
Acidi acetici . . . . f 3ij.
Mellis . . . . f 3ss.
Aquæ . . . . f 3xij.
Fiat gargarisma. (*For inflamed fauces.*)
RATIER.

1637—℞ **Cocain. muriatis** . . . . gr. x.
Aquæ destillatæ . . . . f 3ss.—M.
Sig. Cleanse the throat with a spray of chlorate of potassium solution (saturate). After drying it, apply the solution with a brush every two hours. A wineglassful of coca-wine every two hours also aids. (*In the acute form.*) SAJOUS.

1638—℞ Iodol . 3j.
Spts. vini rectificati . . f 3ij.
Glycerini . . . . f 3iv 3ij.—M.
Sig. Apply with a brush or as a coarse spray. WOLFENDEN.

1639—℞ Tincturæ iodi,
Tincturæ opii . . . . āā f 3j.
Aquæ . . . . f 3vj.
Fiat gargarisma.
Sig. Shake well. **Use three or four times a** day. (*With ulceration.*)
ELLIS.

1640—℞ Zinci sulphatis . . . gr. xv.
Aquæ menthæ pip. . f 3vj.—M.
Ft. gargarisma.
Sig. Use as a gargle four times daily.
ENDLER.

1641—℞ Iodol.,
Glycerini . . . . āā f 3j.
Vaselini . . . . f 3vij.—M.
Sig. Warm slightly and **apply locally.** WOLFENDEN

PHLEGMASIA DOLENS.

1642—℞ Pulv. lini,
    Aquæ bullientis . . . . q. s.
Ft. cataplasma.
Sig. Sprinkle with laudanum and apply locally. LEISHMAN.

1643—℞ Acidi hydrochlorici diluti . . . . . . ʒj.
    Potassii chloratis . . . . ʒ-s.
    Decocti hordei . . . . Oij.—M.
Sig. To be taken in divided doses during the day.
                                  MACKENZIE.

1644—℞ Ext. hamamelidis fld. . . . . fʒj.
    Syr. simplicis,
    Elixir. simplicis . . . . āā fʒss.—M.
Sig. One or two teaspoonfuls three or four times daily.
                                   PRESTON.

1645—℞ Phenacetin. . . . . ʒj.
In pilulas (compressas) no. xii div.
Sig. One tablet every three or four hours. (For the relief of pain.)
                                 J. C. WILSON.

PHLEGMON. (See Carbuncle.)

PHTHISIS. (See also Bronchitis, Diarrhœa, Sweating, and Hæmoptysis.)

1646—℞ Creasote (of the beech) . . . . gr. xv.
    Tincture of gentian . . . . fʒj.
    Pure alcohol . . . . fʒviij.
    Tokay wine . . . . fʒxxij.—M.
Sig. A tablespoonful in water three times a day. GUTTMANN.

1647—℞ Creasoti . . . . ♏j-v.
    Spiritus ammonii aromatici . . . . . ♏xv-fʒj.
    Aquæ destillatæ . . . . fʒiss.
Fiat haustus.
                                  KESTEVEN.

1648—℞ Creasoti . . . . fʒiiss.
    Tinct. gentianæ . . . . fʒj.
    Spts. vini rectificati . . . . fʒviij.
    Vini xerici . . . . ad Oij.—M.
Sig. A tablespoonful in a wineglassful of water three times daily. (In incipient tuberculosis.) FRÄNTZEL.

1649—℞ Hydrarg. chloridi mitis . . . . gr. x.
    Pepsini . . . . gr. lvi.
    Tinct. opii . . . . gtt. xxx.
    Ext. phellandrii . . . . q. s.—M.
Fiant pilulæ no. lx.
Sig. One or two daily.
                                 DOCHMANN.

1650—℞ Hydrarg. chloridi mitis . . . . . . gr. ij.
    Glycerini . . . . ♏xv.
    Aquæ . . . . ♏xv.—M.
Sig. Prepare freshly; shake thoroughly; inject deeply into gluteal or deltoid region once in five days. J. C. WILSON.

1651—℞ Morphinæ muriatis . . . . gr. j.
    Acidi muriatici diluti . . . . ♏v.
    Acidi hydrocyanici diluti . . . . . ♏xxx.
    Syrupi scillæ,
    Aquæ destillatæ . . . . āā fʒj.—M.
Sig. A teaspoonful when the cough is troublesome.
                          A. T. THOMPSON.

1652—℞ Tincturæ benzoini compositæ . . . . . fʒj.
    Aquæ bullientis . . . . Oss.—M.
Sig. Inhale twice daily. (Eases cough and lessens expectoration.)
                                 RINGER.

1653—℞ Codeinæ . . . . gr. vj.
    Acidi sulphurici diluti . . . . fʒj.
    Glycerini . . . . fʒss.
    Aquæ laurocerasi . . . . fʒj.
    Syr. pruni virginianæ . . . . . q.s. ad fʒij.—M.
Sig. A teaspoonful occasionally for the relief of cough.
                             J. C. WILSON.

1654—℞ Iodi . . . . gr. iij.
    Potassii iodidi . . . . gr. vj.
    Aquæ destillatæ . . . . f3j.—M.

Sig. Ten drops three times a **day in a draught** of cold water.
(*With glandular disease.*)   S. G. MORTON.

1655—℞ Ferri sulphatis . . . . 3j.
    Magnesiæ . . . . gr. x.
    Sacchari albi . . . . 3j.
    Aquæ cinnamomi . . . . f3viij.—M.

Sig. A tablespoonful **every three hours.** (*As an efficient tonic
in phthisis.*)   DONOVAN.

1656—℞ Tincturæ ferri chloridi,
    Acidi nitrici diluti . . . . āā f3j.
    Syrupi zingiberis . . . . f3xiv.
    Aquæ menthæ viridis . . . . f3iv.—M.

Sig. A tablespoonful every four hours. (*An astringent tonic.*)
     R. BENNETT.

1657—℞ Calcii chloridi . . . . 3j.
    Extracti hyoscyami . . . . 3ss.
    Syrupi glycyrrhizæ . . . . f3j.
    Aquæ destillatæ . . . . f3vj.—M.

Sig. A tablespoonful to be taken four times a day.   BEDDOES.

1658—℞ Acidi tannici . . . . 3ij.
    Glycerini . . . . f3j.—M.

Sig. A teaspoonful **from two to** four times daily.
     ARTHAUD AND RAYMOND.

1659—℞ Olei delphinidæ (porpoise-oil) . . . . . Oss.

Sig. A teaspoonful to a tablespoonful thrice daily, after
meals. (*Aliment in phthisis.*)   WEST.

1660—℞ Sodii iodidi . .   gr. lxxv.
    Sodii bromidi .   3iss.
    Sodii chloridi . .   3v.
    Aquæ destillatæ   f3j.—M.

Sig. **A** teaspoonful every morning in a cupful of milk. "Summer Cod-Liver Oil." Contains the principal constituents of
olei morrhuæ. (*Aliment in phthisis.*)   POTAIN.

1661—℞ Spts. vini gallici vel jamaicensis   f3iiss.
    Olei menthæ pip.   mij.
    Glycerini   f3x.—M.

Sig.—To be taken in divided doses during the day. In cases
which present no sign of abnormal excitability of the
nervous system or heart, the dose of glycerin may be raised
to twelve or fifteen ounces daily. (*Aliment, when patients
cannot take olei morrhuæ.*)   JACCOUD.

1662—℞ Salviæ,
    Eupatorii . . . . āā 3ss.
    Cascarillæ . . . . 3j.
    Aquæ bullientis . . . . Oj.

Digere per horas duas et cola.
Sig. A wineglassful every three or four hours. (*In hectic.*)
     ELLIS.

1663—℞ Acidi nitrici . . . . f3j.
    Sacchari albi . . . . 3j.
    Aquæ . . . . Oij.

Fiat mistura.
Sig. One-eighth part **daily in divided doses.** (*Sometimes
arrests colliquative* **sweats when other remedies fail.**) FERRIAR.

1664—℞ Pulveris opii . . . . gr. iij.
    Pulveris digitalis . . . . gr. vj.
    Quininæ sulphatis . . . . gr. xij.
    Confectionis rosæ . . . . q. s.

Misce et fiant pilulæ no. xii.
Sig. One pill four times a day. (*In pyrexia.*)   NIEMEYER.

1665—℞ Acidi salicylici . . . . 3v.

Divide in partes æquales no. xl, et fiant pilulæ compressæ.
Sig. Two pills two or three times a day. (*For foul breath and
offensive expectoration; also in pyrexia.*)   RINGER.

1666—℞ Antipyrin. . . . . 3j.
    Aquæ ferventis . . . . f3iij.—M.
Sig. From thirty minims to four drachms daily by hypodermic, according to strength of patient.   ZAKRZHEVSKI.

1667—℞ Ext. ergotæ fld. . . . . f3j.
Sig. Twenty drops three times daily. (*To relieve diarrhœa and sweats.*)   A. L. HODGSON.

1668—℞ Acetphenetidin. . . . . 3iss.
In pulv. no. xv div.
Sig. A powder stirred in a little water, two or three times daily. (*For hectic.*)   HINSBERG AND KAST.

1669—℞ Antifebrin. . . . . 3ij.
    Spts. vini gallici . . . . f3iij.—M.
Sig. From a dessertspoonful to a tablespoonful two or three times daily. (*For hectic.*)   FAUST.

1670—℞ Ammonii borstis . . . . 3ij.
    Syr. simplicis,
    Elix. simplicis. . . . . āā f3iss.—M.
Sig. A teaspoonful thrice daily. (*For expectoration and hectic.*)   LASHKEVITCH.

1671—℞ Antipyrin. . . . . gr. lxxv.
    Spts. jamaicensis . . . . f3v.
    Syr. limonis . . . . f3viiss.
    Aquæ destillatæ . . . . f3iiss.—M.
Sig. One to three tablespoonfuls once or twice daily. (*For hectic.*)   VIGIER.

1672—℞ Acidi borici . . . . 3iij.
    Misturæ acaciæ . . . . f3v.
    Vini cocæ . . . . q. s. ad f3iij.—M.
Sig. Shake the vial. A dessertspoonful every four hours. (*For diarrhœa.*)   J. C. WILSON.

1673—℞ Bismuthi subnitratis . . . . 3j.
    Pulveris acaciæ . . . . 3ss.
    Magnesiæ . . . . 3j.
Misce et divide in pulveres xii.
Sig. One powder every four hours. (*In diarrhœa.*)   A. T. THOMPSON.

1674—℞ Chloral. hydratis . . . . 3iij.
    Syrupi tolutani . . . . f3j.
    Aquæ destillatæ . . . . . . q. s. ad f3iij.—M.
Sig. A tablespoonful at bedtime. (*To procure sleep.*) WALSHE.

1675—℞ Chondri crispi electi,
    Aquæ . . . . āā q. s.
Coque ad f3vj, cola, et adde—
    Sodii phosphatis . . . . 3iss.
    Syrupi papaveris . . . . f3iij.—M.
Sig. A tablespoonful every two hours. (*In hæmoptysis.*)   CLARUS.

1676—℞ Balsami copaibæ,
    Syrupi tolutani,
    Aquæ menthæ piperitæ,
    Spiritus vini rectificati . . . . . āā f3j.
    Spiritus ætheris nitrosi . . . . f3j.—M.
Sig. Two teaspoonfuls every two to four hours. (*In obstinate hæmoptysis.*)   NIEMEYER.

1677—℞ Cupri acetatis . . . . gr. ij.
    Sodii carbonatis . . . . gr. xij.
    Glycerini et ext. glycyrrhizæ . . . . . q. s.—M.
Ft. massa et in pil. no. xii div.
Sig. One pill night and morning on an empty stomach.   LUTON.

1678—℞ Sulphuris sublimati . . . . q. s.
Sig. In a close room burn two to five drachms of sulphur for each cubic yard of air-space; close and leave for twelve hours. Patient then enters the room and remains eight hours. This is repeated daily.   SOLLARD.

1679—℞ Pilocarpinæ muriatis . . . . gr. iij.
    Aquæ destillatæ . . . . f ʒij.—M.

Sig. Five minims three times daily by hypodermic. (*In paroxysmal dyspnœa of phthisis.*)   RIESS.

1680—℞ Pulv. agarici . . . . ʒj.
In pulv. no. xii div.
Sig. One powder every two hours (for three doses) if necessary. (*For night-sweats.*)   A. PETER.

1681—℞ Atropinæ sulphatis . . . . gr. j.
    Aquæ destillatæ . . . . ʒv.—M.
Sig. Twelve minims hypodermically. (*For hæmoptysis.*)
    HAUSMANN.

1682—℞ Pyridin . . . . ʒj.
Sig. Six to ten drops, increased to twenty-five drops daily, in three-drop doses. In urgent cases three to five drops may be inhaled directly from a handkerchief. (*For dyspnœa.*)
    LE KENZI.

1683—℞ Tereben . . . . ʒiv.
    Pulv. acaciæ . . . . ʒiij.
    Syr. zingiberis . . . . f ʒviiss.
    Aquæ . . . . f ʒxv.—M.
Sig. A teaspoonful **three times daily**. (***Relieves*** *dyspnœa and flatulence.*)   VIGIER.

1684—℞ Terpin, hydratis . . . . gr. lxxv.
    Spts. vini rectificati (95 per cent.) . . . f ʒv.
    Glycerini . . . . f ʒx.—M.
Sig. A teaspoonful or two in a little sweetened or aromatized water two or three times daily. (*Expectorant.*)   VIGIER.

1685—℞ Terpinol,
    Sodii benzoatis . . . . āā gr. xv.
    Sacchari albi . . . . q. s.—M.
In capsulas no. x div.
Sig. A capsule every hour **or two**. (*To diminish the expectoration and remove its odor.*)   KABOW.

1686—℞ Amyli hydratis . . . . gr. cv.
    Ext. glycyrrhizæ . . . . ʒiss.
    Aquæ destillatæ . . . . f ʒxv.—M.
Sig. The half **to be taken at bedtime**. (***For the*** *insomnia of phthisis.*)   FISCHER.

1687—℞ Amyli hydratis . . . . ʒiss.
    Morphinæ muriatis . . . . gr. ½.
    Ext. glycyrrhizæ . . . . ʒiss.
    Aquæ destillatæ . . . . f ʒxv.—M.
Sig. The half to be taken at bedtime. (*Insomnia of phthisis.*)
    FISCHER.

PILES. (See Hemorrhoids.)

PITYRIASIS. (See Skin Diseases.)

PLEURISY.

1688—℞ Tincturæ iodi compositæ . . . . f ʒij.
Sig. Divide the surface on the affected side into three sections, and paint one section each day. (*For chronic pleuritic effusion.*)   BARTHOLOW.

1689—℞ Hydrarg. chloridi mitis . . . . gr. vj.
    Pulv. opii . . . . gr. iij-vj.
    Antimonii et potassii tart. . . . . . . gr. iss.—M.
In pulv. no. xii div.
Sig. A powder every **three or five hours**. (*In acute pleurisy.*)
    HARTSHORNE.

1690—℞ Potassii acetatis . . . . ʒvss.
    Spts. ætheris nitrosi . . . . ʒij.
    Aquæ . . . . ad ʒviij.—M.
Sig. A tablespoonful every **three or four hours**. (*In pleuritic effusion.*)   HARTSHORNE.

1691—R Magnesii sulphatis . . . . ℨvj-viij.

In pulv. no. viii div.
Sig. A powder in two tablespoonfuls of water before food,
and no fluids for some time afterward. (*In pleuritic effusion.*)
M. HAY.

1692—R Folii jaborandi . . . . fℨj.
Aquæ bullientis . . . . Oj.—M.

Ft. infusum.
Sig. A wineglassful three or four times daily. (*In bad cases
with much effusion.*)
MICHON.

1693—R Potassii acetatis . . . . ℨij.
Infusi digitalis . . . . ℨiij.—M.

Sig. A teaspoonful every three hours to a child of five years.
(*To remove effusion.*)
J. LEWIS SMITH.

1694—R Potassii acetatis . . . . gr. xv.
Spiritus ætheris nitrosi . . . . fℨss.
Vini ipecacuanhæ . . . . gtt. iij.
Syrupi tolutani . . . . fℨss.—M.

Sig. One dose, four times a day. (*In subacute pleurisy.*)
DA COSTA.

1695—R Potassii iodidi . . . . ℨj.
Tincturæ scillæ . . . . fℨj.
Tincturæ opii camphoratæ . . . . . . fℨss.
Misturæ acaciæ . . . . fℨvj.—M.

Sig. A teaspoonful four times a day. (*In chronic pleurisy with
consolidation of lung.*)
DA COSTA.

1696—R Potassii iodidi . . . . gr. j.
Ferri et ammonii citratis . . . . gr. iij.
Syrupi sarsaparillæ compositi . . . . . fℨss.
Aquæ destillatæ . . . . fℨij.—M.

Sig. One dose, three times a day. (*In chronic form with effusion, for children.*)
HAZARD.

1697—R Potassii iodidi . . . . ℨiv.
Aquæ destillatæ . . . . q. s. ad fℨvj.—M.

Sig. One fluidrachm in milk every four hours. BARTHOLOW.

1698—R Tinct. opii deodoratæ . . . . gtt. xx.
Tinct. digitalis . . . . gtt. xvj.
Syr. pruni virginianæ . . . . fℨj.
Aquæ . . . . fℨss.—M.

Sig. A teaspoonful every three hours for a child eighteen
months old. (*For first stage.*)
J. LEWIS SMITH.

1699—R Tinct. aconiti radicis . . . . fℨss.

Sig. Half a drop every third hour for a child three years old.
One drop for six years old. If younger, then give—

1700—R Tinct. digitalis . . . . fℨss.

Sig. One drop every three hours for a two-year-old child.
J. LEWIS SMITH.

1701—R Pulv. sinapis . . . . ℨss.
Pulv. lini . . . . ℨviij.
Aquæ bullientis . . . . q. s.—M.

Ft. cataplasma.
Sig. Make the poultice so wet that it moistens the hands in
holding it. Place it between two pieces of muslin, cover
with oiled muslin, and renew when beginning to cool. (*In
pleurisy of children.*)
J. LEWIS SMITH.

1702—R Syr. ferri iodidi . . . . fℨij.
Syr. simplicis . . . . fℨij.—M.

Sig. A teaspoonful every two hours, with the following:

1703—R Iodi . . . . ℨss.
Potassii iodidi . . . . ℨij.
Aquæ destillatæ . . . . fℨij.—M.

Sig. Apply on the affected side of the chest. NIEMEYER.

1704—R Tincturæ aconiti radicis . . . . fℨij.
Tincturæ opii deodoratæ . . . . fℨvj.—M.

Sig. Eight drops in water every hour or two. (*In acute form
before effusion.*)
BARTHOLOW.

PLEURISY (Continued).

1705—℞ Acidi tannici . . . . gr. xxx.
Confectionis rosæ . . . . q. s.

Misce et fiant pilulæ no. xv.
Sig. Four to eight pills daily, one-half in the morning, the remainder in the evening. (*In purulent pleurisy.*) DEBOUE.

1706—℞ Morphinæ acetatis . . . . gr. ss.
Potassii acetatis . . . . 3ss.
Tincturæ veratri viridis . . . . ♏xxiv.
Syrupi tolutani . . . . f3ss.
Liquoris potassii citratis . . . . f3iiss.—M.

Sig. Two fluidrachms every three hours. (*In dry pleurisy.*)
DA COSTA.

1707—℞ Morphinæ sulphatis . . . . gr. ¼.
Quininæ sulphatis . . . . gr. xv-xx.

Misce et fiat chartula.
Sig. At once. (*To abort a commencing pleurisy.*) BARTHOLOW.

1708—℞ Collodii cum cantharide . . . . f3ss.

Sig. Apply with a brush over a small area, heal quickly, and repeat. (*In pleuritic effusion.*) RINGER.

PLEURODYNIA. (See Neuralgia.)

PNEUMONIA.

1709—℞ Pulv. morphinæ comp. (Tully) . . . . 3ss.

In chart. no xii. div.
Sig. One powder every two hours. J. C. WILSON.

1710—℞ Tinct. aconiti radicis . . . . f3ij.
Tinct. opii . . . . f3ij.—M.

Sig. Thirteen drops at once followed by five drops every hour or two. (*In the stage of congestion.*) BARTHOLOW.

1711—℞ Ammonii carbonatis . . . . 3ij.
Infusi serpentariæ . . . . f3iv.—M.

Sig. A tablespoonful every three hours. (*About the period of crisis.*) BARTHOLOW.

1712—℞ Potassii iodidi . . . 3j.
Ammonii muriatis . . 3ss.
Mist. glycyrrhizæ comp. . . . f3vj.—M.

Sig. A tablespoonful four times daily, to promote absorption, together with blisters to the chest. DA COSTA.

1713—℞ Pulv. digitalis . . . . gr. vj.
Quininæ sulphatis . . . . gr. xij.
Ext. opii,
Ext. ipecacuanhæ . . . . ââ gr. iij.—M.

Ft. massa et in pil. no. xii. div.
Sig. One pill thrice daily with the preceding mixture.
DA COSTA.

1714—℞ Tinct. veratri viridis ♏xl.
Spts. ætheris nitrosi f3vj.
Liq. potassii citratis f3ivss.
Syr. zingiberis . . ad f3vj.—M.

Sig. A tablespoonful every three hours. (*In the early stage.*)
DA COSTA.

1715—℞ Liq. trinitrin . . . . f3j.

Sig. One to three drops in water **every four** hours or oftener.
(*To relieve embarrassed heart.*) J. C. WILSON.

1716—℞ Antimonii et potassii tartratis . . . . . gr. ij.
Morphinæ sulphatis . . . . gr. iij.
Ammonii chloridi . . . . 3iij.
Syrupi glycyrrhizæ . . . . f3iv.—M.

Sig. A tablespoonful every four hours.

And

1717—℞ Pulveris opii . . . . gr. iij.
Pulveris ipecacuanhæ,
Hydrargyri chloridi mitis . . . . ââ gr. vj.
Sacchari albi . . . . gr. xxx.

Misce et fiant chartulæ no. vi.
Sig. One powder every four hours, alternately with the preceding prescription; at the end of twenty-four hours omit powders, and, if typhoid symptoms persist, give the following instead:

1718—℞ Quininæ sulphatis. . . . . gr. ij.
    Ammonii carbonatis . . . . gr. iv.

Misce et fiat chartula.
Sig. One dose. If delirium or morbid vigilance is troublesome, add

1719—℞ Chloroformi . . . . ℳx-xij

to each dose of the above. (*In typhoid pneumonia.*)
                                N. S. DAVIS.

1720—℞ Tinct. ipecac. comp. (Squibb) . . . . gtt. xxxij.
    Tinct. aconiti radicis . . . . gtt. xvj.
    Syr. tolutani,
    Aquæ . . . . āā f ℥j.—M.

Sig. A teaspoonful every three hours to a child of five years.
(*In the congestive stage.*)   J. LEWIS SMITH.

1721—℞ Morphinæ sulphatis . . . . gr. j.
    Syr. ipecacuanhæ . . . . f ℥ss.
    Syr. tolutani . . . . f ℥iiiss.—M.

Sig. A teaspoonful every three hours to a child of five years.
(*In the stage of hepatization.*)   J. LEWIS SMITH.

1722—℞ Pulv. sinapis . . . . ℥ss.
    Pulv. seminis lini . . . . ℥viij.—M.

Ft. cataplasma.
Sig. Make as large and thin as a book-cover, and apply to the
chest, covering with oiled silk.   J. LEWIS SMITH.

1723—℞ Morphinæ sulphatis . . . . gr. ¼ ad ½.
    Quininæ sulphatis . . . . gr. vi-x.

Misce et fiat chartula.
Sig. One dose. Within twenty-four hours after the chill, to
abort the attack.   A. B. PALMER.

1723*bis*—℞ Acidi salicylici . . . . gr. xx.

Fiat chartula.
Sig. One every two hours until four or five are taken. (*To
abort an impending attack.*)   L. L. SILVERTHORN.

1724—℞ Potassii iodidi . . . . ℥iss.
    Aquæ destillatæ . . . . f ℥viij.—M.

Sig. A tablespoonful every two hours. (*In double pneumonia,
complicated with pleurisy.*)   M. RIEBE.

1725—℞ Ammonii carbonatis . . . . gr. iv.
    Spiritus chloroformi . . . . ℳxx.
    Aquæ camphoræ . . . . f ℥x.—M.

Sig. To be given every three or four hours. (*In uncomplicated
cases.*)   A. T. H. WATERS.

1726—℞ Quininæ sulphatis . . . . ℥ss.
    Acidi sulphurici aromatici . . . . . f ℥iss.
    Olei caryophylli . . . . gtt. iv.
    Mucilaginis acaciæ . . . . f ℥j.
    Aquæ menthæ pip. . . . . ad f ℥iv.—M.

Sig. A teaspoonful or two every three or four hours. (*In
asthenic pneumonia.*)   HARTSHORNE.

1727—℞ Ext. ergotæ fld. . . . . f ℥iv.
    Tinct. digitalis . . . . f ℥j.
    Plumbi acetatis . . . . gr. vj.
    Aquæ cinnamomi . . . . f ℥ij.

Sig. A tablespoonful every two hours till the blood disappears
from the sputa.   WELLS.

1728—℞ Tinct. strophanth. hispid. (1-20.) . . . f ℥j.

Sig. Ten drops in water four or five times daily. (*In the cardiac
lesions of pneumonia.*)   DRASCHE.

1729—℞ Ammonii muriatis . . . . ℥j.
    Ext. glycyrrhizæ . . . . ℥j.
    Spts. ætheris sulph. . . . . f ℥ij.
    Aquæ . . . . f ℥iv.—M.

Sig. A tablespoonful every two or three hours. (*In advanced
stages of pneumonia.*)   WARING.

1730—℞ Acidi salicylici . . . . f ℥j.
  Ammonii carbonatis . . . . ℈iij.
  Syr. simplicis . . . . f℥j.
  Aquæ cinnamomi . . . . ad f ℥vj.—M.
  Sig. A tablespoonful every hour or two till the fever declines.
                                                      FLIESBURG.

1731—℞ Ext. veratri viridis fld. . . . . f ℥j.
  Sig. Four to six minims every hour until the pulse falls to
    sixty-five or seventy per minute.   STROUD.

1732—℞ Thallin. sulphatis . . . . gr. xxxij.
  Aquæ aurantii flor. . . . . f ℥j.—M.
  Sig. A teaspoonful every three hours till the fever declines.
                                                      OSLER.

PORRIGO (ECZEMA CAPITIS). (See Skin Diseases.)

PORRIGO DECALVANS (ALOPECIA AREATA). (See
    Skin Diseases.)

PORRIGO FAVOSA (FAVUS). (See Skin Diseases.)

PRIAPISM. (See Nymphomania.)

PRICKLY HEAT. (See Skin Diseases.)

PROSTATITIS.

1733—℞ Liq. potassæ . . . . f ℥ij–iv.
  Ext. hyoscyami . . . . ℈j–iv.
  Syr. aurantii cort.,
  Aquæ cinnamomi . . . . āā f ℥ij.—M.
  Sig. A tablespoonful in a wineglassful of water every eight
    hours.   VAN BUREN AND KEYES.

1734—℞ Ext. opii aquosi . . . . gr. viij.
  Olei theobromæ . . . . f ℥iv.—M.
  Fiant suppositoria no. viii.
  Sig. Use one as often as required to modify desire to urinate,
    and to ease pain.   VAN BUREN AND KEYES.

1735—℞ Carbonis animalis   gr. iij.
  Ammonii chloridi   . ℈j.
  Extracti conii .   . . gr. ij.
  Pulveris glycyrrhizæ   q. s.
  Fiat bolus.
  Sig. One three times a day. (In swelled and scirrhous prostate.)
                                                      MAGENDIE.

1736—℞ Iodoformi . . . . ℈ss.
  Olei theobromæ,
  Ceræ flavæ . . . . āā q. s.
  Misce et fiant suppositoria no. v.
  Sig. Use two daily. (In chronic enlargement.)   MORÉTIN.

1737—℞ Ammonii chloridi   ℈ss.
  Syrupi glycyrrhizæ   . . . . f ℥j.
  Aquæ destillatæ .   q. s. ad f ℥vj.—M.
  Sig. A tablespoonful three or four times daily.   VANOYE.

1738—℞ Liquoris potassæ . . . . f ℥ss.
  Tincturæ humuli . . . . f ℥iss.
  Infusi calumbæ . . . . f ℥iv.
  Syrupi aurantii corticis . . . . f ℥j.
  Fiat mistura.
  Sig. A tablespoonful three times a day. (With acid urine.)
                                                      H. GREEN.

1739—℞ Tincturæ cantharidis . . . . ♏xvj.
  Syrupi simplicis   . . . . . . f ℥ss.
  Aquæ destillatæ .   . . . . . f ℥iss.—M.
  Sig. A teaspoonful every four hours.   RINGER.

PROSTATORRHŒA.

1740—℞ Collodii cum cantharide . . f℥ss.

Sig. Paint on one side of the perineum, confining the patient
in bed. Paint the other side as soon as the soreness of the
first application subsides.   VAN BUREN AND KEYES.

1741—℞ Potassii citratis . . . . 3ss-j.
    Spts. limonis . . . . f℥ss.
    Syr. simplicis . . . . f℥ij.
    Aquæ . . . . f℥j.—M.

Sig. A dessertspoonful, largely diluted with water, three or
four times daily.   VAN BUREN AND KEYES.

1742—℞ Tinct. ferri muriatis . . . . f℥vj.
    Tinct. cantharidis . . . . f℥ij.—M.

Sig. Fifteen drops in a wineglassful of water three times
daily.   BARTHOLOW.

1743—℞ Extracti hydrastis fluidi . . . . f℥j.
Sig. Twenty drops three times a day.   BARTHOLOW.

1744—℞ Tincturæ nucis vomicæ . . . . f℥j.
    Tincturæ ferri chloridi . . . . f℥ij.—M.

Sig. Twenty drops three times a day. (*In debilitated cases.*)
    GROSS.

PRURIGO, PRURITUS.

1745—℞ Acidi carbolici . . . . 3j.
    Potassæ fusæ . . . . 3ss.
    Aquæ . . . . f℥x.—M.
Sig. Apply locally.   J. C. WILSON.

1746—℞ Naphthol. . . . . gr. ccxxv.
    Saponis viridis . . . . 3xliss.
    Cretæ præparatæ . . . . 3iiss.
    Adipis . . . . 3cxxv.—M.
Fiat unguentum.
Sig. Apply to the parts, and then powder them with starch.
    KAPOSI.

1747—℞ Acidi carbolici . . . . gr. vj.
    Aquæ . . . . f℥j.—M.
Sig. Apply three times daily. (*In pruritus ani.*)
    CHRISTOPHER HEATH.

1748—℞ Acidi carbolici . . . . gr. x.
    Morphinæ acetatis . . . . gr. viij.
    Acidi hydrocyanici diluti . . . . . . f℥j.
    Glycerini . . . . f℥iv.
    Aquæ . . . . q. s. ad f℥iv.
Fiat lotio.
Sig. Twice daily. (*In pruritus vulvæ.*)   LOMBE ATTHILL.

1749—℞ Sodii salicylatis . . . . 3iij.
    Syr. acaciæ . . . . f℥j.
    Aquæ menthæ pip. . . . . ad f℥ij.—M.
Sig. A dessertspoonful three times daily. (*With rheumatic or
diabetic diathesis.*)   ICARD.

1750—℞ Sodii biboratis . . . . 3ss.
    Morphinæ sulphatis . . . . gr. vj.
    Aquæ rosæ . . . . f℥viij.
Fiat lotio.
Sig. Apply twice daily. (*In pruritus vulvæ.*)   MEIGS.

1751—℞ Sodii hyposulphitis . . . . 3viiss.
    Acidi carbolici . . . . gr. lxxv.
    Glycerini . . . . f℥iv.
    Aquæ . . . . f℥viiss.—M.
Fiat lotio.
Sig. Bathe with cold water, and apply the solution every day
or two. (*For pruritus ani.*)   JOHNSTON.

1752—℞ Ext. nucis vomicæ,
    Ext. belladonnæ . . . . āā gr. iv.—M.
In pil. no. xvi div.
Sig. One pill morning and evening. (*In senile pruritus.*)

144

1753—℞ Liquoris ammonii acetatis . . . . . . f ȝij.
     Acidi hydrocyanici diluti . . . . f ȝj.
     Tincturæ digitalis . . . . f ȝiij.
     Aquæ rosæ. . . . . f ȝv.

Fiat lotio.
Sig. Apply to affected part twice daily. (*In senile prurigo.*)
                    A. T. THOMPSON.

1754—℞ Olei staphisagriæ . . . . f ȝj.
     Adipis. . . . . ȝj.

Fiat unguentum.
Sig. Apply once or twice daily.   BALMANNO SQUIRE.

1755—℞ Aquæ laurocerasi . . . . f ȝj.
     Acidi nitrici diluti . . . . f ȝss.
     Acidi hydrocyanici diluti . . . . . . f ȝiv.
     Glycerini . . . . f ȝj.
     Lactis amygdalæ . . . . ȝxij.

Fiat lotio. (*In pruritus vulvæ.*)   GREENHALGH.

1756—℞ Plumbi iodidi . . . . gr. xij.
     Unguenti ceræ albæ . . . . ȝj.
     Chloroformi . . . . ♏ viij–xij.
     Glycerini . . . . f ȝj.

Misce et fiat unguentum. (*In obstinate cases.*)   NELIGAN.

1757—℞ Lanolini . . . . ȝj.

Sig. Rub in a portion on the affected surface. (*In senile prurigo.*)
                    WULFSBERG.

1758—℞ Cocainæ muriatis . . . . gr. v.
     Lanolini. . . . . ȝj.—M.

Fiat unguentum.
Sig. Apply locally after washing with warm water. (*In pruritus ani.*)
                    BESNIER.

1759—℞ Zinci oxidi . . . . ȝiss.
     Potassii bromidi . . . . ȝiss.
     Ext. cannabis indicæ . . . . ȝss.
     Glyceriti amyli . . . . ȝviiss.—M.

Sig. Wash the parts with very hot lotions of flaxseed, and then apply the above. (*In vulvar pruritus.*)   MÉNIÈRE.

1760—℞ Hydrargyri chloridi corrosivi . . . . . gr. j.
     Pulv. aluminis. . . . . ȝj.
     Pulv. amyli . . . . ȝiss.
     Aquæ . . . . f ȝvj.—M.

Sig. Apply locally.   GOODELL.

1761—℞ Acidi hydrocyanici diluti . . . . f ȝij.
     Sodii boratis. . . . . ȝj.
     Aquæ rosæ . . . . f ȝviij.—M.

Sig. Lotion.   FOX.

1762—℞ Potassii cyanidi . . . . gr. vj.
     Pulv. cocci . . . . gr. j.
     Ungt. aquæ rosæ. . . . . ȝj.—M.

Fiat unguentum.
Sig. Apply locally.   ANDERSON.

1763—℞ Argenti nitratis . . . . gr. xx.
     Aquæ destillatæ . . . . f ȝj.—M.

Sig. Paint over the affected parts. (*In pruritus vulvæ.*)
                    BARTHOLOW.

1764—℞ Iodoformi . . . . ȝj.
     Adipis . . . . ȝj.

Fiat unguentum.
Sig. Apply to affected part once or twice daily.   TANTURRI.

1765—℞ Extracti nucis vomicæ . . . . gr. iij.
     Fellis bovini . . . . gr. vj.
     Extracti taraxaci . . . . gr. xxiv.
     Pulveris myrrhæ . . . . gr. xviij.

Misce et divide in pilulas xxv.
Sig. One three times a day.   NELIGAN.

1766—℞ Morphinæ sulphatis . . . . gr. vj.
   Sodii boratis . . . . ʒiv.
   Aquæ camphoræ . . . . f ʒvj.—M.
 Ft. lotio.
 Sig. Wash the parts with warm water and castile soap and
  apply the lotion twice daily.   BAER.

1767—℞ Chloral. hydratis,
   Pulv. camphoræ . . . . āā ʒj.
   Vaselini . . . . ʒx.—M.
 Sig. Use twice daily. (In hemiplegic prurigo.) KOEBNER.

1768—℞ Chloral. hydratis . . . . gr. lxxv-cl.
   Aquæ laurocerasi . . . . f ʒxiiss.
   Aquæ destillatæ . . . . f ʒl.—M.
 Ft. solutio.
 Sig. Apply locally.   VIDAL.

1769—℞ Iodoformi . . . . ʒj.
   Ceræ flavæ . . . . ʒvj.
   Olei olivæ . . . . q. s. ut ft. ungt.
 Ft. unguentum.
 Sig. Apply locally.   GREGORY.

PSORIASIS. (See Skin Diseases.)

PTYALISM.

1770—℞ Acidi tannici . . . . ʒj.
   Mellis rosæ . . . . f ʒij.
   Aquæ . . . . f ʒvj.—M.
 Sig. Use as a mouth-wash.   BARTHOLOW.

1771—℞ Potassii chloratis . . . . ʒij.
   Infusi rhois glabri radicis . . . . . . Oj.—M.
 Sig. Mouth-wash.   FAHNESTOCK.

1772—℞ Potassii chloratis . . . . ʒj.
   Aquæ . . . . f ʒvj.—M.
 Sig. Use as a mouth-wash, and internally in teaspoonful doses
  four or five times daily.   STURGIS.

1773—℞ Potassii permanganatis . . . . gr. xxv.
   Sodii biboratis,
   Pulveris aluminis . . . . āā ʒij.
   Potassii chloratis . . . . ʒss.
   Tincturæ capsici . . . . f ʒj.
   Aquæ coloniensis,
   Tincturæ myrrhæ,
   Tincturæ krameriæ . . . . āā f ʒj.
   Tincturæ cinchonæ . . . . f ʒij.
   Aquæ destillatæ . . . . f ʒviij.—M.
 Sig. For a mouth-wash.   J. E. GARRETSON.

1774—℞ Sulphuris præcipitati . . . . ℈j-iv.
   Potassii chloratis . . . . ℈j-ʒj.
   Liquoris morphinæ sulphatis . . . . . . f ʒj-iss.
   Misturæ amygdalæ . . . . f ʒvij
 Misce bene.
 Sig. Two tablespoonfuls every three or four hours.
             STYRAP.

1775—℞ Potassii iodidi . . . . ʒj.
   Aquæ destillatæ . . . . f ʒij.—M.
 Sig. A half fluidrachm three times a day. HAMMOND.

1776—℞ Potassii permanganatis . . . . gr. ij-x.
   Aquæ destillatæ . . . . f ʒj.—M.
 Sig. Use as a mouth-wash. (To correct the fetor.)
          J. E. GARRETSON.

1777—℞ Liquoris plumbi subacetatis . . . . . ʒj.
   Aquæ destillatæ . . . . f ʒviij.—M.
 Sig. As a mouth-wash, every hour or two. GROSS.

1778—℞ Pulv. aluminis . . . . ʒss.
    Decocti quercus albæ . . . . Oss.—M.
Sig. Use as a gargle every hour, to remove the fetor of breath
of mercurial salivation. KORTÜM.

1779—℞ Acidi hydrochlorici . . . . f ʒij.
    Syr. rubi . . . . f ʒxv.—M.
Sig. In obstinate salivation, add enough of the above to
acidify strongly a portion of sage-tea. Gargle every hour
with the mixture. KOPP.

1780—℞ Atropinæ sulphatis . . . . gr. j.
    Aquæ destillatæ . . . . f ʒij.—M.
Sig. Four minims three times daily. BARTHOLOW.

1781—℞ Tinct. iodi . . . . f ʒij.
    Aquæ rosæ . . . . f ʒviij.—M.
Sig. Use as a mouth-wash every hour or two. RINGER.

PUERPERAL CONVULSIONS. (See also Convulsions.)

1782—℞ Naphthol . . . . gr. xxxviij.
    Sacchari,
    Bismuthi salicylatis . . . . āā gr. xxxj.
Misce et div. in capsulas no. viij.
Sig. One capsule three times a day. (*Preventive.*) RIVIÈRE.

1783—℞ Aquæ destillatæ,
    Syrupi pruni virginianæ . . . . . āā f ʒij.
    Chloral. hydratis,
    Sodii bromidi . . . . āā ʒss-ʒj.—M.
Sig. A tablespoonful in water every hour. RIVIÈRE.

PUERPERAL FEVER. (See Fever.)

PUERPERAL MANIA. (See Mania.)

PUERPERAL PERITONITIS. (See Peritonitis.)

PURPURA.

1784—℞ Sodii sulphatis . . . . ʒij.
    Ferri sulphatis . . . . gr. iij.
    Acidi sulphurici **diluti** . . . . ♏xv.
    Tinct. hyoscyami . . . . ♏xl.
    Infusi calumbæ . . . . f ʒij.—M.
Sig. To be taken in the morning. TANNER.

1785—℞ Quininæ sulphatis . . . . gr. ix.
    Acidi phosphorici diluti,
    Tincturæ ferri chloridi . . . . . āā f ʒiss.
    Liquoris arsenici chloridi . . . . . . ♏xv-xl.
    Syrupi zingiberis . . . . f ʒvj.
    Infusi quassiæ . . . . f ʒviij.—M.
Sig. One-sixth **part** after breakfast, dinner, and supper.
TANNER.

1786—℞ Strychninæ sulphatis . . . . gr. ss.
    Quininæ sulphatis . . . . ʒj.
    Ferri sulphatis exsiccati . . . . ʒij.—M.
Fiant pilulæ **no.** xx.
Sig. One thrice **daily.** NAPHEYS.

1787—℞ Liq. potassii arsenitis . . . . ʒss.
Sig. Five drops in water, after meals, three times daily. (*When
due to iodism.*) PHILLIPS.

1788—℞ Syr. ferri superphosphatis,
    Liq. hydrogenii perox. (10 vol.),
    Glycerini puri . . . . āā f ʒiss.
    Aquæ destillatæ . . . . ad f ʒvj.—M.
Sig. A tablespoonful thrice daily. GUITÉRAS.

1789—℞ Ext. hamamelidis fld. . . . . f℥ij.
Sig. A teaspoonful every one to three hours.
J. V. SHOEMAKER.

1790—℞ Olei terebinthinæ . . . . f℥iij.
Extracti digitalis fluidi . . . . f℥j.
Mucilaginis acaciæ . . . . : f℥ss.
Aquæ menthæ piperitæ . . . . f℥j.
Misce et fiat emulsio.
Sig. A teaspoonful every three hours. (*In the hemorrhagic form.*)
BARTHOLOW.

1791—℞ Acidi gallici . . . . ℥ss.
Acidi sulphurici diluti . . . . f℥j.
Tincturæ opii deodoratæ . . . . . . f℥j.
Infusi rosæ compositi . . . . f℥iv.—M.
Sig. A tablespoonful every four hours or oftener.
BARTHOLOW.

1792—℞ Extracti ergotæ aquosi . . . . ℈j.
Pulveris ipecacuanhæ . . . . gr. x.
Acidi gallici . . . . ℈j.
Misce et fiant pilulæ no. xx.
Sig. One pill every hour or two. (*With hemorrhage.*)
BARTHOLOW.

PYÆMIA.

1793—℞ Quininæ sulphatis . . . . gr. v-xx.
Ft. pulv. no. i.
Sig. To be taken every four hours. RINGER.

1794—℞ Olei eucalypti . . . . ℥j.
Dispensa in capsulas no. xvi.
Sig. One capsule every three hours. J. C. WILSON.

1795—℞ Acidi sulphurosi . . . . f℥ss-j.
Aquæ . . . . f℥ij.—M.
Ft. haustus.
Sig. To be taken every two to four hours. TANNER.

1796—℞ Acidi salicylici . . . . ℥ss.
Sodii biboratis . . . . ℥j.
Glycerini . . . . f℥j.
Aquæ menthæ piperitæ . . . . f℥v.—M.
Sig. A tablespoonful every two or three hours. BARTHOLOW.

PYROSIS. (See also Acidity.)

1797—℞ Magnesii sulphatis . . . . ℥j.
Tinct. hyoscyami . . . . ♏xv.
Aquæ . . . . f℥ij.—M.
Ft. haustus.
Sig. To be taken three times daily. AITKEN.

1798—℞ Sodii bicarbonatis . . . . ℥iss.
Olei anisi . . . . gtt. j.
Syrupi aurantii florum,
Aquæ destillatæ . . . . ãã f℥j.—M.
Sig. One dose. PIORRY.

1799—℞ Quininæ sulphatis . . . . gr. xxij.
Pepsini . . . . ℈vss.
Extracti absinthii . . . . q. s.
Misce et fiant pilulæ no. xl.
Sig. Two before each meal. PIORRY.

1800—℞ Tinct. nucis vomicæ . . . . f℥ij-iv.
Acidi nitrici diluti . . . . f℥v.
Syr. zingiberis . . . . ad f℥iij.—M.
Sig. A teaspoonful in a wineglassful of water. PHILLIPS.

1801—℞ Extracti nucis vomicæ . . . . gr. iss.
Argenti nitratis . . . . gr. ij.
Extracti lupuli . . . . gr. xij.
Misce et divide in pilulas vi.
Sig. One pill three times a day. BARLOW.

1802—℞ Acidi carbolici . . . . gr. j.
Alcoholis . . . . f ʒij.—M.
Sig. Twenty-five drops in a wineglassful of water before each
meal. PODMORE JONES.

1803—℞ Terebene . . . . gr. ccxxv.
Pulv. acaciæ . . . . ʒiv.
Aquæ . . . . ʒxv.
Pulv. sacchari albi . . . . ʒxlv.
Pulv. tragacanthæ . . . . ʒij.—M.
Ft. trochisci no. c.
Sig. One three **times daily.** VIGIER.

1804—℞ Quininæ sulphatis . . . . gr. xij.
Acidi sulphurici diluti,
Spts. chloroformi . . . . āā f ʒij.
Tinct. aurantii corticis . . . . . . ad f ʒiss.—M.
Sig. A teaspoonful, in water, three times daily. J. R. **MARTIN.**

1805—℞ Acidi sulphurosi . . . . ʒss-j.
Aquæ . . . . f ʒij.—M.
Ft. haustus.
Sig. To be taken shortly **before meals.** LAWSON.

QUINSY

1806—℞ Acidi boracici . . . . ʒij.
Eau de Pagliari . . . . f ʒx.
Aquæ . . . . f ʒvij ʒviss.
Misce et flat gargarisma.
Sig. Use **as** a gargle **several times daily, and each time follow**
by an application of—

1807—℞ Iodoformi . . . . ʒj.
Collodii flexilis . . . . ʒvij.—M.
Sig. "Iodoform collodion." LEBRUN.

1808—℞ Tinct. guaiaci,
Glycerini . . . . āā f ʒiss.—M.
Sig. A teaspoonful every hour or two. RINGER.

1809—℞ Tinct. guaiaci ammoniatæ . . . . . . f ʒij.
Sig. A teaspoonful in half a glassful of milk three or four times
daily. (*In the early stage.*) SAJOUS.

1810—℞ Pulv. resinæ guaiaci . . . . . . ʒiv.
Sig. Put as much as will lie on a one-cent piece on the back
of the tongue, and let it remain as long as possible. SAJOUS.

1811—℞ Tinct. belladonnæ . . . . f ʒss.
Sig. Five drops in a **tablespoonful of water** every one to
three hours. PHILLIPS.

1811bis—℞ Tinct. aconiti radicis . . . . . f ʒss.
Sig. Half a drop or a drop every ten minutes **or quarter of an**
hour for two hours, and afterwards hourly. RINGER.

1812—℞ Quininæ sulphatis . . . . gr. x-xv.
Fiat chartula.
Sig. Take before pus forms. (*To abort an impending attack.*)
BARTHOLOW.

1813—℞ Acidi citrici . . . . gr. xv.
Potassii bicarbonatis . . . . ʒj.
Tincturæ guaiaci . . . . ℳx.
Mucilaginis acaciæ . . . . f ʒj.—M.
Sig. One dose. To be taken while effervescing. (*For children.*)
HAZARD.

1814—℞ Hydrargyri chloridi corrosivi . . . . . gr. j.
Aquæ destillatæ . . . . f ʒj.—M.
Sig. Five minims every two hours. Or—

1815—℞ Hydrargyri chloridi mitis . . . . . . gr. ss.
Sacchari lactis . . . . ʒss.
Misce et flant chartulæ no. **x.**
Sig. One powder every two hours. Or—

RACHITIS, RICKETS, SCROFULA, STRUMA (Continued).

1843—℞ Calcii chloridi . . . . 3j.
Extracti conii . . . . gr. xv.
Aquæ cinnamomi . . . . f3ss.

Solve.
Sig. Shake well. Eight to sixteen drops three times a day, to a child ten years old. PHŒBUS.

1844—℞ Calcii chloridi . . . . 3ss.
Syr. simplicis . . . . f3iv.—M.

Sig. For children, a teaspoonful thrice daily. For adults, three times the dose is taken. SPILLMANN.

1845—℞ Acidi hydrocyanici dil. . . . . f3j.
Glycerini . . . . f3ij.
Acidi nitrici dil. . . . . f3ilj.
Infusi quassiæ . . . . ad f3xiiiss.—M.

Sig. A tablespoonful thrice daily. AITKEN.

1846—℞ Quininæ sulphatis . . . . gr. j.
Acidi sulphurici dil. . . . . mj-ij.
Vini ferri . . . . f3j-ij.—M.

Sig. To be taken three times daily. WM. JENNER.

1847—℞ Carbonis animalis,
Pulveris glycyrrhizæ . . . . āā 3vj.

Misce et detur in scatula.
Sig. Half or a whole teaspoonful twice a day. RADIUS.

1848—℞ Pulveris glandis quercus torrefactæ . 3j.
Aquæ bullientis . . . . Oj.

Fiat infusum.
Sig. Three or four teacupfuls during the day, and augmented. (*In commencing rachitis, glandular swellings, etc. Continue for a long time.*) HUFELAND.

1849—℞ Ferri bromidi . . . . gr. xij.
Confectionis rosæ . . . . gr. xviij.

Misce et fiant pilulæ no. xx.
Sig. One three times a day. (*In strumous dyspepsia.*) ROBERT DICK.

RATTLESNAKE-BITE.

1850—℞ Hydrargyri chloridi corrosivi . . . . . gr. j.
Potassii iodidi . . . . gr. ij.
Brominii . . . . 3iiss.
Alcoholis diluti . . . . 3xxx.—M.

Ft. sol.
Sig. A teaspoonful in wine or brandy as often as necessary. BIBRON.

1851—℞ Aquæ ammoniæ . 3j.
Aquæ . . . . 3iij.—M.

Sig. Inject thirty minims hypodermically into a superficial vein above the seat of injury. HALFORD.

1852—℞ Potassii permanganatis . . . . 3ss.
Aquæ destillatæ . . . . 3iij.—M.

Sig. Apply to the wound, and inject hypodermically above the seat of injury. At the same time take internally the following :

1853—℞ Aquæ ammoniæ . . . . 3iv.

Sig. A half-teaspoonful in water, repeated every ten or fifteen minutes. HAWACK AND ARBOC.

REMITTENT FEVER. (See Fever.)

RENAL CALCULI. (See Calculi.)

RENAL DROPSY. (See Dropsy.)

RENAL HEMORRHAGE. (See Hæmaturia.)

1854—℞ Acidi salicylici . . . . 3iij.
   Potassii bicarbonatis . . . . 3v.
   Aquæ . . . . f3ij.—M. ..
 Sig. A teaspoonful every three hours.   DONNELLY.

1855—℞ Sodii salicylatis . . . . 3ss.
   Tinct. lavandulæ comp. . . . . f3iv.
   Glycerini . . . . f3ss.
   Aquæ . . . . ad f3viij.—M.
 Sig. A tablespoonful every hour or two until pain and fever
 abate, then at longer intervals.   F. MINOT.

1856—℞ Acidi **salicylici** . . . . 3ss.
   Ferri **pyrophosphatis** . . . . 3j.
   Sodii **phosphatis**. . . . . 3x.
   Aquæ . . . . f3vj.—M.
 Sig. A tablespoonful every two hours until the improvement
 justifies less frequent doses, or unless constitutional effects
 are produced.   G. L. PEABODY.

1857—℞ Sodii **salicylatis** . . . . 3vj.
   Glycerini . . . . 3iv.
   Aquæ cinnamomi . . . . ad f3vj.—M.
 Sig. A tablespoonful every two or three hours until tinnitus
 aurium is produced; then every four to six hours until the
 acute symptoms have abated. Then give—

1858—℞ Sodii bicarbonatis . . . . 3iv-vj.
 In pulv. no. xii div.
 Sig. A powder in a half-glassful of water every four hours
 until the urine is alkaline to test-paper. If the patient is
 anæmic, omit the salicylate and begin on the soda at once,
 and give cod-liver oil and iron from the first. (*In robust
 cases.*)   A. L. LOOMIS.

1859—℞ Ergotinæ   gr. xv
   Sodii salicylatis   3iss.
   Aquæ destillatæ . .   . f3vj.—M.
 Sig. A tablespoonful every hour. (*The ergot obviates thickening
 of the tympanum.*)   SCHILLING.

1860—℞ Sodii salicylatis .   gr. xv.
   Sodii bicarbonatis .   gr. xxx.
   Aquæ menthæ pip.   .   f3ss.—M.
 Sig. To be taken every third or fourth hour. When **the acute**
 symptoms abate, then give—

1861—℞ Mist. ferri et ammonii acetatis (U.S.P.) 3iv.
 Sig. A dessertspoonful or two in a wineglassful of water,
 thrice daily.   J. C. WILSON.

1862—℞ Acidi salicylici . . . . 3ij.
   Sodii boratis . . . . gr. xv.
   Aquæ menthæ pip. . . . . ad f3vj.—M.
 Ft. sol.
 Sig. One-third **to** be taken during twenty-four hours. If there
 be no improvement in three or four days, discontinue, and
 use—

1863—℞ Ammonii **bromidi** . . . . 3iij-iv.
 In pulv. no. xii div.
 Sig. A powder in a half-glassful of water every four hours.
 When the acute symptoms abate, add twelve to sixteen
 grains of quinine daily.   DA COSTA.

1864—℞ Sodii bicarbonatis.
   Ammonii carbonatis . . . . āā gr. v.
   Acidi salicylici . . . . gr. xx
   Aquæ destillatæ . . . . f3j.—M.
 Sig. One dose. (*This avoids unpleasant cerebral symptoms, sick
 stomach, and rapid collapse.*)   PRIDEAUX.

1865—℞ Lithii bromidi . . . . 3ij.
   Vini cocæ . . . . f3iv.—M.
 Sig. A dessertspoonful in water every two or three hours.
   J. C. WILSON.

1866—℞ Salicinæ . . . . gr. xv.
Fiat chartula.
Sig. This amount every three hours.　　　T. J. McLagan.

1867—℞ Olei gaultheriæ . . . . f ʒj.
Sig. Fifteen or twenty minims to be given in capsules or
floated on milk or water every two hours until the acute
symptoms abate; then gradually diminish to one drachm
daily until convalescence; then combine iron. If any
joint-stiffness remains, then give—

1868—℞ Lithii salicylatis . . . . ℈ij-iij.
Sig. To be given, dissolved in water, during the twenty-four
hours.　　　Kinnicutt.

1869—℞ Sodii bicarbonatis. . . . . ʒiss.
Potassii acetatis . . . . ʒss.
Liquoris ammonii acetatis . . . . . . f ʒij.
Aquæ destillatæ. . . . . f ʒiss.—M.
Sig. One dose. To be taken in a state of effervescence, in
combination with—

1870—℞ Acidi citrici . . . . ʒss.
Aquæ destillatæ . . . . f ʒij.—M.
　　　　　　　　　　　　　　　　　Fuller.

1871—℞ Ammonii chloridi,
Potassii bromidi . . . . āā ʒss.
Tincturæ cinchonæ compositæ . . . . f ʒij.
Syrupi zingiberis,
Aquæ destillatæ . . . . āā f ʒj.—M.
Sig. One fluidrachm every two hours. With—

1872—℞ Iodoformi deodorati . . . . ʒiss.
Vaselini . . . . ʒj.—M.
Sig. Apply well to the inflamed parts.　　W. C. Boteler.

1873—℞ Tincturæ aconiti (B.P.) . . . . ℳxij.
Ammonii sulphidi . . . . ℳxvj.
Aquæ menthæ piperitæ . . . . f ʒvj.—M.
Sig. A fourth part every fourth hour until the fever is abated.
　　　　　　　　　　　　J. Mortimer Granville.

1874—℞ Potassii nitratis . . . . : gr. xv.
Pulveris ipecacuanhæ compositi . . . gr. iij.
Misce et fiat chartula.
Sig. One dose. To be taken every fourth hour. (In subacute
rheumatism.)　　　　　　　　　　Da Costa.

1875—℞ Pulveris colchici　　　　. . . . gr. iij.
Potassii sulphatis . .　　　. . . . gr. iv.
Potassii bicarbonatis　　　　gr. iij.
Tere simul ut fiat pulvis.
Sig. One every three or four hours. (In subacute rheumatism.)
　　　　　　　　　　　　　　　　　Haden.

1876—℞ Aquæ camphoræ . . . . .　　f ʒiss.
Liquoris ammonii acetatis　　f ʒss.
Vini antimonii . . . . .　　gtt. xl.
Tincturæ opii deodoratæ　　gtt. xx.
Misce et fiat haustus.
Sig. At bedtime.　　　　　　　　　Blanc.

1877—℞ Hydrochinon. . .　　　　ʒss.
Aquæ cinnamomi　　　. . f ʒiij.—M.
Sig. One-half to three teaspoonfuls two to four times daily
until the fever abates.　　Sylvestrini and Picchini.

1878—℞ Antifebrin. . . . . ʒj.
Fiant capsulæ no. xvi.
Sig. One or two capsules three to six times daily.
　　　　　　　　　　　　　　　　　Eisenhart.

1879—℞ Antipyrin. . . . . ʒij.
Syr. aurantii cort. . . . . f ʒj.
Aquæ . . . . ad f ʒiij.—M.
Sig. A dessertspoonful in water thrice daily. (In afebrile
cases.)　　　　　　　　　　　　Germain Sée.

1880—℞ Propylaminæ . . . . gr. xxiv.
Aquæ menthæ pip. . . . . f3vj.—M.
Sig. A tablespoonful every two or three hours.   Jas. Tyson.

1881—℞ Sodii bicarbonatis . . . . ℈ij.
Acidi salicylici . . . . ℈iij.
Glycerini,
Aquæ destillatæ . . . . ā ā f3ij.—M.
Sig. One teaspoonful every four hours.   N. B. Kennedy.

1882—℞ Liq. ammonii ichthyosulphatis (30 per
cent.) . . . . ℈ij.
Lanolini . . . . ℥j.—M.
Ft. unguentum.
Sig. To be rubbed over **the swollen joints. Take internally**
the following:

1883—℞ Ichthyol. . . . . ℈j.
Fiant capsulæ no. xx.
Sig. Three to six capsules during the twenty-four hours.   (In
both acute and chronic cases.)   Schmidt.

1884—℞ Sodii salicylatis,
Potassii citratis . . . . ā ā gr. xv.
Aquæ . . . . f3ss.—M.
Sig. To be given every two hours **until the pain and fever**
abate. Also the following:

1885—℞ Liq. opii sedativi . . ℥j.
Potassii bicarbonatis ℈iv.
Glycerini . . . f3ij.
Aquæ bullientis . . . . . f3ix.—M.
Sig. "Fuller's Lotion." Soak a piece of flannel or spongio-
piline in the above hot solution, and wrap it around the
painful joint.   Osler.

1886—℞ Pimentæ . . . . ℥vj 3ij.
Aquæ ammoniæ . . . . f3iij 3j.
Ess. thymi,
Chloral. hydratis . . . . ā ā 3ifss.
Spts. vini rectificati (60°) . . . . . . Oij.—M.
Ft. linimentum.
Sig, "Apone." Use pure or mixed with **olive oil.**   (For fric-
tion about rheumatic joints.)   Poulet.

RHEUMATISM, CHRONIC.

1887—℞ Lithiæ citratis . . . . 3ij.
Strychninæ . . . . gr. j.
Tinct. strophanthi . . . . f3ss.
Aquæ menthæ pip. . . . . . . q. s. ad f3iv.—M.
Sig. A teaspoonful before each meal, in water.   Brower.

1888—℞ Aloes . . . . gr. ij.
Pulv. ipecac. . . . . gr. j.
Pulv. rhei,
Ferri sulph. exsiccati,
Ext. hyoscyami . . . . ā ā gr. x.—M.
Divide in capsulas no. x.
Sig. One at bedtime.   Brower.

1889—℞ Lithii salicylatis . . . . 3ij.
Syrupi simplicis . . . . f3j.
Aquæ aurantii flor. . . . . ad f3vj.—M.
Sig. A tablespoonful thrice daily.   Vulpian.

1890—℞ Pulveris guaiaci resinæ,
Potassii iodidi . . . . ā ā gr. x.
Tincturæ colchici **seminis** . . . . . . f3ss.
Aquæ cinnamomi,
Syrupi simplicis . . . . . . ā ā q. s. ad f3j.—M.
Sig. A dessertspoonful to a tablespoonful thrice daily.
Philadelphia Hospital.

1891—℞ Pulveris guaiaci . . . . ℨj.
　　　Pulveris rhei . . . . ℨij.
　　　Potassii bitartratis,
　　　Sulphuris sublimati . . . . āā ℨj.
　　　Pulveris nucis moschatæ . , ... ℨij.
　　　Mellis . . . . ℔j.
Ft. mistura.
Sig. Two large spoonfuls night and morning. (*In old chronic cases. Used in civil and military hospitals.*) AITKEN.

1892—℞ Potassii bicarbonatis . . . . ℨss.
　　　Vini colchici radicis . . . . f℥ij.
　　　Tincturæ guaiaci . . . . f℥ij.
　　　Syrupi aurantii corticis . . . . f℥ij.—M.
Sig. A dessertspoonful **thrice daily** in water. (*In rheumatic arthritis.*) DA COSTA.

1893—℞ Olei terebinthinæ,
　　　Spts. camphoræ,
　　　Aquæ ammoniæ,
　　　Olei olivæ . . . . āā f℥j.—M.
Ft. linimentum.
Sig. Use locally. HARTSHORNE.

1894—℞ Potassii iodidi . . . . ℨj-ij.
　　　Aquæ cinnamomi . . . . f℥vj.—M.
Sig. A tablespoonful thrice daily. HARTSHORNE.

1895—℞ Tinct. guaiaci æth. . . . . f℥j.
　　　Tinct. cannabis indicæ æth. . . . . . f℥vj.
　　　Tinct. colchici æth. . . . . f℥ij.—M.
Sig. Twenty-five to thirty drops on sugar every four hours. ATLEE.

1896—℞ Potassii iodidi . . . . ℨij.
　　　Vini colchici sem.,
　　　Tinct. opii camph. . . . . āā f℥ij.
　　　Tinct. stramonii . . . . f℥vj.
　　　Tinct. cimicifugæ . . . . f℥ij.—M.
Sig. A teaspoonful thrice daily. *St. Luke's Hospital, N.Y.*

1897—℞ Potassii et sodii tartratis . . . . . . ℨss.
　　　Potassii nitratis . . . . ℨv.
　　　Vini colchici sem. . . . . f℥ij.
　　　Aquæ . . . . q. s. ad f℥ij.—M.
Sig. A teaspoonful thrice daily. *Bellevue Hospital, N.Y.*

1898—℞ Potassii et sodii tartratis . . . . . . ℨss.
　　　Vini colchici sem. . . . . f℥ij.
　　　Aquæ . . . . q. s. ad f℥ij.—M.
Sig. A teaspoonful thrice daily. *Charity Hospital, N.Y.*

1899—℞ Sassafras radicis corticis . . . . . . ℨiss.
　　　Mezerei . . . . ℨiv.
　　　Taraxaci radicis . . . . ℨiij.
　　　Aquæ ferventis . . . . Oj.
Misce et fiat infusum.
Sig. From one to one and a half fluidounces three times a day, with a plentiful use of diluents. FULLER.

1900—℞ Iodoformi,
　　　Ferri redacti . . . . āā gr. xliij.
　　　Extracti glycyrrhizæ . . . . q. s.
Misce et divide in pilulas no. ix.
Sig. Two to be taken thrice daily. KNOLL.

1901—℞ Liquoris potassii **arsenitis** . . . . . . f℥ij.
　　　Potassii iodidi . . . . ℨij.
　　　Syrupi simplicis . . . . f℥ij.—M.
Sig. A teaspoonful **thrice daily, in water,** between meals. (*In rheumatic arthritis.*) DA COSTA.

1902—℞ Calcii chloridi . . . . ℨij.
　　　Syr. simplicis . . . . f℥iv.
　　　Olei gaultheriæ . . . . gtt. iv.—M.
Sig. A tablespoonful thrice daily for adults. One-third dose for children. Also use externally—

1903—℞ Calcii chloridi . . . . ℨj.
    Aquæ . . . . f℥xliss.—M.
Ft. lotio.
Sig. Soak lint in the solution and wrap it about the joints.
                                    DUCKWORTH.

1904—℞ Tinct. aconiti,
    Chloroformi,
    Aquæ ammoniæ . . . . āā f℥ij.
    Linimenti saponis comp. . . . . . ad f℥viij.—M.
Ft. linimentum.
Sig. Use locally.   *Jefferson Hospital, Phila.*

1905—℞ Linimenti aconiti (B.P.),
    Linimenti belladonnæ   āā f℥j.
    Glycerini   . . .   . . . ad f℥ij.—M.
Ft. linimentum.
Sig. Apply locally over the seat of pain.   FOTHERGILL.

1906—℞ Tincturæ iodi,
    Alcoholis . . . . āā f℥ss.—M.
Sig. Apply morning and evening.   DA COSTA.

1907—℞ Aconitinæ . . . . gr. v.
    Olei olivæ . . . . f℥ss.
Tere simul et adde—
    Adipis . . . . ℨviiss.
    Olei bergamii . . . . ℳx.
    Olei santali . . . . ℳij.—M.
Ft. unguentum. (*In neuralgic rheumatism.*)   FULLER.

1908—℞ Olei cajuputi,
    Tincturæ opii . . . . āā f℥ij.
    Olei terebinthinæ . . . . f℥iv.
    Linimenti ammoniæ . . . . f℥j.—M.
Ft. linimentum.   FULLER.

1909—℞ Chloroformi,
    Tincturæ aconiti radicis . . . . . āā f℥ij.
    Olei terebinthinæ . . . . f℥ss.
    Olei sassafras . . . . ℳxx.
    Linimenti saponis camphorati . . . . f℥iiss.—M.
Ft. linimentum.   J. C. WILSON.

1910—℞ Acidi salicylici . . . . ℨj-iss.
    Lanolini . . . . ℨiij.
    Olei olivæ . . . . q. s. ad f℥vj.—M.
Sig. Apply as directed.   ZEBALD.

1911—℞ Olei monardæ . . . . f℥ss.
    Tincturæ opii . . . . f℥ij.
    Tincturæ camphoræ . . . . f℥ij.—M.
Ft. linimentum.   W. ATLEE.

RHINITIS. (See also Catarrh.)

1912—℞ Menthol . . . . gr. ij.
    Caffeæ tostæ,
    Sacchari albi . . . . āā gr. l.—M.
Ft. pulv.
Sig. To be used like ordinary snuff.   RABOW.

1913—℞ Cocainæ hydrochloratis . . . . gr. iss.
    Caffeæ tostæ,
    Sacchari albi . . . . āā gr. l.—M.
Ft. pulv.
Sig. To be used as snuff. (*Used in rare cases where the preceding is ineffectual.*)   RABOW.

1914—℞ Naphthol, (β) . . . . ℨij.
    Spts. vini rectificati (90°) . . . . f℥ij.—M.
Sig. A teaspoonful in a pint and a half of tepid water. Use as a douche, or with an atomizer. (*In ozæna and purulent rhinitis.*)   A. RUAULT.

RICKETS. (See Rachitis.)

RINGWORM. (See Skin Diseases.)

RUBEOLA. (See Fever.)

RUPIA. (See Skin Diseases.)

SALIVATION. (See Ptyalism.)

SARCINÆ ET TORULÆ.

1915—℞ Acidi sulphurosi . . . . f℥j-iss.
Infusi calumbæ . . . . f℥xij.—M.
Ft. haustus.
Sig. A wineglassful ten minutes before meals.   LAWSON.

1916—℞ Acidi sulphurosi . . . . f℥ss-j.
Aquæ . . . . f℥ij.—M.
Ft. haustus.
Sig. To be taken thrice daily.   TANNER.

1917—℞ Acidi sulphurosi . . . . f℥ij.
Syrupi aurantii corticis . . . . f℥ij.
Aquæ destillatæ . . . . q. s. ad f℥vj.—M.
Sig. One to two tablespoonfuls every four hours.
RUSSELL REYNOLDS.

1918—℞ Sodii hyposulphitis . . . . ℥ij.
Infusi quassiæ . . . . f℥vj.
Ft. solutio.
Sig. A tablespoonful three times daily.   R. NEALE.

1919—℞ Sodii sulphitis . . . . ℥ss.
Aquæ destillatæ . . . . f℥iss.
Misce et fiat haustus.
Sig. Three times a day. (*The dose may be increased.*)
JENNER.

SATYRIASIS. (See Nymphomania.)

SCABIES. (See also Lice.)

1920—℞ Oil of sweet almonds . . . . f℥ij.
Salol . . . . ℥j.—M.
Sig. Anoint the body with this mixture every night, and then
rub lightly with flowers of sulphur.
St. Louis Hospital, Paris.

SCARLATINA. (See also Fever and Diphtheria.)

1921—℞ Ammonii carbonatis . . . . ℥j-iss.
Syr. simplicis . . . . f℥j.
Aquæ . . . . ad f℥iss.—M.
Sig. A teaspoonful every hour, or every two or three hours,
according to the severity of the case.   PEART.

1922—℞ Ammonii carbonatis . . . . ℥j.
Syrupi acaciæ . . . . f℥vj.
Liquoris ammonii acetatis . . q. s. ad f℥ij.—M.
Sig. A teaspoonful every two hours.   DA COSTA.

1923—℞ Infusi digitalis . . . . f℥iv.
Sig. One-half to one teaspoonful every two, three, or four
hours.   BARTHOLOW.

1924—℞ Tincturæ digitalis . . . . f℥ss.
Syrupi simplicis . . . . f℥ss.
Aquæ destillatæ . . . . q. s. ad f℥ij.—M.
Sig. A teaspoonful every hour or two, according to age.
BARTHOLOW.

1925—℞ Tincturæ aconiti radicis . . . . . . ℥j-iij.
Syrupi simplicis . . . . f℥ss.
Aquæ destillatæ . . . . f℥iss.—M.
Sig. A teaspoonful every hour or two, according to age.
BARTHOLOW.

1926—℞ Tinct. aconiti radicis . . . . f℥ss.

Sig. One-half to one drop in a teaspoonful of water every quarter-hour for two hours; afterwards hourly. If there is much prostration, with feeble pulse, a smaller dose should be given. RINGER.

1927—℞ Acidi carbolici . . ʒss.
Olei olivæ ad ℥x.—M.

Ft. solutio.
Sig. Anoint all the body except the face (on which pure olive oil is used) twice daily for four or six weeks, and follow by a warm bath at night. BROWN.

1928—℞ Acidi carbolici gr. xxx.
Thymoli . . . . gr. x.
Vaselini . . . . ℥j.
Cerati simplicis ℥j.—M.

Sig. Apply to the whole body night and morning. A warm bath to be given at night. Also paint the patient's throat with—

1929—℞ Boroglyceride (50 **per cent.**) . . . . . . ℥ij.
Sig. Apply frequently to **the patient's throat with a brush.**
(*To prevent contagion.*) JAMIESON.

1930—℞ Resorcin. . . . . ℥ij.
Lanolini . . . . ʒiss.
Olei sesami . . . . f℥ss.—M.

Ft. unguentum.
Sig. Rub into the skin. (*To hasten desquamation, and to elimi-
nate the specific poison.*) JAMIESON.

1931—℞ Acidi carbolici cryst. . . . . ℥x.
Aquæ . . . . ℥j.—M.

Sig. Three to six minims every two hours day and night during the first three days. If the patient is doing well, give every three hours for four or five days; then every four hours until all danger is passed, then thrice daily until convalescent. Do not exceed eight minims at a dose, but give until the urine is smoky or almost black. Also give one minim thrice daily to all exposed persons.
WIGLESWORTH.

1932—℞ Antifebrin. . . . . gr. xv.
Sacchari albi . . . . gr. xxx.—M.

In pulv. no. x div.
Sig. A powder as required by the fever. For a child three or four years old. WIDOWITZ.

1933—℞ Hydrargyri biniodidi . . . . gr. j-vj.
Ext. glycyrrhizæ . . . . . gr. xij.—M.

Ft. massa et in pil. no. xxiv div.
Sig. A pill every four hours. CLEMENT DUKES.

1934—℞ Tinct. ferri chloridi . . . . ℥ij.
Potassii chloratis . . . . ℥j-ij.
Syr. simplicis . . . . f℥iv.—M.

Sig. A teaspoonful every **hour or two to a** child of four or five years. J. LEWIS SMITH.

1935—℞ Acidi hydrochlorici . . . . ℳv.
Syrupi aurantii florum . . . . f℥ss.
Aquæ destillatæ . . . . f℥iss.—M.

Sig. A teaspoonful **every two hours.** ELLIS.

1936—℞ Quininæ sulphatis. . . . . gr. viij.
Acidi sulphurici aromatici . . . . gtt. viij.
Syrupi rubi idæi . . . . f℥ss.
Aquæ destillatæ . . . . f℥iss.—M.

Sig. A teaspoonful every two hours. HOOD.

1937—℞ Chloral. hydratis . . . . gr. xlviij.
Syrupi acaciæ vel lactucarii . . . f℥j.
Aquæ . . . . f℥ij.—M.

Sig. A teaspoonful in cold water every two, three, or four hours, to produce light continued somnolence. (*For child of three or four years.*) J. C. WILSON.

SCIATICA. (See also Neuralgia.)

1938—℞ Extracti belladonnæ . . . . gr. ⅙.
Extracti stramonii . . . . gr. j.
Extracti cannabis indicæ . . . . gr. ¼.
Extracti aconiti . . . . gr. ⅓.
Extracti opii . . . . gr. ½.
Extracti hyoscyami . . . . gr. ⅔.
Extracti conii . . . . gr. j.
Pulveris glycyrrhizæ . . . . q. s.

Misce et fiat pilula.
Sig. Three, four, and even five pills in a day, *pro re nata.*
BROWN-SÉQUARD.

1939—℞ Morphinæ sulphatis . . . . gr. ½-⅔.
Atropinæ sulphatis . . . . gr. 1/72.

Misce et fiat pulvis.
Sig. For one hypodermic injection, in twenty drops of distilled water. BROWN-SÉQUARD.

1940—℞ Aquæ ammoniæ . . . . fʒv.
Olei terebinthinæ,
Olei amygdalæ dulcis . . . . āā fʒj.—M.

Fiat linimentum.
Sig. Rub on three times a day. (*In obstinate sciatica.*)
LABORDE.

1941—℞ Tinct. colchici sem. . . . . gtt. xv.
Potassii iodidi . . . . gr. x.
Tinct. zingiberis . . . . gtt. x.
Syrupi simplicis,
Aquæ . . . . āā q. s. ad f℥ij.—M.

Ft. haustus.
Sig. Apply a strip of blistering plaster over the course of the nerve, and give the above draught in water thrice daily between meals. DA COSTA.

1942—℞ Tinct. aconiti rad.,
Tinct. colchici sem.,
Tinct. belladonnæ,
Tinct. cimicifugæ . . . . āā fʒj.—M.

Sig. Twelve drops every four to eight hours. J. T. METCALF.

1943—℞ Olei terebinthinæ . . . . fʒij.
Olei ricini . . . . fʒiv.
Tincturæ cardamomi compositæ . . . fʒj.
Mucilaginis acaciæ,
Aquæ destillatæ . . . . āā q. s. ad f℥ij.

Misce et fiat emulsio.
Sig. One dose. W. A. JAMIESON.

1944—℞ Olei terebinthinæ . . . . f℥viij.
Chloroformi,
Tincturæ opii . . . . āā fʒij.

Fiat linimentum.
Sig. To be rubbed on several times a day. LABORDE.

1945—℞ Potassii iodidi . . . . ℈j.
Decocti sarsaparillæ comp. . . . . f℥ij.—M.

Ft. haustus.
Sig. To be taken thrice daily. (*In subacute or chronic cases.*)
WARING.

1946—℞ Chloroformi . . . . ♏v-xv.

Sig. For one injection. Insert the needle at the ischiatic notch deeply to near the trunk of the nerve. BARTHOLOW.

1947—℞ Chloroformi . . . . fʒj.
Olei vaselini . . . . fʒiv.—M.

Sig. Inject fifteen to twenty minims hypodermically, and repeat if necessary. MEUNIER.

1948—℞ Arsenici sulphidi . . . . gr. ij.

In pil. no. c div.
Sig. One pill three times a day. J. C. WILSON.

1949—℞ Pulv. sulphuris sublimati . . . . . . ℥iv.

Sig. Dust thickly on the limb and envelop it in soft flannel.
RINGER.

1950—℞ Veratriæ . . . . ∋j-ij.
Adipis . . . . ℨj.—M.
Ft. unguentum.
Sig. Rub into the painful part for half an hour twice daily.
TURNBULL.

1951—℞ Antipyrin. . . . . ℨij.
Syr. aurantii cort. . . . . f ℨss.
Aquæ aurantii flor. . . . . . . ad f ℨij.—M.
Sig. A dessertspoonful every hour to four hours, until three
to six doses are taken. GERMAIN SÉE.

1952—℞ Methyl. chloridi . . . . f ℨss.
Sig. Apply with an atomizer locally, but with care. DEBOVE.

1953—℞ Saloli . . . . ℨss.
Olei vaselini f ℨv.—M.
Sig. Inject twenty or thirty minims hypodermically over the
course of the nerve. MEUNIER.

1954—℞ Saloli,
Sacchari lactis . . . . āā ℨiij.—M.
In pulv. no. xii div.
Sig. A powder every four to six hours. ASCHENBACH.

1955—℞ Quininæ sulphatis . . . . ℨss-ℨj.
Tincturæ ferri chloridi . . . . f ℨij.
Spiritus ætheris nitrosi . . . . . . f ℨiv.
Syrupi simplicis . . . . f ℨij.
Vini xerici . . . . q. s. ad f ℨiv.—M.
Sig. A tablespoonful every three or four hours.
H. V. SWERINGEN.

1956—℞ Extracti ergotæ fluidi . . . . f ℨij.
Aquæ cinnamomi . . . . f ℨij.—M.
Sig. A dessertspoonful in water every three or four hours.
(Tinct. ferri chloridi may be added if indicated.)
EDWARD WAAKES.

1957—℞ Emplastri epispastici, 1½ × 3 in.
Sig. Apply over affected part for five or six hours, poultice,
remove the cuticle, and dress with—

1958—℞ Morphinæ sulphatis . . . . gr. ¼.
Pulveris marantæ . . . . gr. ij.
Misce et fiat chartula.
Sig. Sprinkle over blister. **Ten grains of** Dover's powder at
night. DA COSTA.

1959—℞ Acidi osmici . . . . gr. ij.
Aquæ destillatæ . . . . ℥cc.—M.
Sig. Sixteen minims hypodermically at **the** seat of pain, at
first daily, then less frequently. STEKOULIA.

SCIRRHUS. (See Cancer.)

**SCLEROSIS (POSTERIOR SPINAL). (See also Loco-
motor Ataxia.)**

1960—℞ Argenti nitratis . . . . gr. ¼.
Aquæ . . . . q. s.—M.
Sig. Inject with hypodermic syringe. ROSENBAUM.

1961—℞ Potassii iodidi . . . . ℨvj-ℨviij.
Ferri et ammonii citratis . . . . . . ℨij.
Tincturæ aurantii corticis,
Syrupi simplicis . . . . āā f ℨiij.
Aquæ menthæ piperitæ q. s. ad f ℨiv.—M.
Sig. **A teaspoonful in** water about an hour after each meal.
H. V. SWERINGEN.

1962—℞ Argenti nitratis,
Extracti belladonnæ . . . . āā gr. vj-viij.
Extracti gentianæ . . . . q. s.
Misce et fiant pilulæ no. xxiv.
Sig. One after each meal. A. McL. HAMILTON.

SCLEROSIS (POSTERIOR SPINAL) (Continued).

1963—℞ Extracti belladonnæ . . . . gr. iv.
Olei terebinthinæ . . . . f ℥ij
Olei theobromæ . . . . q. s.—M.
Fiant capsulæ no. xii.
Sig. One thrice daily.   A. McL. Hamilton.

1964—℞ Tincturæ ferri chloridi,
Tincturæ nucis vomicæ,
Acidi phosphorici diluti,
Syrupi simplicis . . . . āā f ℥j.—M.
Sig. A teaspoonful in water about an hour before each meal.
       H. V. Sweringen.

1965—℞ Acidi phosphorici diluti . . . . f ℥vj.
Syrupi simplicis . . . . f ℥iij.—M.
Sig. A teaspoonful in water thrice daily, gradually increased
to a dessertspoonful. (*Along with electricity.*) W. Lambert.

1966—℞ Antipyrin . . . . ℨij.
Syr. sarsaparillæ comp. . . . . f ℥ij.
Aquæ cinnamomi . . . . ad f ℥vj.—M.
Sig. A tablespoonful every hour or two until relieved.
       Suckling.

1967—℞ Ætheris . . . . f ℥iij.
Sig. Spray over the painful area or nerve-trunk with an
atomizer.   Raison.

SCROFULA. (See Rachitis.)

SCURVY.

1968—℞ Succi limonis . . . . f ℥viij.
Sig. Two tablespoonfuls daily. More may be given. With
potatoes and other fresh vegetables.   Parkes.

1969—℞ Succi limonis . . . . f ℥vj.
Sig. Use locally and generally *ad libitum.*   Garrod.

1970—℞ Acidi hydrochlorici . . . . f ℥j.
Mellis,
Aquæ rosæ . . . . āā f ℥j.
Misce et fiat linctus.
Sig. Apply to affected gums three or four times a day.
       Brande.

1971—℞ Potassii nitratis . . . . gr. xx.
Acidi citrici . . . . ℨss.
Syrupi aurantii corticis . . . . f ℥vj.
Aquæ destillatæ . . . . f ℥vj.—M.
Sig. The sixth part three or four times a day. McLachlan.

1972—℞ Potassii bitartratis . . . . ℨj.
Olei limonis . . . . ♏xv.
Sacchari albi . . . . ℨij.
Aquæ bullientis . . . . Oij.—M.
Ft. haustus.
Sig. Use when cold as a drink.   Tanner.

1973—℞ Sodii chloridi . . . . ℨx.
Potassii chloratis . . . . ℨss.
Potassii et sodii tartratis . . . . . . ℨv.
Sodii phosphatis . . . . ℨiiss.
Succi limonis recentis . . . . f ℥vj.
Syr. limonis . . . . f ℥xiv.
Aquæ . . . . Ovij.—M.
Sig. To be taken as a drink, iced or not, as agreeable.
       Tanner.

SEA-SICKNESS.

1974—℞ Antipyrin . . . . gr. lxxv.
Cocainæ hydrochloratis . . . . gr. ias.
Caffeini . . . . gr. iv.
Strychnine sulphatis . . . . gr. ⅟₂.
Spis. vini gallici . . . . f ℥iiss.
Aquæ destillatæ . . . . f ℥xxiiss.—M.
Sig. A tablespoonful before embarking, and two others
during the day, or three during the twenty-four hours.
       Rouquette.

1975—℞ Amyli nitritis . . . . f℈ij.

Sig. Inhale three to five drops from a handkerchief, with care.
BARTHOLOW.

1976—℞ Cerii oxalatis . . . . **gr. ij.**
Tincturæ valerianæ ammoniatæ . . . f℥j.
Aquæ destillatæ . . . . f℥j.
Misce et fiat haustus.
Sig. Every half-hour.
WALSH.

1977—℞ Spiritus chloroformi,
Tincturæ cardamomi compositæ . āā f℥ij.—M.

Sig. A teaspoonful in water **every** half-hour.
BARTHOLOW.

1978—℞ Cocainæ hydrochloratis . . . . . 0.15.
Spiritus vini rectificati q. s. ut fiat solutio.
Dein adde—
Aquæ destillatæ . . . . 150.00.—M.
MANASSEIN.

1979—℞ Cocainæ hydrochloratis . . . . . gr. xxx.
Aquæ destillatæ . . . . f℥vss.—M.
Sig. Four or five drops on a small piece of ice thrice daily.
W. OTTO.

1980—℞ Sodii bromidi . . . . ℨj.
Ammonii bromidi . . . . ℨss.
Aquæ menthæ pip. . . . . f℥v.—M.
Sig. A tablespoonful before meals and at bedtime. To be used for three days before embarking.
BEDARD.

1981—℞ Chloroformi . . . . f℥ss.

Sig. Two to five minims on sugar every half-hour until relieved.
BARTHOLOW.

1982—℞ Chloral. hydratis . . . . ℨss.
Aquæ camphoræ . . f℥j.—M.
Sig. One dose.
PRIESTLEY.

1983—℞ **Sol. nitro-glycerin.** (1 per cent.) . ℨij.
Sig. One **or two drops** two or three times daily.
TRUSSEWITSCH.

1984—℞ Hyoscyaminæ,
Strychninæ . . . . āā gr. ss.
Ext. gentianæ . . . . ℈j.—M.
In pil. no. xxxiii div.
Sig. One every ten minutes.
EMBLETON.

1985—℞ Chloral. hydratis . . . . ℨss.
Syr. aurantii cort. . . . . f℥j.
Aquæ aurantii flor. . . . . ad f℥ij.—M.
Sig. One or two teaspoonfuls in water every four hours.
RINGER.

SEPTICÆMIA. (See Pyæmia.)

SHINGLES. (See also Skin Diseases, Herpes Zoster.)

1986—℞ Collodii . . . . f℥j.
Sig. Paint over the affected parts.
WARING.

1987—℞ Collodii **flexilis** . . . . f℥j.
Sig. Apply with **a brush to** the affected area constantly, to exclude the air.
ANSTIE.

1988—℞ Magnesii carbonatis . gr. xx.
Vini colchici radicis,
Tincturæ opii . . . . āā f℥ss.
Aquæ camphoræ . . . . f℥j.
Misce et fiat haustus. (**To relieve** the deep-seated pain in chest.)
A. T. THOMPSON.

1989—℞ Sulphuris sublimati . ℈j.
Hydrargyri ammoniati ℨss.
Unguenti simplicis ℨj.
Misce et fiat unguentum.
Sig. Apply two or three times a day.
CORFE.

SHINGLES (Continued).

1990—℞ Zinci phosphidi,
  Ext. nucis vomicæ . . . . āā gr. x.—M.
Ft. massa et in pil. no. xxx div.
Sig. One pill every two to four hours.   BULKLEY.

1991—℞ Pulv. amyli . . . . ℨiv.
Sig. Dust over the eruption and on a muslin band sewed
  tightly around the body, to protect it from the friction of
  the clothes.   BULKLEY.

1992—℞ Liq. sodæ chlorinatæ . . . . f ℨiv.
  Aquæ . . . . f ℨij.—M.
Ft. lotio.
Sig. Apply to the ulcerated vesicles.   FOURNIER.

1993—℞ Bismuthi subnitratis . . . . ℨiv.
  Hydrarg. chloridi mitis,
  Zinci oxidi . . . . āā ℨj.—M.
Ft. pulvis.
Sig. Dust on cotton, and apply to the ulcerated vesicles after
  washing them with the solution of chlorinated soda.
          FOURNIER.

1994—℞ Veratriæ . . . . ℈j–ij.
  Vaselini . . . . ℨj.—M.
Ft. unguentum.
Sig. Apply locally. (*For the neuralgia following shingles.*)
          RINGER.

SICK HEADACHE. (See Headache.)

SINGULTUS. (See Hiccough.)

SKIN DISEASES.

1995—℞ Sulphuris præcip. . . . . ℨiv.
  Glycerini . . . . ℨiss.
  Spts. camphoræ . . . . f ℨj.
  Aquæ . . . . f ℨiv.—M.
Sig. Apply with a brush to the affected part before retiring
  at night. (*In acne.*)   LAILLER.

1996—℞ Potassii acetatis . . ℨiv.
  Tinct. nucis vomicæ . f ℨij.
  Ext. rumicis fld. . . . . . ad f ℨiv.—M.
Sig. One teaspoonful, well diluted, after meals, thrice daily.
  (*In acne.*)   BULKLEY.

1997—℞ Magnesii sulphatis . . . . . ℨss.
  Acidi sulphurici aromatici   ℳxx.
  Ferri sulphatis . . . gr. iij.
  Quininæ sulphatis . gr. j.
  Vini colchici radicis   ℳx.
  Syrupi zingiberis   f ℨj.
  Aquæ destillatæ . . . . f ℨj.
Misce et fiat haustus.
Sig. To be taken twice or thrice a day, with an aperient pill,
  if necessary. (*In acne.*)   TILBURY FOX.

1998—℞ Hydrargyri oxidi rubri,
  Hydrargyri ammoniati . . . . . . āā gr. v.
  Adipis . . . . ℨj.—M.
Fiat unguentum. (*In acne.*)   TILBURY FOX.

1999—℞ Creasoti . . . . ℳv–xv.
  Adipis . . . . ℨss.—M.
Fiat unguentum. (*In acne.*)   JOY.

2000—℞ Zinci oxidi . . . . ℨij.
  Pulveris amyli . . . . ℨiv.—M.
Fiat pulvis. (*In eczema, acne, impetigo.*)   CAZENAVE.

2001—℞ Sulphuris præcip. . . . . ℥j-iss.
    Glycerini . . . . f℥j.
    Spts. vini rectificati . . . . f℥ss.
    Aquæ rosæ . . . . ad f℥iv.—M.

Ft. lotio.
Sig. To be painted on at night, after steaming the face and washing it with sand-soap. To be washed off in the morning with warm gruel, and the face powdered with—

2002—℞ Zinci oleatis,
    Pulv. talci . . . . āā ℥j.—M.

Sig. To be dusted on every morning. (*In acne.*)   JAMIESON.

2003—℞ Acidi chrysophanici . . . . gr. xxiv.
    Vaselini . . . . ℥j.—M.

Ft. unguentum.
Sig. Wash the skin with soap and dry it at night. Rub the ointment well in. Repeat every night until a sharp dermatitis is produced. Cease inunction until the dermatitis disappears; then repeat the process. (*In acne.*)
          J. T. METCALF.

2004—℞ Saponis mollis . . . ℥iv.
    Aquæ coloniensis . . . . f℥ij.—M.

Sig. Moisten a flannel with hot water, then dip it into the solution, and rub firmly over the skin. Wash well with warm water, dry with friction, and anoint with zinc ointment. (*In acne, with thick, sluggish skin.*)   JAMIESON.

2005—℞ Potassii acetatis . . . . ℥j.
    Acidi acetici . . . . ℥ss.
    Spts. ætheris nitrosi . . . . f℥iss.
    Ext. taraxaci fld. . . . . f℥ij.—M.

Sig. A teaspoonful before meals, in water. (*In acne indurata.*)
          BULKLEY.

2006—℞ Calcis vivæ . . . . ℥j.
    Sulphuris sublimati . . . . ℥ij.
    Aquæ . . . . f℥x.—M.

Coque ad f℥vi.
Sig. Apply after bathing with hot water at night. Wash off with gruel in the morning, and apply the powder. (*In acne rosacea.*)   VLEMINCKX.

2007—℞ Sulphuris præcip.,
    Cretæ præcip.,
    Aquæ laurocerasi,
    Spts. vini rectificati,
    Glycerini . . . . āā ℥ij.—M.

Ft. lotio.
Sig. Bathe the face with hot water and dry it with friction, then apply the lotion. (*In acne of the face.*)   LEROY.

2008—℞ β-Naphthol . . . . 10 gram.
    Vaselini flavi,
    Saponis viridis . . . . āā 20 gram.
    Sulphuris præcip. . . . . 50 gram.

Sig. To be applied by the physician, and to remain fifteen to sixty minutes, then gently removed and replaced by powder or white paste. This is repeated, after the peeled surface is healed, or the following may remain over-night:

2009—℞ Resorcin . . . . 2.5-5.0 gram.
    Zinci oxidi,
    Amyli . . . . āā 5 gram.
    Vaselini flavi . . . . 12.5 gram.—M.

Ft. pasta. (*In acne vulgaris and rosacea.*)   LASSAR.

2010—℞ Bismuthi oxidi,
    Pulv. amyli . . . . āā gr. xxx.
    Kaolin . . . . ℥j.
    Glycerini . . . . f℥iss.
    Aquæ rosæ . . . . q. s.—M.

Sig. To be painted on the spots and allowed to dry. Wash carefully before making a new application. (*In chloasma.*)
          UNNA.

2011—℞ Zinci oxidi . . . . gr. iij.
Hydrargyri ammoniati . . . . gr. iss.
Olei theobromæ,
Olei ricini . . . . āā ℨiss.
Ess. rosæ . . . . gtt. x.—M.

Sig. Apply to the **face night and morning**. (*In the chloasma of pregnancy.*) MONIN.

2012—℞ Ext. opii . . . . gr. x-xx.
Acidi tannici . . . . ℨj.
Unguenti . . . . ℥j.—M.

Sig. Apply after the inflammatory condition has been subdued with lead lotion. (*In idiopathic ecthyma.*) TILBURY FOX.

2013—℞ Hydrargyri iodidi rubri . . . . . . gr. xij.
Cerati simplicis . . . . ℨviiss.—M.

Ft. unguentum.
Sig. Apply locally. (*In ecthyma syphilitica.*) DIDAY.

2014—℞ Quininæ sulphatis . . . . ℨss.
Acidi sulphurici aromatici . . . . . f ℨss.
Tincturæ cardamomi compositi . . . f ℨiss.
Aquæ destillatæ . . . . q. s. ad f ℨv.—M.

Sig. A dessertspoonful three times a day. (*In ecthyma.*) RINGER.

2015—℞ Sodii biboratis . . . . ℨij-iij.
Aquæ rosæ . . . . f ℨvj.—M.

Fiat lotio.
Sig. Apply two or three times daily. (*In ecthyma.*) COPLAND.

2016—℞ Chrysarobin . . . . gr. xx.
Ætheris . . . . f ℨj.—M.

Sig. Use as a spray. (*In mycotic eczema.*) HEBRA.

2017—℞ Naphthol . . . . 5 grammes.
Black soap . . . . 50 "
Powdered chalk . . . . 10 "
Prepared lard . . . . 100 "

Mix.
Sig. Twice daily. (*In eczema.*) KAPOSI.

2018—℞ Liquoris carbonis detergentis . . . . . f ℨj.
Zinci oxidi . . . . ℨij.
Calaminæ puræ . . . . ℨij.
Glycerini . . . . f ℨij.
Aquæ calcis . . . . f ℨx.—M.

Fiat lotio. (*In eczema.*) DUCKWORTH.

2019—℞ Acidi hydrocyanici diluti . . . . ♏ xl.
Olei cadini . . . . f ℨj.
Saponis viridis . . . . ℨij.
Olei rosmarini . . . . f ℨiss.
Aquæ destillatæ . . . . q. s. ad f ℨv.—M.

Fiat linimentum. (*In eczema.*) ANDERSON.

2020—℞ Acidi boracici . . . . gr. lxxxj.
Vaselini . . . . ℨj.
Balsami peruviani . . . . gr. viiss.—M.

Sig. Apply to the parts affected. (*In infantile eczema.*) DELAPERT.

2021—℞ Citrine ointment,
Chaulmoogra ointment . . . of each ℨss.—M.

Sig. Apply once daily. (*In obstinate chronic eczema, scrofuloderma, lupus, leprosy, and tuberculosis of the skin.*) SHOEMAKER.

2022—℞ Oil of cade . . . . f ℨiss.
Ammoniated mercury . . . . gr. xl.
Chaulmoogra ointment . . . . ℨj.—M.

Sig. Apply thoroughly. (*In chronic eczema, psoriasis, lichen, and scleroderma.*) SHOEMAKER.

2023—℞ Balsam of Peru . . . . ℨj.
Sulphuretted potash ointment . . . . ℨj.—M.

Sig. Apply thoroughly. (*In chronic eczema, psoriasis, and in itch and ringworm.*) SHOEMAKER.

2024—℞ Oil of cade . . . . ℈ss.
Iodide of sulphur ointment . . . . . ℥j.—M.

Sig. Apply thoroughly. (*In* alopecia circumscripta, chronic eczema, and psoriasis.) SHOEMAKER.

2025—℞ Cocaine hydrochlorate . . . . gr. j.
Potassii bromidi . . . . gr. x.
Aquæ destillatæ,
Glycerini . . . . āā f℥iiss.—M.

Sig. Apply to the gums. (*In the eczema of dentition.*) BESNIER.

2026—℞ Sodii bromidi . . . . gr. ivss-vliss.
Syr. aurantii flor. . . . . f℥ij.—M.

Sig. One teaspoonful every two hours. (*In the eczema of dentition.*) BESNIER.

2027—℞ Zinci oxidi . . . . ℥ij.
Vaselini . . . . ℥vj.—M.

Sig. Apply locally and cover with a rubber mask. (*In the eczema of dentition.*) BESNIER.

2028—℞ Crystallized acetic acid . . . . 2 parts.
Glycerin . . . . 50 "
Cherry-laurel water (dist.) . . . . . . 200 " —M.

Sig.—Paint on the eyelid once a day. (*In palpebral eczema.*) LAILLER.

2029—℞ Liquoris plumbi subacetatis . . . . . . ℀xl.
Vini opii . . . . f℥j.
Aquæ rosæ . . . . f℥viij.

Misce et fiat lotio. (*In eczema.*) BURGESS.

2030—℞ Potassii iodidi . . . . gr. viij.
Decocti dulcamaræ . . . . f℥iv.
Decocti ulmi . . . . f℥xij.—M.

Sig. A wineglassful at bedtime. (*In eczema.*) NELIGAN.

2031—℞ Extracti staphisagriæ,
Zinci oxidi . . . . āā ℈ss.
Adipis benzoatæ . . . . ℥j.—M.

Fiat unguentum. (*In chronic eczema.*) BAZIN.

2032—℞ Infusi cinchonæ . . . . f℥vj.
Aquæ calcis . . . . f℥ixss.
Tincturæ lupulinæ,
Succi conii . . . . āā f℥ij.—M.

Sig. A wineglassful three times a day. (*In chronic eczema.*) NELIGAN.

2033—℞ Hydrargyri oxidi rubri,
Hydrargyri ammoniati . . . . . . āā gr. vj.
Adipis . . . . ℥j.—M.

Sig. Apply locally (*In ecthyma syphiliticm.*) STARTIN.

2034—℞ Acidi citrici . . . . gr. xv.
Aquæ lauroceras. . . . . ℥j.
Olei rusci [birch] . . . . gtt. xv.
Ungt. aquæ rosæ . . . . ℥x.—M.

Sig. Use thrice daily. Use starch-powder between the applications. Carefully attend to diet. (*In acute eczema.*) MONIN.

2035—℞ Acidi boracici . . . . gr. xv
Pulv. acaciæ . . . . ℥j.
Olei vaselini . . . . ℥viiss.
Aquæ . . . . f℥xv.—M.

Fiat emulsio.
Sig. Apply locally. Bismuth, zinc, sulphur, or other substance may be added. (*In eczema.*) KNAGGS.

2036—℞ Pulv. acidi salicyllci . . . . gr. xv-xxx.
Pulv. zinci oxidi,
Pulv. amyli . . . . āā ℥iij gr. viij.
Vaselini puri . . . . ℥vj gr. xv.

Misce et fiat unguentum.
Sig. Apply locally, and cover with cotton after rubbing the ointment in. (*In papulous or squamous eczema, or infantile intertrigo.*) LASSAR.

2037—℞ Sodii arseniatis   gr. ¾.
     Aquæ destillatæ . .   ʄ ʒiv ʒij.-M.

Sig. A teaspoonful thrice daily. With saline purgative twice weekly. Apply locally the following:

2038—℞ **Hydrargyri ammoniati** . . . . **gr. xv.**
     Vaselini . . . . ʒv.
     Ess. rosæ . . . . ♏ij.—M.

Sig. Apply gently every evening. Every eight or ten days use the following:

2039—℞ Pilocarpinæ nitratis   gr. iss.
     Aquæ destillatæ . . . . ♏lxxv.—M.

Sig. Six drops to be injected hypodermically. Contra-indicated in diseases of the heart and great vessels. (*In eczema about the menopause.*)   J. CHÉRON.

2040—℞ Olei cadini,
     Saponis mollis,
     Spiritus rectificati . . . . āā ʄ ʒj.
     Olei lavandulæ . . . . ʄ ʒiss.—M.

Sig. After washing, rub in firmly night and morning. (*In eczema.*)   ANDERSON.

2041—℞ Zinci oxidi . . . . ʒij.
     Glycerini . . . . ʄ ʒij.
     Liquoris plumbi **subacetatis** . . . . . ʄ ʒss.
     Aquæ calcis . . . . q. s. ad ʄ ʒvj.—M.

Ft. lotio. (*In eczema.*)   TILBURY FOX.

2042—℞ **Bismuthi subnitratis** . . . . ʒss.

Detur in scatula.
Sig. Dust the affected **parts.** (*In erythema of the genitals, etc., of infants.*)   BARTHOLOW.

2043—℞ Tinct. belladonnæ . . . . ʄ ʒss.

Sig. Five drops thrice daily to a child of two years. The dose should cause dryness of the throat, that it may affect the cutaneous circulation. (*In infantile eczema.*)   BARTHOLOW.

2044—℞ Zinci oxidi,
     Picis liquidæ . . . . āā partes æquales.

Misce et fiat cataplasma.
Sig. Apply locally. (*In impetiginous eczema after the crusts are removed.*)   ELLIOTT.

2045—℞ Pulv. oryzæ . . . . ʒiiss.
     Plumbi oxidi,
     Glycerini . . . . āā ʒviiss.
     Acidi acetici diluti . . . . ʄ ʒxv.—M.

Coque ad ʒxx.
Sig. Use locally. (*In eczema of the hands and fingers. Useful also in painful fissures of the genitals.*) This paste resembles, in color, the skin.   UNNA.

2046—℞ Acidi acetici cryst. . . . . gr. iij.
     Glycerini . . . . ♏lxxv.
     Aquæ laurocerasi . . . . ʄ ʒv.—M.

Sig. Apply daily with a stiff camel's-hair brush. (*In eczema of the eyelids.*)   LAILLER.

2047—℞ Olei cadini . . . . ʒ-s.
     Glycerini . . . . ʒj.
     Ungt. diachyli. . . . . ʒiss.—M.

Ft. unguentum.
Sig. Apply locally. (*In squamous eczema with thickened skin.*)   TILBURY FOX.

2048—℞ Glyceriti amyli . . . . ʒviiss.
     Acidi tannici,
     Hydrarg. chloridi mitis . . . . . āā gr. xv.—M.

Sig. Apply morning and evening. (*In dry eczema with itching.*)   VIDAL.

2049—℞ Acidi salicylici . . . . gr. xlv.
     Zinci oxidi . . . . ʒiij.
     Pulv. amyli . . . . ʒv.—M.

Sig. Dust the surface and cover with wadding. (*In acute eczema.*)   ELLIOTT.

2050—℞ Ungt. hydrargyri oxidi rubri . . . . . ʒij.
Ungt. sulphuris . . . . ʒij.
Acidi carbolici . . . . gr. iij.
Ungt. simplicis . . . . ʒss.—M.
Sig. Apply to the affected parts. (*In chronic eczema.*)
Da Costa.

2051—℞ Antipyrin . . . . ʒiss.
Aquæ laurocerasi . . . . fʒiij.—M.
Ft. lotio.
Sig. Apply as a lotion or on compresses. (*In chronic eczema.*)
Chenneviere.

2052—℞ Hydrargyri ammoniati . . . . gr. xv.
Unguenti simplicis . . . . ʒv.—M.
Ft. unguentum.
Sig. For local use night and morning. (*In dry eczema, or chapped lips.*)
Royer.

2053—℞ Resorcin . . . . ʒij.
Vaselini puri . . . . ʒxviij.—M.
Ft. unguentum.
Sig. Rub in three times daily, and dust on rice-powder. (*In acute eczema of the hands.*)
Wiss.

2054—℞ Potassii chloratis . . . . gr. xj.
Vini opii . . . . ℧xx.
Aquæ . . . . Oj.—M.
Sig. Wet compresses with the solution, and apply them to the affected parts. If the inflammation is very acute, give first a hot sitz-bath, and use poultices, sprinkled on the surface with precipitated chalk. (*In eczema.*)
Martin.

2055—℞ Pulv. camphoræ . . . . ʒss.
Pulv. zinci oxidi . . . . ʒiij.
Glycerini . . . . ℧xl.
Unguenti benzoini . . . . ʒj.—M.
Sig. Apply locally at once, or some isolating powder, as talc, bismuth, or lycopodium, may be used first. (*In vesiculous eczema.*)
Duhring.

2056—℞ Pulv. camphoræ . . . . ʒss-j.
Spts. vini rectificati . . . . fʒj.
Sodii boratis . . . . ʒij.
Aquæ rosæ . . . . fʒviij.—M.
Ft. lotio.
Sig. Apply locally several times daily. (*In erythema. Also in pruritus and eczema.*)
Tilbury Fox.

2057—℞ Hydrargyri ammoniati . . . . gr. x.
Acidi carbolici cryst. . . . . gr. viiss.
Ungt. petrolei,
Ungt. zinci oxidi . . . . āā ʒss.
Olei olivæ . . . . ʒss.—M.
Sig. Apply two or three times daily. (*In general infantile eczema.*)
Stelwagon.

2058—℞ Resorcin,
Zinci oxidi . . . . āā ʒj.
Ungt. aquæ rosæ . . . . ʒx.—M.
Ft. unguentum.
Sig. Apply locally. (*In chronic indurated eczema of infants.*)
Fliesburg.

2059—℞ Olei morrhuæ . . . . ʒij.
Vitell. ovi . . . . no. j.
Liq. sodii arseniatis . . . . fʒj.
Syrupi simplicis . . . . fʒij.
Aquæ . . . . fʒiv.—M.
Sig. A half-teaspoonful thrice daily. (*In chronic infantile eczema.*)
Doyon.

2060—℞ Ungt. zinci oxidi,
Ungt. plumbi subacetatis . . . . . āā ʒss.
Chloral. hydratis,
Pulv. camphoræ . . . . āā gr. xv.—M.
Ft. unguentum.
Sig. Use two or three times daily, after bathing with warm water. (*In general eczema.*)
Gross.

169

2061—℞ Ferri et ammonii citratis . . . . ℨj.
Potassii citratis . . . . ℨij.
Liq. potassii arsenitis . . . . f ℨj-ij.
Tinct. nucis vomicæ . . . . f ℨij.
Tinct. cinchonæ comp. . . . . . . ad f ℥iv.—M.

Sig. A teaspoonful in water after meals, as a tonic and alterative. (*In eczema.*)　　　　　　　BULKLEY.

2062—℞ Liq. plumbi subacetatis . . . . f ℨj.
Glycerini,
Aquæ . . . . āā f ℥iv.—M.

Sig. To be applied two to four times daily with a camel's-hair pencil. (*In infantile eczema, when the surface is red, angry-looking, and discharging a thin, watery secretion.*)
　　　　　　　J. LEWIS SMITH.

2063—℞ Pulv. camphoræ . . . . ℨss-j.
Zinci oxidi . . . . ℨiv.
Pulv. amyli . . . . ℥j.—M.

Sig. Dust on lightly, and do not allow to cake upon the skin. (*In erythema.*)　　　　　　　BULKLEY.

2064—℞ Petrolei,
Balsami peruviani . . . . āā ℨss.
Unguenti laurini [bay-leaf] (Ph. P.) . . gr. xvj.—M.

Ft. unguentum.
Sig. Apply with a camel's-hair pencil. Wash off, after remaining three hours, with warm water. (*In erythema following mercurial inunction.*)　　　　　　　HEBRA.

2065—℞ Quininæ sulphatis . . . . ℨss.
Acidi sulphurici **aromatici** . . . . . . ℨss.
Ext. taraxaci fld. . . . . ℨvj.
Aquæ . . . . q. s. ad f ℥iv.—M.

Sig. A dessertspoonful **thrice daily**. (*In erythema nodosum, with impaired vital forces.*)　　　　　　　BARTHOLOW.

2066—℞ Zinci acetatis . . . . gr. ij.
Aquæ rosæ . . . . f ℨj.
Unguenti aquæ rosæ . . . . ℥j.—M.

Ft. unguentum. (*In erythema and herpes.*)　　　NEUMANN.

2067—℞ Collodii . . . . f ℨj.
Morphinæ . . . . gr. vijj.—M.

Sig. Paint the affected surfaces. (*In herpes zoster.*) BOURDON.

2068—℞ Potassii chloratis . . . . ℨij.
Acidi hydrochlorici **diluti**,
Spiritus chloroformi,
Liquoris cinchonæ . . . . āā f ℨj.
Aquæ destillatæ . . . . q. s. ad f ℥vj.—M.

Sig. Two **tablespoonfuls** three times a day. (*In herpes zoster.*)
　　　　　　　CHARLES STURGES.

2069—℞ Ferri arseniatis . . . . gr. iij.
Extracti lupulinæ . . . . ℨj.
Pulveris althææ . . . . ℨss.
Syrupi simplicis . . . . q. s.

Misce et fiant pilulæ no. xlviij.
Sig. One pill daily. (*In herpetic **ulcers and cancerous diseases.***)
　　　　　　　BIETT.

2070—℞ Ulmi corticis . . . . ℨiss.
Aquæ bullientis . . . . Oj.—M.

Ft. decoctum.
Sig. Two to four fluidounces thrice **daily**. (*In ichthyosis.*)
　　　　　　　LETTSOM.

2071—℞ Pulveris camphoræ . . . . gr. x.
Unguenti zinci oxidi . ℨj.

Misce et fiat unguentum. (*In ichthyosis.*) ERASMUS WILSON.

2072—℞ Zinci sulphatis . . . . . . ℨj.
Cerati simplicis . . . . ℨj.—M.

Ft. unguentum. (*In ichthyosis.*) ERASMUS WILSON.

2072bis—℞ Sodii bicarbonatis gr. xv-ℨss.
Adipis . . . . ℨj.—M.

Ft. unguentum. (*In ichthyosis.*) DEVERGIE.

2073—℞ Potassii carbonatis . . . . ℨj.
Adipis . . . . ℥j.—M.

Ft. unguentum.
Sig. Smear over the eruption at night, and wash off in the
morning with the following :

2074—℞ Potassii carbonatis . . . . ℨss.
Aquæ . . . . Oj.—M.

Ft. lotio.
Sig. Use in the morning locally, as directed.   (*In herpes.*)
NELIGAN.

2075—℞ Aquæ coloniensis . . . . f℥ij.
Sig. Apply locally with a camel's-hair pencil. (*In herpes
labialis.*)
HARTSHORNE.

2076—℞ Magnesii carbonatis . . . . ℨss.
Spiritus ammoniæ aromatici . . . . . f℥ij.
Tincturæ rhei . . . . f℥iij.
Aquæ calcis . . . . f℥vss.—M.
Sig. One fluidounce twice daily. (*In acute herpes labialis.*)
BURGESS.

2077—℞ Hydrargyri chloridi mitis . . . . gr. x.
Adipis . . . . ℥j.—M. ·

Ft. unguentum.
Sig. Apply three times daily. (*In chronic herpes labialis.*)
NELIGAN.

2078—℞ Hydrargyri chloridi corrosivi . . . . . gr. iij.
Alcoholis . . . . q. s.
Solve et adde—
Extracti conii . . . . ℨj.
Misce et divide in pilulas no. xl.
Sig. Six pills to be taken in the day, and the quantity grad-
ually increased to nine or ten. (*In herpetic eruptions.*)
KOPP.

2079—℞ Ferri arseniatis . . . . gr. iv.
Ext. gentianæ,
Ext. glycyrrhizæ . . . . . . ãã q. s. ut ft. massa.
Ft. massa et in pilulas no. lx div.
Sig. One pill thrice daily. (*In herpes.*)
DUPARC.

2080—℞ Pulv. camphoræ.
Chloral. hydratis .   ãã ℨiv.—M.
Sig. Apply locally with a camel's-hair brush. (*In herpes labi-
alis and herpes præputialis.*)
JAMIESON.

2081—℞ Hydrargyri chloridi mitis . . . . ℨj.
Unguenti simplicis . . . . ℨj.—M.
Ft. unguentum.
Sig. Apply locally. (*In herpes.*)
PAREIRA.

2082—℞ Glycerini . . . .   ℨj.
Pulv. tragacanthæ comp.   ℨij.
Mellis . . . .   ℨij.
Liq. calcis saccharati   f℥ss.
Emulsionis amygdalæ   . . f℥viij.—M.
Sig. Apply **locally.** (*In herpes.   Also in burns, chapped hands,
etc.*)
TILBURY FOX.

2083—℞ Sodii boratis . . . . ℨss.
Morphinæ sulphatis . . . . gr. vj.
Aquæ rosæ . . . . f℥viij.—M.
Sig. Apply locally. (*In herpes.*)
MEIGS.

2084—℞ Aluminis . . . . ℨj.
Aquæ . . . . f℥j.—M.
Ft. lotio.
Sig. Wet a piece of **lint** with the solution, and apply to the
glans penis. (*In herpes præputialis.*)
WARING

2085—℞ Morphinæ acetatis . . . . gr. v.
Chloroformi . . . . ♏xl.
Unguenti simplicis . . . . ℨv.
Olei amygdalæ dulcis . . . . ♏cc.—M.
Sig. Apply two or three times daily. (*In herpes.   Also in pru-
ritus pudendi.*)
ELLEAUME.

2086—℞ Creasoti . . . . f 3ss.
Aquæ destillatæ . . . . Oj.—M.
Ft. lotio. (*In impetigo.*) DUNGLISON.

2087—℞ Acidi hydrocyanici **diluti** . . . . f 3ij.
Spiritus rectificati . . . . f 3ss.
Aquæ destillatæ . . . . f 3vij.—M.
Ft. lotio.
Sig. To be applied with lint covered with oiled silk. (*In impetigo, after removal of scabs.*) PLUMBE.

2088—℞ Tincturæ ferri chloridi . f 3ss.
Magnesii sulphatis . 3ij.
Tincturæ calumbæ f 3iss.
Infusi quassiæ . . . . f 3xvij.—M.
Sig. A wineglassful every morning. (*In impetigo.*) NELIGAN.

2089—℞ Hydrargyri protiodidi . . . . **gr. iv.**
Hydrargyri cum cretâ,
Sodii carbonatis . . . . āā **gr. xij.**
Pulveris myrrhæ . . . . **gr. vj.**
Mucilaginis acaciæ . . . . **q. s.**
Misce et fiant pilulæ no. xii.
Sig. One three times a day. (*In chronic impetigo.*) NELIGAN.

2089bis—℞ Syr. hypophosphitum comp. f 3vj.
Sig. A teaspoonful thrice daily, in water. (*In impetigo of the anæmic.*) JAMIESON.

2090—℞ Plumbi acetatis . . . . **gr. vij.**
Acidi hydrocyanici diluti . . . . . . f 3ij.
Spiritus rectificati . . . . f 3ss.
Aquæ destillatæ . . . . f 3viiss.—M.
Ft. lotio.
Sig. Poison. (*In impetigo.*) PARIS.

2091—℞ Sodii carbonatis . 3ij.
Syrupi violæ . . . . . . f 3xij.—M.
Sig. A tablespoonful night and morning. (*Apply at the same time a poultice containing one drachm of sulphur. In impetigo.*) BIETT.

2092—℞ Hydrargyri chloridi corrosivi . . . . . **gr. iss.**
Olei theobromæ,
Vaselini . . . . āā **gr. ccxxv.**
Misce et ft. unguentum.
Sig. Apply in a thin layer over the eruption. (*In impetigo of the scalp.*) JORISSENNE.

2093—℞ Hydrargyri ammoniati gr. v.
Adipis . . 3j.—M.
Sig. Apply to the surface after the scabs have been removed by poulticing or warm fomentations. (*In impetigo contagiosa.*) TILBURY FOX.

2094—℞ Hydrargyri sulphureti **rubri** . . . . . **gr. xxiss.**
Plumbi oxidi rubri . . . . **gr. xxxviiss.**
Emplastri diachyli . . . . ad 3j.—M.
Ft. emplastrum.
Sig. "Vidal's Emplâtre Rouge." Remove the crusts by poulticing: wash with dilute spirit of camphor, and cover all the points involved with the paste, renewing daily, after washing with dilute spirit of camphor. A sulphur-bath every two days is desirable; also the following:

2095—℞ Syr. ferri iodidi f 3j.
Sig. Ten to fifteen drops thrice daily, with cod-liver oil and other supporting treatment. (*In impetigo.*)
VIDAL ET THURIES.

2096—℞ Glyceriti acidi tannici . . . . . . 3ij.
Sig. Apply with a hair-pencil during the day. Poultice at night to remove the crusts. (*In impetigo.*) RINGER.

2097—℞ Acidi borΛcici . . . . ℨj.
Aquæ . . . . f℥x.—M.

Ft. lotio.
Sig. Wet a compress, and apply to the face as a mask. Place three or four of these compresses the one on the other, and cover with a sheet of thin rubber cloth. Renew this dressing every hour. In forty-eight hours cover the secreting surfaces with adhesive plaster. (*In impetigo of the face.*) E. BESNIER.

2098—℞ Olei terebinthinæ . . . . ℥v.

Sig. Cut the hair close, and rub the scalp well with the lotion. Let it remain about five minutes, and then wash it off with warm water and carbolic acid soap, and then with clean warm water. Then apply the following:

2099—℞ Iodi . . . . ℈ij.
Olei terebinthinæ . . . . f℥v.—M.

Sig. Apply once or twice daily. (*In impetigo.*) SAERES.

2100—℞ Acidi salicylici . . . . gr. xv.
Pulv. zinci oxidi,
Pulv. amyli . . . . āā ℨij.
Lanolini . . . . ℥vj gr. xv.

Misce et fiat unguentum.
Sig. Apply locally. (*In impetigo.*) LIEBREICH.

2101—℞ Acidi carbolici . . . . gr. x.
Glycerini,
Aquæ rosæ . . . . āā f℥j.—M.

Ft. lotio. (*In impetigo.*) HEADLAND.

2102—℞ Sulphuris . . . . gr. xxv-l.
Unguenti simplicis . . . . ℨj.—M.

Ft. unguentum.
Sig. Rub in nightly. (*In ichthyosis or zeroderma.*) UNNA.

2103—℞ Resorcin. . . . . gr. xv.
Adipis . . . . ℨj.—M.

Ft. unguentum.
Sig. Rub in locally in mild cases. In more severe cases, increase the strength of the ointment from two to six times that given above. (*In ichthyosis.*) ANDEER.

2104—℞ Zinci sulphatis . . . . ℨj.
Adipis . . . . ℨj.—M.

Sig. Use locally. (*In ichthyosis.*) ERASMUS WILSON.

2105—℞ Acidi salicylici . . . . ℨij.
Collodii flexilis . . . . ℨj.—M.

Sig. Use locally with a brush. (*In spinous formations in ichthyosis hystrix.*) LIVEING.

2106—℞ Sodii bicarbonatis . . . . ℨij-iij.
Aquæ . . . . Oj.—M.

Ft. lotio.
Sig. Use two or three times daily as a wash. (*In ichthyosis or zeroderma.*) DEVERGIE.

2107—℞ Unguenti zinci oxidi . . . . ℨj.

Sig. Apply locally. (*In indolent impetigo.*) RINGER.

2108—℞ Ammonii sulpho-ichthyolati . . . . . gr. ii.
Coumarini . . . . gr. viij-xv.
Unguenti petrolei . . . . ℨv.—M.

Ft. unguentum.
Sig. Apply with the finger after bathing and drying the child. (*In intertrigo.*) LORENS.

2109—℞ Bismuthi subnitratis . . . . ℨj.

Detur in scatula.
Sig. Dust over the inflamed part. (*In intertrigo.*) BARTHOLOW.

2110—℞ Acidi tannici . . . . ℨss.
Glycerini . . . . f℥ij.—M.

Sig. Apply locally. (*In intertrigo.*) BARTHOLOW.

2111—℞ Linimenti aquæ calcis . . . . f℥vj.
Sig. Use locally. (*In intertrigo.*)   TILBURY FOX.

2112—℞ Pulv. amyli . . . . ℥iv.
     Zinci oxidi . . . . ℥j.
     Zinci carbonatis . . . . ℥ss.—M.
Sig. Use as a dusting-powder. (*In intertrigo.*) TILBURY FOX.

2113—℞ Hydrargyri chloridi mitis . . . . ℨj–ij.
     Adipis . . . . ℥j.—M.
Ft. unguentum. (*In intertrigo, pruritus vulvæ et ani, eczema of
the scrotum, etc.*)   TOURNIE.

2113*bis*—℞ Acidi boracici . . . . ℨiss.
     Vaselini . . . . ℥j.—M.
Ft. unguentum.
Sig. Apply locally, after washing and drying the parts. (*In
intertrigo.*)   WARING.

2114—℞ Calcii sulpho-carbolatis . . . . ℨj.
     Liquoris potassii arsenitis . . . . . . ℳxviij.
     Tincturæ aurantii . . . . f℥vj.
     Aquæ destillatæ . . . . q. s. ad f℥vj.—M.
Sig. A sixth part before breakfast and dinner. (*In itching
skin-diseases.*)   DONELI.

2115—℞ Plumbi acetatis . . . . gr. xvj.
     Acidi hydrocyanici diluti . . . . f℥iss.
     Spiritus rectificati . . . . f℥ij.
     Aquæ destillatæ . . . . f℥viiss.—M.
Ft. lotio. (*To allay itching in cutaneous diseases.*)
     A. T. THOMPSON.

2116—℞ Plumbi carbonatis . . . . ℥ij.
     Calcis præparatæ . . . . ℥ss.
     Unguenti aquæ rosæ . . . . ℥ij.—M.
Ft. unguentum. (*In popular and itching eruptions.*) BURGESS.

2117—℞ Potassii cyanidi . . . . gr. xij.
     Misturæ amygdalæ . . . . f℥vj.—M.
Ft. lotio. (*In itching eruptions.*)   LOUIS.

2118—℞ Acidi arseniosi . . . . gr. x–xxx.
     Adipis . . . . ℥j.—M.
Ft. unguentum.
Sig. Over a patch of skin three or four inches square, rub
the ointment in well once daily for a fortnight. Then treat
a fresh portion. (*In lepra.*)   TILBURY FOX.

2119—℞ Olei anacardii [cashew-nut] . . . . . f℥iv.
Sig. Soap-and-water baths are used twice daily, followed by
frictions over the whole body with cocoanut oil or olive oil.
After the oil has remained on for three or four hours, the
body is thoroughly cleansed by a soap-and-water bath.
Then the oil of cashew-nut is applied on a sponge to a
small portion of the skin, as large as the hand. A week or
ten days later another application of cashew-nut oil may
be made. If any herpetic or other eruption is present, then
use the following:

2120—℞ Spts. vini rectificati . . . . f℥j.
     Iodi . . . . q. s. ad ft. sat. sol.
Dein adde—
     Liq. sodæ caust. . . . . ad excess.
Dein adde—
     Olei olivæ. . . . . f℥xxxiv.—M.
Ft. linimentum.
Sig. Use locally on herpetic or other eruptions that occur.
Shake well before using. If there be a squamous or scurfy
condition of the skin, then use the following:

2121—℞ Vitell. ovi . . . . no. ij.
     Balsami copaibæ . . . . f℥vss.—M.
Ft. emulsio et adde—
     Olei olivæ. . . . . Oj.—M.
Ft. linimentum.
Sig. To be used instead of the oil baths, when the skin is
scurfy. For the feet, hot baths (100° F.) of cocoanut oil are
used twice daily. (*In lepra.*)   BEAUPERTHUY.

2122—℞ Hydrargyri chloridi corrosivi . . . . . gr. ij–iiss.
Iufusi calumbæ . . . . f℥v.—M.

Sig. A teaspoonful twice daily. Fresh meat and fresh vegetable diet, with good hygienic surroundings, are essential to success. (*In lepra.*) BEAUPERTHUY.

2123—℞ Quininæ diarsenitis . . . . gr. iv.
Misæ panis . . . . q. s.

Fiant pilulæ no. xii.
Sig. Two, three, or four per day. (*In lepra.*) KINGDON.

2124—℞ Acidi arsenicei gr. j.
Piperis . . . . gr. xij.
Tere simul in pulverem subtilissimum, et adde—
Pulveris acaciæ . . . . gr. ij.
Aquæ destillatæ . . . . q. s.

Misce et fiant pilulæ no. xvi.
Sig. One morning and night. (*In tuberculous lepra.*)
Paris Codex.

2125—℞ Unguenti hydrargyri nitratis . . . ℨj.
Sig. Use twice **daily**; dilute if necessary. (*In lepra.*)
WARING.

2126—℞ Unguenti picis liquidæ . . . . ℨj.
Sig. Apply to affected parts. (*In lepra.*) McCALL ANDERSON.

2127—℞ Sodii carbonatis . . . . ℨss–j.
Aquæ . . . . f℥vj.—M.
Sig. A dessertspoonful, well diluted, twice daily. (*In lepra where mercurials are contra-indicated.*) BEAUPERTHUY.

2128—℞ Iodoformi . . . . ℨj.
Unguenti petrolei . . . . ℨj.—M.

Sig. Apply to the affected parts. (*In lepra.*) GLOVER.

2129—℞ Arsenici iodidi . . . . gr. j.
Extracti conii . . . . ℨij.

Fiat massa et divide in pilulas no. xvi.
Sig. One pill night and morning. (*In lepra, impetigo, cancer.*)
ELLIS.

2130—℞ Acidi carbolici . . . . gr. ij.
Menthol . . . . gr. iij.
Talci . . . . ℨj.—M.

Sig. Use as a dusting-powder. (*In acute eczema.*) J. C. WILSON.

2131—℞ Menthol . gr. xxxvij.
Olei olivæ ℨij–iij.
Lanolini . . . . . ℨss.—M.

Sig. Apply frequently. (*In pruritus.*) LASSAR.

2132—℞ Menthol . . . . gr. xxij–xxxvij.
Spts. vini rectificati . . . . ℨiss.—M.

Sig. Apply at intervals as required. (*In pruritus.*) LASSAR.

2133—℞ Liquoris potassæ . . . . . fℨj.
Acidi hydrocyanici diluti . fℨj.
Misturæ amygdalæ f℥viij.

Misce et fiat lotio. (*In lichen.*) BURGESS.

2134—℞ Cretæ præparatæ . . . . ℨvj.
Sulphuris sublimati,
Olei cadini . . . . ââ ℨix.
Saponis nigris,
Adipis . . . . ââ ℨxxv.

[Melt the lard at a gentle heat. Then add the black soap and other ingredients, stirring until cold.]
Sig. Apply locally. (*In lichen.*) HEBRA.

2135—℞ Sodii arseniatis . . . . gr. iss.
Aquæ destillatæ . . . . f℥xxv.—M.

Sig. A teaspoonful every morning at meal-time. At the end of a week increase to two teaspoonfuls. If the eruption is dry, add tonics, as cod-liver oil and phosphate of lime. (*In lichen.*) E. VIDAL.

2136—℞ Sodii carbonatis . . . . ℈j.
    Aquæ rosæ . . . . f℥vj.
    Glycerini . . . . f℥ij.—M.
Ft. lotio.
Sig. Apply to the eruption. (*In infantile lichen or strophulus.*)
                                    TILBURY FOX.

2137—℞ Glyceriti amyli . . . . ℥v.
    Pulv. acidi tartarici . . . . gr. xv.—M.
Sig. Apply locally. (*In chronic lichen simplex.*)   E. VIDAL.

2138—℞ Bismuthi subnitratis . . . . ℈ij.
    Pulv. zinci oxidi . . . . ℈ij.
    Tinct. digitalis . . . . f℈ss.
    Aquæ . . . . q. s. ad f℥vj.—M.
Ft. lotio.
Sig. To be used as a lotion, after an alkaline bath, as bicarbonate of sodium with bran. (*In lichen planus.*)
                                   TILBURY FOX.

2139—℞ Olei cadini . . . . ℈ij.
    Glyceriti amyli . . . . ℥iss.—M.
Sig. Apply locally. Gradually increase the oil of cade to equal portions. (*In chronic lichen of the genitals.*) E. VIDAL.

2140—℞ Potassii cyanidi . . . . gr. iv.
    Chloroformi . . . . ℳviij.
    Glycerini . . . . ℥j.
    Cerati simplicis . . . . ℥vj.—M.
Ft. unguentum.
Sig. Apply locally. (*In lichen agrius. Also in pruritus.*)
                                   NELIGAN.

2141—℞ Acidi salicylici . . . . gr. x.
    Vaselini . . . . ℥ss.
    Zinci oxidi.
    Pulv. amyli . . . . āā ℥ij.—M.
Ft. pasta.
Sig. Apply locally. (*In lichen marginatus.*)   LASSAR.

2142—℞ Hydrarg. chloridi corrosivi . . . . . . gr. viiss.
    Cretæ præparatæ . . . . ℈iss.
    Acidi carbolici.
    Olei olivæ . . . . āā ℥v.
    Ungt. zinci oxidi . . . . ℥xv ℥v.—M.
Ft. unguentum.
Sig. Rub diligently into the affected skin. (*In lichen planus.*)
                                    UNNA.

2143—℞ Ferri arseniatis . . . . gr. iij.
    Pulveris glycyrrhizæ . . . . ℈ss.
    Syrupi simplicis . . . . q. s.
Misce bene, et fiant pilulæ no. xlviii.
Sig. One to three pills daily. (*In lichen, elephantiasis, lepra, lupus, herpetic and squamous affections.*) BIETT AND DUPARC.

2144—℞ Potassii cyanidi . . . . gr. xij.
    Olei amygdalæ . . . . f℥ij.
    Unguenti ceræ albæ . . . . ℥ij.—M.
Ft. unguentum. (*In lichen.*)   BURGESS.

2145—℞ Sodii biboratis . . . . ℥ss.
    Acidi hydrocyanici diluti . . . . . . f℥ij.
    Aquæ rosæ . . . . f℥viij.—M.
Ft. lotio. (*In lichen agrius.*)   NELIGAN.

2146—℞ Rosæ petalæ . . . . ℈j.
    Aquæ ferventis . . . . f℥viij.
    Acidi nitrici diluti . . . . f℥iiss.—M.
Macera, cola, et fiat lotio. (*In lichen.*)   HOOPER.

2147—℞ Liquoris ammonii acetatis . . . . . . f℥ij.
    Spiritus rectificati . . . . f℥v.
    Aquæ rosæ . . . . f℥iv.—M.
Ft. lotio. (*In lichen.*)   BURGESS.

2148—℞ Chloroformi . . . . ℳxx.
    Olei olivæ . . . . f℥j.—M.
Sig. After a tepid bath, and well dried. (*In lichen.*)
                                    NELIGAN.

2149—℞ Liquoris plumbi subacetatis . . . . . . f℥j-ij.
  Infusi althææ . . . . f℥xvj.—M.
Ft. lotio. (*In lichen.*)   BURGESS.

2150—℞ Pulv. lycopodii . . . . . . ℈ss.
 Sig.—Use as a dusting-powder after the bullæ are cut. Then
 use zinc ointment or an astringent solution; and then use
 the following :

2151—℞ Argenti nitratis .   gr. iij-iv.
  Adipis .   ℥j.—M.
 Ft. unguentum.
 Sig. Apply locally (*In chronic ulceration following pemphigus.*)
             TILBURY FOX.

2152—℞ Linimenti **calcis** . . . . ℥j.
 Sig. Apply after the bullæ have burst or have been punctured.
 The parts should be fixed, and no motion allowed. (*In
 pemphigus.*)   CHAMBARD.

2153—℞ Argenti nitratis . . . . gr. ij.
  Aquæ destillatæ . . . . f℥j.
 Misce et fiat solutio. (*In pemphigus after the bullæ have burst.*)
           ERASMUS WILSON.

2154—℞ Unguenti hydrargyri nitratis . . . . . ℥ij.
  Unguenti simplicis . . . . ℥vj.—M.
 Sig. Use twice daily. (*In pemphigus.*)   WARING.

2155—℞ Liquoris potassii arsenitis   . . . . f℥ij.
  Aquæ destillatæ . . . . . q. s. ad f℥iij.—M.
 Sig. A teaspoonful **after each** meal. (*In the more chronic form
 of pemphigus.*)   McCALL ANDERSON.

2156—℞ Sulphuris loti . . . . ℥j.
  Vaselini . . . . ℥j.—M.
 Ft. unguentum.
 Sig. Apply to the scalp every morning. Anoint it with sweet
 almond oil every evening. (*In pityriasis.*)   JACKSON.

2157—℞ Sodii sulphureti.
  Sodii carbonatis . . . . āā ℥ij.
  Unguenti simplicis . . . . ℥iss.—M.
 Ft. unguentum. (*In pityriasis.*)   BAREGES.

2158—℞ Tinct. ferri chloridi . . .   gtt. xx.
  Liq. sodii arseniatis   . .   gtt. v.
  Syrupi simplicis,
  Aquæ . . . . āā q. s. ad f℥j.—M.
 Sig. To be taken thrice daily. (*In pityriasis.*)   DA COSTA.

2159—℞ Vitell. ovi . . . . no. iij.
  Liq. calcis . . . . Oj.
 Ft. emulsio, dein adde—
  Spts. vini rectificati . . . . f℥ss.—M.
 Sig. Use as a shampoo. (*In pityriasis.*)   JACKSON.

2160—℞ Pilulæ hydrargyri . . . . gr. ix.
  Sodii carbonatis . . . . gr. vj.
  Extracti taraxaci . . . . gr. xij.
  Extracti hyoscyami . . . . gr. iij.
 Misce et fiant pilulæ no. vi.
 Sig. One pill two or three **times a** day, half an hour before
 meals. (*In pityriasis.*)   NELIGAN.

2161—℞ Potassii sulphureti . . . . ℥j.
  Aquæ destillatæ . . . . f℥iij.—M.
 Ft. lotio.
 Sig. Use once daily. (*In pityriasis capitis.*)   WINZAR.

2162—℞ Sodii hyposulphitis   ℈ss.
  Aquæ destillatæ .   f℥j.—M.
 Ft. lotio. (*In pityriasis versicolor.*)   HARLEY.

2163—℞ Liquoris potassii arsenitis . . . . ꭑiv.
　　Decocti cinchonæ . . . . f3x.
　　Syrupi aurantii corticis . . . . f3ij.
　　Tincturæ opii . . . . ꭑv.—M.

Ft. haustus.
Sig. Twice daily after meals. (*In chronic pityriasis.*) BURGESS.

2164—℞ Hydrargyri sulphatis flavæ . . . . . . gr. xlv.
　　Vaselini puri . . . . 3xv.
　　Ess. bergamii vel limonis . . . . . . gtt. xx.—M.

Sig. Keep in a porcelain jar. Anoint the scalp every evening.
Wash with tepid water every morning. (*In pityriasis capitis.*)
　　　　　　　　　　　　　　　　　　　　P. VIGIER.

2165—℞ Sulphuris loti . . . . gr. vliss.
　　Tinct. benzoini . . . . ꭑxlv.
　　Medullæ ossium bovinum [beef-mar-
　　　row] . . . . 3vliss.
　　Olei amygdalæ dulcis . . . . f3iiss.—M.

Ft. unguentum.
Sig. Use daily or semi-weekly, according to the severity of
the case. Wash off the next morning. (*In pityriasis capitis.*)
　　　　　　　　　　　　　　　　　　　　FOURNIER.

2166—℞ Liquoris iodi compositi,
　　Liquoris potassii arsenitis . . . . . āā f3ij.—M.

Sig. Ten drops three times daily. (*In pityriasis, psoriasis, and
lepra.*)
　　　　　　　　　　　　　　　　　　　　ELLIS.

2167—℞ Liq. arsenici et hydrargyri iodidi . . . gtt. lxxx.
　　Syrupi zingiberis . . . . f3ss.
　　Aquæ destillatæ . . . . f3viij.—M.

Sig. One fluidounce every third hour. (*In pityriasis.*)
　　　　　　　　　　　　　　　　　　　　OSBREY.

2168—℞ Acidi carbolici . . . . 3ij.
　　Glycerini . . . . f3ss.
　　Aquæ destillatæ . . . . f3viij.—M.

Ft. lotio.
Sig. Twice daily. (*In pityriasis.*) J. C. WILSON.

2169—℞ Amygdalarum amararum . . . . . . no. xxx.
　　Aquæ destillatæ . . . . f3viij.—M.

Ft. emulsio. (*A lotion for prickly heat.*) WARING.

2170—℞ Acidi hydrocyanici diluti . . . . . . ꭑx-xi.
　　Glycerini . . . . f3j.—M.

Ft. lotio. (*In prickly heat.*) WARING.

2171—℞ Zinci carbonatis præcip. . . . . . . 3iv.
　　Zinci oxidi . . . . 3ij.
　　Glycerini . . . . f3ij.
　　Aquæ rosæ . . . . f3viij.—M.

Ft. lotio.
Sig. Apply locally. (*In prickly heat. Also in eczema, when
the surface is red and tender.*) TILBURY FOX.

2172—℞ Acidi hydrocyanici diluti . . . . . . f3j.
　　Liq. potassæ . . . . f3ij.
　　Mist. amygdalæ . . . . f3viij.—M.

Ft. lotio.
Sig. Use locally. (*In prickly heat [lichen tropicus].*) BURGESS.

2173—℞ Acidi hydrocyanici diluti . . . . . . f3iss.
　　Aquæ rosæ . . . . f3viiss.—M.

Ft. lotio.
Sig. Use locally. (*In prickly heat.*) A. T. THOMPSON.

2174—℞ Sodii arseniatis . . . . gr. ss.
　　Ext. gentianæ . . . . gr. xlv.—M.

Ft. massa et in pil. no. xxx div.
Sig. Two or three pills after each meal. Also the following:

2175—℞ Acidi pyrogallici　　　　　　　3iiss-iv.
　　Adipis　　　　　　　　　　　　3ij.—M.

Ft. unguentum.
Sig. To be rubbed in twice daily. Also, a thorough cleansing
with soap every two days. (*In psoriasis.*) GUIBOUT.

2176—℞ Chrysarobini . . . . gr. xx–xl.
    Lanolini,
    Vaselini . . . . āā 3ss.—M.
  Sig. Apply every second day. (*In psoriasis.*)   HEBRA.

2177—℞ Tincturæ cantharidis,
    Liquoris potassii arsenitis . . . . . āā f3ss.—M.
  Sig. Ten minims twice daily, gradually increasing to fifteen,
  carefully watching effects. (*In psoriasis.*)   BENNETT.

2178—℞ Hydrargyri biniodidi . . . . gr. j.
    Extracti sarsaparillæ
    Extracti gentianæ . . . . āā ⊝j.
  Misce et divide in pilulas no. x.
  Sig. One pill three times a day. (*In psoriasis.*)   BURGESS.

2179—℞ Hydroxylamine . . . . 1 part.
    Glycerin,
    Alcohol . . . . of each 500 parts.
  Mix.
  Sig. Apply with a camel's-hair pencil to each spot. (*In
  psoriasis.*)   HEBRA.

2180—℞ Chrysarobin . . . . gr. xx.
    Collodioi . . . . f3j.
  Mix.
  Sig. Apply to each spot. (*In psoriasis.*)   HEBRA.

2181—℞ Acidi salicylici . . . . 3ss.
    Acidi pyrogallici . . . . 3iss–ij.
    Collodii . . . . f3ij.—M.
  Ft. collodium.
  Sig. Preserve in a dark-colored bottle. After a warm bath
  to loosen the scales, the collodion is painted on the patches
  and a half-inch beyond the border. Reapply every day,
  preceding the application by a warm bath. If the eruption
  is general, treat successively the different parts. (*In
  psoriasis.*)   ELLIOTT.

2182—℞ Ungt. hydrargyri nitratis . . . . 3j–ij.
    Zinci oxidi . . . . 3ij.
    Liq. plumbi subacetatis . . . . f3ss.
    Acidi carbolici . . . . gtt. ij.
    Olei olivæ . . . . f3j–iss.—M.
  Ft. unguentum.
  Sig. Apply after **removing the scales.** (*In psoriasis.*)
    TILBURY FOX.

2183—℞ Acidi salicylici . . . . 3iss.
    Olei cadini,
    Glyceriti amyli āā 3xxv.
    Ess. caryophylli 3iss.—M.
  Ft. glyceritum.
  Sig. The scales are first removed with hot water and tar soap,
  and then a weak alkaline bath is given. The glyceröle is
  then rubbed in. If too much irritation follow, diminish
  the salicylic acid or the oil of cade. (*In psoriasis.*)
    L. BROCQ.

2184—℞ Acidi pyrogallici,
    Acidi chrysophanici . . . . āā gr. lxxv.
    Ætheris,
    Alcoholis . . . . āā q. s. ad ft. sol.
    Collodii . . . . f3xxv.—M.
  Ft. collodium.
  Sig. A prolonged (three hours') hot bath, twice weekly. After
  the bath, rub the surface well to detach the scales; then
  cover with the collodion, which should remain on until
  the next bath, if possible. Observe strict diet, and use internally the following:

2185—℞ Liquoris potassii arsenitis . .   f3ss.
  Sig. Three to ten drops, well diluted, thrice daily after meals.
  (*In psoriasis circinatus.*)   BESNIER.

2186—℞ Olei cadini,
    Ungt. hydrargyri . . . . āā 3ij.
    Vaselini . . . . 3j.—M.
  Ft. unguentum.
  Sig. Apply locally. (*In psoriasis palmaris et plantaris syphi-
  litica.*)   MAURIAC.

2187—℞ Hydrargyri chloridi corrosivi,
Ammonii muriatis . . . . ãã gr. xv.—M.

Ft. pulv. no. j.
Sig. Dissolve the powder in two quarts of tepid water, and
bathe the parts for fifteen minutes, morning and evening.
(*In psoriasis palmaris et plantaris syphilitica.*)
GILLES DE LA TOURETTE.

2188—℞ Hydrargyri chloridi corrosivi . . . . . ʒj.(!)
Alcoholis . . . . fʒj.—M.

Fiat lotio.
Sig. Paint the affected spot. (*In psoriasis.*) NIEMEYER.

2189—℞ Tincturæ guaiaci ammoniatæ fʒj.
Tincturæ serpentariæ fʒss.
Mucilaginis acaciæ ℥xx.
Decocti mezerei fʒviss.
Infusi dulcamaræ fʒj.—M.

Fiat haustus.
Sig. Thrice daily. (*In psoriasis guttata.*) NELIGAN.

2190—℞ Liquoris potassii arsenitis . . . . fʒss.
Liquoris potassæ . . . . fʒj
Spiritus ætheris nitrosi . . . . fʒij.
Infusi gentianæ compositi . . . . . . fʒvij.—M.

Sig. Two tablespoonfuls three times a day. (*In psoriasis.*)
S. WRIGHT.

2191—℞ Unguenti picis liquidæ,
Unguenti sulphuris . . . . ãã ʒj.—M.
(*In psoriasis.*) Guy's Hospital.

2192—℞ Liquoris potassii arsenitis . . . . . . ℥v.
Tincturæ ferri chloridi . . . . . . ℥xx.
Infusi quassiæ . . . . fʒj.

Misce et fiat haustus.
Sig. Three times a day. (*In psoriasis inveterata.*) GUY.

2193—℞ Cupri oleatis . . . . ʒss.
Sig. Apply twice daily. (*In ringworm.*) F. LE SIEURE WEIR.

2194—℞ Sodii biboratis . . . . ʒj.
Aceti destillatæ . . . . fʒij.—M.
Fiat lotio. (*In ringworm of the scalp.*) ABERCROMBIE.

2195—℞ Hydrargyri protiodidi . . . . gr. xij-xx.
Unguenti simplicis . . . . ʒj.—M.
(*In rupia.*) BIETT.

2196—℞ Unguenti hydrargyri oxidi rubri . . . ʒj.
(*In rupia, frambœsia, etc.*) WARING.

2197—℞ Hydrargyri chloridi corrosivi . . . . . gr. iv.
Acidi nitrici diluti,
Acidi hydrocyanici diluti . . . . . ãã fʒj.
Glycerini . . . . fʒij.
Aquæ . . . . fʒviij.—M.

Ft. lotio.
Sig. Apply locally. (*In rupia. Also in pityriasis, chloasma,*
etc.)

2198—℞ Hydrargyri oxidi rubri,
Hydrargyri ammoniati . . . . . ãã gr. vj.
Adipis . . . . ʒj.—M.
Ft. unguentum.
Sig. Apply locally. (*In rupia.*) STARTIN.

2199—℞ Potassii bitartratis . . . . ʒj.
Reducetur in pulverem subtilissimum, et detur in scatula.
Sig. Dust over ulcer. (*In rupia.*) RAYER.

2200—℞ Hydrargyri iodidi rubri . . . . gr. j-ij.
Ext. gentianæ . . . . ɔiij.—M.

Ft. massa et in pil. no. xij div.
Sig. One pill twice daily. (*In rupia and other syphilodermata.*)
TILBURY FOX.

2201—℞ Hydrargyri cyanidi . . . . **gr. vj.**
Cerati simplicis . . . . **ʒj.—M.**

Ft. unguentum.
Sig. Use locally. (*In rupia when the crusts become loosened.
Also in syphilitic ulcers.*)   TILBURY FOX.

2202—℞ Hydrargyri iodidi rubri . . . . gr. iij.
Potassii iodidi . . . . ʒj-ij.
Alcoholis . . . . f ʒij.
Syr. zingiberis . . . . f ʒiv.
Aquæ . . . . ad f ʒiss.—M.

Sig. Thirty drops **thrice daily.** (*In rupia and other syphilitic
eruptions.*)   PUCHE.

2203—℞ Hydrargyri chloridi corrosivi . 　ʒj.
Potassii iodidi . . 　ʒvj.
Tinct. iodi comp. 　. . . f ʒij.
Aquæ . . 　. . . ad f ʒxv).—M.

Sig. One-half to one teaspoonful thrice daily. (*In rupia and
other syphilodermata.*)   STARTIN.

2204—℞ Hydrargyri bicyanidi . . . . **gr. j.**
Quinine . . . . ʒj.
Ext. gentianæ . . . . **ʒss.—M.**

Ft. massa et in pil. no. xx **div.**
Sig. One pill twice daily. (*In ordinary syphilitic eruptions.*)
TILBURY FOX.

2205—℞ **Sulphuris loti** . . . . gr. cexxv.
Olei ricini . . . . f ʒxiiss.
Olei theobromæ . . . . ʒij.
Balsami peruviani . . . . ʒss.—M.

Ft. unguentum.
Sig. Apply night **and morning.** (*In dry seborrhœa of the scalp.*)
VIDAL.

2206—℞ Olei amygdalæ dulcis . . . . ♏j.
Acidi carbolici . . . . gr. v.
Alcoholis . . . . **q. s. ad** f ʒj.
Olei bergamii . . . . q. s.—M.

Ft. unguentum.
Sig. Soak the scalp at night with sweet oil, and shampoo it
in the morning with the officinal tincture of green soap, to
remove the crusts. Shampoo twice a week, and apply the
ointment every night. (*In dry seborrhœa of the scalp.*)
HYDE.

2207—℞ Sulphuris loti . . . 　ʒij.
Balsami peruviani . . . . 　ʒss.
Vaselini . 　. . 　ʒx.—M.

Ft. unguentum.
Sig. Bathe the part with soap and hot water, dry, and apply
the ointment lightly with the finger. (*In seborrhœa.*)
G. H. FOX.

2208—℞ Zinci sulphatis,
Potassii sulphureti . . . . āā **gr. xxx.**
Alcoholis . . . . ♏c.
Aquæ rosæ . . . . **q. s. ad** f ʒij.—M.

Ft. lotio.
Sig. Wet a soft linen rag with ether, rub the nose with it
vigorously at night, and then apply the lotion. (*In obstinate
seborrhœa of the nose.*)   G. H. FOX.

2209—℞ Potassii carbonatis . . . . ʒij.
Sodii chloridi . . . . ʒij.
Aquæ aurantii flor. . . . . f ʒij.
Aquæ rosæ . . . . f ʒviij.—M.

Ft. lotio.
Sig. Face-wash. (*In tan and freckles.*)   BARTHOLOW.

2210—℞ Hydrargyri chloridi corrosivi . . . . . gr. j.
Zinci oxidi . . . . ʒij.
Zinci carbonatis . . . . ʒss.
Glycerini . . . . f ʒij.
Aquæ rosæ . . . . f ʒviij.—M.

Ft. lotio.
Sig. Apply with a sponge. (*In freckles and sunburn.*)
TILBURY **FOX.**

2211—℞ Liq. potassæ . . . . 3j.
 Aquæ rosæ . . . . f3ij.—M.
Ft. lotio.
Sig. Face-wash. (*In tan and freckles.*)   TODD.

2212—℞ Plumbi acetatis . . . . gr. xv.
 Acidi hydrocyanici diluti . . . . ℳxx.
 Alcoholis . . . . f3ss.
 Aquæ . . . . q. s. ad f3vj.—M.
Ft. lotio.
Sig. Apply with a sponge. (*In freckles and sunburn.*)
      TILBURY FOX.

2213—℞ Lactis recentis . . . . f3xliss.
 Glycerini . . . . f3viiss.
 Acidi hydrochlorici . . . . ℳlxxv.
 Ammonii muriatis . . . . 3j.—M.
Ft. lotio.
Sig. Apply morning and evening with a camel's-hair brush.
 (*In tan and freckles.*)   MONIN.

2214—℞ Unguenti hydrargyri nitratis . . . . . 3ss.
 Unguenti picis liquidæ . . . . 3j.—M.
 (*In tinea capitis.*)   ELLIS.

2215—℞ Olei juniperi . . . . f3iss.
 Olei anisi . . . . ℳvj.
 Axungiæ . . . . 3ij.
Misce bene ut fiat unguentum. (*In tinea capitis.*)   SULLY.

2216—℞ Sodii bicarbonatis . . . . 3ij.
 Acidi hydrocyanici diluti . . . . f3ss.
 Lactis vaccæ . . . . f3viij.
Misce et fiat lotio. (*In milk crust.*)   A. T. THOMPSON.

2217—℞ Pulveris carbonis . . . . 3iij.
 Adipis . . . . 3j.—M.
Fiat unguentum. (*In tinea capitis.*)   ALIBERT.

2218—℞ Sodii hyposulphitis . . . . 3iij.
 Acidi sulphurosi diluti . . . . f3ss.
 Aquæ . . . . q. s. ad Oj.—M.
Ft. lotio.
Sig. Apply thoroughly to the scalp, to loosen the crusts. (*In
 tinea favosa.*)   STARTIN.

2219—℞ Acidi sulphurosi . . . . f3ij.
 Aquæ destillatæ . . . . f3viij.
Sig. Apply constantly. (*In tinea favosa.*)   W. JENNER.

2220—℞ Iodi . . . . . . gr. x.
 Potassii iodidi . . gr. xv.
 Tinct. iodi comp. . f3j.—M.
Sig. Apply to the scalp after the crusts have been removed
 by soaking in oil or poulticing. (*In tinea favosa.*)
      TILBURY FOX.

2221—℞ Sodii hyposulphitis . . . . 3j.
 Aquæ destillatæ . . . . f3xij.
Misce et fiat lotio. (*In tinea favosa.*)   TILBURY FOX.

2222—℞ Sulphuris loti . . . . f3j.
 Olei cadini,
 Hydrarg. chloridi corrosivi . . . . āā gr. v.—M.
Sig. Apply four times daily, on the hairy portion of the skin
 and scalp. (*In tinea favosa.*)   BAZIN.

2223—℞ Sulphuris iodidi . . . . 3j.
 Unguenti simplicis . . . . 3iss.
Ft. unguentum. (*In tinea favosa.*)   DONAVAN.

2224—℞ Acidi salicylici,
 Acidi chrysophanici . . . . . . āā 3ij gr. viiss.
 Cretæ præparatæ . . . . 3ij gr. xlv.
 Vaselini . . . . 3xviiss.—M.
Ft. unguentum.
Sig. Remove the crusts, epilate the hairs, and rub in the oint-
 ment for fifteen minutes at night. (*In tinea favosa.*) MONOE.

2225—℞ Hydrargyri chloridi corrosivi . . . . . **gr. x.**
    Aquæ destillate , ... f ℥j.

Solve.
Sig. Apply with **a camel's-hair** brush, after epilation. (*In tinea sycosa.*)   **HARLEY.**

2226—℞ Iodi . . . . ℥j-ij.
    Olei picis decolorate . . . . f ℥j.—M.

Ft. pasta.
Sig. Apply every fourth or sixth day. When the mass begins to flake off, wash well, and reapply the paste. (*In tinea tonsurans, or ringworm of the scalp. Also in tinea circinata.*)   COSTER.

2227—℞ Hydrargyri oleatis (5-10 per cent.) . ℥j.
Sig. Paint over the affected part. (*In tinea sycosa.*)   LEONARD **CANE.**

2228—℞ Liquoris arsenici et hydrargyri iodidi . f ℥ij.
    Syrupi zingiberis . . . . . f ℥j.
    Aquæ destillate . . . . q. s. ad f ℥iij.—M.

Sig. A teaspoonful after each meal. (*In tinea sycosa.*)   ERASMUS WILSON.

2229—℞ Acidi carbolici . . . . ℥j.
    Glycerini . . . . f ℥ss-j.—M.

Ft. lotio.
Sig. Use locally night **and morning, rubbing in well.** (*In tinea tonsurans.*)   **TILBURY FOX.**

2230—℞ Hydrargyri ammoniati,
    Hydrargyri oxidi rubri . . . . . . ãã **gr. vj.**
    Adipis . . . . ℥j.—M.

Ft. unguentum.
Sig. Use after epilation and washing. (*In tinea tonsurans.*)   STARTIN.

2231—℞ Sulphuris loti . . . . ℥ij.
    Spts. camphoræ . . . . f ℥ss.
    Glycerini . . . . f ℥ss.
    Hydrargyri bisulphidi . . . . ℈ss.
    Pulv. amyli . . . . ℥j.
    Aquæ . . . . q. s. ad Oj.—M.

Ft. lotio.
Sig. Use locally **night and morning.** (*In tinea tonsurans.*)   STARTIN.

2232—℞ Aceti cantharidis . . . . **℥ss.**
Sig. Apply lightly with a camel's-hair pencil ; **epilate around** the patch, and use the following :

2233—℞ Hydrargyri chloridi corrosivi . . . . . gr. lj.
    Adipis . . . . ℥j.—M.

Ft. unguentum.
Sig. Rub in well for ten days **or a** fortnight; then **stimulate** with cantharidal ointment. (**In tinea decalvans.**)   TILBURY **FOX.**

2234—℞ Naphthol . . . . ℥j-iiss.
    Saponis viridis,
    Cretæ præparatæ,
    Sulphuris loti,
    Lanolini . . . . ãã ℥vj gr. xv.

Misce et fiat unguentum.
Sig. Apply locally. (*In tinea sycosis.*)   **LIEBREICH.**

2235—℞ **Acidi acetici glacialis** . . . . ℥j.
Sig. Use as a paint, once or more, and dry off with blotting-paper if it produces much irritation. (*In tinea circinata.*)   TILBURY FOX.

2236—℞ Cupri carbonatis . . . . ℥ij.
    Adipis . . . . ℥j.—M.

Ft. unguentum.
Sig. Rub in well. (*In tinea sycosis.*)   DEVERGIE.

2237—℞ Hydrargyri nitratis . . . . **℥iss.**
    Adipis . . . . ℥j.—M.

Ft. unguentum.
Sig. Rub in night **and morning, for a** day or two. (*In tinea circinata.*)   TILBURY FOX.

2238—℞ Ungt. hydrargyri nitratis . . . . ℨiv.
   Sulphuris . . . . ℨij.
   Creasoti . . . . gtt. x.
   Adipis . . . . ℨj-ij.—M.

Ft. unguentum.
Sig. Rub in well. (*In tinea sycosis. See also tinea tonsurans.*)
           TILBURY FOX.

2239—℞ Hydrargyri chloridi corrosivi . . . . . gr. ij.
   Adipis . . . . ℨj.—M.

Ft. unguentum.
Sig. Use locally, rubbing in well. (*In tinea circinata.*)
           TILBURY FOX.

2240—℞ Hydrargyri ammoniati . . . . gr. v.
   Adipis . . . . ℨj.—M.

Ft. unguentum. (*In tinea circinata, where the surface is discharging.*)
           TILBURY FOX.

2241—℞ Acidi sulphurosi . . . . ℨij.
   Aquæ . . . . ℨviij.—M.

Ft. lotio.
Sig. Wash the surface with soap and water, and apply the
lotion, night and morning, on compresses of lint covered
with oiled silk for at least one hour. (*In tinea circinata,
where the disease is more or less general.*) TILBURY FOX.

2242—℞ Resorcin . . . . ℨj-iiss.
   Olei ricini . . . . ℨxiss.
   Alcoholis . . . . ℨxxxviiss.
   Balsami peruviani . . . . gr. viiss.—M.

Ft. lotio.
Sig. Apply locally. (*In tinea versicolor. Also in seborrhœa and
alopecia areata.*)   IHLE.

2243—℞ Sodii hyposulphitis . . . . ℨiv-vj.
   Aquæ . . . . ℨvj.—M.

Ft. lotio.
Sig. Wash the parts well with yellow soap (sapo terebinthinæ),
then sponge with weak vinegar and water, and apply the
lotion freely, even after the disease has vanished. (*In tinea
versicolor.*)   TILBURY FOX.

2244—℞ Acidi salicylici . . . . gr. xxx.
   Sulphuris loti . . . . ℨiiss.
   Lanolini . . . . ℨxxv.—M.

Ft. unguentum.
Sig. Apply with friction. (*In tinea versicolor.*) LIEBREICH.

2245—℞ Acidi salicylici . . . . gr. xlv.
   Sulphuris loti . . . . ℨiiss.
   Lanolini,
   Vaselini . . . . āā ℨxiiss.—M.

Ft. unguentum.
Sig. After rubbing well with tar-soap, rub in the ointment
well every evening. Wash off in the morning. (*In tinea
versicolor.*)   E. BESNIER.

2246—℞ Acidi carbolici . . . . ℨj.
   Glycerini . . . . f ℨix.—M.

Ft. solutio.
Sig. Cut the eyelashes short. Scrape off all crusts and the
surface of the exposed ulcerations. Paint the raw surface
with the solution. Dress with iodoform. (*In tinea tarsi.*)
           TEALE.

2247—℞ Sodii bicarbonatis . . . . ℨij-x.
   Aquæ ferventis (90°-95° F.) . . . . cong. xx-xxx.

Misce.
Sig. Alkaline bath. (*In eczema, psoriasis, urticaria, lichen, and
prurigo, where there is much local irritation.*) TILBURY FOX.

2248—℞ Potassii carbonatis . . . . ℨij-vj.
   Sodii boratis . . . . ℨij.
   Aquæ ferventis (90°-95° F.) . . . . cong. xx-xxx.

Misce.
Sig. Alkaline bath. Use the same as the preceding.
           TILBURY FOX.

2249—℞ Acidi sulphurosi,
Aquæ destillatæ . . . . āā partes æquales.
Misce et fiat lotio. (*In fungous skin diseases.*)　　BIETT.

2250—℞ Hydrargyri chloridi corrosivi . . . . ℈j.
Hydrargyri oxidi rubri,
Cupri subacetatis,
Cupri sulphatis . . . . āā ℈ij.
Adipis . . . . ℥v.—M.
Ft. unguentum. (*For fungous growths and granulations.*)
B. C. BRODIE.

2251—℞ Cupri sulphatis . . 　　　℈ss.
Spiritus rectificati . 　　　f℥j.
Aquæ destillatæ . 　　. . . f℥j.—M.
Ft. lotio. (*In chronic molluscum.*)　　NELIGAN.

2252—℞ Acidi nitrici diluti . . . . . f℥ss.
Spiritus lavandulæ compositi . . . . f℈ss.
Syrupi aurantii corticis . . . . . f℥ss.
Aquæ destillatæ . . . . . . Oiss.—M.
Sig. A wineglassful three or four times a day. (*In chronic, obstinate ulcers and skin diseases.*)　　M RYAN.

2253—℞ Amygdalæ dulcis excorticatæ . . . . . ℈j.
Aquæ florum aurantii . . . . f℥ij.
Aquæ rosæ . . . . f℥vij.
Fiat emulsio, et adde—
Ammonii chloridi . . . . ℈j.
Tincturæ benzoini . . . . f℈ij.—M.
Fiat lotio cosmetica. (*In pimples, freckles, and dryness of the skin.*)　　HERMANN.

2254—℞ Sodii arseniatis . . . . gr. ij.
Aquæ destillatæ . . . . q. s.
Solve et adde—
Pulveris guaiaci . . . . ℈ss.
Antimonii sulphurati . . . . ℈j.
Mucilaginis acaciæ . . . . q. s.
Misce caute et divide in pilulas xxiv.
Sig. Two to three pills daily. (*In **chronic** skin diseases.*)
ERASMUS WILSON.

2255—℞ Phosphori . . 　　　gr. ij)–℈j.(!!)
Olei caryophylli . . 　　　♏x–f℈j.
Mucilaginis acaciæ . . . . . q. s. ut fiant pilulæ xii.
Sig. One twice a day. (*In obstinate, scaly, tubercular, and syphilitic skin diseases.*)　　BURGESS.

2256—℞ Hydrargyri chloridi mitis . . . ℈j–℈j.
Adipis benzoatæ . . . . ℈j.—M.
Ft. unguentum. (*In most chronic eruptions.*)　　BURGESS.

2257—℞ Hydrargyri biniodidi . . . . gr. j.
Unguenti simplicis . . . . ℥v.—M.
Sig. Strength **may be gradually increased**. (*In elephantiasis Arabum.*)　　WARING.

2858—℞ Acidi arseniosi . . . . gr. j.
Piperis nigri . . . . gr. x.
Tere simul per horam dimidiam; dein adde—
Mucilaginis acaciæ . . . . . q. s. ut fiant pilulæ xv.
Sig. One pill once or twice daily. (*In elephantiasis.*)
HENRY BEASLEY.

2259—℞ Hydrargyri sulphureti . . 　　　℈ss.
Pulveris olibani . . . . 　　. ℈ij.—M.
Sig. To be thrown on a red-hot iron, and the diseased parts *only* exposed to the fumes. (*In chronic skin disease.*)　FOY.

2260—℞ Iodi . . . . ℈j–℈j.
Sulphuris **sublimati** . . . . ℈ss–℈ss.
Misce et fiat pulvis.
Sig. One twelfth of a part to be used as a fumigation in *skin-diseases*　　HOOPER.

2261—℞ Menthol . . . . gr. xlviij.
Balsami peruviani . . . . gr. xcvj.
Unguenti zinci benzol.,
Lanolini puri . . . . āā ad ℈ij.—M.
Sig. Apply twice daily. (*In prurigo.*)　　SAALFELD.

2262—℞ Potassii sulphureti . . . . ℨij-ℨiv.
Aquæ calidæ . . . . ℔c-℔cc.
Solve et adde—
Ichthyocollæ . . . . ℔j-℔ij, in
aquæ bullientis solutæ, ℔x.
Fiat balneum. (*Bath for skin diseases.*) DUPUYTREN.

2263—℞ Sodii carbonatis,
Sodii liboratis . . . . ãã ℥v.
Aquæ pluvialis (caloris grad. 76°-98° F.) cong. xxx.
Solve ut fiat balneum alkalinum. (*For many skin diseases.*)
NELIGAN.

2264—℞ Acidi nitrici vel muriatici . . . . . . ℥j.
Aquæ ferventis . . . . cong. xxx.
Misce. Fiat balneum acidum. (*In chronic lichen and pruigo.*)
TILBURY FOX.

2265—℞ Sodii hyposulphitis,
Sulphuris sublimati . . . . ãã ℥ij.
Aquæ pluvialis (caloris grad. 80° F.) . cong. xxx.
Solve. **Fiat balneum sulphureum.** (*For scaly diseases of the skin.*)
NELIGAN.

2266—℞ Furfuris [bran] . . . . ℔ij-vj.
vel lini seminis . . . . ℔j.
Aquæ ferventis . . . . cong. xx-xxx.
Misce.
Sig. Emollient bath. (*In erythematous, itchy, and scaly diseases.*)
TILBURY FOX.

2267—℞ Potassii sulphidi . . . . ℥ij-iv.
Aquæ ferventis . . . . cong. xxx.-M.
Sig. Sulphuret of potash **bath.** (*In scabies,* chronic eczema, *lichen, and psoriasis.*)
TILBURY FOX.

SLEEPLESSNESS. (See Insomnia.)

SMALL-POX.

2268—℞ Aristol. . . . . ℥j.
Sig. Use as a dusting-powder from the appearance of the pustules. J. J. LEVICK.

2269—℞ Acidi salicylici . . . . gr. xx.
Sodii bicarbonatis,
Ammonii carbonatis . . . . ãã gr. iv.
Misce et fiat chartula.
Sig. This amount in water every two to four hours, according to severity. (In the later stage, ferri et ammonii citras may be added.) PRIDEAUX.

2270—℞ Acidi carbolici,
Acidi acetici . . . . ãã f℥j-iss.
Tincturæ opii,
Spiritus chloroformi . . . . ãã fℨj.
Aquæ destillatæ . . . . q. s. ad f℥viij.—M.
Sig. A tablespoonful every **four hours.** NAPHEYS.

2271—℞ Sodii sulphitis . . . . ℈j.
Aquæ destillatæ . . . . f℥j.
Misce et fiat haustus.
Sig. To be taken every four hours. A. E. SANSOM.

2272—℞ Xyloli puri . . . . gr. xlv.
Mucilaginis acaciæ,
Syrupi cinnamomi . . . . ãã f℥iss.
Aquæ menthæ pip.,
Aquæ destillatæ . . . . ãã f℥iiss.—M.
Sig. A dessertspoonful **every two hours.** OETTOES.

2273—℞ Pulv. iodoformi . . . . ℨss.
Pulv. camphoræ . . . . ℈j.
Vaselini . . . . ℥j.—M.
Sig. **Apply to the affected parts.**

2274—℞ Pulv. folii belladonnæ . . . . gr. vj-xij.
Sacchari lactis. . . . . ℈j.—M.

In pulv. no. xii div.
Sig. A powder every three to six hours, till dilatation of the
pupils and some stupor follow. WARING.

2275—℞ Liquoris ammonii acetatis . . . . . . f℥iiiss.
Spiritus ætheris nitrosi . . . . f℥ss.—M.

Sig. A tablespoonful every two or three hours, in a wineglassful of water. HARTSHORNE.

2276—℞ Sodii salicylatis . . . . ℈ij.
Glycerini . . . . f℥j.
Aquæ menthæ pip. . . . . ad f℥iij.—M.

Sig. One or two teaspoonfuls three or four times daily.
REIMER.

2277—℞ Hydrargyri chloridi corrosivi . . . . gr. ij-iv.
Aquæ . . . . f℥vj.—M.

Ft. lotio.
Sig. Wet compresses and apply to the eruption. SKODA.

2278—℞ Calcis calcinatæ . . . . ℥iv.
Sulphuris . . . . ℥viij.
Aquæ . . . . Ov.—M.

[Boil in an earthenware pan, evaporate to three pints, and
filter.]
Sig. Apply locally as a lotion to the eruption. (*To prevent
pitting and secondary fever.*) PETERS.

2279—℞ Collodii flexilis . . . . ℥j.

Sig. Apply every day or two with a brush to the eruption.
(*To prevent pitting.*) RINGER.

2280—℞ Argenti nitratis . . . . ℈ij.
Aquæ destillatæ . . . . f℥ij.—M.

Sig. Paint the skin that is exposed to the light. (*To prevent
pitting.*) RINGER.

2281—℞ Zinci oxidi . . . . ℥j.
Zinci carbonatis . . . . ℥ij.
Olei olivæ . . . q. s. ut fiat unguentum.
BENNETT.

2282—℞ Atropinæ sulphatis . . . . gr. j.
Aquæ destillatæ . . . . f℥ss.—M.

Sig. Three to five minims every three or four hours.
W. HITCHMAN.

2283—℞ Acidi carbolici,
Gelatinæ . . āā ℥j.
Glycerini f℥vj.
Aquæ . . f℥xxvj.—M.

Sig. For local use. (Daily, after bathing, paint over the body.
After the pustules in the face are filled, prick them, and
apply the lotion frequently.) PRIDEAUX.

SPERMATORRHŒA.

2284—℞ Pulv. opii . . . . gr. v.
Pulv. camphoræ . . . . ℥iv.
Pulv. acaciæ,
Syr. simplicis . . . . . āā q. s. ut ft. massa.—M.

In pil. no. xl dividenda.
Sig. Two pills thrice daily. WARING.

2285—℞ Tinct. cantharidis . . . . ℈j.
Tinct. ferri chloridi . . . . ℈vj.—M.

Sig. Twenty drops in water thrice daily. (*In impotence, with
spermatorrhœa.*) H. C. WOOD.

2286—℞ Pulv. ergotæ . . . . ℥ss.
Pulv. nucis vomicæ . . . . gr. vj.
Sacchari albi . . . . ℈j.—M.

In pulv. no. xx div.
Sig. One or two powders at meal-time. SINÉTY.

SPERMATORRHŒA (Continued).

2287—℞ Potassii bromidi . . . . 3j.
    Aquæ destillatæ . . . . q. s. ad f 3ij.—M.
Sig. A teaspoonful three times a day. (*In the strong and plethoric.*)
                                     BARTHOLOW.

2288—℞ Quininæ sulphatis . . . . gr. vj.
    Acidi sulphurici diluti . . . . f 3j.
    Tincturæ cardamomi compositæ . . . f 3iij.
    Aquæ cinnamomi . . . . f 3vss.—M.
Sig. Two tablespoonfuls twice daily.   MILTON.

2289—℞ Tincturæ cimicifugæ . . . . f 3iij.
Sig. A teaspoonful three times a day.   MORSE.

2290—℞ Digitalinæ . . . .   . gr. j.
    Pulveris acaciæ .   Əij.
    Syrupi simplicis .   q. s.
Fiat massa, in pilulas no. xxxv dividenda.
Sig. One pill three times a day.   CORVISART.

2291—℞ Pulveris opii . . . . gr. v.
    Camphoræ . . . . Əiv.
    Pulveris acaciæ,
    Syrupi simplicis . . . . āā q. s.
Fiat massa, in pilulas no. xl dividenda.
Sig. Two pills three times a day.   WARING.

2292—℞ Pulveris digitalis   . gr. ij.
    Lupulinæ   gr. xv.
Misce et fiat chartula.
Sig. Daily at bedtime.   PESCHECK.

2293—℞ Ext. belladonnæ,
    Pulv. belladonnæ . . . . āā gr. iij.
    Confect. rosæ . . . . . . q. s. ut ft. massa.—M.
In pulv. no. x div.
Sig. From one to three pills at bedtime, and during the day
from fifteen to sixty grains of potassium bromide in divided
doses.   SINÉTY.

2294—℞ Antipyrin . . . . 3ij.
    Syr. acaciæ . . . . 3ss.
    Aquæ cinnamomi . . . . nd f 3iv.—M.
Sig. A dessertspoonful or two on retiring. (*When due to
neurasthenia.*)   THOR.

2295—℞ Potassii bromidi   . 3j.
    Sodii bicarbonatis   gr. xv.
    Infusi digitalis . .   3ss.
    Atropinæ sulphatis   gr. ⅟₆₀.—M.
Sig. To be taken at bedtime.   GROSS.

2296—℞ Tinct. gelsemii . . . . 3j.
    Tinct. belladonnæ . . . . 3ij.—M.
Sig. Fifteen drops at bedtime.   BARTHOLOW.

2297—℞ Lupulinæ . . . . gr. x.
    Pulv. camphoræ . . . . gr. vj.
    Ext. belladonnæ . . . . gr. ij.—M.
In pil. no. xii div.
Sig. One pill thrice daily.   BARTHOLOW.

2298—℞ Infusi digitalis   . . . . 3iv.
Sig. One or two teaspoonfuls twice or thrice daily. RINGER.

2299—℞ Argenti nitratis .   gr. v-x.
    Aquæ destillatæ   3j.—M.
Sig. Inject into the prostatic portion of the urethra, using a
deep urethral syringe.   VAN BUREN AND KEYES.

2300—℞ Acidi tannici . . . . 3j.
    Glycerini . . . . q. s.—M.
Ft. pasta.
Sig. Apply to the deep urethra with a cupped sound, placing
the paste in the cups.   VAN BUREN AND KEYES.

SPLEEN, ENLARGEMENT OF. (See Fever, Intermittent, and Leucocythæmia.)

STOMATITIS. (See Aphthæ.)

STRANGURY.

2301—℞ Ext. belladonnæ. . . . . gr. j-iv.
Olei theobromæ . . . . ℥ss.—M.
Ft. suppositorium no. j.
Sig. Introduce into the bowel, and repeat in four hours, if it
be necessary. HARTSHORNE.

2302—℞ Pulv. opii . . . . gr. ij-iv.
Olei theobromæ . . . . ℥j.—M.
Fiant suppositoria no. ij.
Sig. Introduce one into the bowel, and repeat, if necessary, in
four hours. HARTSHORNE.

2303—℞ Pulv. opii . . . . . . gr. iv.
Pulv. folii hyoscyami gr. xx.
Olei theobromæ ℥j.—M.
Fiant suppositoria no. ij.
Sig. Introduce one into the rectum. PHILLIPS.

2304—℞ Tincturæ cannabis indicæ . . f ℥j.
Sig. A half-teaspoonful every few hours. (*Especially with
bloody urine, and when due to spinal disease.*) RINGER.

2305—℞ Aceti scillæ,
Spiritus ætheris nitrosi . . . . . . āā f ℥ss.—M.
Sig. A half-teaspoonful in some demulcent tea every hour or
oftener. WARING.

2306—℞ Balsami copaibæ . . . . ℥ss.
Acidi benzoici . . . . ℥j.
Vitell. ovi . . . . no. j.
Aquæ camphoræ . . . . f ℥vij.—M.
Sig. Two tablespoonfuls **twice a day.** (*In dysuria senilis.*)
SODEN.

2307—℞ Ext. nucis vomicæ . . . . gr. viij.
Ext. glycyrrhizæ. . . . . q. s.—M.
Ft. massa et in pil. no. l div.
Sig. Two pills on retiring. (*For strangury and dysuria of old
age.*) FISCHER.

STRUMA. (See Rachitis.)

STYE (HORDEOLUM).

2308—℞ Acidi boracici . . . . ℨiv.
Aquæ destillatæ . . . . ℥v.—M.
Ft. lotio.
Sig. Apply to the eyelids several times daily. ABADIE.

2309—℞ Hydrarg. oxidi rubri gr. xv.
Ungt. aquæ rosæ . . . . ℥j.—M.
Sig. Apply night and morning, after bathing with hot water
containing a pinch of salt to the cupful. J. C. WILSON.

2310—℞ Calcii sulphidi . . . . gr. lx.
In pil. (gelatin-coated) i.o. xxx. div.
Sig. One pill after each meal and at bedtime. J. C. WILSON.

SUPPURATION. (See Abscess.)

SWEATING. (See Phthisis.)

SWEATING, LOCAL. (See Bromidrosis.)

SYCOSIS. (See also Tinea, in Skin Diseases.)

2311—℞ Acidi tannici . . . . gr. xlv.
Sulphuris præcip. . . . . ℥ss.
Zinci oxidi,
Amyli . . . . āā ℨiv.
Vaselini . . . . ℥j.—M.
Sig. Use twice daily. ROSENTHAL.

2312—℞ Vitell. ovi . . . . no. ij.
    Pulv. sacchari albi . . . . ℨiv.
    Olei amygdalæ amaræ . . . . gtt. ij.
    Aquæ aurantii flor. . . . . f ℨij.
    Olei morrhuæ . . . . f ℨv.—M.

Sig. From a teaspoonful to a tablespoonful thrice daily. (*In strumous synovitis.*)   HEDER.

2313—℞ Saponis mollis . . . . ℨij.
    Alcoholis vel aquæ coloniensis . . . . ℨj.—M.

Sig. Soak linen rags in the solution and apply about the joint.
     KAPPESSER.

2314—℞ Tinct. iodi . . . . f ℨj.

Sig. Apply with a brush every second or third day. RINGER.

2315—℞ Morphinæ . . . . gr. viij.
    Hydrargyri oleatis (5-10 per cent.) . . . ℨj.—M.

Sig. Apply twice daily with a soft brush. (*In the acute form.*)
     MARSHALL.

2316—℞ Emplastri cantharidis . . . . 1 in. × 2 in.

Sig. Apply every night until the skin is well reddened. If this does not avail, leave on until a bleb is formed, which may be cut, poulticed, and dressed with simple cerate. (*In the chronic form.*)   RINGER.

2317—℞ Argenti nitratis . . . . ℨj.
    Aquæ destillatæ . . . . f ℨj.

Solve.
Sig. Apply almost to vesication. (*In acute synovitis.*)
     FURNEAUX JORDAN.

2318—℞ Ungt. hydrargyri . . . . ℨij.
    Pulv. ammonii chloridi . . . . ℨj.—M.

Sig. For inunction.   DUPUYTREN.

2319—℞ Iodi . . . . ℨiv.
    Potassii iodidi . . . . ℨj.
    Aquæ destillatæ . . . . f ℨvj.—M.

Sig. Apply externally, with a brush.   LUGOL.

2320—℞ Unguenti hydrargyri . . . . ℨj.

Sig. As an inunction to the **previously** blistered surface. (*In the subacute form.*)   W. ADAMS.

SYPHILIS.

2321—℞ Hydrargyri protiodidi,
    Lactucarii . . . . āā gr. xv.
    Ext. opii . . . . gt. iij½.
    Ext. guaiaci . . . . ℨss.—M.

Ft. massa et in pil, no. xx div.
Sig. One pill at breakfast and after supper, followed by a draught of water.   DIDAY.

2322—℞ Hydrargyri chloridi corrosivi . .   gr. viiss.
    Amyli . . . . ℨj.
    Syrupi acaciæ . . . . q. s.

Misce et fiant pilulæ no. lx.
Sig. One pill three times a day.   TROUSSEAU.

2323—℞ Hydrargyri chloridi corrosivi,
    Ammonii chloridi . . . . āā gr. iiss.
    Aquæ destillatæ . . . . f ℨiv.—M.

Ft. solutio et adde—
    Potassii iodidi . . . . ℨj.
    Aquæ destillatæ . . . . f ℨxvj.—M.

Sig. A tablespoonful **before each meal.**   BESNIER.

2324—℞ Hydrargyri chloridi **corrosivi** . . . . . gr. ss.(!)
    Extracti cinchonæ . . . . gr. x.
    Extracti opii aquosi . . . . gr. ss.—M.

Fiant pilulæ ii.
Sig. One or two pills daily, closely watching. DUPUYTREN.

2325—℞ Pilulæ hydrargyri . . . . ʒss.
Divide in pilulas no. x.
Sig. One pill night and morning. ("One of the best methods
of treatment in the *secondary form*.")   ELLIS.

2326—℞ Pil. hydrargyri . . . . ɔij.
Ferri sulphatis exsiccatæ . . . . ɔj.
Ext. opii aquosi . . . . gr. v.—M.
In pil. no. xx div.
Sig. One pill thrice daily.   F. N. OTIS.

2327—℞ Hydrargyri chloridi corrosivi,
Ammonii chloridi . . . . āā gr. iij.
Tinct. cinchonæ comp.,
Aquæ . . . . āā fʒiij.—M.
Sig. A teaspoonful thrice daily.   BUMSTEAD.

2328—℞ Hydrargyri cyanidi . . . . gr. iv.
Aquæ destillatæ . . . . fʒvij.—M.
Sig. A teaspoonful three times a day. The *Liqueur Anti-syphi-
litique* of   CHAUSSIER.

2329—℞ Potassii iodidi . . . . ɔj.
Syrupi aurantii corticis . . . . fʒj.
Aquæ destillatæ . . . . fʒv.—M.
Sig. A tablespoonful night and morning, in hop-tea.
LISFRANC.

2330—℞ Hydrargyri protiodidi . . . . gr. iij.
Potassii iodidi . . . . ʒij.
Tincturæ gentianæ compositæ,
Syrupi sarsaparillæ compositi . . . āā fʒij.—M.
Sig. A teaspoonful thrice daily.   HORACE GREEN.

2331—℞ Hydrargyri iodidi rubri . . . . gr. ij.
Ammonii carbonatis . . . . ɔj.
Potassii iodidi . . . . ʒiij.
Tinct. gentianæ comp. . . . . ad fʒiv.—M.
Sig. A teaspoonful in water, after meals. (*Mixed treatment.*)
G. H. FOX.

2332—℞ Hydrargyri iodidi rubri . . . . gr. iij.
Potassii iodidi . . . . ʒiij–vj.
Tinct. aurantii cort.,
Syr. aurantii cort. . . . . āā fʒj.
Aquæ . . . . fʒviij.—M.
Sig. A teaspoonful in water thrice daily, after meals. (*Mixed
treatment.*)   F. N. OTIS.

2333—℞ Hydrargyri iodidi rubri . . . . gr. j.
Potassii iodidi . . . . ʒiv.
Syr. sarsaparillæ comp.,
Aquæ . . . . āā fʒij.—M.
Sig. A teaspoonful thrice daily, after meals. (*Mixed treatment.*)
R. W. TAYLOR.

2334—℞ Hydrargyri biniodidi . . . . gr. j.
Potassii iodidi . . . . ʒj.
Aquæ destillatæ . . . . fʒj.
Syrupi simplicis . . . . fʒv.—M.
Sig. A tablespoonful thrice daily.   *Hôpital Saint-Louis.*

2335—℞ Hydrargyri chloridi corrosivi . . . . . gr. j.
Tincturæ ferri chloridi . . . . fʒij.
Aquæ destillatæ . . . . q. s. ad fʒvj.—M.
Sig. A tablespoonful three times a day. ERNEST GOODMAN.

2336—℞ Hydrargyri chloridi corrosivi . . . . . gr. j.
Potassii iodidi . . . . ʒij.
Tinct. gentianæ comp. . . . . fʒiij.—M.
Sig. A teaspoonful thrice daily, after meals. (*Mixed treat-
ment.*)   *Charity Hospital, N.Y.*

2337—℞ Hydrargyri chloridi corrosivi . . . . . gr. iv.
Tinct. benzoini . . . . ʒss.
Aquæ coloniensis . . . . fʒj.
Aquæ rosæ . . . . fʒvss.—M.
Ft. lotio.
Sig. Apply locally with a sponge to the skin for twenty
minutes. (*For squamous syphilides*.)   S. W. GROSS.

2338—℞ Hydrargyri chloridi mitis,
Lycopodii . . . . āā ℈ij.—M.
Sig. Use as snuff thrice daily. (*In syphilitic lesions of the nose.*)
S. W. Gross.

2339—℞ Potassii Iodidi . . . . ℈ij.
Sacchari albi . . . . ℥j.
Extracti sarsaparillæ fluidi . . . . . . f ʒss.
Aquæ destillatæ . . . . f ℥iij.—M.
Sig. A tablespoonful three times a day. Ellis.

2340—℞ Potassii iodidi . . . . gr. iij.
Aquæ destillatæ . . . . f ℥j.
Solve et adde—
Hydrargyri biniodidi . . . . . . gr. ivss.—M.
Sig. From two to five drops three times a day, much diluted.
Channing.

2341—℞ Auri chloridi . . . . gr. j.
Extracti aconiti . . . . ℈ss.
Pulveris glycyrrhizæ . . . . ℈ij.
Syrupi simplicis . . . . q. s.
Misce intime, et fiant pilulæ no. xx.
Sig. One pill three times a day. Neligan.

2342—℞ Potassii Iodidi . . . . ℥ij.
Ammonii carbonatis . . . . ℈ss.
Tinct. cinchonæ comp. . . . . f ℥iv.
Syr. aurantii cort. . . . . f ℥iss.
Glycerini . . . . f ℥j.—M.
Sig. A teaspoonful, well diluted, after each meal.
E. L. Keyes.

2343—℞ Auri chloridi . . . . gr. j.
Lycopodii præparati . . . . gr. xv.
Misce et fiant chartulæ no. xvi.
Sig. Rub one on the tongue and gums daily. (Afterwards the
same quantity to be divided successively into twelve and
ten powders.) Chrestien.

2344—℞ Acidi nitro-muriatici diluti . . f ℥iss.
Syrupi stillingiæ compositi . . f ℥xiijss.
Aquæ destillatæ . . . . f ℥ij.—M.
Sig. One to two teaspoonfuls three times a day, with denu-
trition. (*In cases saturated with the approved remedies, but
still presenting patches on the skin and mucous membranes.*)
Bartholow.

2345—℞ Hydrargyri salicylatis . . . . gr. viiss.
Confectionis rosæ . . . . ℈ss.—M.
Ft. massa et in pil. no. lx div.
Sig. One thrice daily, after meals. Chaves.

2346—℞ Hydrargyri chloridi corrosivi,
Ammonii chloridi . . . . āā gr. iij.
Aquæ destillatæ . . . . f ℥iss.—M.
Ft. solutio et adde—
Albuminis ovi . . . . ℥iss.
Aquæ destillatæ . . . . f ℥v.
Misce, cola, et adde—
Aquæ destillatæ . . . . q. s. ad f ℥x.—M.
Sig. For hypodermic use. Three to ten minims to be used
for each injection. ℥j contains corrosive sublimate, gr. ₇₂₀.
Potter.

2347—℞ Hydrargyri carbolatis . . . . gr. xviij.
Ext. glycyrrhizæ,
Pulv. glycyrrhizæ . . . . āā q. s. ut ft. massa.—M.
Ft. massa et in pil. no. lx div.
Obduc balsamo tolutano.
Sig. Two to four pills daily. Szadek.

2348—℞ Hydrargyri oxidi flavi . . . . ℥iss.
Hydrargyri chloridi corrosivi . . . . . gr. ¾.
Glycerini puri . . . . f ℥xxv.—M.
Sig. For hypodermic use. Twelve and a half minims to be
used for each injection. De Smet.

2349—℞ Hydrargyri chloridi mitis . . . . . . gr. xij.
    Olei vaselini . . . . ℳcccxxv.
Misce.
Sig. For hypodermic injection. Twenty to thirty minims to
be used.   BALZER.

2350—℞ Hydrargyri chloridi mitis . . . . . . gr. iss.
    Glycerini . . . . ℳxv.—M.
Sig. For hypodermic injection. To be used each time. Two
or three injections required for an average case, before the
symptoms yield.   SCARENZIO.

2351—℞ Hydrargyri chloridi mitis,
    Sodii chlorati . . . . āā gr. xv.
    Aquæ destillatæ . . . . f ℨiss.—M.
Sig. For hypodermic injection. Twenty to thirty minims to
be used.   KRECKE.

2352—℞ Hydrargyri chloridi mitis . . . . . . gr. xv.
    Olei olivæ . . . . f ℨiss.—M.
Sig. For hypodermic injection. Twenty to thirty minims to
be used.   KOPP.

TABES MESENTERICA. (See Marasmus.)

TAPE-WORM. (See Worms.)

TETANUS.

2353—℞ Extracti physostigmatis,
    Pulveris zingiberis . . . . āā gr. j.
Misce et fiat pilula.
Sig. Every hour or two until effects are noted. (Or begin with
one-third of a grain hypodermically.)   E. WATSON.

2354—℞ Extracti physostigmatis   gr. ij.
    Aquæ destillatæ   f ℨj.—M.
Ft. solutio.
Sig. Ten minims every two hours hypodermically, as required.
To be pushed just short of arresting the breathing.
                                 FRASER.

2355—℞ Curaris . . . . gr. j-ij.
    Aquæ . . . . gtt. c.—M.
Ft. solutio.
Sig. Ten drops hypodermically, and repeated every four or
five hours, to control the spasm.   DEMME.

2356—℞ Tincturæ cannabis indicæ . . . . . . f ℨss.
    Mucilaginis acaciæ . . . . f ℨij.
    Aquæ cinnamomi . . . . f ℨss.
Ft. haustus.
Sig. At once, and repeat in two hours, or sooner, if permis-
sible.   NÉLIGAN.

2357—℞ Chloral. hydratis   ℨss.
    Syr. aurantii cort.   f ℨiss.
    Aquæ   ad f ℨiij.—M.
Sig. A dessertspoonful as required.   BARTHOLOW.

2358—℞ Pilocarpinæ muriatis .   gr. ij.
    Aquæ destillatæ .   f ℨj.—M.
Ft. solutio.
Sig. Ten minims hypodermically daily, with chloral hydrate
at night to produce sleep. (In rheumatismal tetanus.)
                                BRUNAUER.

2359—℞ Pulveris opii . . . . gr. iss.
    Moschi optimi,
    Pulveris camphoræ . . . . āā gr. vj.
Misce et fiat pulvis.
Sig. In syrup.   W. AINSLIE

TETANUS (Continued).

2360—℞ Pulv. opii . . . . ʒj.
　　　 Pulv. camphoræ . . . . gr. xv.
　　　 Adipis præp. . . . . ʒss.—M.
Ft. unguentum.
Sig. To be rubbed on the parts affected with the spasm.
　　　　　　　　　　　　　　　　　　　　THOMAS.

2361—℞ Extracti belladonnæ . . . . gr. ss–j.
Ft. pilula.
Sig. One every two hours; to be increased pro re nata.
　　　　　　　　　　　　　　　　　　　　HUTCHINSON.

2362—℞ Extracti conii . . . . gr. v.
Divide in pilulas ii.
Sig. One dose. Every three hours. (The succus is more reli-
able.)　　　　　　　　　　　　　　　　　CORRY.

2363—℞ Cocainæ muriatis.
　　　 Morphinæ muriatis . . . . āā gr. xij.
　　　 Aquæ destillatæ . . . . f ʒj.—M.
Sig. Twenty to sixty minims hypodermically, as required.
　　　　　　　　　　　　　　　　　　　　LOPEZ.

2364—℞ Liquoris potassii arsenitis . . . . . . f ʒj.
Sig. Five to eight drops, well diluted, every three hours.
　　　　　　　　　　　　　　　　　　　　DALTON.

2365—℞ Strychninæ sulphatis . . . . gr. j.
　　　 Aquæ bullientis . . . . f ʒj.—M.
Ft. solutio.
Sig. Eight to sixteen minims hypodermically, as required.
　　　　　　　　　　　　　　　　　　　　BARTHOLOW.

2366—℞ Potassii bromidi . . . . ʒiss.
In pulv. no. xii div.
Sig. A powder dissolved in water every three or four hours.
　　　　　　　　　　　　　　　　　　　　H. C. WOOD.

2367—℞ Nicotinæ . . . . gr. ss.
　　　 Aquæ destillatæ . . . . f ʒij.—M.
Sig. For hypodermic use. (Ten minims contain ¹⁄₆₀ of a grain.)
　　　　　　　　　　　　　　　　　　　　ERLENMEYER.

2368—℞ Nicotinæ . . . . gtt. ss–iiss.
　　　 Vini xerensis,
　　　 Aquæ destillatæ . . . . āā f ʒss.—M.
Sig. One dose. Several times a day.　　　 HAUGHTON.

2369—℞ Tincturæ aconiti (Ph. Br.) . . . . . . ♍xv.
　　　 Spiritus vini gallici . . . . f ʒij–f ʒss.
　　　 Aquæ destillatæ . . . . q. s. ad f ʒiss.
Misce et fiat haustus.
Sig. Every fourth hour.　　　　　　　　　 H. JONES.

THREAD-WORMS. (See Worms.)

THRUSH. (See Aphthæ.)

TIC DOULOUREUX. (See Neuralgia.)

TINEA. (See Skin Diseases.)

TINNITUS AURIUM.

2370—℞ Arnicæ . . . . ʒij.
　　　 Aquæ bullientis . . . . Oss.
Macera per horas duas et cola. Dein adde—
　　　 Tincturæ arnicæ . . . . f ʒij.
　　　 Tincturæ cardamomi . . . . f ʒvj.—M.
Sig. A tablespoonful three times a day.　　 WILDE.

2371—℞ Acidi hydrobromici diluti (10 per cent.) f ʒj.
Sig. One-half to one teaspoonful, in a wineglassful of
sweetened water, thrice daily.　　　　　　FOTHERGILL.

2372—℞ Tincturæ cimicifugæ . . . . ℔clx.
Aquæ . . . . f℥ij.—M.
Sig. A teaspoonful thrice daily. PATTON.

2373—℞ Quininæ muriatis . . . . gr. lx.
In pil. no. xxx div.
Sig. One pill four times a day. J. C. WILSON.

2374—℞ Sodii salicylatis . . . . ℥ij.
Vini cocæ . . . . f℥iv.—M.
Sig. A dessertspoonful in water three or four times a day;
gradually reduce the dose. J. C. WILSON.

TONSILLITIS. (See also Quinsy.)

2375—℞ Potassii bromidi . . . . ℥iv.
Potassii chloratis . . . . ℥j.
Tinct. ferri chloridi . . . . f℥iss.
Ext. glycyrrhizæ . . . . ℥j.
Aquæ . . . . q. s. ad f℥iv.—M.
Sig. A teaspoonful **in water every two** hours. Gargle and
swallow. CARL SEILER.

2376—℞ Creolin . . . . gr. xv–xxx.
Aquæ destillatæ . . . . Oj.
Aquæ menthæ pip. . . . ℥ij.—M.
Sig. Use as a gargle. SCHNITZLER.

2377—℞ Creolin . . . gr. xv–lxxv.
Aquæ destillatæ . . . . f℥iss–ij.—M.
Sig. For local application with brush. SCHNITZLER.

2378—℞ Creolin . . . . gr. iss–viiss.
Acidi borici . . . . ℈xxx.
Olei menthæ pip. . . . . gtt. xx.—M.
Sig. For insufflation. SCHNITZLER.

TOOTHACHE.

2379—℞ Pulv. acidi **arseniosi,**
Iodoformi . . . . partes æq.
Sol. acidi carbolici (5 per cent.) q. s.—M.
Ft. pasta.
Sig. Carry the paste to the nerve on a piece of cotton the size
of a pin's head. Cover with red gutta-percha to retain it.
(*In exposed nerve.*) TRUMAN.

2380—℞ Acidi arseniosi . . . . **gr. ij.**
Morphinæ sulphatis . . . . **gr. j.**
Creasoti . . . . **q. s.—M.**
Ft. pasta.
Sig. Apply by a **bit of cotton-wool to carious portion.**
BARTHOLOW.

2381—℞ Pulv. acidi arseniosi,
Cocainæ hydrochloratis āā gr. xxx.
Menthol, crystal. gr. viiss.
Glycerini q. s.—M.
Ft. pasta.
Sig. Apply to the carious cavity, and retain with a cotton or
rubber plug. (*For devitalizing exposed nerves.*) E. C. KIRK.

2382—℞ Mastiches . . gr. x.
Acidi tannici . . . ℈j.
Ætheris sulphurici f℥ss.—M.
DRUITT.

2383—℞ Linimenti aconiti (B.P.),
Chloroformi . . . . āā ℥ij.
Tinct. capsici . . . . ℥j.
Tinct. pyrethri,
Olei caryophylli,
Pulv. camphoræ . . . . āā ℈ss.—M.
Sig. A few drops on cotton placed **in the cavity.** MASON.

2384—℞ Olei caryophylli,
Olei cajuputi . . . . āā f3j.
Pulveris opii,
Camphoræ . . . . āā ǯss.
Spiritus rectificati . . . . q. s.—M.
Ft. solutio. COPLAND.

2385—℞ Morphinæ sulphatis . . . . gr. iv.
Atropinæ sulphatis . . . . gr. j.
Aquæ destillatæ . . . . f3j.—M.
Sig. A few drops on cotton placed in the cavity.
BARTHOLOW.

2386—℞ Creasoti . . gr. lxxv.
Tincturæ pyrethri . . f3iss.—M.
Sig. Put in the hollow tooth by means of a little cotton.
TROUSSEAU ET RÉVEIL.

2387—℞ Creasoti . . . . ǯij.
Sig. Moisten a pledget of cotton and lay it in the carious
cavity. HENSON.

2388—℞ Liq. cocainæ muriatis (3 per cent.) . . ǯvij.
Morphinæ sulphatis . . . . gr. xij.
Gossypii absorbentis . . . . ǯvij.—M.
[Saturate the cotton and dry with a gentle heat, and then re-
card the cotton.]
Sig. Moisten a small piece with a few drops of water, and
place it in the cavity of the tooth. ELLER.

2389—℞ Olei caryophylli . . . . f3ij.
Sig. Moisten a piece of cotton and insert it into the cavity.
HARTSHORNE.

2390—℞ Collodii flexilis,
Acidi carbolici crystal. . . . . . . āā ǯij.—M.
Sig. Apply to the tooth-cavity by means of a probe wrapped
on the end with cotton. GUILD.

2391—℞ Tinct. iodi . . . . f3iv.
Tinct. aconiti . . . . f3j.—M.
Sig. Paint the gums twice daily around the painful tooth.
(In dental periostitis.) RODIER.

2392—℞ Pulv. camphoræ,
Chloral. hydratis . . . . āā gr. xxx.
Cocainæ hydrochloratis . . . . gr. vj.—M.
[Heat to the boiling-point of water, and an oily fluid results.]
Sig. Introduce a small quantity of the mixture into the
carious tooth. GSELL-FELS.

2393—℞ Ext. opii alcoholici,
Pulv. camphoræ,
Balsami peruviani . . . . āā gr. viiss.
Mastiches . . . . gr. xv.
Chloroformi . . . . f3iss.—M.
Sig. Wet a bit of cotton with the solution, and place it in the
carious cavity. L'Union Médicale.

TRICHINOSIS.

2394—℞ Sodii sulphocarbolatis . . . . gr. ij-x.
Aquæ . . . . f3ij.—M.
Ft. haustus.
Sig. To be repeated three or four times daily. FUREY.

2395—℞ Extracti ergotæ fluidi . . . . f3iij.
Sig. A teaspoonful in water, night and morning. RHODE.

2396—℞ Acidi sclerotinici . . . . gr. vj.
Acidi carbolici . . . . gr. ½.
Aquæ . . . . f3ss.—M.
Sig. Twenty minims, hypodermically, once a day.
J. C. WILSON.

TRISMUS NEONATORUM. (See also Tetanus.)

2397—℞ Chloral. hydratis . . . . gr. j–ij.
Syrupi simplicis . . . . f3j.—M.
Sig. To be given every two hours, unless there be profound sleep. Double the dose if given by the rectum.
WIDERHOFER.

2398—℞ Chloral. hydratis . . . . gr. j–v.
Syrupi simplicis . . . . f3j.—M.
Sig. One dose.
BARTHOLOW.

2399—℞ Tincturæ opii . . . . gtt. v.
Tincturæ asafœtidæ . . . . f3iss.
Syrupi simplicis . . . . f3v.
Aquæ . . . . ad f3xv.—M.
Sig. A half-teaspoonful hourly.
EBERLE.

2400—℞ Tincturæ opii . . . . f3iv.
Sig. One drop every three hours, alternating with the following:

2401—℞ Pulveris ipecacuanhæ comp. . . . . . gr. xxiv.
Zinci sulphatis . . . . 3j.—M.
In pulv. no. xii div.
Sig. A powder every three hours.
FURLONGE.

2402—℞ Extracti gelsemii fluidi . . . . ℥viij–xvj.
Syrupi simplicis . . . . f3j.
Aquæ destillatæ . . . . q. s. ad f3ss.—M.
Sig. A half-teaspoonful every two to four hours.
BARTHOLOW.

2403—℞ Tincturæ opii . . . . ℥j.
Olei ricini . . . . f3j.—M.
Sig. A teaspoonful every four hours, with a warm bath.
DRUITT.

TUBERCULOSIS. (See Rachitis and Phthisis.)

TYMPANITES. (See also Fever.)

2404—℞ Olei terebinthinæ . . . . f3j.
Olei amygdalæ **expres.** . . . . f3ss.
Tinct. opii . . . . f3ij.
Mucil. acaciæ . . . . f3v.
Aquæ laurocerasi . . . . f3ss.—M.
Sig. A teaspoonful every three **to six hours.**
BARTHOLOW.

2405—℞ Olei ricini,
Olei terebinthinæ,
Mucilaginis acaciæ,
Aquæ menthæ piperitæ . . . . . . āā f3ss.
Misce et fiat haustus.
HOOPER.

2406—℞ Olei terebinthinæ . . . . 3j.
Olei olivæ . . . . 3iss.
Camphoræ . . . . gr. xx.
Decocti avenæ . . . . f3viij.—M.
Ft. enema.
Sig. Inject into the bowel. (In hysterical tympanites.)
COPLAND.

2407—℞ Olei terebinthinæ,
Olei ricini . . . . āā f3iij.
Olei cajaputi . . . . ℥vj.
Magnesiæ calcinatæ . . . . 3j.
Aquæ menthæ piperitæ . . . . f3iss.
Misce et fiat haustus.
JOY.

2408—℞ Olei terebinthinæ . . . . f3j.
Pulveris acaciæ . . . . q. s.
Misce et adde—
Decocti hordei . . . . f3xix.
Ft. enema.
HOOPER.

2409—℞ Pulv. capsici . . . . gr. vj–xxiv.
Sacchari lactis . . . . 3iss.—M.
In pulv. no. xii div.
Sig. A powder every four hours.
PHILLIPS.

TYMPANITES (Continued.)

2410—℞ Olei terebinthinæ . . . . f℥ij-viij.
Olei ricini . . . . f℥ij.
Vitell. ovi . . . . no. j.
Decocti hordei . . . . f℥viij-xvj.
Misce et fiat enema.
Sig. Inject into the bowel. BARTHOLOW.

2411—℞ Olei terebinthinæ . . . . f℥j.
Olei olivæ . . . . f℥iss.
Camphoræ . . . . ℈j.
Decocti avenæ . . . . f℥viij.
Misce et fiat enema. (*In hysterical tympanites.*) COPLAND.

TYPHOID AND TYPHUS FEVER. (See Fever.)

ULCER. —U—

2412—℞ Creasoti . . . . ℳiv.
Aquæ destillatæ . . . . f℥vj.—M.
Sig. In tablespoonful doses. (*In chronic gastric ulcer.*)
NIEMEYER.

2413—℞ Argenti oxidi,
Extracti hyoscyami . . . . . . āā gr. v.
Misce et fiant pilulæ no. x. (*In gastric ulcer.*) BARTHOLOW.

2414—℞ Argenti nitratis . . . . gr. v.
Pulv. opii . . . . gr. iiss.—M.
Ft. massa et in pil. no. xx div.
Sig. One pill thrice daily. (*In gastric ulcer.*)
HARTSHORNE.

2415—℞ Bismuthi subnitratis . . . . . . ℥ij.
Pulv. opii . . . . gr. iij.—M.
In pulv. no. xli div.
Sig. One powder thrice daily, followed continuously by—

2416—℞ Argenti nitratis . . . . gr. v.
Tinct. opii . . . . f℥iss.
Aquæ anisi . . . . ad f℥ijss.—M.
Sig. A teaspoonful thrice daily, with rest to the stomach. (*In gastric ulcer.*) W. H. THOMPSON.

2417—℞ Liq. potassii arsenitis . . . . f℥ss.
Sig. One drop, repeated as required, to **relieve** the pain and vomiting. (*In gastric ulcer.*) BARTHOLOW.

2418—℞ Skimmed milk two parts and liquor calcis one part, mixed, as a steady diet. (*In gastric ulcer.*) DA COSTA.

2419—℞ Argenti nitratis fusæ . . . . q. s.
Sig. Apply to the surface and edges, and strap with diachylon adhesive plaster. (*In leg-ulcers.*) T. M. MARKOE.

2420—℞ Balsami copaibæ . . . . ℥ij.
Mucilaginis acaciæ . . . . f℥ss.
Misce et adde—
Aquæ calcis . . . . f℥vj.
Fiat injectio. (*In ulceration of the urethra, rectum, or vagina.*)
ABERNETHY.

2421—℞ Creasoti . . . . ℳiv.
Tincturæ galbani . . . . f℥ij.
Aquæ destillatæ . . . . f℥ij.—M.
Ft. lotio. (*In indolent ulcers with excessive discharge.*)
NELIGAN.

2422—℞ Zinci sulpho-carbolatis . . . . . . ℥vj.
Aquæ destillatæ . . . . f℥viij.—M.
Sig. Each portion to be used to be mixed with three parts of water. (*A lotion for fetid ulcers.*) H. LEE.

2423—℞ Emplastri plumbi . . . . ℥ij.
Ungt. hydrargyri . . . . ℥ss.
Olei cadini . . . . ℥ij.—M.
Ft. unguentum.
Sig. Spread on linen and apply. (*In inflamed syphilitic ulcers.*)
BUMSTEAD AND TAYLOR.

-U-

2424—℞ Chloral. hydratis . . . . ʒss–ij.
Aquæ . . . . f ʒvj.—M.
Ft. lotio.
Sig. Use as a wash. (*In sluggish ulcers.*) KEYES.

2425—℞ Hydrargyri chloridi corrosivi . . . . gr. xv.
Acidi carbolici . . . . ♏xxx.
Aquæ . . . . q. s. ad ʒiv.—M.
Ft. lotio.
Sig. Pack on cotton and renew daily. (*In syphilitic ulcers.*)
FOX.

2426—℞ Unguenti hydrargyri nitratis,
Unguenti simplicis . . . . āā ʒj.—M.
Ft. unguentum.
Sig. Apply locally. (*In serpiginous ulcers.*) KEYES.

2427—℞ Tincturæ iodi . . . . f ʒj.
Acidi tannici . . . . . . q. s. ad saturandum.—M.
(*An application to ulcers of the rectum and anus, fissure in ano.*)
BARTHOLOW.

2428—℞ Iodoformi pulverizati . . . . ʒj.
Detur in scatula.
Sig. Use as a dusting-powder. BARTHOLOW.

2429—℞ Acidi nitrici . . . . ♏xij.
Aquæ destillatæ . . . . f ʒxvj.—M.
Ft. lotio. (*In indolent ulcers.*) E. HOWE.

2430—℞ Aluminis . . . . ʒij.
Aquæ destillatæ . . . . f ʒviij.—M.
Ft. lotio. (*In foul ulcers.*) PENNYPACKER.

2431—℞ Acidi nitrici diluti . . . . ♏x.
Extracti opii . . . . gr. v.
Aquæ destillatæ . . . . f ʒj.—M.
Ft. lotio. (*In sloughing incised wounds.*) ERICHSEN.

2432—℞ Acidi pyrogallici,
Pulv. amyli . . . . āā ʒij.
Vaselini . . . . ʒvj.—M.
Ft. unguentum.
Sig. Preserve in a glass-stopped jar. Spread on lint and
apply once daily. (*In venereal ulcerations.*) TERRILLON.

2433—℞ Zinci sulphatis . . . . gr. xvj.
Tinct. lavandulæ comp.,
Spts. rosmarini . . . āā f ʒij.
Aquæ . . f ʒviij.—M.
Ft. lotio.
Sig. Apply lint wet with the lotion. The granulations may
be touched from time to time with nitrate of silver. (*In
weak ulcers.*) ERICHSEN.

2434—℞ Pulv. camphoræ,
Carbonis animalis . . . . āā ʒj.—M.
Ft. pulvis.
Sig. Use as a dusting-powder, and pack the ulcer. To cleanse
and relieve pain. (*In deep chronic ulcers.*) BARBACCI.

2435—℞ Acidi tannici . . . . gr. lxxv.
Hydrargyri nitratis acid . . . . gtt. xij.
Adipis . . . . ʒviiss.—M.
Ft. unguentum.
Sig. Apply as a dressing. (*For chronic syphilitic ulcers.*)
VENOT.

2436—℞ Calcii phosphatis . . . . ʒj.
Aquæ . . . . f ʒx.—M.
Ft. lotio.
Sig. Saturate compresses and apply, renewing three or four
times daily. (*In leg-ulcers.*) GROSSICH.

2437—℞ Ext. colocynth. comp. . . . . gr. xiv.
   Hydrargyri chloridi mitis . . . . gr. vj.—M.

In pil. no. iv div.
Sig. To be taken at once, and in four hours followed by one
 ounce of compound infusion of senna.   JOHNSON.

2438—℞ Olei tiglii . . . . gtt. viij.
   Elaterii . . . . gr. ss-j.
   Micæ panis . . . . q. s.—M.

Ft. massa et in pil. no. viij div.
Sig. One or two pills to produce watery stools. Use cautiously.
            BARTHOLOW.

2439—℞ Olei tiglii . . . . gtt. v.
   Olei caryophylli . . . . gtt. ij.
   Micæ panis . . . . q. s.

Misce et fiant pilulæ no. v.
Sig. One every two, three, or four hours pro re nata. PARIS.

2440—℞ Hydrargyri chloridi mitis . . . . gr. vj.
   Pilulæ colocynthidis compositæ . . . gr. xiv.—M.

Fiant pilulæ ii.
Sig. One dose, to be followed in four hours by a dose of compound liquorice powder.   GEORGE JOHNSON.

2441—℞ Pulv. scillæ,
   Pulv. scammonii,
   Pulv. digitalis . . . . āā gr. xv.—M.

Ft. massa et in pil. no. xx div.
Sig. Four to six pills daily for five or six days. LANCEREAUX.

2442—℞ Ext. pilocarpi alc,
   Ext. scillæ,
   Resinæ jalapæ,
   Resinæ scammonii . . . . āā gr. xv.—M.

Ft. massa et in pil. no. xx div.
Sig. Four or five pills daily for four or five days. Strict milk
 diet is requisite.   ROLLAND.

2443—℞ Pilocarpinæ muriatis . . . . gr. ij.
   Aquæ destillatæ . . . . ℥ij.—M.

Ft. solutio.
Sig. Inject hypodermically five minims; for a child of six
 years. Ten minims for an adult. E. R. STONE.

2444—℞ Acidi benzoici . . . . ℈v.

Divide in chartulas no. v.
Sig. One powder every three hours, largely diluted.
            DA COSTA.

2445—℞ Sodii benzoatis . . . . ℥iij.

In pulv. no. xii div.
Sig. One powder in solution, or in capsules, every three hours.
            PARZEVSKI.

2446—℞ Chloral. hydratis . . . . ℈viij.
   Syr. aurantii cort. . . . . ℥j.
   Aquæ . . . . ad f℥iv.—M.

Sig. A dessertspoonful as the initial dose, followed by teaspoonful doses, repeated as necessary to relieve the convulsions.   JAS. ANDREW.

2447—℞ Tincturæ scillæ . . . . f℥ij.
   Liquoris ammonii acetatis . . . . . . f℥ij.
   Decocti scoparii . . . . q. s. ad f℥vj.—M.

Sig. Two tablespoonfuls three times daily. CHARTERIS.

2448—℞ Tincturæ hyoscyami . . . . f℥iij.
   Spiritus ætheris nitrosi . . . . f℥ss.
   Liquoris ammonii acetatis . . . . . . f℥j.
   Aquæ camphoræ . . . . . . q. s. ad f℥vj.—M.

Sig. A tablespoonful every three hours. (Inhalation of
 chloroform during convulsions, or chloral hydrate by the
 mouth or hypodermically. In sudden attacks in plethoric
 persons, as sometimes in pregnancy, free venesection.)
           CHARTERIS.

URIC ACID DIATHESIS. (See also Gout.)

2449—℞ Lithii carbonatis . . . . ℨiiss.
   Ext. gentianæ   gr. lxxv.-M.

Ft. massa et in pil. no. c div.
Sig. One pill after each meal. *(In chronic cases with no com-plication.)*   PIERRE VIGIER.

2450—℞ Lithii carbonatis,
   Sodii iodidi . . . . āā ℨiss.
   Ext. gentianæ,
   Pulv. acaciæ . . . . āā gr. xxiij.
   Ext. glycyrrhizæ . . . . ℈v.-M.

Ft. massa et in pil. no. c div.
Sig. Preserve in a well-stopped bottle. One pill after meals. *(In chronic cases with tophi in the joints.)* PIERRE VIGIER.

2451—℞ Lithii carbonatis,
   Potassii iodidi . . . . āā ℨiss.
   Pulv. acaciæ . . . . . . gr. xxiij.
   Ext. gentianæ . . . . ℨiiss.-M.

Ft. massa et in pil. no. c div.
Sig. One pill after each meal. *(In chronic cases with tophi in the joints.)*   PIERRE VIGIER.

2452—℞ Lithii benzoatis . . . . ℨiiss.
   Ext. gentianæ . . . . gr. cv.—M.

Ft. massa et in pil. no. c div.
Sig. A pill morning and evening. *(When complicated with nephritic colic.)*   PIERRE VIGIER.

2453—℞ Sodii bicarbonatis . . . . ℨj.
   Tincturæ calumbæ . . . . f ℨij.
   Infusi quassiæ . . . . f ℨij.—M.

Sig. A tablespoonful four **times a day**. HAZARD.

2454—℞ Sodii carbonatis . . . . ℨij-ℨss.
   Aquæ calidæ . . . . Oij.

Misce et fiat potus.
Sig. To be taken *ad libitum.*   PROUTT.

2455—℞ Sodii boratis . . . . ℨij.
   Sodii bicarbonatis,
   Potassii nitratis . . . . āā ℨiss.—M.

In pulv. no. xii div.
Sig. One powder in a full draught of water. DRUITT.

2456—℞ Liq. potassii arsenitis . . . . ♏v.
   Potassii bicarbonatis,
   Ferri et potassii tartratis . . . . . āā gr. v.
   Infusi quassiæ . . . . f ℨj.—M.

Ft. haustus.
Sig. To be taken thrice **daily, two hours** after meals. *(In asthenic cases.)*   FOTHERGILL.

2457—℞ Acidi hydrochlorici **diluti** . . . . . . f ℨj.
   Acidi lactici . . . . f ℨij.
   Syrupi simplicis . . . . f ℨss.
   Aquæ destillatæ . . . . f ℨij.—M.

Sig. A dessertspoonful after each meal. *(When the excess of acid is due to faulty digestion.)* BARTHOLOW.

URTICARIA. (See also Pruritus.)

2458—℞ Potassii bromidi . . . . . ℨss.
   Aquæ destillatæ . . . . q. s. ad f ℨij.—M.

Sig. A dessertspoonful four times a day. MCCALL ANDERSON.

2459—℞ Pulv. jaborandi,
   Resinæ guaiaci . . . . āā ℨj.
   Lithii benzoatis   ℨij.—M.

Ft. massa et in pil. **no.** xl div.
Sig. Two pills daily, to be increased to four daily. A course of sulpho-arsenical waters is to be used with the pills.
       GUÉNEAU DE MUSSY.

2460—℞ Quininæ sulphatis . . . . gr. xij.
Pulveris rhei . . . . gr. xxiv.
Misce et fiant pilulæ no. xii.
Sig. One pill three times a day. *(When intermittent.)*
WARING.

2461—℞ Plumbi acetatis,
Ammonii carbonatis . . . . āā 3j.
Tincturæ opii . . . . f3ss.
Aquæ rosæ . . . . f3viij.—M.
Sig. Apply locally.
HAZARD.

2462—℞ Acidi benzoici . . . . gr. x–xx.
Aquæ destillatæ . . . . f3viij.
Misce et fiat lotio. *(To allay itching in chronic cases.)* RINGER.

2463—℞ Ammonii carbonatis . . . . . . 3j.
Plumbi acetatis . . . . . 3ij.
Aquæ rosæ . . f3viij.—M.
Ft. lotio.
Sig. Apply locally.
WM. AITKEN.

2464—℞ Sodii biboratis . . . . 3ss.
Aquæ destillatæ . . . . f3viij.—M.
Ft. lotio. *(Also in chloasma, or liver-spots.—PEREIRA.)*
WARING.

2465—℞ Chloroformi . . . . f3j.
Glycerini . . . . f3iv.—M.
Ft. lotio.
Sig. Apply locally with a brush.
DUPARC.

2466—℞ Acidi benzoici . . . . gr. viij.
Aquæ . . . . f3iv.—M.
Ft. lotio.
Sig. Apply locally as a wash.
SQUIRE.

2467—℞ Hydrargyri chloridi corrosivi . . . . gr. iss.
Chloroformi . . . . ♏xx.
Glycerini . . . . f3ij.
Aquæ rosæ . . . . f3vj.—M.
Ft. lotio.
Sig. Use locally. *(Also used in pruritus and in papular and vesicular diseases.)*
BURGESS.

2468—℞ Sodii bicarbonatis . . . . 3j.
Glycerini . . . . 3ss.
Aquæ sambuci . . . . f3viss.—M.
Ft. lotio.
Sig. Apply to allay the itching.
TILBURY FOX.

2469—℞ Potassii cyanidi . . . . gr. vj.
Pulv. cocci . . . . gr. j.
Ungt. aquæ rosæ . . . . 3j.—M.
Ft. unguentum.
Sig. Apply locally. *(Also used in pruritus.)*
ANDERSON.

2470—℞ Sodii boratis . . . . 3ij.
Aquæ laurocerasi . . . . f3j.
Aquæ sambuci . . . . f3xj.—M.
Ft. lotio.
Sig. Use as a wash, to allay the itching. *(Also used in lichen.)*
NELIGAN.

2471—℞ Hydrargyri chloridi corrosivi . . . . . gr. j.
Acidi hydrocyanici diluti . . . . 3j.
Misturæ amygdalæ . . . . f3vj.—M.
Ft. lotio.
Sig. Apply locally, to allay the itching. *(Also used in lichen and in the syphilodermata.)*
TILBURY FOX.

UTERUS, SUBINVOLUTION OF.

2472—℞ Ext. ergotæ fld.,
Ext. viburni fld. . . . . āā f3j.—M.
Sig. A teaspoonful in water three times a day, after meals.
ELLWOOD WILSON.

2473—℞ Strychninæ sulphatis . . . . gr. ⅒.
Quininæ sulphatis . . . . gr. ij.
Ext. ergotæ . . . . gr. j.
Misce et fiat pil. no. I.
Sig. One pill three times a day.   B. C. HIRST.

UVULA, RELAXATION OF.

2474—℞ Trochisci acidi tannici . . . . no. xx.
Sig. Let one dissolve slowly in the mouth every two or three
hours.   WILLIAM AITKEN.

2475—℞ Zinci chloridi . . . . ℨj.
Aquæ . . . . f ℨij.—M.
Sig. Apply to the soft palate and uvula. MORELL MACKENZIE.

2476—℞ Pulveris capsici . . . . ℨss.
Potassii nitratis.
Ammonii chloridi . . . . āā ℨj.
Misce bene et detur in scatula.
Sig. Apply by means of a camel's-hair pencil.
    B. GRANVILLE.

2477—℞ Liq. **ferri perchloridi** . . . . ℨij.
Aquæ . . . . f ℨij.—M.
Sig. Apply to the **soft palate and uvula.** MORELL MACKENZIE.

2478—℞ Acidi tannici . . . . ℨss.
Glycerini . . . . f ℨij.
Misce cum leni calore.
Sig. Apply with a camel's-hair brush.   **HILLIER.**

2479—℞ Acidi tannici . . ℨss.
Aquæ . f ℨvj.—M.
Ft. gargarisma.
Sig. Use as a gargle every two or three hours. SAJOUS.

2480—℞ Pulv. aluminis . ℨij.
Aquæ . . . . . . f ℨvj.—M.
Ft. gargarisma.
Sig. Use as a gargle every two or three hours. **SAJOUS.**

2481—R Aluminis . . . . ℨj.
Infusi galllæ . . . . . f ℨvj.—M.
Ft. gargarisma. (*With hypertrophied tonsils.*) WARING.

VAGINISMUS.

2482—℞ Iodoform . . . . gr. xv.
Extract of belladonna . . . . gr. viij.
Cacao butter . q. s.—M.
For one suppository.
Sig. Use at night.   LUTAUD.

VAGINITIS.

2483—℞ Tincturæ cubebæ . . . . f ℨij.
Sig. A teaspoonful three times a day.   PIORRY.

2484—℞ Acidi boracici . . . . ℨiiss.
Glycerini . . . . ℨxxx.—M.
Sig. Three or four dessertspoonfuls in a quart of water as a
vaginal injection twice daily, or upon a cotton tampon.
    CHÉRON.

2485—℞ Cubebæ . . . . ℨj.
Aquæ . . . . Oj.—M.
Ft. infusum. (*As a vaginal injection.*) PIORRY.

2486—℞ Glycerini . . . . f ℨiv.
Acidi tannici . . . . ℨj.—M.
(*A local application for adults and children.*) BRAXTON HICKS.

2487—℞ Aluminis . . . . ℨj.
Aquæ . . . . Oj.—M.
Ft. lotio. (*In vulvitis of children.*) RINGER.

VAGINITIS (Continued).

2488—℞ Liquoris plumbi subacetatis . . . . . f℥j.
      Tincturæ hyoscyami . . . . f℥ij.
      Aquæ camphoræ . . . . f℥viij.
Misce et fiat lotio.
Sig. Apply constantly, tepid, with saturated cloths. (*In vulvitis of adults and children.*)   WARING.

2489—℞ Glyceriti acidi tannici . . . . ℥j.
Sig. Apply locally, or diluted, as an injection. (*In chronic vaginitis of children.*)   RINGER.

2490—℞ Argenti nitratis   ℈j.
      Aquæ destillatæ . . . . f℥j.—M.
Sig. Apply on a cotton pledget, within the cervical canal and over the vaginal mucous membrane.   EMMET.

2491—℞ Ext. hydrastis fld. .   . f℥iv.
Sig. Apply freely to the cervix and vagina, and leave a cotton tampon smeared with vaseline between the vulvæ and in the vagina. (*When nitrate of silver fails.*)   MUNDÉ.

2492—℞ Balsami gurjunæ . . . . ℥ij.
      Liquoris calcis . . . . f℥iv.—M.
Sig. Saturate a **cotton tampon, and leave it** in the vagina twenty-four hours.   VIDAL.

2493—℞ Glycerini . .   ℥iv.
      Acidi tannici . . .   . . . ℈ss.
      Morphinæ sulphatis   . . gr. ⅓.—M.
Sig. Paint the whole vaginal canal with nitrate of silver solution (1 to 8), then saturate a cotton tampon with the above solution, and pack it in the vagina to slightly distend it. Leave the tampon in for two days. (*In the subacute form.*)
                               T. G. THOMAS.

2494—℞ Acidi tannici . . . . ℥j.
      Morphinæ sulphatis . . . . gr. iij.
      Olei theobromæ . . . . ℥v.—M.
Ft. suppositoria no. x.
Sig. One *per vaginam,* **every night and** morning, after free syringing.   T. G. THOMAS.

VALVULAR DISEASE. (See Heart-Disease.)

VARICOSE VEINS.

2495—℞ Ext. hamamelidis fld.   f℥iij.
Sig. A teaspoonful three or four times daily, with compresses applied externally.   MUSSER.

2496—℞ Ext. ergotini **aquosi** . . . . ℥j.
      Glycerini . . . . f℥j.
      Aquæ destillatæ . . . . f℥vij.—M.
Sig. Fifteen minims hypodermically, near the veins.
                               BARTHOLOW.

2497—℞ Barii chloridi .   gr. xxx.
      Aquæ destillatæ . .   q. s. ut ft. sol.
      Lanolini . .   gr. ccxxv.
      Olei amygdalæ dulcis . . . . .   𝕸lxxv.—M.
Ft. unguentum.
Sig. Use three times daily, with friction, where blue veins shine through the skin.   KOBERT.

2498—℞ Sodii chloridi . . . . gr. xv.
      Aquæ destillatæ . . . . q. s. ad ft. sol.
      Lanolini . . . . gr. ccxxv.
      Olei olivæ . . . . 𝕸lxxv.—M.
Sig. Rub in thrice daily over the varicose veins.   ROBERT.

VARIOLA. (See Small-Pox.)

VENEREAL DISEASE. (See Syphilis, Chancroid, etc.)

2499—℞ Pil. hydrargyri,
Pil. rhei comp.,
Ext. hyoscyami . . . . āā ᴣj.—M.

In pil. no. xij div.

Sig. Two pills **occasionally at bedtime.** (*In plethoric cases.*)
A. TANNER.

2500—℞ Hydrargyri chloridi corrosivi . . . . . gr. j.
Glycerini . . . . ᴣj.
Tinct. cinchonæ comp. . . . . . . ad ᴣiij.
Olei menthæ pip. . . . . . . ♏xxv.—M.

Sig. One teaspoonful in a wineglassful of water thrice daily.
(*In vertigo of the aged.*) TANNER.

2501—℞ Pulv. jalapæ . . . . gr. xij.
Hydrargyri chloridi mitis . . . . . . gr. iij.
Potassii sulphatis . . . . gr. vij.—M.

Ft. pulvis.

Sig. To be taken at bedtime. (*In bilious vertigo.*)
A. T. THOMPSON.

2502—℞ Hydrargyri chloridi corrosivi . . . . . gr. j.
Glycerini . . . . fᴣj.
Tincturæ cinchonæ compositæ . . . . fᴣij.
Olei menthæ piperitæ . . . . ♏xxv.—M.

Sig. A teaspoonful in a wineglassful of water three times a
day. (*In the vertigo and dizziness of the aged.*)
C. HANDFIELD JONES.

2503—℞ Pulveris rhei . . . . ᴣj.
Sodii bicarbonatis,
Pulveris gentianæ . . . . āā ᴣij.
Aquæ menthæ piperitæ,
Aquæ destillatæ . . . . āā fᴣiij.—M.

Sig. A tablespoonful **before each meal.** (*When due to indigestion.*)
E. C. MANN.

2504—℞ Potassii bitartratis . . . . ᴣvj.
Pulveris jalapæ . . . . . . ᴣij.—M.

Sig. A teaspoonful, in milk or syrup, every two or three hours.
(*In plethoric cases.*) H. V. SWERINGEN.

2505—℞ Potassii bicarbonatis . . . . . ᴣij.
Tincturæ nucis vomicæ . . . . . . fᴣss.
Tincturæ cardamomi compositæ . fᴣiij.
Liquoris lacto-peptini . . fᴣj.
Syrupi simplicis . . . . fᴣij.
Aquæ menthæ piperitæ . q. s. ad fᴣiv.—M.

Sig. A tablespoonful in water every three or four hours. (*In gastric vertigo.*) H. V. SWERINGEN.

2506—℞ Tinct. gelsemii . . . . fᴣj.

Sig. Ten minims thrice daily. (*In aural vertigo.*) RINGER.

2507—℞ Tinct. digitalis . . . . fᴣj.

Sig. Twelve drops in water three or four times a day. (*In weak heart.*) J. C. WILSON.

VOMITING. (See also Morning Sickness and Sea-Sickness.)

2508—℞ Menthol . . . . gr. xv.
Spiritus vini . fᴣv.
Aquæ destillatæ . fᴣv.—M.

Sig. A spoonful hourly. GOTTSCHALK.

2509—℞ Acidi carbolici . . . . gr. iv.
Bismuthi subnitratis ᴣij.
Mucilaginis acaciæ . fᴣj.
Aquæ menthæ piperitæ fᴣiij.—M.

Sig. A tablespoonful every two, three, or four hours. (*When due to acute stomachal and intestinal disorder.*) BARTHOLOW.

2510—℞ Creasoti . . . . ♏vj.
Pulveris tragacanthæ . . . . ᴣss.
Aquæ camphoræ . . . . fᴣvj.—M.

Sig. A sixth part to be taken for a dose. (*In obstinate vomiting.*) KESTEVEN.

2511—℞ Creasoti . . . . ♏iv.
Aquæ . . . . f℥vj.—M.
Sig. A tablespoonful, repeated as necessary. NIEMEYER.

2512—℞ Liquoris calcis,
Lactis recentis . . . . āā f℥iv.—M.
Sig. A tablespoonful every half-hour or hour. WOOD.

2513—℞ Vini ipecacuanhæ . . . . f℥ss.
Sig. One drop **every hour to thrice daily**. (*Suitable in all cases.*) RINGER.

2514—℞ Extracti nucis vomicæ . . . . gr. j.
Extracti conii . . . . gr. xij.
Misce et fiant pilulæ no. vi.
Sig. One three times a day. (**When due** *to malignant disease of the stomach.*) BARLOW.

2515—℞ Sodii bicarbonatis . . . . gr. xv.
Acidi hydrocyanici diluti . . . . . . ♏iss.
Aquæ camphoræ . . . . f℥x.—M.
Ft. haustus.
Sig. To be taken **thrice daily after meals**. (*When due to acidity.*) CHAMBERS.

2516—℞ Cocainæ hydrochloratis . . . . gr. vj.
Aquæ destillatæ . . . . f℥viiss.—M.
Sig. Two tablespoonfuls every hour, until six grains of cocaine have been taken during the twenty-four hours. To avoid vertigo, the recumbent posture is necessary. (*In vomiting of pregnancy.*) DUJARDIN-BEAUMETZ.

2517—℞ Ext. nucis vomicæ . . . . gr. xv.
Ext. belladonnæ,
Ext. opii . . . . āā gr. iij.—M.
Ft. massa et in pil. no. xx div.
Sig. One pill at night. (*In vomiting of uterine catarrh.*) AUDHOUL.

2518—℞ Bismuthi subnitratis . . . . ℈ij.
Acidi hydrocyanici diluti . . . . f℥ss.
Mucilaginis acaciæ,
Aquæ menthæ piperitæ . . . . . āā f℥ij.—M.
Sig. A tablespoonful thrice daily. (*With gastric ulcer.*) DA COSTA.

2519—℞ Ext. belladonnæ,
Ext. physostigmatis,
Ext. nucis vomicæ,
Aloini . . . . āā gr. xv.
Ferri sulphatis exsiccatæ . . ℈j.—M.
Ft. massa et in pil. no. lx div.
Sig. One pill at bedtime. One grain of permanganate of potash, in distilled water, is also taken thrice daily. (*In hysterical vomiting.*) BARTHOLOW.

2520—℞ Ammonii carbonatis . . . . ℈ij.
Pulveris tragacanthæ . . . . . . ℈j.
Aquæ destillatæ . . . . . . f℥vij.—M.
Sig. A tablespoonful every hour. (*When due to acidity.*) EUDERMACHER.

2521—℞ Aloini . . . . gr. v.
Strychninæ sulphatis . . . . gr. j.
Ext. colocynth. comp. . . . . gr. v.
Ext. hyoscyami . . . . ℈j.—M.
Ft. massa et in pil. no. lx div.
Sig. One pill after each meal. (*In obstinate vomiting* **due to** *chronic constipation.*) DA COSTA.

2522—℞ Tincturæ benzoini compositæ,
Acidi sulphurici diluti . . . . . . āā f℥ss.—M.
Sig. **Thirty drops, with sugar.** E. G. CLARK.

2523—℞ Acidi hydrobromici . . . . f℥j.
Sig. Thirty minims in a half-wineglassful of water four times daily. (*In vomiting due to gastric ulcer.*) RINGER.

VOMITING (Continued).

2524—℞ Potassii iodidi . . . . ℨiv.
  Infusi quassiæ . . . . f ℨviij.—M.
Sig. A tablespoonful three times a day. (*In sympathetic vomiting.*) SELKIRK.

2525—℞ Chloroformi . . . . f ℨj.
Sig. Two to **five minims, on sugar.** (*In non-inflammatory vomiting.*) RINGER.

2526—℞ Tinct. nucis vomicæ . . mij.
  Aquæ laurocerasi .   f ℨj.—M.
Sig. **Ten** drops night and morning. (*In pregnancy.*) KROYLA.

2527—℞ Hydrargyri cum cretâ gr. iv.
  Sacchari lactis gr. x.—M.
In pulv. no. xii div.
Sig. A powder dry on the tongue every two hours. (*In children with clayey stools.*) RINGER.

2528—℞ Potassii nitratis . . . . . ℨj.
  Acidi hydrocyanici diluti . gtt. vj.
  Syr. simplicis . . . . f ℨss.
  Aquæ destillatæ . . . . f ℨiss.—M.
Sig. A quarter to a half-teaspoonful thrice daily. (*In infantile vomiting.*) EUSTACE SMITH.

2529—℞ Liq. potassii arsenitis . . . . **f ℨss.**
Sig. A drop every half-hour, for six or eight doses. (*In vomiting of drunkards and of pregnancy.*) A. A. SMITH.

VULVITIS. (See Vaginitis.)

WAKEFULNESS. (See Insomnia.)

WARTS. (See also Condylomata.)

2530—℞ Acidi salicylici,
  Alcoholis . . . . . . āā ℨij.
  Æther. sulph. ℨv.
  Collodii . . . . ℨx.—M.
Sig. Paint the warts with the solution daily. E. VIDAL.

WHITLOW. (See Onychia.)

WHOOPING-COUGH.

2531—℞ Ext. castaneæ fld. . . . . f ℨiiiss.
  Glycerini . . . . f ℨss.
  Potassii bromidi . ℨij.—M.
Sig. A teaspoonful in water every two or three hours, for a child six years old. J. C. WILSON.

2532—℞ Powdered belladonna-root . . . . gr. ¼.
  Dover's powder . gr. ½
  Sublimed sulphur . . gr. iv.
  White sugar . . . . gr. x.—M.
Sig. Take in one dose from two to ten times a day, according to age of patient and effect produced. GERMAIN SÉE.

2533—℞ Cocainæ muriatis . . . . . . gr. iij.
  Aquæ amygdalæ amaræ . . . . . . f ℨiiss.—M.
Sig. **Ten to fifteen drops several times daily.** WEINTRAUB.

2534—℞ Antipyrin. . . . . **gr. ij.**
  Sacchari albi . . . . **ℨj.—M.**
In pulv. no. xiv div.
Sig. A powder three times during the day and once during the night, for very young children. Dose increased up to fifteen grains for adults. SONNENBERGER.

2535—℞ Acidi nitrici diluti . . . . f℥ij.
Syrupi simplicis . . . . f℥iss.
Aquæ destillatæ . . . . f℥j.—M.
Sig. A teaspoonful every three **hours.** HAZARD.

2536—℞ Tincturæ lobeliæ,
Syrupi scillæ . . . . āā f℥j.
Extracti belladonnæ . . . . gr. iv.—M.
Sig. Thirty drops three times a day. **HAZARD.**

2537—℞ Sol. cocainæ muriatis (5 per cent.) . . ℥ss.
Sig. Paint the **throat** and fauces repeatedly, with a camel's-hair brush. LABRIC.

2538—℞ Ext. cannabis indicæ . . . . gr. xv.
Ext. belladonnæ . . . . gr. vliss.
Alcoholis absoluti,
Glycerini . . . . . . āā ℳlxxv.—M.
Sig. Four **or** five drops to a child of eight months to one year; one to two years, five to eight drops; over twelve years, and adults, fifteen to twenty drops. VETLESEN.

2539—℞ Potassii carbonatis . ℈j.
Pulveris cocci ℈ss.
Sacchari albi ℥j.
Aquæ destillatæ . . . . . . f℥iv.—M.
Sig. Dose for children, a teaspoonful every two or three hours.
N. CHAPMAN.

2540—℞ **Liquoris hydrogenii** peroxidi (10 vols.) ℥vj.
Glycerini puriss. ℥iv.
Aquæ destillatæ . . . . ad ℥iij.—M.
Sig. A tablespoonful in a wineglassful of water, five or six
times daily. B. W. RICHARDSON.

2541—℞ **Acidi carbolici** . . . . ℥ss.
Potassii chloratis . . . . ℥ij.
Glycerini . . . . ℥iv.
Aquæ . . . . q. s. ad ℥vj.—M.
Sig. Use with a steam atomizer three times daily.
J. LEWIS SMITH.

2542—℞ Acidi carbolici puri . . . . . gtt. xv-xx.
Sig. Drop on cotton or in an inhaler, and inhale for several hours daily. Renew the cotton three times a day. PICK.

2543—℞ Sodii benzoatis . . . . ℈iv.
Aquæ menthæ pip.,
Aquæ destillatæ . . . . āā ℥x.
Syr. aurantii . . . . ℥ij.—M.
Sig. A dessertspoonful every hour or two. LETZERICH.

2544—℞ Quininæ sulphatis . . . gr. c.
Pulv. benzoini . . . gr. x.—M.
In pulv. no. vii div.
Sig. One powder to be insufflated into the nose during the day. BACHEN.

2545—℞ Ext. aconiti . . . . gr. j.
Syr. ipecac. . . . . . ℳxlv.
Aquæ lauroccrasi . . . ℥j.
Mucilaginis acaciæ . . . . ℥viss.—M.
Sig. A teaspoonful to a tablespoonful, according to age, every hour. DERVIEUX.

2546—℞ Pulv. benzoini.
Bismuthi salicylatis . . . . āā ℥iss.
Quininæ sulphatis . . . . gr. xxx.—M.
Sig. **Insufflate** the fauces several **times daily.** MOIZARD.

2547—℞ Pulv. acidi **boracici** . . . ℥j-iss.
In pulv. no. xxx div.
Sig. Insufflate one powder into each nostril three times during the day and once at night. HOLLOWAY.

2548—℞ Quininæ sulphatis . . . . gr. j.
    Acidi sulpharici . . . . gtt. xxx.
    Aquæ destillatæ . . . . ℥v ℥v.—M.

Sig. Use as a spray to the fauces every two hours for the first
three days, and every three hours for the remainder of the
first week, after which it will be unnecessary. KOLOVER.

2549—℞ Olei terebinthinæ . . . . f ℥j-iv.
    Olei ricini . . . . f ℥j.
    Mucilaginis acaciæ . . . . f ℥ij.—M.

Sig. One dose. (In tape-worm.) McPHAIL.

2550—℞ Olei terebinthinæ,
    Oleoresinæ filicis maris . . . . . . āā ℥j.
    Mucilaginis acaciæ . . . . f ℥ij.—M.

Ft. emulsio.
Sig. Day before treatment, a milk or thin soup diet, and one
drachm of compound jalap powder. The emulsion is
taken the following morning, fasting, and a half-hour later
a dose of castor oil. (In tape-worm.) F. A. A. SMITH.

2551—℞ Pulveris kamalæ . . . . gr. v-x.
    Syrupi aurantii florum . . . . f ℥ss.
    Mucilaginis tragacanthæ . . . . ℥j.
    Aquæ destillatæ . . . . f ℥j.

Misce et fiat haustus.
Sig. Take early in the morning four hours after a purge.
(For a child from two to five years. In tape-worm.) TANNER.

2552—℞ Olei tiglii . . . . gtt. j.
    Chloroformi . . . . f ℥j.
    Glycerini . . . . f ℥viss.—M.

Sig. At night give a saline purge; the following morning before breakfast the above mixture. (In tænia.) B. PEESH.

2553—℞ Peponis decort. . . . . ℥v-x.
    Sacchari albi . . . . ℥v) gr. xv.
    Lactis recentis . . . . f ℥xv.—M.

Ft. emulsio.
Sig. To be given before breakfast. Two hours later to be followed by castor oil. (In tape-worm.) DUPONT.

2554—℞ Pelletierine sulphatis . . . . gr. vj-viiss.
    Pulv. acidi tannici . . . . gr. viiss.
    Syr. simplicis . . . . f ℥j.—M.

Sig. Take a little milk for supper, and a simple enema at bedtime. Take the mixture the following morning before
breakfast, and lie down to prevent vertigo. In a quarter- or
a half-hour take an ounce of castor oil. (In tape-worm.)
LABBÉ.

2555—℞ Pelletierine tannatis . . . . gr. vij.
    Syr. simplicis . . . . f ℥ss.—M.

Sig. Milk diet the day before. Before breakfast, a dose of
infusion of senna. One hour later, half the medicine, and
the rest a half-hour later. A half-hour later, an ounce of
castor oil. Patient to remain in bed during treatment. A
large vessel of warm water should be ready to receive the
worm. (In tape-worm.) BÉRENGER-FÉRAUD.

2556—℞ Thymoli . . . . ℥ij.

In pulv. no. xii div.
Sig. A powder every fifteen minutes. A dose of castor oil
should precede and follow the powders. (In tape-worm.)
N. CAMPI.

2557—℞ Chloroformi . . . . f ℥j.
    Syr. simplicis . . . . f ℥j.—M.

Sig. To be given in three doses, at intervals of two hours;
taken fasting, and followed by castor oil. (In tape-worm.)
THOMPSON.

2558—℞ Oleoresinæ filicis maris,
    Tinct. vanillæ . . . . āā ℥xlv.
    Syr. terebinthinæ . . . . f ℥vij ℥xv.
    Pulv. acaciæ . . . . gr. xxx.
    Aquæ destillatæ . . . . f ℥vj ℥xv.

Misce.
Sig. To be taken at one dose, in an equal quantity of milk.
Castor oil should be given a few hours later. (In tape-
worm.) EILLARD.

2559—℞ Ext. filicis maris fl. . . . . ƒ ʒj.
Hydrargyri chloridi mitis . . . . gr. vij.
Sacchari . . . . ʒij.

Mix, and add a sufficient quantity of gelatin to make a jelly
of a proper consistency.
Sig. (*For children.*)   DESCROIZILLES.

2560—℞ Ext. filicis maris fl. . . . . ƒ ʒss-ƒ ʒij.
Ess. anisi . . . . ♏ x.
Aquæ menthæ pip. . . . . ƒ ʒss.
Aquæ anthemidis . . . . ƒ ʒj.
Syrupi,
Syrupi aurantii cort. . . . . . . āā ƒ ʒvj.—M.

Sig. (*For children.*)   DUCHENNE.

2561—℞ Olei tiglii . gtt. j.
Chloroformi . . ʒj.
Glycerini ʒx.—M.
Sig. One dose.   KAISER.

2562—℞ Olei chenopodii . . gtt. lx-ƒ ʒj.
Mucilaginis acaciæ . . . . ƒ ʒij.
Syrupi simplicis . . . . ƒ ʒj.
Aquæ cinnamomi . . . ƒ ʒij.—M.

Sig. A dessertspoonful three times a day for three days, and
repeat after three days. (*In lumbrici. For a child of two
years.*)   MEIGS AND PEPPER.

2563—℞ Santonini . . . . . . gr. viij.
Extracti sennæ et spigeliæ fluidi . . . ƒ ʒj.—M.

Sig. One teaspoonful to a child of five years. (*In lumbrici and
ascarides.*)   J. LEWIS SMITH.

2564—℞ Hydrargyri chloridi mitis . . . . gr. ij.
Santonini . . . . gr. iss.
Sacchari lactis . . . . gr. xv.

Misce et fiat pulvis.
Sig. One dose, in honey. (*Infant two years old. In lumbrici.*)
EUGENE BOUCHUT.

2565—℞ Mucunæ . . . . ʒij-ʒj.
Syrupi simplicis . . . . ʒss.—M.

Sig. A teaspoonful every morning before breakfast for three
days, and a dose of castor oil after the last dose. (*Children
from two to five years old. In lumbrici.*)   CORREA.

2566—℞ Tinct. rhei . . . . gtt. lij.
Tinct. zingiberis . . . . gtt. j.
Magnesii carbonatis . . . . ʒv.
Aquæ . . . . ƒ ʒij.—M.

Sig. This dose should be taken three or four times daily,
according to the effect on the bowels. (*In oxyuris.*)
SYDNEY MARTIN.

2567—℞ Sodii chloridi . . . . ʒx.
Aquæ . . . . ƒ ʒvj.—M.

Ft. solutio.
Sig. **To be injected by the rectum.** (*In oxyuris.*)   EILLARD.

2568—℞ Acidi tannici . . . . gr. xv.
Olei theobromæ . . . . ʒj.—M.

Ft. suppositorium no. i.
Sig. To be introduced into the **rectum.** (*In thread-worms.*)
EILLARD.

2569—℞ Tinct. ferri chloridi . . . . ʒss.
Aquæ . . . . Oj.—M.

Sig. **One-fourth to one-third, as a rectal enema.** (*In seat-
worms.*)   RINGER.

2570—℞ Trochisci **santonini** (U.S.P.) no. xxiv.

Sig. One to six at bedtime for children, with a dose **of** castor
oil the following morning. (*In ascarides.*)   BARTHOLOW.

2571—℞ Infusi quassiæ . . . . ʒvj.
Sig. Use as a rectal injection. (*In seat-worms.*)   RINGER.

2572—℞ Santonini . . . . gr. xij.
   Olei theobromæ . . . . ℥j.—M.
Fiant suppositoria nos. iv.
Sig. One at bedtime, introduced into the bowel. (*For seat-worms.*)   HARTSHORNE.

2573—℞ Tincturæ ferri chloridi . . . . f℥ss.
   Aquæ . . . . f℥vlij.—M.
Ft. enema. (*In ascarides.*)   DARWALL.

2574—℞ Fuliginis ligni . . . . ℥j.
   Aquæ . . . . f℥v.—M.
Coque per quartam partem horæ et cola.
Ft. enema. (*In ascarides.*)   TROUSSEAU.

2575—℞ Sodii chloridi . . . . ℥ij.
   Infusi quassiæ . . . . Oj.—M.
Ft. enema.
Sig. Use once a day. If this fails to dislodge them completely, give—

2576—℞ Ferri sulphatis,
   Quininæ sulphatis,
   Pilulæ aloës cum myrrhâ,
   Pilulæ galbani compositæ . . . . āā gr. l.
Misce et fiant pilulæ no. l.
Sig. Take one pill three times a day. Keep up for a fortnight.
  Adult dose. (*In oxyuris vermicularis.*) W. DALE.

WOUNDS.

2577—℞ Acidi carbolici,
   Olei ricini . . . . āā f℥ss.
   Collodii . . . . f℥j.—M.
Sig. "Carbolized collodion"

2578—℞ Acidi tannici . . . . ℥iss.
   Alcoholis absoluti . . . . f℥ss.
   Ætheris . . . . f℥iiss.
   Collodii . . . . f℥xij.—M.
Sig. "Styptic colloid."

2579—℞ Iodoformi . . . . ℥j.
   Collodii flexilis . . . . ℥vj).—M.
Sig. Hold or stitch the edges of the wound together, and apply with a brush. (*In superficial wounds.*) BRUNS.

2580—℞ Salol,
   Ætheris . . . . āā ℥j.
Solve et adde—
   Collodii flexilis . . . . f℥viiss.—M.
Sig. Apply with a camel's-hair brush. NICOT.

2581—℞ Hydrargyri chloridi corrosivi . . . . . gr. viiss.
   Aquæ ferventis . . . . Oij.—M.
Sig. "Sublimate solution (1 to 2000)." (*For washing wounds, irrigating cavities, or saturating dressings.*)

2582—℞ Pulv. acidi salicylici . . . . ℥j.
Sig. Use as a dusting-powder.   THIERSCH.

2583—℞ Iodoformi . . . . ℥ij.
Sig. Use as a dusting-powder, and apply dry dressings.
            BARTHOLOW.

2584—℞ Pulv. aloes . . . . ℥j.
Sig. Dust over the wound, and apply dry dressings. Remove only at long intervals.   MILLET.

2585—℞ Acidi boracici . . . . ℥iss.
   Glycerini . . . . f℥iij.
   Infusi caryophylli (℥iv ad Oj) . . . . Oij.
   Olei menthæ pip. . . . . ♏vj).—M.
Sig. "Aseptin."   MAGNUS TROILIUS.

WOUNDS (Continued).

2586—℞ Pulv. saloli,
      Pulv. amyli . . . . āā ʒss.—M.
  Sig. Use as a dusting-powder.   CREYX ET JARRY.

2587—℞ Pulv. naphthol. . . .   . . ʒj.
  Sig. Use as a dusting-powder.   BOUCHARD.

2588—℞ Iodoformi . . . . gr. c.
      Thymoli . . . . gr. cc.
      Sacchari lactis . . . . gr. j.—M.
  Ft. pulvis.
  Sig. Apply as a powder thrice daily.   R. G. REYNOLDS.

2589—℞ Tincturæ arnicæ   f ʒij.
      Aquæ destillatæ .   f ʒiv.—M.
  Ft. lotio.   GRAEFE.

2590—℞ Phenol sodique . . . . f ʒvj.
  Sig. In all wounds and surgical operations.   J. E. GARRETSON.

2591—℞ Acidi carbolici . .   ʒj.
      Glycerini   . .   f ʒj.—M.
       HAZARD.

2592—℞ Tincturæ eucalypti . . . . f ʒij.
      Aquæ destillatæ . . . . f ʒiv.—M.
       GIMBERT.

2593—℞ Ext. calendulæ fld.   f ʒj.
      Alcoholis   f ʒij.—M.
  Sig. Use as a dressing.   R. G. REYNOLDS.

2594—℞ Iodol. . . . . ʒj.
      Glycerini . . . . f ʒj.
      Vaselini . . . . ʒvij.—M.
  Ft. unguentum.
  Sig. Use locally.   WOLFENDEN.

2595—℞ Acidi boracici . . . . ʒiss.
      Ess. eucalypti . . . . f ʒiss.
      Vaselini . . . . ʒxxv.—M.
  Ft. unguentum.
  Sig. To be used as a dressing. *(The boracic acid may be re-*
  placed by mercuric chloride corr., gr. iss., if desired.) BRONDEL.

XERODERMA. (See Ichthyosis.)

YELLOW FEVER. (See Fever.)

Z Nothing listed

-XYZ-

II

Special List of New Remedies, with their Dosage, Solubilities, and Therapeutic Applications.

Acetophenone.

Syn. Hypnone; Phenyl-Methyl Ketone.

Dose, 1½ to 5 minims, in almond emulsion or with mucilage or syrup, in peppermint water, or in capsules with oil.

Insoluble in water, but soluble in alcohol, ether, and oil.

As a hypnotic; useful in nervous affections and insomnia without pain; act on uncertain.

Acidum Phenylaceticum—Phenylacetic Acid.

Syn. Alphatoluic Acid.

Dose, 1 to 3 grains, in alcoholic or oily solution.

Soluble 1 in 1 of spirit, 1 in 29 of oils.

Phthisis, in doses of 10 to 20 minims of a 1 in 6 alcoholic solution, freely diluted, three times a day.

Acidum Phenylpropionicum — Phenylpropionic Acid.

Syn. Hydrocinnamic Acid; Homotoluic Acid.

Dose, 1 to 3 grains, in alcoholic or oily solution.

Soluble 1 in 1 of spirit, 1 in 5 of oils.

In phthisis, same dose as preceding, but less useful.

Adonis Vernalis

Dose, in powder, 3 **to 6 grains;** of the infusion, 1 in 40, 4 drachms.

Adonidin.

Dose, ¼ to ½ grain daily.

Cardiac tonic and diuretic.

Useful in the præcordial pains of cardiac disease.

Agaricin.

Dose, ⅒ to ¼ grain.

In night-sweats.

Aldehyde, Diluted.

A mixture of spirit and aldehyde, containing **15 per cent.** of the latter.

Dose for inhalation, 10 minims in a pint of hot water.

In catarrhal congestion and ozena.

Metaldehyde.

Dose, 2 to 8 grains, in cachets or pills.

Insoluble in water, slightly soluble in alcohol and ether.

Sedative and hypnotic.

Paraldehydum—Paraldehyde.

Dose, 30 to 60 minims, in diluted syrup or almond mixture.

Soluble 1 in 10 of water.

Hypnotic; resembling chloral in its effects, but without its depressing influence upon the heart. Is sedative rather than anodyne.

Amyl Nitrite.

Dose, by inhalation, the vapor of 2 to 5 minims; **by the mouth,** ¼ to 1 minim.

Soluble in spirit, insoluble in water.

In angina pectoris, sea-sickness, ague, spasmodic asthma, migraine, neuralgic dysmenorrhœa, post-partum hemorrhage, **as an** antidote to chloroform, to ward off epileptic attacks, **and** for the **spasm** of false croup and whooping-cough.

Sold in **the shops in glass capsules, 1, 2, 3, or 5 minims.**

Isobutyl Nitrite.

When pure, has effects analogous to the above, for which it may be used as a substitute.

Amylene, Hydrate of.

Syn. Dimethyl-Ethyl Carbinol.
Dose, 30 to 80 minims, flavored with extract of liquorice.
Soluble in 12 parts of water, and in spirit.
Hypnotic: intermediate in its effects between chloral and paraldehyde.

Anacardium Occidentale—Cashew-Nut.

Best given in the form of a 10-per-cent. tincture, of which the dose is 2 to 10 minims.
In leprosy; also as a vermifuge. Locally in ringworm and obstinate ulcers.

Aniline.

Syn. Phenylamine, Mono-Phenylamine.
In phthisis, by inhalations from a specially-designed inhaler, 1 part of aniline to 7 parts of oil of eucalyptus, anise, peppermint, or gaultheria.

Anthrarobin.

Five to ten per cent. ointment, or as a tincture.
Sparingly soluble in chloroform and ether, but readily so in alcohol or weak alkaline solutions.
In psoriasis.

Antifebrin. (Patented under this name.)

Syn. Acetanilide; Phenylacetamide.
Dose, 4 to 15 grains, in cachets, or suspended by means of mucilage of tragacanth or acacia in an aqueous vehicle.
Almost insoluble in cold water, but freely soluble in spirit; neutral in reaction.
As a febrifuge and antipyretic, hypnotic, sedative, anti-epileptic, anti-arthritic, and nervine.
Useful in alcoholic delirium and in the hectic of phthisis; also for the relief of the pains of locomotor ataxia and in sciatica.
Applied locally in psoriasis, erysipelas, and eczema.

Antipyrin. (Patented.)

Syn. Analgesine; Dimethyloxychinizin (?); Phenyldimethylpyrazolon.
Dose, 4 to 30 grains, in cachets or aqueous solution.
Readily soluble in water.
An analgesic, febrifuge, hæmostatic; especially useful in various forms of neuralgia; may be employed hypodermically.
A measly rash has been observed after its use.
Incompatible with spirit of nitrous ether and other nitrites in the presence of free acid, a brilliant bluish-green compound being formed, which appears to be inert.
Also incompatible with the cinchona alkaloids.
Liquefactions occur on trituration with butyl-chloral hydrate or sodium salicylate or with β-naphthol.

Antithermin.

Syn. Phenyl-Hydrazin-Levulinic Acid.
Dose, 8 grains.
Allied to antipyrin; apt to cause gastric irritation.

Arbutin.

Dose, 15 to 60 grains.
In chronic cystitis and vesical catarrh.

Aristol.

Syn. Di-Thymol Iodide.
Insoluble in water, soluble in ether and oils. Useful in psoriasis, mycosis, and lupus, and as a dusting-powder for wounds and burns.

Auri Bromidum—Bromide of Gold—Auric Bromide.

Dose, $\frac{1}{64}$ to $\frac{1}{32}$ grain, increased to $\frac{1}{8}$ grain, well diluted.
In epilepsy and migraine.

Benzanilide.

Syn. Phenyl Benzamide.
Dose, 3 to 12 grains.
Insoluble in water, soluble 1 in 60 of spirit.
Chemically and therapeutically allied to acetanilide.
Especially useful in the treatment of diseases of children.

Beberine, Sulphate of.

Dose, 1 to 10 grains, in pills with glycerin of tragacanth, or in aqueous solution.
Soluble 1 in 80 of water, slightly in spirit.
In neuralgia and as an antiperiodic.

Blatta Orientalis—Cockroach.

Dose, 2 to 8 grains, in powder.
A Russian domestic remedy for dropsy; it has recently attracted some attention.

Boldoa Fragrans.

Tincture of Boldo, 1 in 5 of rectified spirit.
Dose, 10 to 20 minims.
In dyspepsia, liver-affections, rheumatism, and as a diuretic.

Boldin.

A glucoside.
Hypnotic properties; local anaesthetic like cocaine.

Bromal, Hydrate of.

Dose, 2 to 5 grains—3 grains to relieve pain or produce sleep.
Less soluble in water than chloral hydrate.
Physiologically more active than chloral; not suitable for internal administration, by reason of producing vomiting and diarrhoea.

Bromoform.

Dose, 5 to 20 drops per diem.
A limpid, sweet liquid, with an agreeable odor.
Soluble in alcohol and ether, slightly soluble in water.
Useful in whooping cough.

Cactus Grandiflorus.

Tincture, 1 to 20.
Dose, 1 to 5 minims.
In cardiac asthenia with dropsy.

Caffeinæ Sodio-Salicylas.

Dose, 1 to 4 grains, hypodermically.

Caffeinæ Tri-Iodidum.

Dose, 2 to 4 grains.

Caffeinæ Valerianas.

Dose, ½ to 3 grains.

The above three preparations are tonic and stimulant, useful in cardiac failure with dropsy.
In unilateral headache and in bronchial asthma.

Carbon, Tetrachloride of.

By inhalation.
Anaesthetic, hay fever, dysmenorrhœa, and tic-douloureux.
Locally for neuralgia.

Caulophyllin.

Dose, 1 to 4 grains, in a pill with glycerin of tragacanth.
An emmenagogue, parturient, and antispasmodic.

Chaulmoogra Oil.

Dose, 2 to 15 grains, filled into empty capsules, or in cod-liver oil or milk.
Used externally and internally in leprosy, phthisis, scrofula, marasmus, psoriasis, and lupus; also locally in chronic rheumatism and rheumatic gout.

Chekan.

Dose of the fluid extract, ½ to 3 drachms.
In chronic coughs and bronchitis.

Chinolinum—Chinoline.

Dose, 3 to 10 minims.
Soluble in alcohol, insoluble in water.
Locally in diphtheria, 5 per cent. in solution of equal parts of spirit and water.

Chinolini Tartras.

Dose, 5 to 15 grains, in chloroform water with syrup of orange, or in wafer paper.
Soluble 1 in 10 of water.
Chinolini salicylas is less soluble than the above.
Antipyretic, anti-neuralgic, local antiseptic.

Chloral, Hydrate of.

Dose, 5 to 30 grains, in aqueous solution or in chloroform water well diluted.

Soluble 3 in 1 of water, freely soluble in rectified spirit, and in ether, 1 in 4 of chloroform, also in oils and fats.

A pure hypnotic. Contra-indicated in heart-affections, feeble circulation, Bright's disease, and asthenic conditions. An antidote to strychnine-poison; useful in tetanus, chorea, and hysteria. There is danger of formation of the chloral habit.

As a vesicant.

Toxic effects best treated, after emesis, by hypodermic injection of sulphate of strychnine and inhalations of amyl nitrite. Picrotoxin is also an antidote.

Chloralamide.

Syn. Chloral Formamide.

Dose, 20 to 50 grains, in weak spirituous or acidulated solution. Incompatible with alkalies.

Soluble 1 in 9 of water, 1 in 2 of spirit; decomposed at a temperature of 120° F.

Hypnotic without analgesic effects.

Chloral cum Camphora, B.P.C.—Pigmentum Chloral et Camphorae.

Locally in neuralgia and rheumatism.

Hydrate of Butyl-Chloral.

Syn. Croton-Chloral Hydrate,—wrongly so called.

Dose, 2 to 15 grains or more.

Soluble 1 in 100 of cold water, freely soluble in rectified spirit, and about 1 in 4 of glycerin.

Facial neuralgia, toothache, neuralgic toothache; hypnotic.

Chrysarobin.

Syn. Araroba Powder, Goa Powder, Pó di Bahía.

Dose, ⅓ to ½ grain.

Pure Chrysarobin.

Dose, ⅛ to ½ grain.

Freely soluble in hot benzene, hot chloroform, hot oil of turpentine, and certain volatile oils.

Insoluble in water, rectified spirit, and ether.

Parasiticide in many skin-affections.

Cocaina—Cocaine.

Dose, ⅟₁₂ to 1 grain, in a pill or tablet.

The alkaloid soluble 1 in 700 of water, 1 in 20 of alcohol, freely in chloroform, ether, oil of cloves, etc., 1 in 10 of vaseline and castor oil, 1 in 3 of benzol, toluol, and amylic alcohol. The salts are soluble in water.

A powerful local anaesthetic on mucous surfaces. Mydriatic, and paralyzes the accommodation. Irritability of inflamed mucous surfaces much relieved by applications of solutions of the cocaine salts. Useful in hay fever, influenza, coryza, bronchitis, spasmodic asthma, laryngitis, and pharyngitis. Much employed as a local anaesthetic in minor gynæcological operations. In dentistry it deadens the sensibility of exposed pulp. Acts as a cardiac stimulant. Morphine and cocaine appear to be mutually antagonistic. A valuable stomachic.

Condurango.

Dose of the fluid extract, 20 to 40 drops.

Alterative. Has been unsuccessfully used in the treatment of cancer and syphilis. Said to be a useful stomachic tonic.

Convallaria Majalis—Lily of the Valley.

Convallarin.

Dose, 2 to 4 grains.

Soluble in alcohol, insoluble in water.

No effect other than purgative.

Convallamarin.

Dose, ½ to 2 grains.

Soluble in water and alcohol.

Said to contain the active principles of the drug.

Extractum Convallariæ.

Dose, 2 to 8 grains.

Extractum Convallariæ Fluidum.

Dose, 2 to 10 minims.

Tinctura Convallariæ.

Dose, 5 to 30 minims.

The physiological action of convallaria approaches that of digitalis; its action is cumulative; it is a powerful diuretic.

In mitral and aortic regurgitation, dilatation of the heart, senile hypertrophy, chronic pericarditis, anæmia, and diabetes.

Coumarinum.

A neutral crystalline principle obtained from the Tonka bean, also synthetically from salicylic aldehyde.

Readily soluble in hot water, dilute acids, and alcohol.

It has an agreeable aromatic odor, and is employed to disguise the odor of iodoform.

Creolin.

A dark alkaline liquid prepared from coal tar, forming a white emulsion with water.

Dose, 1 to 5 grains.

Used in the form of lotion, strength of 1 to 100 or more of water.

An antiseptic and sedative.

Crotalus.

A solution of the pure venom of the rattlesnake, 1 to 1000.

Dose, 3 drops every three hours.

Has been used in malignant scarlet fever.

Diuretin.

A sodio-salicylic compound of theobromine, about 50 per cent.

Dose, 90 grains, daily, in divided doses.

Diuretic.

Emblic Myrobalan Fruit.

Dose, 1, 2, or more, as required.

Stomachic and purgative.

Ethidene, Dichloride of.

Syn. Monochlorethyl Chloride—Chlorinated Chloride of Ethyl.

An anæsthetic.

Eugenol.

Syn. Eugenic Acid.

An oxidation product of oil of cloves.

Antiseptic and antiputrescent.

Lowers sensibility of the mucous membranes; does not produce anæsthesia.

Exalgin.

Syn. Methylacetanilide.

Dose, 2 to 6 grains, in cachets or aqueous or weak alcoholic solutions.

Soluble 1 in 60 of water, freely soluble in spirit.

An analgesic, antipyretic, and antiseptic.

Toxic effects, with cyanosis, have followed its employment.

Ferri Albuminati Liquor—Solution of Albuminated Iron.

Dose, 1 to 4 drachms.

Ferri Peptonati Liquor—Solution of Peptonated Iron.

Dose, 1 to 4 drachms.

Ferri Pomati Tinctura.

Dose, 15 to 30 minims.

Fuchsine—Rosaniline Mono-Hydrochlorate.

Syn. Magenta; Roseine.

Dose, ½ to 1 grains, in a pill with glycerin of tragacanth.

Freely soluble in water.

In albuminuria.

Apt to contain arsenic in variable quantities.

Guaiacol.

Dose. ½ to 2 minims.
Soluble in alcohol, ether, fats, oils, and glycerin, slightly soluble in water.
In phthisis.
Capsules containing 1 minim sold in the shops.

Gurjun Balsam—Wood Oil.

Dose, ½ to 2 drachms.
Not fully soluble in ether or alcohol.
In leprosy, and, in an emulsion of acacia, in gonorrhœa.

Gynocardic Acid.

Dose, ½ to 3 grains.
Supposed to be the active principle of Chaulmoogra oil.

Hamamelin

Syn. Hamamelidin.
Dose, ½ to 2 grains, in a pill with mucilage of acacia.
Hæmostatic.
In hæmoptysis, hemorrhoids, menorrhagia, and all passive hemorrhages.

Hydracetin.

Syn. Acetyl-Phenyl-Hydrazin.
Dose, ½ to 3 grains daily, in one or two doses.
Soluble 1 in 50 of water, freely in alcohol.
Administration requires caution; must not be continuous.
An impure preparation sold under the name of pyrodin.
A somewhat uncertain antipyretic.
Ten-per-cent. ointment in psoriasis. Its absorption apt to be followed by toxic effects.

Hydrargyri Naphtholacetas—Mercur-β-Naphthol Acetate.

Dose, ½ to 1 grain.
A mild antisyphilitic.

Hydrargyri Succinimidum — Succinimide or Imido-Succinate of Mercury.

Used hypodermically in 2-per-cent. solution in the treatment of syphilis.

Hydrargyri Thymolacetas—Mercury Thymolacetate.

Dose, ¾ to 1½ grains, in pill, also hypodermically.
Antisyphilitic.

Hydrogen, Peroxide of.

Syn. Hydroxyl, in aqueous solution.
Dose, ½ to 2 drachms.
As made for medical purposes, the solution contains ten times its volume of active oxygen.
It possesses disinfecting and bleaching properties.
Readily decomposed.

Ozonic Ether.

Dose, ½ to 1 drachm.
Ether containing in solution peroxide of hydrogen in 30-volume strength with the addition of alcohol.
In diabetes, whooping-cough, scarlet fever, diphtheria, rheumatism, albuminuria, etc.

Hydroquinone.

Syn. Quinol; Hydrochinon (German).
Dose, ½ to 5 grains.
Soluble 1 in 20 of water, also in alcohol and ether; slightly soluble in olive oil.
Antiseptic and antipyretic.

Hydroxylamine.

Results from the action of nascent hydrogen on nitric acid.
Aqueous solution odorless and colorless.
Has powerful reducing properties.
The hydrochlorate is freely soluble in water.
Used in solution 1 in 1000 in the treatment of lupus and parasitic skin-diseases.

Ichthyol.

Syn. Sulpho-Ichthyolate of Ammonium.
Dose, 10 to 30 grains per diem.

Lithii Sulpho-Ichthyolas.

Dose, 10 to 30 grains per diem.

Sodii Sulpho-Ichthyolas.

Dose, 10 to 30 grains per diem.

Zinci Sulpho-Ichthyolas.

These preparations are miscible with water, glycerin, fats, oils, vaseline, and lanolin, and may be combined with preparations of lead and mercury, without the formation of sulphide.

Used locally in chronic skin-diseases, such as eczema, psoriasis, acne, and favus, also used in chronic rheumatism.

Iodoform.

Dose, ½ to 3 grains.
Soluble 1 in 8 of ether, 1 in 12 of chloroform, 1 in 80 of rectified spirit, 1 in 14 of oil of eucalyptus, 1 in 10 of collodium, 1 in 60 of vaseline and oil of almond; insoluble in water.

Iodoformi Pulvis.

Minute crystals

Iodoformum Præcipitatum.

A primrose-yellow-colored impalpable powder.

Iodoformum Aromaticum.

Is scented with coumarin, 1 in 50.
Powerful antiseptic, sedative, and alterative.
Especially useful in the treatment of surgical and other wounds, the ulcerative processes of chronic infectious diseases, etc.

Iodol.

Syn. Tetra-iodo-Pyrrol.
Dose, 1 to 3 grains.
Insoluble in water; soluble 1 in 31 of glycerin, 1 in 6 of alcohol, and free y in ether.
Useful for the same purposes as the preceding.

Sozoiodol.

Dose, 20 grains 3 times a day.
Soluble 1 in 14 of water.

Iodo-Salicylic Acid and Di-iodo-Salicylic Acid.

Dose, 20 to 60 grains in the course of twenty-four hours.
Slightly soluble in water; soluble in alcohol, ether, and fixed oils.
Antiseptic, analgesic, and antithermic.

Syrupus Acidi Hydriodici.

Dose, 20 to 40 minims.
A mild preparation of Iodine.

Iodide of Ethyl.

Syn. Hydriodic Ether.
Soluble in alcohol and ether, not readily soluble in water.
By inhalation in asthma and laryngitis; also in nervous dyspnœa and certain forms of bronchial catarrh.
Dispensed in the shops in glass capsules containing 5 minims each.

Jambul.

Dose, 5 to 10 grains.
Said to check the diastasic conversion of starch into sugar. In diabetes.

Kava-Kava.

Fluid extract dose, **15 to 60 minims; extract, 3 grains.**
A bitter tonic.

Kairine. (Patented.)

Syn. Oxychinoline-Ethyl Hydrochloride.

Dose, 5 to 8 increased to 15 grains, in pills with glycerin of tragacanth, or in cachets.

Freely soluble in water, less soluble in alcohol; insoluble in ether.

Taste saline, bitter, and nauseous.

Powerful antipyretic.

Lanolin.

Syn. Adeps Lanæ—Wool Fat.

Lanolinum Anhydricum—Anhydrous Lanolin.

Sapolanolin.

Lanolin 5 parts, soft soap 4 parts.

In acne, eczema.

Agnine.

These preparations consist of a purified fat from sheep's wool.

Used as a basis for ointments, and readily absorbed by the integument.

Lipanin.

A mixture of olive oil with 6 per cent. of oleic acid.

Has been used as a substitute for cod-liver oil.

Maidis Stigmata.

Dose of the fluid extract, 1 drachm.

Demulcent and diuretic.

In acute and chronic affections of the kidney and bladder; also in cardiac dropsy.

Maidis Ustilago.

Dose, 15 to 60 grains; of the fluid extract, ½ to 1 drachm.

Used in parturition instead of ergot.

Manganesii Hypophosphis—Hypophosphite of Manganese.

Dose, 1 to 10 grains.

Manganesii Oxidum Præcipitatum.

Dose, 3 to 10 grains or more, in pills with syrup.

Manganesii Phosphas—Phosphate of Manganese—Manganous Phosphate.

Dose, 1 to 5 grains.

In gastrodynia and amenorrhœa, chlorosis, jaundice.

Mandragorine.

A crystallized alkaloid from mandrake root.

A solution of the sulphate acts as a mydriatic.

Menthol.

Dose, ½ to 2 grains or more, in a pill with powdered soap, or in solution in olive oil.

Insoluble in glycerin, soluble 2 in 3 of rectified spirit, also freely in ether, chloroform, and fixed and volatile oils; sparingly soluble in water.

Internally a diffusible stimulant; externally sedative and anæsthetic.

Methacetin.

Syn. Para-Acetanisidin; Oxymethylacetanilide.

Dose, 2 to 6 grains, in cachets or mucilaginous fluid.

Soluble 1 in 200 of water, freely soluble in alcohol, chloroform, and glycerin.

Resembles phenacetin in its action.

Methyl Chloride.

This gas is used as a local anæsthetic. Applied as a jet, it produces intense cold and freezes the part.

Useful in various small operations, such as opening abscesses and in scraping lupus; also in neuralgia, lumbago, muscular pains.

Employed in microscopical work to freeze specimens for section-cutting.

Methylal.

Dose, 15 to 30 minims, in aqueous mixture.
Topically as an anæsthetic.
Used internally in angina pectoris, **delirium** tremens.

Methylene.

Syn. Methylene Dichloride; **Dichlormethane**; formerly called Bichloride of Methylene.
Used as an anæsthetic.

Mollin.

A white, inodorous, superfatted soap, **containing about 17** per cent. excess of fat.
A basis for ointments, readily **washed off with water, with** which it forms a lather.

Monobromacetanilide.

Syn. Monobromphenylacetanide.
A bromine substitution compound of acetanilide.
Dose, 5 to 15 grains.
Facial neuralgia, neuritis, and rheumatism.
Its employment has been followed by cyanosis.

Morrhuol.

Dose, in capsules containing 0.20 gramme, 1 **or 2, each** equivalent to 5 grammes of cod-liver oil.

Nitrate of Muscarine.

Dose, (?) ¼ to ¾ grain hypodermically, etc.
Muscarine and its alkaloid, the nitrate of muscarine, **are** uncrystallizable. The latter is a viscid, yellowish-brown liquid, hygroscopic, soluble in water. Applied topically to the eye it dilates the pupil, but given internally it contracts it. Causes salivation, perspiration, flow of tears, and purgation.
Useful in **checking night sweats.**

Myrtol.

Dose, 2 to 4 minims, in capsules.
In putrid affections of the lungs and air-passages.

β-Naphthol.

Syn. Naphthyl Alcohol.
Dose, 2 to 15 grains.
Soluble in alcohol, ether, and benzene; sparingly soluble in hot water; soluble 1 in 8 of olive oil and lard, and 1 in 80 of vaseline.
Powerfully antiseptic and germicide.
In scabies, psoriasis, and hyperidrosis of palms, soles, and axillæ; has been administered in enteric fever. In various gastric and intestinal disorders, and by inhalation in pharyngitis, catarrh, and bronchitis.

α-Naphthol.

Powerfully antiseptic, and less poisonous than β-naphthol.

Acidum α-Oxynaphthoicum — α-Oxynaphthoic Acid.

Syn. α-Naphthol-Carbonic Acid; α-Carbonaphtholic Acid.
Powerfully antizymotic; said to possess this property to five times the degree of salicylic acid.

Naphthol cum Camphora—Naphthol Camphor.

β-Naphthol 1, Camphor 2, mixed to form a viscid liquid.
A powerful non-toxic antiseptic; has been used to protect surgical instruments.

Hydronaphthol.

A commercial preparation in the form of a grayish-white crystalline powder, with a faint odor of iodine.
A non-toxic antiseptic in solution or dusting-powder.

Naphthalene.

Dose, 2 to **15 grains or more, in cachets or** pills with mucilage and syrup.
Insoluble in water; soluble in ether, **in** hot alcohol, and in fats, also in fixed and volatile oils.

Naphthalene Tetrachloride.

Syn. **Naphthalon** Hydrochlorate.
Dose, 3 to **12 grains,** in cachets or pills.

α-Dichloronaphthalene.

Naphthalene, not being absorbed by the system, acts only on the mucous membrane of the bowel.

In dysentery and the catarrhal diarrhœa of enteric fever and phthisis.

Used locally in foul ulcers, etc.; also very useful in fetid urine.

Nitroglycerin.

Syn. Glonoine; Trinitrate of Glycerol; Nitric Ether of Glycerin (formerly considered as the Trinitrite of Glycerol or Nitrous Ether of Glycerin); Trinitrine.

Dose, $\frac{1}{100}$ to $\frac{1}{50}$ grain, increased to $\frac{1}{5}$ grain.

Slightly soluble in water, freely in ether and in absolute alcohol, 1 in 6 of almond oil, 1 in 15 of rectified spirit.

Nervous sedative and muscular depressant; an active depressant of the inhibitory apparatus of the heart and of the vaso-motor centres and muscular coats of the blood-vessels.

In angina pectoris, and in spastic neuralgias, asthma, headaches, sea-sickness, and Bright's disease.

Less fugacious in its effects than nitrite of amyl, and more powerful than the other nitrites.

Has been used in myxœdema, puerperal convulsions, epileptic vertigo, epilepsy, and specially in *petit mal*.

Acidum Oleicum—Oleic Acid.

Dissolves many of the metallic oxides, with the resulting formation of oleic solutions of the oleates in an excess of oleic acid. Also dissolves alkaloids, but not their salts.

The following are used in medicine:

Oleatum Cocainæ.

Cupri Oleas.

Oleatum Hydrargyri.

5 per cent., 10 per cent., and 20 per cent.

Quininæ Oleatum.

Oleatum Zinci.

Chartazine.

Tissue-paper saturated with oleate of zinc.
In chronic ulcers.

The metallic oleates are made by the double decomposition of soluble metallic salts and castile soap; they contain no free oleic acid.

Pulvis Zinci Oleatis.

An example of the above.

A fine white powder, resembling chalk.

Used in moist eczema and for the relief of excessive perspiration; especially useful in hyperidrosis and osmidrosis.

Oleanodyne.

A preparation of oleic acid holding in solution the alkaloids aconite, atropine, morphine, and veratrine.

Rapidly absorbed.

Powerfully anodyne.

It can be diluted with chloroform, rectified spirit, or oils.

Orexine.

Syn. Orexine Hydrochloride; Hydrochloride of Phenyldihydrochinazolin.

Dose, in coated pills, 3 grains each, 1 to 3 once or twice daily, with a cup of broth or hot fluid.

Freely soluble in water and alcohol.

In failure of appetite.

Acts as a stomachic and appetizer, stimulating the gastric secretion.

Osmic Acid.

Syn. Tetroxide of Osmium; Perosmic Acid; Hyerposmic Acid.

Soluble slowly, 1 to 5 of water.

Hypodermically for neuralgia, especially obstinate sciatica, enlarged glands, sarcoma, and cancer; also in muscular rheumatism.

Phenacetin.

Syn. Para-Acet-Phenetidin.
Dose, 4 to 8 increased to 15 grains, in cachets, or suspended in mucilaginous fluids.
Inodorous and tasteless.
Insoluble **in water or** glycerin; freely soluble in hot alcohol. **Insoluble in** both acid and alkaline solutions.
Antipyretic **and** anodyne.
Rheumatism, neuralgia, migraine, hysteria, **pertussis.**
Causes neither rashes nor cyanosis.

Picric Acid.

Syn. Carbazotic Acid; Trinitrophenic Acid.
Dose, ¼ to 2 grains.
Soluble 1 in 90 of water, 1 in 15 of rectified spirit.
In ague, albuminuria, and certain forms of headache; also locally in erysipelas and dermatitis.

Ammonium Picrate.

Dose, ¼ to 1½ grains four or five times a day.
In ague and malarial fevers.

Potassii Cobalto-Nitris—Cobalto-Nitrite of **Potassium.**

Dose, ½ grain every two or four hours.
Slightly soluble in water.
Relieves arterial tension.
In dyspnœa of uræmia and asthma; **also in arterial capillary fibrosis.**

Priodate, Crystals and **Powder.**

Dose, 1 to 15 grains.
Slightly soluble in water.
Antiseptic and deodorant.
A weak germicide.

Pyridine.

Dose, **5 to 10** increased to 25 minims daily.
Miscible with water, alcohol, ether, and oils.
Used by inhalation in a closet or small room.
In asthma; also as a heart-stimulant, and in angina pectoris.

Pyrogallic Acid.

Syn. Pyrogallol.
Dose, ¼ to 1½ grains, **in aqueous solution,** or in a pill with syrup.
Soluble in 2½ parts of water and in 10 parts of melted lard.
In hæmoptysis, and locally in psoriasis; also used in the preparation of hair-dyes.

Resorcin.

Dose, 5 to 15 or 30 grains.
Soluble in 2 parts of water, in 20 of olive **oil.**
A powerful antiseptic.
Internally, action analogous **to that of** quinine, but with excessive diaphoresis.
Used locally in diphtheria, gonorrhœa, vesical catarrh, cancer, eczema, psoriasis, condylomata and mucous patches, and internally, well diluted with water and flavored with syrup of orange, **or** in infusion of chamomile, in whooping-cough, sea-sickness.

Rubidium-Ammonium Bromide.

Dose, 30 grains three times daily.
In epilepsy.

Saccharin.

A harmless drug, valuable as a substitute for sugar in cases of diabetes.
Syn. Benzoyl-Sulphonic-Imide; Benzoic Sulphinide; Anhydro-Ortho-Sulphamine-Benzoic Acid.
Dose, ¼ to 2 grains, or more,—ad libitum is recommended.
Soluble 1 in 500 volumes of cold and 1 in 160 of hot water, 1 in 35 of rectified spirit, 1 in 30 of proof spirit, 1 in 160 of ether, 1 in 50 of chloroform, 1 in 50 of glycerin.
Sweetening power variously estimated as from 100 to 300 times that of sugar. 1 part in 10,000 parts of distilled water is perceptibly sweet, and it is possible to detect 1 part in 70,000,—about a grain in a gallon.

Saccharinum Solubile.

Dose, ⅛ to 2 grains or more.
This substance consists of saccharin, 99 per cent., in combination with soda.

Safrol.

Dose, 20 to 30 minims.
In subacute rheumatism.

Salicylic Acid.

Dose, 5 to 20 grains, in cachets.
Soluble in 760 parts of water, 4 of spirit, 2 of ether, 120 of olive oil, 100 of castor oil, 200 of glycerin; also in melted fats and vaseline. Solubility in water much increased by the addition of borax.
Internally its effects are analogous to those of quinine.
Used in rheumatism, sciatica, Ménière's disease; is a powerful antiseptic.

Bismuthi Salicylas.

Dose, 5 to 20 grains.
Insoluble in water, alcohol, and glycerin.
In diarrhœa, typhoid fever, etc.; also in gastric catarrh.

Cresol Salicylas.

Syn. Para-Cresol Salicylate; Cresalol.
Dose, (?)
Insoluble in water; freely soluble in spirit.
Has been used in acute rheumatism.

Ferri Salicylas.

Dose, 3 to 10 grains, in pills.
Slightly soluble in water.
In certain forms of diarrhœa of infancy.

Quinine Salicylas.

Dose, 2 to 6 grains.
Soluble in water 1 to 900.
Best administered in pills.
In rheumatic gout.

Sodii Salicylas.

Dose, 10 to 30 grains, in water.
Soluble in its own weight of water, also in rectified spirit.
Antipyretic: chiefly useful in acute rheumatism. Used also in enteric fever, tonsillitis, vesical catarrh, neuralgia, gouty headaches, diarrhœa, influenza, and in vertigo with auditory-nerve symptoms.
Over-doses produce headache, suffusion of the eyes, deafness, flushed face, muscular trembling and weakness.

Sodii Di-Thio-Salicylas.

Dose, 3 grains, morning and evening.
Soluble 1 in 1 of water.
In articular and gonorrhœal rheumatism.

Salicinum—Salicin.

Dose, 5 to 30 grains, in aqueous solution.
Soluble 1 in 20 parts of water, 1 in 50 of spirit; insoluble in ether.
In rheumatism and ague.

Salol.

Syn. Phenyl Ether of Salicylic Acid. (Patented.)
Dose, 4 to 30 grains, in cachets or suspended in milk.
Insoluble in water, faintly soluble in glycerin, soluble in alcohol, ether, and fixed oils.
Antiseptic and antipyretic.
Useful in sciatica: chiefly valuable in acute rheumatism; also employed in the treatment of summer diarrhœas.

Salol cum Camphora—Salol Camphor.

3 parts of salol heated with 2 parts of camphor combine to form a viscid liquid which has been used as an antiseptic.

Betol.

The salicylate of β-naphthol-ether.
Dose, 3 to 8 grains, in cachets or pills, or suspended in almond emulsion or milk.
Insoluble in water, soluble in alcohol.
Rheumatism, cystitis, and intestinal catarrh.

Simnio.

Used in the treatment of nervous diseases, especially **hysteria** and epilepsy.

Somnal.

A liquid preparation believed **to be a combination of** chloral alcoholate and urethane.
Dose, ½ drachm.
Hypnotic.

Sparteine **Sulphate.**

Dose, ½ to 1 grain, increased.
Soluble 2 in 3 of water.
Cardiac tonic, non-cumulative; valuable diuretic.

Strophanthus Hispidus.

Two crystalline substances have been isolated, strophanthin and ineis.
The dose of strophanthin, hypodermically, is from 1-120th to 1-160th of a grain; it has been used as a cardiac tonic and diuretic. Its chemical nature has not been fully determined, and it is not a safe therapeutic.
The preparations of strophanthus most available for therapeutic purposes are

Tincture of Strophanthus,

Dose, 2 to 10 minims, and

Pills of Strophanthus

Contain 2 to 4 minims of the tincture combined with sugar **of milk.**
Dose, 1 to 2.

Sulphonal.

Syn. Diethyl-Sulphon-Dimethyl-Methane.
Dose, 15 to 30 grains (?), in cachets or suspended in water with mucilage.
Soluble 1 in 500 of **water, freely** soluble in boiling water and in alcohol and ether.
A pure hypnotic, not affecting the digestion, pulse, or temperature.
Especially useful in insomnia of nervous subjects, in mania, delirium tremens, and meningitis, and in the control of night-sweats.

Terebene, Pure.

Dose, 5 to 30 minims.
Not miscible with water.
Powerful antiseptic, disinfectant, deodorizer.
In phthisis, dysentery, and winter cough.
Used by inhalation and internally.

Terpin Hydrate.

Syn. Terpene Hydrate; Hydrate of Oil of Turpentine.
Dose, 2 to 6 grains or more
Soluble 1 in 200 of water, 1 in 20 of alcohol, 1 in 6 of oils.
In chronic and subacute bronchitis.
Also diuretic.

Terpinol.

An aromatic liquid resulting from the action of dilute hydrochloric or sulphuric acid on terpene.

Tetronal.

Syn. Diethyl-Sulphon-Diethyl-Methane.
Dose, 10 to 20 grains, in cachet.
Soluble 1 in 450 of water, 1 in 15 of spirit.

Thalline—Tetrahydroparamethyloxychinoline, or Tetrahydroparach nanisol. (Patented.)

Syn. Thalline Sulphas—Sulphate of Thalline.
Dose, 2 to 8 grains.
Soluble 1 in 5 of cold water.
An irregular and dangerous **antipyretic.**

Tiuol.

Dose, (dry) 2 to 10 grains, in pills.

Thiol Liquidum.

A syrupy liquid containing about 40 per cent. of thiol.

Thiol is soluble in water, alcohol, and ether. It is precipitated by acids; analogous to ichthyol, and used for the same purposes.

Thio-Resorcin.

Insoluble in water, slightly soluble in ether and alcohol. Used as a substitute for iodoform as a dusting-powder, or in 10 per cent. ointment.

Thymol.

Dose, ½ to 2 grains or more, in pills with powdered soap, or in oily or aqueous solution.
Soluble 1 in 800 of water, 1 in 200 of glycerin, 1 in 8 of equal parts of alcohol and glycerin mixed; also in fats and oils; freely soluble in alcohol and ether.
Powerfully antiseptic and antiputrefactive.
Used in surgical dressings, and as an intestinal antiseptic.

Trimethylamine.

Syn. Secalin; Propylamine (?).
Dose of the solution, 20 to 50 minims every two to four hours.
Commercial preparation miscible with water.
In acute articular rheumatism.
Propylamine is isomeric with trimethylamine.

Trimethylaminæ Hydrochloras.

Dose, 2 to 8 grains three to five times daily.
Very soluble in water.
In acute articular rheumatism.

Trional. (?)

Intermediate in hypnotic effect between sulphonal and tetronal.

Ulexine.

Ulexine Hydrobromate.

Dose of each, ⅓ to ⅒ grain.
Powerful diuretic.

Uralium.

Syn. Ural.
A compound of chloral and urethane.
Dose, 15 to 45 grains.
Hypnotic.

Uranium, Nitrate of.

Dose, ½ to 5 grains.
Soluble in half its weight of water.
Used in solution, 10 grains to the ounce, as a spray for the throat. Has been used in the treatment of diabetes. Not a safe remedy.

Urethane.

Syn. Ethyl Carbamate.
Dose, 10 to 20 grains.
Soluble in water.
A pure hypnotic.
Very useful in diseases of children, in delirium tremens, and in acute mania.

Yerba Santa.

Dose of the fluid extract, 10 to 40 minims; aromatic and expectorant.
In bronchitis, phthisis, and pulmonary catarrh.

III

A Table of Formulæ for Suppositories.

A.—RECTAL.

The quantity given is to be thoroughly incorporated with a sufficient quantity of cacao butter—gr. xxx., U.S.P.—to form one suppository.

1. Anodyne.

Pulv. opii . . . gr. ½-iv.
Ext. opii aq. . . . gr. ½-ij
Morphinæ sulph. . . gr. ½-j.
Morphinæ acetatis . gr. ½-j.
Ext. belladonnæ . . gr. ½-j.
{ Pulv. opii . . . . . gr. ½.
{ Ext. belladonnæ . gr. ½.
{ Pulv. opii . . . . . gr. j.
{ Ext. belladonnæ . gr. ¼.
{ Pulv. opii . . . . . gr. ij.
{ Ext. belladonnæ . gr. ½.
{ Pulv. opii . . . . . gr. iij.
{ Ext. belladonnæ . gr. ½.
{ Ext. opii aq. . . . gr. ½.
{ Ext. belladonnæ . gr. ¼.
{ Ext. opii aq. . . . gr. i.
{ Ext. belladonnæ . gr. ½.
{ Ext. opii aq. . . . gr. iss.
{ Ext. belladonnæ . gr. ½.
{ Ext. opii aq. . . . gr. ij.
{ Ext. belladonnæ . gr. j.
{ Pulv. opii . . . . . gr. ½.
{ Pulv. ipecacuanhæ . gr. j.
{ Pulv. opii . . . . . gr. j.
{ Pulv. ipecacuanhæ . gr. ij.

Ext. hyoscyami . . **gr. iij.**
Ext. hyoscyami . . **gr. v.**
{ Ext. hyoscyami . . **gr. ij.**
{ Ext. opii aq. . . . . **gr. j.**
{ Morphinæ sulph. . . **gr.** ⅓.
{ Atropinæ sulph. . . **gr.** ₁₅₀.
{ Morphinæ sulph. . . gr. ½.
{ Atropinæ sulph. . . gr. ₁₅₀.
{ Cocain. hydrochlor. gr. ½.
{ Morphinæ sulph. . . gr. ½.
{ Atropinæ sulph. . . gr. ₁₅₀.
{ Cocain. hydrochlor. gr. ¼.
{ Morphinæ sulph. . . gr. ½.
{ Atropinæ sulph. . . gr. ₁₅₀.
{ Cocain. hydrochlor. gr. ½.
{ Ext. cannabis ind. . gr. ½.
{ Codeinæ . . . . . . gr. j.
{ Ext. hyoscyami . . gr. ij.
{ Ext. cannabis ind. . gr. j.
{ Codeinæ . . . . . . gr. ij.
{ Ext. hyoscyami . . gr. ij.
{ Ext. cannabis ind. . gr. ij.
{ Ext. cannabis ind. gr. ½.
{ Ext. hyoscyami . . gr. j.
{ Ext. coca . . . . . gr. ij.

2. Anodyne and Hypnotic.

{ Chloral. hydrat. . . **gr. x.**
{ Atropinæ sulph. . . **gr.** ₁₅₀.
{ Morphinæ sulph. . . **gr.** ½.
{ Chloral. hydrat. . . **gr. xv.**
{ Morphinæ sulph. . . **gr.** ¼.
{ Atropinæ sulph. . . **gr.** ₁₅₀.
{ Chloral. hydrat. . . gr. xx.
{ Morphinæ sulph. . . gr. ½.
{ Atropinæ sulph. . . gr. ₁₅₀.

{ Chloral. hydrat. . . gr. xxx.
{ Atropinæ sulph. . . gr. ₁₅₀.
{ Morphinæ sulph. . . gr. ½.
{ Ext. opii . . . . . . gr. ½.
{ Ext. cannabis ind. . gr. j.
{ Lupulini . . . . . . gr. v.
{ Ext. hyoscyami . . gr. j.
{ Ext. opii . . . . . . gr. j
{ Ext. cannabis ind. . gr. ij.
{ Lupulini . . . . . . gr. xv.
{ Ext. hyoscyami . . gr. ij.

3. Hypnotic.

{ Chloral. hydrat. . . gr. xv.
{ Camph. monobrom. gr. v.
{ Hyoscyam. hydroch. gr. ₁₂₀.
{ Chloral. hydrat. . . gr. xx.
{ Camph. monobrom. gr. x.
{ Hyoscyam. hydroch. gr. ₁₂₀.
Urethane . . . . . . **gr. x.**
Urethane . . . . . . **gr. xv.**
{ Ext. cannabis ind. . **gr.** ½.
{ Lupulini . . . . . . **gr. v.**
{ Ext. hyoscyami . . **gr. j.**
{ Camph. monobrom **gr. ij.**

{ Ext. cannabis ind. . gr. j.
{ Lupulini . . . . . . gr. xv.
{ Ext. hyoscyami . . gr. ij.
{ Camph. monobrom. gr. v.
{ Hyoscinæ **hydro-**
{ brom. . . . . gr. ₁₅₀.
{ Codeinæ . . . . . . gr. j.
{ Lupulini . . . . . . gr. v.
{ Hyoscinæ **hydro-**
{ brom. . . . . **gr.** ₇₅.
{ Codeinæ . . . . . . **gr. ij.**
{ Lupulini . . . . . . **gr. x.**

4. Antiseptic.

{ Iodoformi . . . . . gr. ij.
Thymol. . . . . . gr. j.
Resorcin. . . . . . gr. v.

Acidi borici . . . gr. x.
Thymol. . . . . . . gr. j.
Ol. eucalypti . . . ♏ij.

{ Iodoformi . . . . . gr. v.
Thymol. . . . . . gr. j.
Resorcin. . . . . . gr. x.

Acidi benzoici . . . gr. v.
Hydrarg. chlor. cor. gr. ⅒.
Resorcin. . . . . . gr. x.

{ Iodoformi . . . . . gr. v.
Acidi tannici . . . gr. x.

Acidi benzoici . . . gr. x.
Hydrarg. chlor. cor. gr. ½.
Resorcin. . . . . . gr. x.

{ Iodoformi . . . . . gr. v.
Acidi tannici . . . gr. xx.

Naphthalini . . . . gr. ij.
Sodii biborat. . . . gr. x.
Hydrarg. chlor. cor. gr. ½.
Ol. eucalypti . . . ♏ij.

Acidi borici . . . gr. v.
Thymol. . . . . . gr. ij.
Ol. eucalypti . . . ♏ij.

Acidi salicylici . . gr. x.
Acidi borici . . . . gr. x.
Thymol. . . . . . gr. v.

Naphthalini . . . . gr. v.
Sodii biborat. . . . gr. x.
Hydrarg. chlor. cor. gr. ½.
Ol. eucalypti . . . ♏ij.

Iodoformi . . . . . gr. ij.

{ Acidi salicylici . . . gr. v.
Acidi borici . . . . gr. v.
Thymol. . . . . . gr. ij.

Iodoformi . . . . . gr. iij.
Acidi borici . . . gr. vj.

5. Astringent.

{ Pulv. opii . . . . . gr. j.
Acidi tannici . . . gr. ij.

Ext. krameriæ . . . gr. iij.

{ Pulv. opii . . . . . gr. j.
Acidi tannici . . . gr. ij.

Ext. krameriæ . . . gr. v.

{ Pulv. opii . . . . . gr. j.
Acidi tannici . . . gr. v.

Ext. krameriæ . . . gr. x.

{ Pulv. opii . . . . . gr. ij.
Acidi tannici . . . gr. v.

Acidi tannici . . . gr. v.
Acidi gallici . . . gr. ij.
Ext. krameriæ . . . gr. j.

{ Pulv. opii . . . . . gr. j.
Plumbi acetat. . . . gr. ij.

Acidi tannici . . . gr. x.
Ext. krameriæ . . . gr. v.
Acidi gallici . . . gr. iv.

{ Pulv. opii . . . . . gr. ij.
Plumbi acetat. . . . gr. ij.

Acidi gallici . . . gr. ij.
Ext. ergotæ . . . . gr. v.
Digitalis . . . . . gr. j.

{ Pulv. opii . . . . . gr. j.
Plumbi acetat. . . . gr. v.

Acidi gallici . . . gr. v.
Ext. ergotæ . . . . gr. x.
Digitalis . . . . . gr. ij.

{ Pulv. opii . . . . . gr. ij.
Plumbi acetat. . . . gr. v.

Bismuthi subnitrat. . gr. x.
Acidi tannici . . . . gr. v.

{ Ext. belladonnæ . . gr. ¼.
Plumbi acetat. . . . gr. iss.

Bismuthi subnitrat. gr. xx.
Acidi tannici . . . . gr. x.

{ Ext. belladonnæ . . gr. ½.
Plumbi acetat. . . . gr. iij.

Bismuthi subnitrat. gr. x.
Thymol. . . . . . . gr. ij.

Acidi tannici . . . gr. ij.

Bismuthi subnitrat. gr. xx.
Thymol. . . . . . . gr. j.

Acidi tannici . . . gr. v.

Acidi tannici . . . gr. v.
Eucalyptol. . . . . ♏ij.
Iodoformi . . . . . gr. ij.

Acidi tannici . . . gr. x.

{ Ext. stramonii . . . gr. j.
Plumbi acetat. . . . gr. ij.

Acidi tannici . . . gr. xx.
Eucalyptol. . . . . ♏ij.
Iodoformi . . . . . gr. v.

{ Ext. stramonii . . . gr. ½.
Acidi tannici . . . gr. ½.
Plumbi carbonat. . . gr. j.
Liquor plumbi sub-
  acetat. . . . . ♏ij.
Creasoti . . . . ♏½.

Acidi tannici . . . gr. v.
Bismuthi subnitrat. gr. x.
Hydrarg. chlor. cor. gr. ½.

Plumbi iodidi . . . gr. iij.
Ext. belladonnæ . . gr. ½.
Morphinæ sulph. . . gr. ¼.
Acidi tannici . . . gr. v.

Acidi tannici . . . gr. v.
Bismuthi subnitrat. gr. x.
Hydrarg. chlor. cor. gr. ½.

{ Ext. stramonii . . . gr. j.
Acidi tannici . . . gr. v.

6. Laxative.

Glycerin. Containing 95 per cent. of glycerin.

7. Antiperiodic.

Quininæ bisulphatis . . . . gr. j–vj.

248

B.—VAGINAL.

Iodoformi . . . . . . gr. v.
Hydrarg. chlor. cor. . gr. $\frac{1}{25}$.

Iodoformi . . . . . . gr. x.
Hydrarg. chlor. cor. . gr. $\frac{1}{16}$.

Iodoformi . . . . . . gr. v.
Acidi tannici . . . . gr. xv.

Iodoformi . . . . . . gr. v.
Acidi tannici . . . . gr. xxx.

Acidi tannici . . . . gr. xx.
Acidi borici . . . . . gr. v.

Acidi tannici . . . . gr. xl.
Acidi borici . . . . . gr. x.

Acidi salicylici . . . gr. x.
Acidi borici . . . . . gr. v.
Acidi tannici . . . . gr. xx.

Acidi salicylici . . . gr. xv.
Acidi borici . . . . . gr. v.
Acidi tannici . . . . gr. xx.

Bismuthi subnitrat. . gr. xx.
Acidi tannici . . . . gr. xx.

Bismuthi subnitrat. . gr. xl.
Acidi tannici . . . . gr. xx.

Plumbi nitrat. . . . gr. ij.
Plumbi acetat. . . . gr. v.

Plumbi nitrat. . . . gr. v.
Plumbi acetat. . . . gr. x.

Bismuthi subcarb. . gr. x.
Plumbi carbonat. . . gr. v.
Eucalyptol . . . . . . ℳij.

Bismuthi subcarb. . gr. xx.
Plumbi carbonat. . . gr. x.
Eucalyptol . . . . . . ℳij.

Zinci oxidi . . . . . gr. v.
Zinci sulphocarbolat. gr. x.
Thymol. . . . . gr. ij.

Zinci oxidi . . . . . gr. x.
Zinci sulphocarbolat. gr. xx.
Thymol. . . . . gr. v.

Resorcin. . . . . . . gr. v.
Bismuthi subnitrat. . gr. xx.
Salicini . . . . gr. x.

Resorcin. . . . . . . gr. x.
Bismuthi subnitrat. . gr. xxx.
Salicini . . . . gr. x.

Cocain. hydrochlor. gr. ½.
Salicini . . . . gr. xx.

Cocain. hydrochlor. gr. j.
Salicini . . . . gr. xxx.

C.—URETHRAL.

Zinci sulph. . . . . . gr. ¼.

Zinci chlor. . . . . . gr. ¼.

Iodoformi . . . . . . gr. j.

Hydrastis canad. . . gr. v.

Zinci sulph. . . . . . gr. j.
Ext. opii aq. . . . . gr. j.

Zinci sulph. . . . . . gr. j.
Ext. belladonnæ . . gr. j.

Zinci sulph. . . . . . gr. j.
Ext. opii aq. . . . . gr. j.
Ext. belladonnæ . . gr. j.

Zinci sulph. . . . . . gr. j.
Morphinæ sulph. . . gr. ¼.

Zinci chlor. . . . . . gr. ¼.
Ext. opii aq. . . . . gr. j.

Zinci chlor. . . . . . gr. ¼.
Ext. belladonnæ . . gr. j.

Plumbi acetat. . . . gr. j.
Ext. opii aq. . . . . gr. j.

Sol. plumbi subacet. gr. v.
Ext. opii aq. . . . . gr. j.

Zinci sulph. . . . . . gr. j.
Acidi carbolici . . . gr. ½.

Iodoformi . . . . . . gr. iij.
Ext. belladonnæ . . gr. ½.

Iodoformi . . . . . . gr. v.

Zinci sulph. . . . . . gr. ¼.
Plumbi acetat. . . . gr. ½.
Ext. opii aq. . . . . gr. j.

Iodoformi . . . . . . gr. v.
Ol. eucalypti . . . . gr. x.

Zinci sulph. . . . . . gr. ¼.
Zinci oxidi . . . . . gr. ij.

Iodoformi . . . . . . gr. iij.
Ext. opii aq. . . . . gr. j.

Zinci sulph. . . . . . gr. ¼.
Zinci oxidi . . . . . gr. ij.
Hydrastis canad. . . gr. v.

Bismuthi subnitrat. gr. iij.
Hydrastis canad. . . gr. v.

Zinci acetat. . . . . gr. ¼.
Iodoformi . . . . . . gr. ij.
Ext. belladonnæ . . gr. ¼.

Ext. belladonnæ . . gr. ¼.
Ext. opii aq. . . . . gr. j.
Ext. hyoscyami . . . gr. ij.

Ext. gelsemii fld. . gr. v.
Ext. belladonnæ . . gr. ¼.
Ext. aconiti rad. fld. gr. j.
Ext. opii aq. . . . . gr. j.

Boroglyceridi . . . . gr. v.

Iodoformi . . . . . . gr. v.
Boroglyceridi . . . . gr. v.

Zinci sulph. . . . . . gr. ¼.
Boroglyceridi . . . . gr. v.
Iodoformi . . . . . . gr. v.

Iodoformi . . . . . . gr. ij.

Iodoformi . . . . . . gr. iij.

Cocain. hydrochlor. gr. ¼.

Zinci sulph. . . . . . gr. ½.

Zinci sulph. . . . . . gr. j.

Zinci sulphocarb. . gr. ½.

Cocain. hydrochlor. gr. ¼.
Morph. sulph. . . . . gr. ½.

Cocain. hydrochlor. gr. ¼.
Morph. sulph. . . . . gr. ½.
Atropinæ sulph. . . gr. $\frac{1}{100}$.

Cocain. hydrochlor. gr. ¼.
Morph. sulph. . . . . gr. ½.
Iodoformi . . . . . . gr. iij.
Thymol. . . . . gr. ½.

Iodoformi . . . . . . gr. iij.
Morph. sulph. . . . . gr. ¼.

Bismuthi subcarb. . gr. ij.
Plumbi carb. . . . . gr. ij.

Bismuthi subcarb. . gr. ij.
Plumbi carb. . . . . gr. j.

Bismuthi subcarb. . gr. iij.
Plumbi carb. . . . . gr. j.

Hydrastin. muriat. . gr. j.

Hydrastin. muriat. . gr. j.
Iodoformi . . . . . . gr. ij.

Zinci sulph. . . . . . gr. j.
Plumbi acetat. . . . gr. ½.
Ext. opii aq. . . . . gr. j.
Ext. belladonnæ . . gr. ¼.

Zinci oxidi . . . . . gr. ij.
Morph. sulph. . . . gr. ¼.
Iodoformi . . . . . gr. iij.

Hydrarg. chlor. cor. gr. 1/24.
Hydrarg. chlor mit gr. ij.
Ol. eucalypti . gr. v.

Hydrarg. chlor. cor. gr. 1/24.
Hydrarg. chlor. mit. gr. v.
Ol. eucalypti . . . . ♏j.

Iodol . . . . gr. ij.

Iodoformi . . . . . gr. iij.
Ergotini . . . . . . gr. v.
Ext. belladonnæ . . gr. ¼.

Bismuthi subiodidi . gr. iij.

Thallin. sulph. . . . gr. j.
Iodoformi . . . . . gr. j.
Ext. opii aq. . . gr. ½.
Ext. belladonnæ . gr. ¼.

Copaibæ . . . . . . ♏ij.
Acidi tannici . . . . gr. ij.

Copaibæ . . . . . . ♏ij.
Acidi tannici . . . . gr. v.

Copaibæ . . . . ♏ij.
Bismuthi subnitrat. gr. iij.

Copaibæ . . . . ♏iij.
Bismuthi subnitrat. gr. v.

Hydrarg. chlor. mit. gr. j.
Potassii chlorat. . gr. j.

Hydrarg. chlor. mit. gr. ij.
Potassii chlorat. . . gr. iij.

Hydrastini . . . . . gr. ½.
Salicini . . . . gr. ij.

Hydrastini . . . . . gr. j.
Salicini . . . . gr. iij.

Salicini . . . . gr. ij.
Copaibæ . . . . . . ♏ij.
Ol. cubebæ . . . . . ♏j.

Salicini . . . . gr. iij.
Copaibæ . . . . . . ♏ij.
Ol. cubebæ . . . . . ♏j.

Zinci sulph. . . . . gr. j.
Cupri sulph. . . . . gr. j.

Zinci sulph. . . . . gr. iij.
Cupri sulph. . . . . gr. j.

Iodoformi . . . . . gr. ij.
Acidi tannici . . . . gr. j.
Thymol. . . . . . . gr. ½.

Iodoformi . . . . . gr. ij.
Acidi tannici . . . . gr. ij.
Thymol. . . . . . . gr. ½.

D.—AURAL.

Bismuthi subnitrat. gr. j.
Acidi benzoici gr. j.

Bismuthi subnitrat. gr. ij.
Acidi benzoici . . . gr. j.

Iodoformi . . . . . gr. j.
Acidi tannici . . . . gr. ij.

Iodoformi . . . . . gr. j.
Acidi tannici . . . . gr. iij.

Acidi borici . . . . . gr. ½.
Acidi tannici . . . . gr. j.

Acidi borici . . . . . gr. j.
Acidi tannici . . . . gr. iij.

Acidi salicylici . . . gr. j.
Acidi borici . . . . gr. ½.
Acidi tannici . . . . gr. ij.

Acidi salicylici . . . gr. ij.
Acidi borici . . . . gr. j.
Acidi tannici . . . . gr. iij.

Zinci sulphocarbol. . gr. ij.
Zinci sulph. . . . . gr. j.

Zinci sulphocarbol. . gr. iij.
Zinci sulph. . . . . gr. j.

Hydrarg. oxidi flav. gr. j.

Hydrarg. oxidi flav. gr. iij.

Hydrarg. chlor. cor. gr. 1/24.
Hydrarg. chlor. mit. gr. ij.

Hydrarg. chlor. cor. gr. 1/24.
Hydrarg. chlor. mit. gr. iij.

Thymol. . . . . . . gr. ½.
Eucalyptol. . . . . ♏j.
Chloral. hydrat. . . gr. ij.

Thymol. . . . . . . gr. j.
Eucalyptol. . . . . ♏ij.
Chloral. hydrat. . . gr. iij.

Morphinæ sulph. . . gr. ¼.
Atropinæ sulph. . . gr. 1/250.

Morphinæ sulph. . . gr. ½.
Atropinæ sulph. . . gr. 1/100.

Cocain. hydrochlor. gr. ½.
Morphinæ sulph. . . gr. ⅛.

Cocain. hydrochlor. gr. j.
Morphinæ sulph. . . gr. ¼.

Cocain. hydrochlor. gr. ½.
Potassii chlorat. . . gr. j.

Cocain. hydrochlor. gr. j.
Potassii chlorat. . . gr. iij.

Morphinæ sulph. . . gr. ¼.
Acidi tannici . . . . gr. ij.

Morphinæ sulph. . . gr. ½.
Acidi tannici . . . . gr. iij.

Morphinæ sulph. . . gr. ¼.
Atropinæ sulph. . . gr. 1/200.
Cocain. hydrochlor. gr. ½.

E.—NASAL.

Hydrastis canad. . . gr. v.

Zinci sulph. . . . . . gr. j.
Acidi carbolici . . . gr. ¼.
Hydrastis canad. . . gr. v.

Iodoformi . . . . . . gr. iij.

Iodoformi . . . . . . gr. v.

Zinci sulph. . . . . . gr. j.
Ex. opii aq. . . . . . gr. ij.

Iodoformi . . . . . . gr. ij.
Ext. belladonnæ . . gr. ¼.

Acidi carbolici . . . gr. ¼.
Liq. iodi comp. . . . ♏ij.

Ergotin. . . . . gr. v.

Iodoformi . . . . . . gr. v.
Ol. eucalypti . . . . ♏iij.

Zinci sulph. . . . . . gr. ½.
Zinci oxidi . . . . . gr. j.
Hydrastis canad. . . gr. v.

Boroglyceridi . . . . gr. v.

Boroglyceridi . . . . gr. v.
Iodoformi . . . . . gr. ij.

Ergotini . . . . gr. iij.
Iodoformi . . . . . . gr. iij.
Ext. opii aq. . . . . gr. j.

{ Bismuthi subnitrat. **gr. iv.**
{ Morphinæ sulph. . . **gr.** ¼.

{ Zinci sulph. . . . . **gr.** 1/16
{ Morphinæ sulph. . **gr.** ½

Zinci sulph. . **gr.** 2/...

Hydrastin. muriatis **gr.** ¼.

{ Hydrastin. muriatis **gr.** ½
{ Bismuth. subcarb. . **gr. iij.**

{ **Plumbi acetatis** . . . **gr.** ½
{ **Ext. opii aq.** . . . . **gr.** ½
{ **Ext. belladonnæ** . . **gr.** ⅛

Sanguinarinæ sulph. gr. 1/16

Cocain. hydrochlor. gr. j.

{ Cocain. hydrochlor. gr. ½
{ Morphinæ sulph. . gr. ½

{ Cocain. hydrochlor. gr. ½
{ Morphinæ sulph. . . gr. ½
{ Atropinæ sulph. . . . gr. 1/64

{ Iodoformi . . . . **gr.** j.
{ Morphinæ sulph. . . **gr.** ½

{ Iodoformi . . . . . . gr. j.
{ Thymol. . . . . . gr. ½
{ Cocain. hydrochlor. gr. ½

{ Iodoformi . . . gr. iij.
{ Hydrastin. muriat. . gr. ½

{ Potassi chlorat. . . gr. iij.
{ Thymol. . . . . . gr. ½

{ Potassi **chlorat.** . . gr. iv.
{ Thymol. . . . . . gr. ½

{ Bismuthi subnitrat. . gr ij.
{ Eucalyptol. . . . . ♏j.

{ Bismuthi subnitrat. . gr. iv.
{ Eucalyptol. . . . ♏j.

{ Iodoformi . gr. ij.
{ Thymol. gr. ½.

{ Iodoformi . . . gr. ij.
{ Acidi tannici . gr. ij.

{ Iodoformi gr. ij
{ Acidi tannici . gr. iij.

{ Hydrarg chlor. cor. . gr. 1/...
{ Potassii chlorat. . gr. j.

{ Hydrarg. chlor. cor. . gr. ...
{ Potassii chlorat. . . gr. ij.

{ Acidi borici . . . . gr. j.
{ Sodii biborat. . . . . gr. iss.
{ Thymol. . . . . . . gr. ½

{ Acidi borici . . . . gr. ij.
{ Sodii biborat. . . . . gr. iv.
{ Thymol . . . . gr. j.

{ Acidi benzoici . . . gr. j.
{ Iodoformi . . . . . . gr. j.
{ Hydrarg. chlor. **cor.** gr. ...

{ Acidi benzoici . . . gr. ij.
{ Iodoformi . . . . . . gr. j.
{ Hydrarg. chlor. cor. gr. ...
{ Cocain. hydrochlor. gr. ½

Cocain. hydrochlor. gr. j.

{ Cocain. hydrochlor. **gr.** j.
{ Morphinæ sulph. . . **gr.** ½

{ Cocain. hydrochlor. gr. j.
{ Morphinæ sulph. . gr. ½

{ Cocain. hydrochlor. gr. j.
{ Morphinæ sulph. . gr. ½
{ Atropinæ sulph. . . gr. 1/64

{ Cocain. hydrochlor. **gr.** j.
{ Morphinæ sulph. . . **gr.** ½
{ Atropinæ sulph. . . . gr. 1/64

{ Cocain. hydrochlor. gr. j.
{ Eucalyptol. ♏ij.
{ Thymol. . . gr. ½

{ Cocain. hydrochlor. gr. j.
{ Eucalyptol. . . . . . ♏ij.
{ Thymol. . . . . . gr. j.

{ Morphinæ sulph. . . **gr.** ½
{ Zinci oxidi . . . . **gr.** ij.

{ Morphinæ sulph. . . **gr.** ½
{ Zinci oxidi . . . . . **gr.** ½
{ Bismuthi subnitrat. . **gr. iij.**

{ Bismuthi subnitrat. . **gr. iij.**
{ Cocain. hydrochlor. **gr.** ¼

{ Acidi tannici . . . . **gr. ij.**
{ Iodoformi . . . . **gr.** j.
{ Cocain. hydrochlor. . **gr.** ¼

IV

A Table of Formulæ for Hypodermic Medication.

Solutions of alkaloids usually undergo speedy alteration; they are not convenient to carry; and it is not always easy to secure by their use accuracy of dosage. For these reasons the soluble compressed tablets manufactured for hypodermic use are preferable. The tablet should be dissolved in a syringeful of water just boiled. The following alphabetical list contains the drugs available for use in this manner, in convenient doses.

Aconitinæ	gr. $\frac{1}{40}$		Morph. bi-mec.	gr. $\frac{1}{4}$
Aconitinæ	gr. $\frac{1}{150}$		Morph. mur.	gr. $\frac{1}{6}$
Aconitinæ	gr. $\frac{1}{250}$		Morph. mur.	gr. $\frac{1}{5}$
Atrop. sulph.	gr. $\frac{1}{50}$		Morph. sulph.	gr. $\frac{1}{2}$
Atrop. sulph.	gr. $\frac{1}{100}$		Morph. sulph.	gr. $\frac{1}{4}$
Atrop. sulph.	gr. $\frac{1}{150}$		Morph. sulph.	gr. $\frac{1}{8}$
Atrop. sulph.	gr. $\frac{1}{200}$		Morph. sulph.	gr. $\frac{1}{6}$
Apomor. mur.	gr. $\frac{1}{10}$		Morph. sulph.	gr. $\frac{1}{3}$
Apomor. mur.	gr. $\frac{1}{20}$		Morph. sulph.	gr. $\frac{1}{12}$
Caffeinæ	gr. $\frac{1}{2}$		Morph. sulph.	gr. $\frac{1}{5}$
Caffeinæ	gr. i.		Atrop. sulph.	gr. $\frac{1}{100}$
Cocainæ mur.	gr. $\frac{1}{6}$		Morph. sulph.	gr. $\frac{1}{6}$
Cocainæ mur.	gr. $\frac{1}{3}$		Atrop. sulph.	gr. $\frac{1}{150}$
Cocainæ mur.	gr. $\frac{1}{10}$		Morph. sulph.	gr. $\frac{1}{4}$
Conin. hydrob.	gr. $\frac{1}{20}$		Atrop. sulph.	gr. $\frac{1}{150}$
Conin. hydrob.	gr. $\frac{1}{40}$		Morph. sulph.	gr. $\frac{1}{2}$
Conin. hydrob.	gr. $\frac{1}{100}$		Atrop. sulph.	gr. $\frac{1}{120}$
Morph. sulph.	gr. $\frac{1}{6}$		Morph. sulph.	gr. $\frac{1}{2}$
Curarin. sulph.	gr. $\frac{1}{40}$		Atrop. sulph.	gr. $\frac{1}{200}$
Curarin. sulph.	gr. $\frac{1}{100}$		Morph. sulph.	gr. $\frac{1}{12}$
Curarin. sulph.	gr. $\frac{1}{150}$		Atrop. sulph.	gr. $\frac{1}{250}$
Digitalin.	gr. $\frac{1}{100}$		Physostyg. salic.	gr. $\frac{1}{40}$
Dubois. mur.	gr. $\frac{1}{50}$		Physostyg. salic.	gr. $\frac{1}{60}$
Dubois. mur.	gr. $\frac{1}{100}$		Picrotoxini	gr. $\frac{1}{20}$
Dubois. mur.	gr. $\frac{1}{150}$		Picrotoxini	gr. $\frac{1}{60}$
Morph. sulph.	gr. $\frac{1}{4}$		Picrotoxini	gr. $\frac{1}{80}$
Dubois. mur.	gr. $\frac{1}{150}$		Strych. sulph.	gr. $\frac{1}{30}$
Morph. sulph.	gr. $\frac{1}{4}$		Pilocarp. mur.	gr. $\frac{1}{4}$
Eserin. sulph.	gr. $\frac{1}{20}$		Pilocarp. mur.	gr. $\frac{1}{3}$
Eserin. sulph.	gr. $\frac{1}{40}$		Pilocarp. mur.	gr. $\frac{1}{10}$
Eserin. sulph.	gr. $\frac{1}{100}$		Pilocarp. mur.	gr. $\frac{1}{2}$
Eserin. sulph.	gr. $\frac{1}{150}$		Pilocarp. mur.	gr. $\frac{1}{6}$
Morph. sulph.	gr. $\frac{1}{6}$		Pilocarp. mur.	gr. $\frac{1}{6}$
Hyoscy. sulph.	gr. $\frac{1}{20}$		Quin. carb. mur.	gr. i.
Hyoscy. sulph.	gr. $\frac{1}{100}$		Quin. carb. mur.	gr. ij.
Hyoscy. sulph.	gr. $\frac{1}{60}$		Quin. carb. mur.	gr. iij.
Morph. sulph.	gr. $\frac{1}{4}$		Spartein. sulph.	gr. $\frac{1}{30}$
Hyoscin. hydrobrom.	gr. $\frac{1}{100}$		Spartein. sulph.	gr. $\frac{1}{60}$
Hyoscin. hydrobrom.	gr. $\frac{1}{75}$		Strych. sulph.	gr. $\frac{1}{60}$
Hydrarg. chlor. cor.	gr. $\frac{1}{50}$		Strych. sulph.	gr. $\frac{1}{100}$
Hydrarg. chlor. cor.	gr. $\frac{1}{20}$		Strych. sulph.	gr. $\frac{1}{120}$
Morph. bi-mec.	gr. $\frac{1}{2}$		Trinitrin.	gr. $\frac{1}{100}$
Morph. bi-mec.	gr. $\frac{1}{3}$		Trinitrin.	gr. $\frac{1}{150}$
Morph. bi-mec.	gr. $\frac{1}{6}$		Trinitrin.	gr. $\frac{1}{250}$

The following substances are to be used in freshly-prepared solutions, etc.: they should be fully dissolved and carefully filtered:

Acidi Carbolici ʒii, *Acidi Tannici* ʒi, *Alcoholis* ʒiv, *Glycerini* ʒi. Dose, 1–5 m. for each hemorrhoid.

Acidi Chrysophanici gr. vi, Aq. Destil. fʒx: one minim = $\frac{1}{80}$ gr. Dose, 7½–15 m. = $\frac{1}{8}$–¼ gr.

Acidi Osmici gr. vi, Aq. Destil. fʒx: one minim = $\frac{1}{80}$ gr. Dose, 7½–15 m. = $\frac{1}{8}$–¼ gr.

Acidi Sclerotici ʒi, Aq. Destil. ʒv: one minim = $\frac{1}{8}$ gr. Dose, 15–30 m. = 3–6 gr.

Agaricin. gr. iii. Alcohol. Absol. fʒivss, Glycerini fʒvss: one minim = $\frac{1}{200}$ gr. Dose, 15–30 m. = $\frac{1}{13}$–¼ gr.

Aloini gr. xii, Aq. Destil. 3i: one minim = ⅛ gr. Dose, 10-15 m.

Aq. Ammoniae 3i, Aq. Destil. 3iii. Dose, 20-30 m.

Antipyrin. gr. xxviiss, Cocain. Mur. gr. iss, Aq. Bullient. f3ii. Dose, 10 m. = Antipyrine 2½ gr. and Cocaine ⅛ gr.

Antipyrin. Hydrochlor. 3i, Aq. Destil. f3i. Heat in a test-tube. One minim = one gr. Dose, 15 m. = 15 gr.

Camphorae gr. v, Alcohol. 3i. Dose, 6-30 m.

Camphorae gr. iii, Ol. Vaselini gr. e. Triturate and filter carefully. Dose, 20-60 m.

Chloral. Hydratis 3i, Aq. Font. 3ii. Dose, 4-16 m.

Chloroformi 3ii. Dose, 5-15 m.

Chloroformi 3i, Ol. Vaselini 3iv. Dose, 15-30 m.

Codeini **Pur.** gr. xv, Æther. Acetic. f3i: one **minim = ¼ gr.** Dose, 10-30 m. = 4-7½ gr.

Daturiae gr. ss, Aq. Font. 3i: one minim = ₂₁₀ gr. Dose, 4-10 m.

Ergotae gr. xv, Alcohol., Glycerini, āā 3iss: one minim = ₂₀ gr. Dose, 5-30 m.

Ext. Ergotae Fl. q. s. Filter carefully. Dose, 10 m.

Eucalypti Ess. ℳxxv, Ol. Vaselini 3v. Triturate and filter carefully. Dose, 15-30 m.

Eucalyptol. Pur. ℳxxv, Iodoformi gr. iv. Triturate and dissolve, and add Ol. Vaselini 3v, shake, and filter carefully. Dose, 15-30 m.

Helleborein. (Merck's) gr. xii, Aq. Destil. f3i: one minim = ₂₁₀ gr. Dose, 5-10 m.

Hydrarg. Chlorid. Corros., Ammonii Chlorid., āā gr. iii, Aq. Destil. f3ss: mix, dissolve and add Albuminis Ovi f3iss, Aq. Destil. f3v: filter, and add Aq. Destil. q. s. ad f3x. One minim = ₂₀₀ gr. Dose, 3-10 m. = ₁₀₀-₆₀ gr.

Hydrarg. *Chlor. Mit.* gr. iss, **Glycerini** ℳxv. **Dose, 15 m.**

Hydrarg. Chlor. Mit. gr. xv, **Ol. Olivæ 3iiss.** Dose, 10-30 m.

Hydrarg. Chlor. Mit. gr. xii, Ol. Vaselini ℳccxxv. Dose, 20-30 m.

Hydrarg. Chlor. Mit., Sodii Chlorat., āā gr. xv, Aq. Dest. 3iiss. Dose, 10-30 m.

Hydrarg. Oxid. Flav. 3iss, Hydrarg. **Chlor. Corros.** gr. ¾, Glycerini 3xxv. Dose, 12½ m.

Hydrarg. et Sodii Iodidi **gr. iii,** Aq. Destil. f3iiiss, dissolve and filter: one minim = ₂₀ gr. **Dose, 10 m. = ½ gr.**

Hyoscyaminæ gr. i, Acid. Sulph. **Dil.** ℳv, Aq. Destil. f3i: one minim = ₁₆₀ gr. Dose, 5 m. = ₃₂ gr.

Iodi gr. i, Olei Vaselini gr. e. Triturate **and filter carefully,** and preserve in a yellow bottle. Dose, 15-30 m.

Iodoformi gr. i, Ol. Vaselini. gr. e. Triturate for a half-hour, adding the vaseline slowly. Filter carefully, and preserve in a yellow glass-stopped vial. Dose, 15-30 m.

Lobelinæ Hydrobrom. gr. i, **Aq. Destil. f3v: one minim = ₂₄₀ gr.** Dose, 3-15 m. = ₁₄₀-₃₂ gr.

Menthol Pur. gr. x, Ol. Vaselini 3iss. Dissolve over a sand-bath at low heat, and filter carefully. Dose, 5-20 m.

Paraldehyde 3iss, Aq. Laurocerasi 17iss, Aq. Destil. **f3ivss.** Warm the solution before using. Dose, 30-60 m. = 6-12 gr.

Pareiræ Hydrochlor. gr. xv, Aq. Destil. f3v: one minim = ₂₀ gr. Dose, 2-10 m. = ₁₀-¼ gr.

Phenol gr. i, Ol. Vaselini gr. e. Dissolve over **a sand-bath at** low heat, and filter carefully. Dose, 5-30 m.

Physostigmatis **Ext. gr.** ii, Aq. Destil. 3i. **Dose, 10 m. = ¼ gr.**

Potassii Arsenitis Liq. Dose, **1-3 m.**

Potassii Iodidi 3i, Aq. Font. 3iv. **Dose, 6-20 m. = 1½-5 gr.**

Potassii Permangan. 3ss, Aq. Destil. 3iii: one minim = ⅓ gr. Dose, 25 m.

Quininæ Hydrobrom. gr. xlviii, **Aq. Destil.** f3iv: one minim = ½ gr. Dose, 20 m. = 4 gr.

Salol. 3ss, Ol. Vaselini 3v: one minim = ₁₆ gr. Dose, 20-30 m.

Sparteinæ Sulph. **gr. i,** Aq. Destil. 3i: one minim = ₂₄₀ gr. Dose, 10 m.

Terebinthinæ Olei gr. xxv, Ol. Vaselini gr. e. Triturate and filter carefully. Dose, 10-30 m.

Thallin. Sulph. 3i, Aq. Destil. f3v: one minim = ½ **gr. Warm** the solution before using. Dose, 5-7½ m. = 1-1½ gr.

Thymol gr. i, Ol. Vaselini gr. e. Dissolve over **a sand-bath at** a low heat, and filter carefully. Dose, 10-30 m.

After drawing the fluid into the syringe, expel all the air, by pointing the syringe upwards and pressing the piston until a drop of the liquid appears at the point of the needle.

Draw the skin tense at the selected point, and thrust the needle through into the **subcutaneous** tissues, immediately but slowly injecting the **fluid into them**; after the needle has been withdrawn, place **the finger over** the puncture for a short time. Gentle circular friction with the finger-top serves to disperse the injected fluid and hasten absorption.

Avoid, in puncturing, **large vessels, inflamed spots, and bony** prominences.

Select for the injection the outer surfaces of the arms, thighs, the calves of the legs, the abdomen, or the back.

Hypodermic injections of the preparations of mercury should be made in the gluteal region and very deep, the needle being entered perpendicularly to the plane of the surface to the extent of one inch or more.

Hypodermic medication should be employed when immediate and decided results are required; when medicines otherwise administered fail of their effect; when medicines are indicated which the patient refuses or is unable to swallow; when there is an irritable state of the stomach precluding exhibition by the mouth.

Solutions intended for hypodermic use should **be neutral,** without acid or alkaline reaction, and non-irritating.

Indications **for the Administration of Medicaments by the Hypodermic Method.**

Arrest of Perspiration.—Pilocarpin.

Asthma.—Lobeline hydrobromate one two-hundredth to **one-**twentieth grain. Also in cardiac asthma and pseudo-angina.

Bubo **has been** aborted by injecting carbolic acid into the swelling.

Bowels, Obstruction of the.—Aloin, in doses of one-half to one grain.

Carcinoma.—Acetic acid, one part to three of water, injected into the cancer.

Chloroform Poisoning.—One-tenth grain of digitaline, **followed** an hour afterwards with one-tenth grain of atropine.

Chorea.—Curare, one-tenth to one-twentieth of a grain, daily. Liquor potassii arsenitis, one to three minims. Lobeline hydrobromate, one-hundredth to one-twentieth of a grain.

Congestive Chills.—Ten drops of tincture of belladonna every fifteen minutes, until the pulse becomes distinguishable, followed by hypodermics of quinine or dextro-quinine, brandy, or whiskey. Pareirine, one-tenth to one half grain, also commended. Quinine muriate and hydrobromate may be used hypodermically.

Convulsions, Puerperal.—Chloral.

Convulsions, Infantile.—Morphine, with inhalations of five drops of nitrite of amyl, immediately following.

Convulsions.—Saturated tincture of gelsemium, **ten** to fifteen drops.

Croup.—Sulphate of atropine, one-per-cent. solution, **three** drops, repeated after four hours.

Diarrhœa.—Cotoin, four to seven and a half grains, hypodermically, every fifteen or twenty minutes, or every hour, except in intestinal ulceration, cirrhosis, and alcoholics. Also useful in cholera, night-sweats, and ptyalism.

Dysentery.—Morphine, in one-third grain doses.

Dysmenorrhœa.—Antipyrine, two and **one-third grains, and** cocaine, one-eighth grain, in combination.

Eczema.—Arseniate of sodium, in solutions of one-fifth, one-half, and one per cent., commencing with ten minims of the weaker, and gradually increasing. Chrysophanic acid, one-fifteenth to one-seventh grain, highly recommended in eczema, lichen, prurigo, and psoriasis. Pilocarpin is also of use.

Enuresis, Nocturnal.—Very small doses of the nitrate of strychnine, injected in the vicinity of the rectum at intervals.

Epilepsy.—Curare, in solution, seven grains in seventy-five minims of water, with two drops of hydrochloric acid. About once a week inject eight drops beneath the skin. Also lobeline hydrobromate, one-hundredth to one-twentieth grain.

Erysipelas.—Carbolic acid, three-per-cent. solution, eight or ten injections at the same time, so as to surround and cover the inflamed regions. Also salicylic acid in the same manner.

Fevers.—Antipyrine, **hypodermically**, is very valuable as an antipyretic in doses of **ten or fifteen grains. Cocaine, one-eighth** grain, may be added. **Thallin sulphate, one to one and a half** grains, **is** also useful.

Fractures, Ununited.—Glacial acetic acid, five to ten minims between the ends of the bones. Iodine also used in the same way.

Foreign Body in the Œsophagus.—Threatened strangulation from impaction of the gullet has been promptly relieved by inducing vomiting; apomorphine, one-tenth grain. Emetics also suggested.

Goitre.—Ergotine, one-third **grain, gradually increased to one** grain.

Hæmoptysis.—Sclerotinic acid, five-per-cent. **solution, injected** in the neck or arm.

Heart-Failure.—Tincture of digitalis, ten to thirty minims. Digitaline and helleborein (Merck's); brandy and whiskey also.

Hemorrhages (Hæmoptysis, Hæmatemesis, and Uterine Hemorrhages).—Ergotine. In pain, add morphine.

Hemorrhoids.—Iodine, carbolic acid, perchloride of iron, a few drops of either injected into each pile, usually operating on only one at a time, waiting several days before repeating.

Hernia.—Morphine, with or without atropine.

Hiccough.—Three-eighths of **a** grain of hydrochlorate of pilocarpin.

Hydrophobia.—Curare.

Mania and Melancholia.—Paraldehyde, six to twelve minims in solution. Hyoscyamia, one-ninety-sixth grain, and hyoscine hydrobromate, one-two-hundredth to one-ninetieth grain, also useful.

Nasal Polypus.—Carbolic acid, one part, glycerin, four parts; twenty drops injected into the tumor.

Neuralgias.—Osmic acid, one-fifteenth to one-seventh grain. Also chloroform and antipyrine.

Night Sweats.—Atropine, one-fortieth grain at bedtime. **Agaricin,** one-tenth grain.

Opium Habit.—Sparteine sulphate.

Opium Poisoning.—Fluid extract of coffee **in thirty-minim** doses. Caffeine citrate and atropine sulphate.

Paralysis.—Strychnine.

Peritonitis.—Morphine and conium.

Sciatica.—Chloroform and salol.

Sepsis.—Iodoform, turpentine, menthol, thymol, **phenol,** iodine, and camphor, dissolved in liquid vaseline.

Skin-Diseases (mycotic).—Sulphuric, carbolic, salicylic, **or** sclerotinic acid, hypodermically, as in erysipelas.

Snake-Bites.—Ammonia, brandy, carbolic or salicylic acid. Also permanganate of potassium.

Strychnine Poisoning.—Caffeine, one grain; alcohol; chloral.

Surgical Shock.—Quinine, six grains, with one-third grain of morphine. Also quinine hydrobromate, four grains.

Suspension of Salivary Secretion.—Pilocarpin.

Syphilis.—Mercurials.

Tetanus.—Curare, physostigmine, morphine, and cornine; also pilocarpin.

Trichinosis.—Tincture of ergot and ergotine.

Urticaria.—Saturated solution of bisulphide of sodium into the part affected. Chrysophanic acid, one-fifteenth to one-seventh grain.

Varicose Veins.—**Ergot or ergotine, injected near the affected** veins.

V.

A List of Drugs for Inhalation.

The doses are calculated for an ordinary steam-atomizer, and are to be added to one ounce of **water.**

Acidi carbolici, gtt. iij to x. In phthisis.

Acidi **tannici, gr. j to xx.** In chronic catarrhal affections and laryngeal ulcerations.

Aluminis, **gr. v to xxx.** In cases of excessive secretions from bronchi.

Ammonii chloridi, **gr. ij to ℨij.** To promote expectoration in acute and chronic catarrh.

Aquæ amygdalæ amaræ ℨj. (Add no water.) In painful affections of the upper air-passages and paroxysmal cough.

Aquæ ferventis. In acute inflammations of the mucous membrane, as in laryngitis.

Argenti nitratis, gr. j to x. In ulcerations and follicular pharyngitis. A face-shield should be worn.

Calcis liquoris, ℨj. (Add no water.) In diphtheria and croup.

Cannabis indicæ ext., **gr. ¼ to j.** In chronic catarrh and emphysema.

Conii ext., **gr. j to vj.** In irritative coughs and asthma.

Cupri sulphatis, **gr. j to xx.** In chronic inflammations and coughs.

Hyoscyami ext., **gr. ½.** In whooping-cough and spasmodic coughs.

Iodi tinct., gtt. j to xx. In inflammatory affections of the larynx and pharynx.

Morphinæ acetatis, **gr. ¼ to ½.** In irritative cough and its constitutional effect.

Opii ext. aquosi, **gr. ¼ to ½.** In irritative cough.

Picis liq. infus., ℨj to ℨij. In offensive bronchial secretions.

Plumbi acetatis, gr. ij to v. In advanced stages of acute **catarrhs.** Astringent and sedative.

Potassii carbonatis, **gr. x to ℨij.** In follicular pharyngitis.

Potassii chloratis, gr. x to **xx.** In chronic and subacute catarrhal affections.

Potassii bromidi, **gr. j to x.** In spasmodic laryngeal affections.

Potassii iodidi, **gr. ij to xx.** In granular inflammations, and chronic bronchitis with emphysema.

Sodæ chloratæ liq., ℨ½ to j. In offensive bronchial secretions.

Terebinthinæ ol., gtt. j to ij. In chronic bronchitis with offensive secretions.

Zinci sulphatis, **gr. j to vj.** In bronchorrhœa, etc.

VI

A List of Common Poisons and their Antidotes.

In cases of poisoning when the substance has been taken by way of the mouth, the stomach must be emptied before proceeding to administer the antidote. This can be done by means of—

(a) *Emetics:*

Large draughts of lukewarm water; mustard-water, a teaspoonful of powdered mustard to the tumblerful of water; alum-water, a dessertspoonful of powdered alum to the tumblerful of water; sulphate of zinc, 10 to 30 grains; **powdered** ipecac, 10 grains; or—

(b) *The stomach pump.*

Where the stomach-pump cannot be promptly obtained, a rubber tube may be used for the purpose of washing out the stomach.

The only exceptions to the above rule are: first, when a considerable period of time—several hours—has elapsed after the ingestion of a small amount of highly poisonous substance; and, second, when highly corrosive substances have been taken which are likely to have partially dissolved the wall of the stomach.

POISONS.	ANTIDOTES.

ACIDS.

Acids. *Sulphuric.* *Hydrochloric.* *Nitric.* *Phosphoric.*	*Alkalies.* Bicarbonate of sodium or potassium. Magnesia. Chalk or whiting. Plaster from the wall; soap, to be followed by copious draughts of tepid water or flaxseed tea; milk; eggs beaten up; olive or almond oil.
Oxalic. *Binoxalate of Potassium.* *Tartaric.* *Acetic.*	Chalk or whiting, or plaster from the wall, with water.
Hydrocyanic.	Alternate hot and cold affusion; artificial respiration; atropine hypodermically; ammonia.
Carbolic.	Saccharated lime; Glauber's or Epsom salts; stimulants; white of egg, milk, or wheat flour.

ALKALIES.

Caustic Potash.	Vinegar, or other dilute acids.
Caustic Soda.	Lemon juice.
Caustic Lime.	**Milk.**
Caustic Ammonia, *Carbonate of Sodium or of Potassium.*	Castor, linseed, almond, or other oil, freely.

MINERAL POISONS.

Antimony.	If vomiting does not occur, **wash out the** stomach with water. Follow **with astringent** infusions, as of galls, **oak bark, very** strong green tea, or tannic **or gallic acid.** Follow this by white of egg.

MINERAL POISONS (Continued).

Arsenic.   Administer freshly-precipitated hydrated ox-ide of iron freely.

[To make hydrated oxide of iron: "Take of solution of tersulphate of iron a pint; water of ammonia, water, each a sufficient quantity. To the solution of tersulphate of iron, previously mixed with three pints of water, add water of ammonia with constant stirring until in slight excess. Then pour the whole on a wet muslin strainer, wash the precipitate with water, pressing the strainer forcibly with the hands until no more liquid passes. Lastly, mix the precipitate with sufficient water to bring the mixture to the measure of a pint and a half, and transfer it to a wide-mouthed bottle, which must be well stopped."—U.S.P.]

or—

Dialyzed iron in tablespoonful doses, followed by 15-grain doses of chloride of sodium, repeated every ten or fifteen minutes.

In the absence of the above, magnesia or oils or fats, as sweet oil, butter, milk, should be freely administered.

Barium Salts.   Epsom or Glauber's salts, or dilute sulphuric acid.

Copper.
Corrosive Subli-mate. } See *Metallic Salts.*

Cyanide of Potas-sium. } See *Hydrocyanic Acid.*

Insect Powder.   See *Arsenic.*

Iodine.
Iodide of Potas-sium. } Starch, wheat flour, or arrow-root, well boiled with water, very freely. Afterwards, vine-gar and water.

Lead.   See *Metallic Salts.*

Metallic Salts.   White of egg, freely, to form insoluble al-buminate. Then wash out stomach and follow by demulcents, poultices to epigas-trium, and opium by suppository, or mor-phine hypodermically.

Phosphorus.   Sulphate of copper; magnesia; copious draughts of water and mucilaginous drinks; oil of turpentine (old); animal charcoal. Avoid oils and fats.

Rat Paste.   See *Phosphorus.*

ALKALOIDS, ETC.

Aconite.   Alcohol, whiskey, brandy, etc.; ammonia; artificial heat; digitalis; atropine.

Alcohol.   Coffee; cold affusion to head; artificial heat to head and feet; strychnine hypodermically.

Atropine.   Coffee and stimulants; hypodermic injections of caffeine; artificial respiration; physo-stigma, cautiously.

Belladonna.   See *Atropine.*

Calabar Bean.   Stimulants; atropine; artificial respiration.

Cannabis Indica.   See *Morphine.*

Cantharides.   Demulcents, freely. Avoid fats and oils.

Cherry-Laurel Water. } See *Hydrocyanic Acid.*

Chloral.   External warmth; strong, hot coffee per rec-tum; strychnine hypodermically, repeated at intervals of fifteen or twenty minutes. Keep the patient roused.

Codeine.   See *Morphine.*

Colchicum.   Tannic or gallic acid; stimulants; opium.

Conium.   Tannic acid; stimulants; coffee.

Creasote.   See *Carbolic Acid.*

Croton Oil.   Demulcents; stimulants; opium.

ALKALOIDS, ETC. (Continued).

Curare.	Artificial respiration: if the poison has been introduced by a weapon, incise the wound freely and suck it. If the wound is upon a limb, tie a bandage above the wound. The bandage should be from time to time loosened for a moment, in order to allow the unremoved poison to pass into the system by degrees.
Digitalis.	Strong **tea**; **tannin**; stimulants; aconite; absolute quiet.
Ergot.	Stimulants.
Gelsemium.	Atropine; stimulants; artificial respiration.
Hyoscyamus.	See *Atropine.*
Lobelia.	Tannin; stimulants; strychnine hypodermically.
Morphine.	Keep the patient aroused and moving; cold affusion; general faradization; alcohol; atropine hypodermically; artificial respiration.
Mushrooms.	Atropine hypodermically; **castor** oil; stimulants.
Nitrite of Amyl.	Stimulants; alternate cold and hot douches; artificial respiration.
Nitroglycerin.	Cold to the head; ergotine; atropine hypodermically.
Oil of Bitter Almonds.	See *Hydrocyanic Acid.*
Opium.	See *Morphine.*
Quinine.	Tannic or gallic acid; strong tea or coffee; alcohol; ammonia; artificial respiration.
Physostigma.	Stimulants; atropine; chloral; strychnine; artificial respiration.
Picrotoxine.	**Chloral;** bromide of **potassium.**
Pilocarpine.	Atropine.
Snake-Bite.	A bandage around the limb; fresh incision and sucking of the wound; actual cautery or permanganate of potassium, locally; alcoholic stimulants freely; ammonia; artificial respiration; strychnine hypodermically.
Stramonium.	See *Atropine.*
Strychnine.	Chloroform; tannin; bromide of potassium; chloral.
Tobacco.	Tannin; **diffusible** stimulants; strychnine.
Turpentine.	Demulcents; sulphate of magnesia.
Veratrine.	Diffusible stimulants; hot coffee; absolute rest in a recumbent posture.

AERIAL POISONS.

Anæsthetics. *Chloroform.* *Ether.* *Nitrous Oxide.* *Bromide of Ethyl, etc.*	Artificial respiration; inversion of the body; flagellation, etc.
Chlorine. *Bromine.* *Iodine Vapor.*	Steam inhalations.
Coal Gas. *Charcoal Fumes.* *Carbonic Acid Gas.* *Choke Damp.* *Marsh Gas.* *Fire Damp.*	Artificial respiration; alternate warm and cold douches; frictions; sinapisms; venesection; inhalations of oxygen.
Carbon Monoxide.	Fresh air; artificial respiration; transfusion.

VII.

A Posological Table.

For hypodermic use the dose should be half that used by the mouth.

For use by the rectum the dose should be twice that by the mouth.

Doses for Different Ages.

Gaubius's Rule:

Regulating the Ordinary Proportion of Doses according to the Age of the Patient.

For an adult, suppose the dose to be	1,	or	1 drachm.
Under 1 year will require	1/12	"	5 grains.
" 2 years " "	1/8	"	8 "
" 3 " " "	1/6	"	10 "
" 4 " " "	1/4	"	15 "
" 7 " " "	1/3	"	1 scruple.
" 11 " " "	1/2	"	1/2 drachm.
" 20 " " "	2/3	"	2 scruples.
From 21 years to 60 years, the full dose	1	"	1 drachm.

Above 60 years an inverse gradation should be observed.

Young's Rule:

For children under 12 years the doses of most medicines must be diminished in the proportion of the age to the age increased by 12. Thus, at 2 years the dose will be 1/7 of that for an adult, viz.

$$\frac{2}{2+12} = \tfrac{1}{7}.$$

Sex, temperament, constitutional strength, and the habits and idiosyncrasies of individuals must be taken into account. Nor does the same rule apply to all medicines. Calomel, for instance, is generally borne better by children than by adults; while opium affects them more powerfully, and requires the dose to be diminished considerably below that indicated in the table.

Table for the Administration of Laudanum.

For a child at birth, or one month old	1/16 to 1/4 drop.
Under a year old	1/4 to 1 "
From one to two years	1 to 3 drops.
" two to five years	2 to 5 "
" five to ten years	5 to 10 "
" ten to fifteen years	10 to 20 "
At fifteen years	15 to 20 "
For an adult	20 to 30 "

It is important, in the employment of laudanum, that it should be of the proper strength and perfectly clear. Thirteen minims represent one grain of opium. Laudanum becomes stronger with age, especially if the bottle be not tightly corked.

A POSOLOGICAL TABLE.

Drug or Preparation.	Dose.	Drug or Preparation.	Dose.
Abstract. bella-donnæ	½ grain.	Auri et sodii chlorid.	1/10 to 1/6 gr.
cannabis ind.	1 grain.	Balsamum gurjunæ	15 to 40 grs.
conii	1 to 3 grs.	peruviani	20 to 30 min.
gelsemii	1 grain.	Beberiæ sulphas: tonic	1 to 3 grs.
hyoscyami	2 grains.	antiperiodic	3 to 10 grs.
nuc. vom.	1 grain.	Belladonnæ fol.	1 to 10 grs.
podophylli	4 grains.	Belladonnæ rad.	1 to 5 grs.
Acetphenetidine	3 to 10 grs.	Benzanilide	4 to 30 grs.
Acet. opii	5 minims.	Berberina	1 to 15 grs.
scillæ	10 to 30 min.	Bismuthi citras	3 to 15 grs.
Acid. acet. dil.	60 minims.	et ammonii citr.	1 to 15 grs.
arsenios.	1/30 to 1/12 gr.	salicylas	2 to 5 grs.
benzoic.	5 to 15 grs.	subnitr.	3 to 15 grs.
boric.	5 to 10 grs.	valer.	1 to 3 grs.
carbolic.	1 to 3 grs.	Caffeina	1 to 5 grs.
gallic.	3 to 15 grs.	Calcii chloridum	10 to 20 grs.
hydrobrom, 34 per cent.	10 to 15 grs.	hippuras	5 to 10 grs.
hydrobrom. dil.	15 to 60 min.	hypophosphis	3 to 15 grs.
hydrochlor.	3 to 10 min.	iodidum	1 to 3 grs.
hydrochlor. dil.	10 to 30 min.	phosphas	15 to 30 grs.
hydrocyan. dil.	2 to 6 min.	santoninas	¼ to 2½ gr.
lactic.	15 to 60 grs.	Calx sulphurata	1/10 to 1 gr.
nitric.	3 to 10 min.	Cambogium	1 to 4 grs.
nitr. dil.	10 to 30 min.	Camphora	3 to 10 grs.
nitrohydrochlor.	3 to 10 min.	monobrom.	2 to 5 grs.
nitrohydrochlor. dil.	5 to 20 min.	Cannabinon	¾ to 1½ grs.
oxalic.	¼ to 2 grs.	Cannabin. tannas	4 to 15 grs.
phosphoric, 50 per cent.	3 to 15 grs.	Cantharis	½ to 2 grs.
phosphoric, dil.	10 to 20 min.	Capsicum	1 to 3 grs.
salicylic.	5 to 15 grs.	Castoreum	6 to 15 grs.
sulphuric.	5 to 10 min.	Catechu	15 to 30 grs.
sulphuric. dil.	10 to 20 min.	Cerii nitras	1 to 3 grs.
sulphuric, arom.	5 to 30 min.	oxalas	1 to 3 grs.
sulphuros	30 to 60 min.	Chinoidinum	3 to 30 grs.
tannic.	2 to 15 grs.	Chinolino	8 to 30 grs.
Aconitina (white cryst.)	1/640 to 1/24 gr.	Chloral.	10 to 30 grs.
Adonidine	1/8 to 1/2 gr.	Chloroformum	1 to 5 min.
Agaricin.	1/16 to 1 gr.	Chrysarobinum	3 to 15 grs.
Aloe	2 to 5 grs.	Cinchona	15 to 60 grs.
Aloinum	1 to 3 grs.	Cinchonidina	1 to 30 grs.
Alumen	5 to 15 grs.	Cinchonina	1 to 30 grs.
Ammonii benzoas	10 to 20 grs.	Cinnamomum	6 to 30 grs.
bromid.	5 to 30 grs.	Coca fol.	¼ to 2 drs.
carb.	3 to 10 grs.	Cocainæ hydrochlor.	1/8 to 1 gr.
Ammonii chlorid.	5 to 30 grs.	Codeina	¼ to 2 grs.
iodid.	5 to 15 grs.	Colocynthin	1/12 to 6 grs.
phosph.	5 to 20 grs.	Colchicin.	1/40 to 1/20 gr.
picras	½ to 1½ grs.	Confectio sennæ	1 to 2 grs.
valer.	3 to 15 grs.	Coniina and its salts	1/60 to 1/8 gr.
Amyl. hydras	15 to 75 min.	Convallamarin.	½ to 4 grs.
nitris	2 to 5 min.	Copaiba	15 to 60 min.
Antifebrin (acetanilide)	2 to 15 grs.	Cotoinum	¼ to 1 gr.
Ant. et pot. tart.: diaphoretic	1/8 to 1/4 gr.	Creasotum	1 to 3 min.
emetic	1 to 2 grs.	Creta præpar.	15 to 75 grs.
Antimonii oxysulphuret.	¼ to 2 grs.	Croton chloral.	1 to 10 grs.
Antipyrin.	5 to 30 grs.	Cubebæ	15 to 60 grs.
Apiol	3 to 15 grs.	Cupri acetas	¼ to 6 grs.
Apomorph. hydrochlor.	1/20 to 1/8 gr.	sulphas	½ to 10 grs.
Aqua ammoniæ	5 to 30 min.	Cuprum ammon.	½ to 1 gr.
amygd. amar	2 fl. drs.	Curare	1/12 to 2/3 gr.
camphoræ	1 to 4 fl. drs.	Decoct. aloes comp.	½ to 2 fl. oz.
chlori	1 to 4 fl. drs.	sarsæ comp.	2 to 6 fl. oz.
creasoti	1 to 4 fl. drs.	Diastase	5 to 15 grs.
laurocerasi	6 to 30 min.	Digitalinum	1/60 to 1/30 gr.
Arbutin	8 to 15 grs.	Digitalis	½ to 3 grs.
Argenti nitras	¼ to ¼ gr.	Duboisina and its salts	1/120 to 1/60 gr.
Arsenii iodidum	1/20 to 1/6 gr.	Elaterinum, U. S. P. 1880	1/20 to 1/6 gr.
Assafœtida	5 to 20 grs.	Elaterinum, U. S. P. 1870	1/8 to 1/2 gr.
Atropina	1/120 to 1/50 gr.	Ergota	15 to 60 grs.
Atropinæ sulph.	1/120 to 1/50 gr.	Ergotinum	2 to 8 grs.
		Eserine and its salts	1/60 to 1/6 gr.
		Ethoxycaffeina	1 to 3 grs.
		Euonymin.	2 to 4 grs.
		Ext. aconiti rad., U. S. P. 1880	1/2 to ¼ gr.

Drug or Preparation.	Dose.
Ext. aconiti [rad.] fl.	1 to 5 min.
aloes aquos.	½ to 3 grs.
angusturæ fl.	15 to 45 min.
angelicæ rad. fl.	30 to 60 min.
anthemidis	2 to 10 grs.
anthemidis fl.	30 to 60 min.
apocyni cannab. fl.	8 to 30 min.
arecæ fl.	45 to 75 min.
arnicæ flor.	3 to 8 grs.
arnicæ fl.	5 to 15 min.
arnicæ rad.	2 to 5 grs.
arnicæ rad. fl.	5 to 15 min.
aromat. fl.	30 to 60 min.
aspidospermæ fl.	15 to 45 min.
aurantii cort. fl.	½ to 2½ fl. drs.
azedarach fl.	15 to 75 min.
baptisiæ fl.	7 to 20 min.
bellad. fol. fl.	3 to 7 min.
bellad. rad.	1/6 to 1/4 gr.
bellad. rad. fl.	1 to 6 min.
brayeræ fl.	2 to 4 fl. drs.
bryoniæ fl.	15 to 60 min.
buchu fl.	½ to 2½ fl. drs.
calami fl.	15 to 60 min.
calend. fl.	15 to 60 min.
calumbæ	3 to 10 grs.
calumbæ fl.	15 to 60 min.
canellæ fl.	15 to 60 min.
cannab. amer. fl.	3 to 15 min.
cannab. ind.	1/6 to 2 grs.
cannab. ind. fl.	3 to 6 min.
cantharidis fl.	1 to 3 min.
capsici fl.	1 to 3 min.
cardam. comp. fl.	15 to 45 min.
cascarillæ fl.	½ to 2½ fl. drs.
caulophylli fl.	15 to 30 min.
chimaph. fl.	½ to 1½ fl. drs.
cimicifugæ fl.	8 to 30 min.
cinchonæ	15 to 30 grs.
cinchonæ fl.	30 to 60 min.
cinchonæ arom. fl.	30 to 60 min.
cinchonæ comp. fl.	½ to 1½ fl. drs.
cocæ	10 to 25 grs.
cocæ fl.	1 to 2 drs.
cocculi fl.	1 to 3 min.
colch. rad.	1/6 to 1½ grs.
colch. rad. fl.	3 to 15 min.
colch. sem. fl.	1½ to 10 min.
colocynth.	1 to 5 grs.
colocynth. comp.	1 to 5 grs.
conii fol. fl.	3 to 15 min.
convallariæ rad. fl.	15 to 30 min.
corn. flor. fl.	30 to 60 min.
coto fl.	5 to 15 min.
cubebæ fl.	15 to 30 min.
cypripedii fl.	15 to 60 min.
damianæ fl.	½ to 2 fl. drs.
digitalis	1/4 to 1/2 gr.
digitalis fl.	1 to 6 min.
droseræ fl.	5 to 10 min.
dulcamaræ	5 to 15 grs.
dulcamaræ fl.	1 to 2 fl. drs.
ergotæ	1 to 8 grs.
ergotæ fl.	15 to 60 min.
erythroxyli fl.	½ to 2 fl. drs.
eucalypti fl.	15 to 60 min.
euonymi fl.	15 to 60 min.
eupatorii fl.	30 to 60 min.
euphorbiæ pil. fl.	10 to 30 min.
gallæ fl.	¾ to 2 fl. drs.
gelsemii	2 to 8 min.
gelsemii fl.	1 to 8 min.
gentianæ fl.	30 to 60 min.
gent. comp. fl.	30 to 60 min.
geranii fl.	15 to 90 min.
gilleniæ fl.	15 to 30 min.
gossypii fl.	15 to 45 min.
granati rad co fl.	¾ to 2 fl. drs.
grind. rob. fl.	30 to 60 min.
Ext. grind. squarr. fl.	30 to 60 min.
guaiaci ligni fl.	30 to 60 min.
guaranæ fl.	15 to 30 min.
hæmatoxyli	8 to 30 grs.
hæmatoxyli fl.	30 to 60 min.
hamamelidis fl.	60 to 90 min.
helleb. nigris	½ to 3 grs.
helleb. nigris fl.	5 to 15 min.
heloniæ fl.	8 to 30 min.
hepaticæ fl.	30 to 60 min.
humuli	3 to 15 grs.
humuli fl.	30 to 60 min.
hydrangeæ fl.	30 to 60 min.
hydrastis	3 to 10 grs.
hydrastis fl.	8 to 30 min.
hyoscyami fol. fl.	3 to 30 min.
hyoscyami sem. fl.	3 to 8 min.
ignatiæ	1/6 to 1¼ grs.
ignatiæ fl.	1 to 6 min.
ipecac. fl.	3 to 60 min.
iridis versicol.	3 to 6 grs.
iridis versicol. fl.	15 to 30 min.
jalapæ, U. S. P. 1870	5 to 10 grs.
jalapæ fl.	15 to 60 min.
juglandis	15 to 30 grs.
juglandis fl.	¾ to 2 fl. drs.
junip fl.	30 to 60 min.
kino fl.	15 to 30 min.
krameriæ	5 to 15 grs.
krameriæ fl.	30 to 60 min.
lactucæ	5 to 15 grs.
lactucæ fl.	15 to 60 min.
lactucarii fl.	8 to 30 min.
leptandræ	3 to 10 grs.
leptandræ fl.	30 to 60 min.
lobeliæ fl.	¼ to 1 fl. dr.
lobeliæ sem. fl.	¼ to ½ fl. dr.
lupulini fl.	10 to 30 min.
lycopi fl.	5 to 30 min.
malti	1 to 2½ drs.
matico fl.	30 to 60 min.
mezerei	½ to 1 gr.
mezerei fl.	3 to 10 min.
nectandræ fl.	1 to 4 fl. drs.
nuc. vom.	½ to 1 gr.
nuc. vom. fl.	1 to 5 min.
opii	¼ to ½ gr.
papaveris	½ to 2 grs.
papaveris fl.	15 to 45 min.
pareiræ fl.	30 to 60 min.
petroselini fl.	1 to 2 fl. drs.
physostigmæ	1/16 to 1/4 gr.
physostigmæ fl.	1 to 3 min.
phytolaccæ bac. fl.	5 to 30 min.
phytolaccæ rad.	1 to 3 grs.
phytolaccæ rad. fl.	5 to 30 min.
pilocarpi fl.	15 to 60 min.
piper. nigr fl.	15 to 45 min.
piscidiæ fl.	15 to 60 min.
podophylli	½ to 1½ grs.
podophylli fl.	8 to 30 min.
prun. virg. fl.	30 to 60 min.
pulsatillæ fl.	2 to 10 min.
quassiæ	1 to 5 grs.
quassiæ fl.	30 to 60 min.
quebracho fl.	20 to 60 min.
quercus fl.	30 to 60 min.
rhamnus purshian. fl.	5 to 90 min.
rhei	5 to 15 grs.
rhei fl.	15 to 45 min.
rhois arom. fl.	15 to 60 min.
rhois glabr. co. fl.	30 to 60 min.
rhois glab. fret. fl.	30 to 60 min.
rhois toxicod. fl.	1 to 6 min.
ricini fol. fl.	½ to 2 fl. drs.
rosæ fl.	½ to 2 fl. drs.
rubi fl.	15 to 60 min.

Drug or Preparation.	Dose.	Drug or Preparation.	Dose.
Ext. sabinæ fl.	5 to 15 min.	Hydrarg. salicylas	⅛ to ¼ gr.
salicis fl.	½ to 2 fl. drs.	subsulphas flav.	¼ to 1 gr.
salviæ fl.	½ to 2 fl. drs.	tannas	½ to 1½ gr.
sanguin. fl.	5 to 15 min.	cum creta	1 to 8 grs.
santali citr. fl.	1 to 2 fl. drs.	Hydrochinon	5 to 30 grs.
santonica fl.	15 to 60 min.	Hyoscin hydrobrom.	1/200 to 1/50 gr.
sarsæ. fl.	½ to 2 fl. drs.	Hyoscyamina and	
sassafras fl.	½ to 2 fl. drs.	salts.	1/10 to 1/4 gr.
scillæ fl.	1 to 5 min.	Hypnone	¾ to 2 grs.
scillæ comp. fl.	1 to 5 min.	Ichthyol	3 to 5 grs.
scoparii fl.	½ to 1 fl. dr.	Infusum digitalis	2 to 4 fl. drs.
senegæ fl.	8 to 15 min.	sennæ comp.	1 to 2 fl. oz.
sennæ fl.	1 to 4 fl. drs.	Iodoformum	1 to 3 grs.
serpent. fl.	30 to 60 min.	Iodol	¼ to 2 grs.
sinsrubo fl.	15 to 30 min.	Iodum	⅙ to ½ gr.
spigeliæ fl.	15 to 60 min.	Ipecacuanha:	
spigeliæ et		expectorant	⅛ to 1 gr.
sennæ fl.	½ to 2 fl. drs.	emetic	15 to 30 grs.
stigmatis maid. fl.	1 to 2 fl. drs.	Iridin	2 to 4 grs.
stillingiæ fl.	½ to 2 fl. drs.	Jalapa	15 to 30 grs.
stillingiæ comp. fl.	½ to 2 fl. drs.	Kairine	4 to 15 grs.
stramonii fol. alc.	½ to ⅔ gr.	Kamala	1 to 2 drs.
stramonii sem.	¼ to ½ gr.	Kino	8 to 30 grs.
stramonii fl.	1 to 6 min.	Kosin	10 to 40 grs.
sumbul fl.	15 to 60 min.	Lactucarium	8 to 15 grs.
taraxaci	5 to 15 grs.	Liq. ammon. acet.	2 to 4 fl. drs.
taraxaci fl.	½ to 2 fl. drs.	acidi arseniosi	2 to 7 min.
trit rep. fl.	1 to 4 fl. drs.	arsen. et hydr. iod.	2 to 7 min.
urticæ rad. fl.	5 to 15 min.	calcii chloridi	30 to 60 min.
ustilag. maid. fl.	15 to 60 min.	ferri chloridi	2 to 10 min.
uvæ ursi fl.	30 to 60 min.	ferri dialys.	10 to 15 min.
valerinæ	5 to 15 grs.	ferri nitrat.	8 to 15 min.
valer. fl.	30 to 60 min.	hydrog. perox. (10	
veratr. vir. fl.	2 to 8 min.	vol.)	⅓ to 4 drs.
viburni [prunif. fl.	1 to 2 fl. drs	pepsini	1 to 4 fl. drs.
xanthoxyli cort. fl.	15 to 30 min.	potassii arsenit.	3 to 7 min.
xanthoxyli fret. fl.	15 to 30 min.	potassii citrat.	2 to 4 fl. drs.
zingiberis fl.	8 to 30 min.	sodæ	5 to 30 min.
Fel bovis purif.	3 to 6 grs.	sodii arseniatis	3 to 7 min.
Ferri arsen.	1/20 to ½ gr.	Lithii benzoas	2 to 5 grs.
benzoas	1 to 5 grs.	bromid.	1 to 3 grs.
bromid	1 to 5 grs.	carb.	2 to 6 grs.
carb. sacch.	4 to 15 grs.	citr.	2 to 5 grs.
chlorid.	1 to 3 grs.	salicylas	2 to 8 grs.
citr.	5 to 10 grs.	Lobeline hydrobro.	1/20 to 1/8 gr.
et ammon. citr.	5 to 10 grs.	Lupulinum	5 to 10 grs.
et ammon. sulph.	5 to 10 grs.	Magnesia	15 to 60 grs.
et ammon. tartr.	8 to 15 grs.	Magnesii carb.	15 to 60 grs.
et cinchonid. citr.	5 to 10 grs.	citr. gran.	2 to 4 drs.
et pot. tartr.	5 to 30 grs.	sulphas	2 to 8 drs.
et quin. citr.	5 to 10 grs.	sulphis	8 to 30 grs.
et strychn. citr.	1 to 5 grs.	Mangani oxidum	
hypophosphis	5 to 10 grs.	nig.	2 to 10 grs.
iodidum	1 to 5 grs.	sulphas	2 to 10 grs.
iodidum sacch.	2 to 10 grs.	Manna	1 to 2 oz.
lactas	1 to 5 grs.	Massa copaibæ	5 to 30 grs.
oxalas	1 to 3 grs.	ferri carb.	5 to 15 grs.
oxid. hydrat.	¼ to 2 oz.	hydrarg.	1 to 10 grs.
phosphas	1 to 5 grs.	Menthol	½ to 1½ gr.
pyrophosphas	1 to 5 grs.	Methylal	1 to 4 drs.
subcarb.	5 to 30 grs.	Mist. ammoniaci	4 to 8 fl. drs.
sulphas	1 to 3 grs.	asafœtidæ	2 to 4 fl. drs.
sulphas exsiccat.	1 to 3 grs.	chloroformi	2 to 4 fl. drs.
valer.	1 to 3 grs.	cretæ	1 to 4 fl. drs.
Ferrum dialysatum	5 to 15 min.	ferri comp.	½ to 2 fl. oz.
redactum	1 to 5 grs.	ferri et amm. acet.	1 to 4 fl. drs.
Guarana	10 to 30 grs.	glycyrrh. comp.	1 to 4 fl. drs.
Helleborein		magnes. et asafœt.	1 to 4 fl. drs.
(Merck's)	1/20 to ¼ gr.	potassii citr.	¼ to 1 fl. oz.
Hydrarg. chlorid.		rhei et sodæ	½ to 1 fl. oz.
corr.	1/16 to 1/8 gr.	Morrhuol	4 to 12 grs.
chlorid. mite	1/10 to 10 grs.	Morphine and its	
cyanid.	⅛ to ½ gr.	salts	⅛ to 1½ gr.
iodid. flav.	⅛ to 1 gr.	Naphthalinum	2 to 10 grs.
iodid. rubr.	1/20 to ½ gr.	Naphthol	5 to 15 grs.
iodid. vir.	⅛ to 1 gr	Narceina	½ to 2 grs.
oxid. flav.	⅛ to ½ gr	Nitroglycerinum	1/100 to 1/50 gr.
oxid. nigr.	1/16 to 1 gr	Nux vomica	1 to 5 grs.
oxid. rubr.	1/16 to ½ gr	Oleoresina aspidii	20 to 40 min.

Drug or Preparation.	Dose.
Oleoresina capsici .	1/4 to 1/2 gr
cubebæ	5 to 30 grs
piperis	1 to 3 grs.
zingiberis	1 to 3 grs.
Oleum copaibæ . .	8 to 15 min.
cubebæ	15 to 30 min.
erigerontis . . .	5 to 15 min.
eucalypti	10 to 30 min.
gaultheriæ . . .	2 to 10 min.
phosphoratum . .	1 to 3 min.
sabinæ	1 to 3 min.
terebinthinæ . . .	5 to 60 min.
tiglii	1 to 4 drops.
Opium (14 per cent. morphine) . . .	1/2 to 1 1/2 grs.
Pancreatin	10 to 20 grs
Papayotin	1 to 5 grs.
Paracotoin	1 1/2 to 3 grs.
Paraldehyde	15 to 90 min.
Pareirin hydrochlor.	1/8 to 1 gr.
Pelletierine sulphas	3 to 6 grs.
tannas .	12 to 24 grs.
Pepsinum purum .	15 grains.
saccharatum*.	30 grains.
Phenacetin	7 to 11 grs.
Phosphorus . . .	1/100 to 1/25 gr.
Physostigminæ salicyl. .	1/100 to 1/64 gr.
sulphas	1/100 to 1/64 gr.
Picrotoxinum .	1/64 to 1/8 gr.
Pilocarpina and salts	1/24 to 1/2 gr.
Pil. aloes . . .	1 to 3 pills.
aloes et asafœt.	2 to 5 pills.
aloes et ferri .	1 to 3 pills.
aloes et mast. .	1 to 3 pills.
aloes et myrrhæ .	2 to 5 pills.
antim. comp. . .	1 to 3 pills.
asafœtidæ	1 to 6 pills.
cathart. comp. . .	1 to 4 pills.
ferri **comp.**	2 to 5 pills.
ferri **iodidi**	1 to 4 pills.
opii	1 to 2 pills.
phosphori	1 to 4 pills.
rhei	2 to 5 pills.
rhei comp.	2 to 5 pills.
Piperinum	1 to 8 grs.
Plumbi acetas . . .	1/2 to 3 grs.
iodidum	1/2 to 3 grs.
Potassa sulphurata .	1 to 10 grs.
Potassii acetas . . .	15 to 60 grs.
bicarb.	8 to 60 grs.
bitartr.	1 to 2 drs.
bromid.	8 to 60 grs.
carb.	8 to 30 grs.
chloras	5 to 30 grs.
citras	15 to 60 grs.
cyanid.	1/16 to 1/4 gr.
et sodii tartr. . .	1/2 to 1 oz.
hypophosphis . .	5 to 15 grs.
iodid.	5 to 60 grs.
nitras	8 to 15 grs.
permanganas . . .	1/4 to 1 gr.
sulphis	15 to 30 grs.
tartras	1 to 8 drs.
Propylamina	2 to 15 grs.
Pulv. antimonialis .	3 to 10 grs.
aromat. . . .	5 to 30 grs
cretæ comp. . .	8 to 30 grs.
glycyrrh. comp.	30 to 60 grs
ipecac. et opii .	5 to 15 grs.
jalapæ comp. . .	30 to 60 grs.
morphinæ comp. .	8 to 15 grs
rhei comp.	30 to 60 grs
Pyridin	2 to 5 drops.
Quinidina and salts	1 to 30 grs
Quinina and salts	1 to 30 grs
Quininæ arsenias .	1/6 to 1 gr.
Resina copaibæ .	2 to 10 grs.
guaiaci .	10 to 30 grs.
Resina jalapæ . . .	2 to 5 grs.
podophylli	1/8 to 1/2 gr.
scammonii	2 to 10 grs.
Resorcin	5 to 30 grs.
Rheum	2 to 30 **grs.**
Saccharin	1/4 to 2 grs.
Salicinum	8 to 30 grs.
Salol	5 to 30 grs.
Santonica	8 to 60 grs.
santoninum	1 to 5 grs.
Scammonium . . .	3 to 15 grs.
Scoparine	1/2 to 1 gr.
Senna	8 to 60 grs.
Sodii acetas	15 to 60 grs.
arsenias	1/64 to 1/16 **gr.**
benzoas	5 to 15 grs.
bicarb.	8 to 30 grs.
bisulphis	8 to 30 grs.
boras	8 to 30 grs.
bromid.	8 **to** 30 grs.
carb.	8 **to** 30 grs.
hypophosphis . .	**8 to** 15 grs.
hyposulphis . . .	**8 to** 30 **grs.**
iodidum	**5 to** 15 grs.
phosphas	**2 to** 15 grs.
salicylas	5 to 30 grs.
santoninas	2 to 10 grs.
sulphas	1 to 2 drs.
sulphis	8 to 30 grs.
Spartein sulphas . .	1/16 to 1 1/2 **grs.**
Spir. æther.	30 to 60 **min.**
æther. nitrosi . .	1/2 to 2 fl. drs.
ammoniæ	8 to 30 min.
ammoniæ arom. .	15 to 60 min.
camphoræ . .	8 to 30 min.
chloroformi	15 to 60 min.
lavand. comp. .	30 to 60 min.
menth. pip.	30 to 60 min.
Strophanthin (Merck's)	1/200 to 1/100 gr.
Strychnina (and salts)	1/64 to 1/20 gr.
Sulphonal	15 to 30 grs.
Sulphur	1/2 **to 4** drs.
Syrup. acidi **hydri**odici	1 to 4 fl. drs.
allii	1 to 4 fl. drs.
calcii lactophos. .	1 to 2 fl. drs.
calcis	15 to 30 min.
ferri bromidi . .	15 to 60 min.
ferri iodidi	15 to 60 min.
ferri oxidi	1 fl. dr.
ferri hypophosph.	1 fl. dr.
fer. quin. et stryc. phos.	**1 fl. dr.**
hypophosphit. . .	**1 fl. dr.**
ipecac.	1/4 to 4 fl. drs.
krameriæ	1/2 to 4 fl. drs.
lactucarii	1 to 3 fl. drs.
rhei	1 to 4 fl. drs.
rhei **arom.**	1 to 4 fl. drs.
rosæ	1 to 2 fl. drs.
rubi	1 to 2 fl. drs.
sarsap. comp. . .	1 to 4 fl. drs.
scillæ	1/2 to 1 fl. dr.
scillæ comp. . . .	15 to 60 min.
senegæ	1 to 2 fl. drs.
sennæ	1 to 4 fl. drs.
Terebene	5 to 15 drops.
Terpene hydrate . .	3 **to 20** grs.
Thallin. sulph. . . .	1 to 5 grs
Thymol	1/2 to 5 grs.
Tinct. aconiti fol. . .	5 to 16 min.
aconiti rad. . . .	1 to 5 min.
aconiti rad., Fleming's . .	3/4 to 2 1/2 min.
aloes (1880)	1/2 to 2 fl. drs.
aloes et myrrhæ	1 to 2 fl. drs.
arnicæ flor.	8 to 30 min.

A POSOLOGICAL TABLE (Continued).

Drug or Preparation.	Dose.	Drug or Preparation.	Dose.
Tinct. arnicæ rad.	15 to 30 min.	Tinct. opii camph.	1 to 4 fl. drs.
asafœtidæ	30 to 60 min.	physostigmatis	5 to 15 min.
belladonnæ	5 to 15 min.	quassiæ	½ to 2 fl. drs.
bryoniæ	15 to 30 min.	rhei	1 to 8 fl. drs.
calendulæ	15 to 30 min.	rhei arom.	30 to 75 min.
calumbæ	1 to 4 fl. drs.	rhei dulc.	1 to 4 fl. drs.
cannabis ind.	15 to 30 min.	sanguinariæ	15 to 60 min.
cantharidis	5 to 15 min.	scillæ	8 to 40 min.
capsici	8 to 15 min.	serpentariæ	½ to 2 fl. drs.
catechu comp.	½ to 2 fl. drs.	stramon. fol.	8 to 15 **min.**
cimicifugæ	30 to 60 min.	stramon. sem.	6 to 15 min.
cinchonæ	½ to 2 fl. drs.	strophanthi (1-20)	5 to 10 min.
cinchonæ comp.	½ to 2 fl. drs.	sumbul	8 to 30 min.
cocæ (1-5)	2 to 30 min.	valerianæ	½ to 2 fl. drs.
colchici rad.	5 to 20 min.	valer. ammon.	½ to 2 fl. drs.
colchici **sem.**	15 to 60 min.	veratri viridis	1 to 10 min.
conii	**5 to 30 min.**	zingiberis	15 to 60 min.
cubebæ	1 to 2 fl. drs.	Trimethylamina	2 to 15 grs.
digitalis	5 to 15 min.	Tritur. elaterini	½ to ½ **gr.**
ferri acet.	15 to 30 min.	Urethane	15 to 60 grs.
ferri chloridi	15 to 60 min.	Veratrina	$\frac{1}{15}$ to $\frac{1}{8}$ gr.
ferri chloridi æther.	15 to 30 min.	Vinum aloes	1 to 2 fl. drs.
gallæ	½ to 2 fl. drs.	antim. { expect. & alt.	1 to 8 min.
gelsemii	5 to 10 min.	antim. { emet.	30 to 75 min.
guaiaci	30 to 60 min.	cocæ	2 to 4 drs.
guaiaci **ammon.**	30 to 60 min.	colch. rad.	8 to 45 min.
hellebori	10 to 15 min.	colch. sem.	5 to 30 min.
humuli	1 to 4 fl. drs.	ergotæ	1 to 4 fl. drs.
hydrastis	30 to 90 min.	ferri amarum	1 fl. dr.
hyoscyami fol.	15 to 60 min.	ferri citrat.	1 fl. dr.
hyoscyami **sem.**	15 to 30 min.	ipecac. { expector.	5 to 15 min.
ignatiæ	5 to 15 min.	ipecac. { emetic	2 to 4 fl. drs.
iodi	5 to 15 min.	opii	5 to 10 min.
ipecac. et opii	5 to 15 min.	rhei	1 to 2 fl. drs.
jalapæ	½ to 2 fl. drs.	Xylolum	5 to 15 grs.
kino	½ to 2 fl. drs.	Zinci acet.	1 to **2** grs.
krameriæ	½ to 2 fl. drs.	bromid.	½ to **2** grs.
lavand. comp.	½ to 2 fl. drs.	cyanid.	$\frac{1}{6}$ to ¼ gr.
lobeliæ	15 to 45 min.	iodid	½ to 3 grs.
lupulini	½ to 2 fl. drs.	oxid.	1 to 10 grs.
matico	½ to 2 fl. drs.	phosphid.	$\frac{1}{8}$ to ¼ gr.
nucis vomicæ	5 to 30 min.	sulphas, emetic	15 to 30 grs.
opii	5 to 25 min.	valerianas	1 **to** 6 grs.

VIII.

A List of Incompatibles.

Those substances are incompatible—

I. Between which chemical reaction may occur, destroying the properties of both. The reaction may or may not occasion the formation of a precipitate.

II. Which introduce a solution of **a substance in a certain** menstruum into a large quantity of **another menstruum in which** the substance is insoluble.

III. Besides such mixtures, those must be **avoided in which** oxidizing agents, or iodine, or bromine, would **come in contact** with combustible substances.

Acids must not be **compounded with alkalies nor alkaline** carbonates.

Liquids containing mucilaginous matters are precipitated by salts of iron, lead, and other heavy metals; also by alcohol, ether, and mineral acids.

Tinctures and fluid extracts containing resins are precipitated **by water.**

Liquids containing tannin or bitter substances are precipitated by salts of iron and other heavy metals. ☞ Chiretta does not contain tannin.

Salts of the alkaloids are usually precipitated by ammonia and other alkalies, the alkaloid being thrown down; they are also precipitated by tannic acid, and many of them by iodine and iodides.

Chromic **acid**, potassium chromate, potassium permanganate, must not be compounded with organic or combustible matters, such as sugar, glycerin, starch, alcohol, sulphur, sulphides, phosphorus. Neither potassium chlorate nor potassium nitrate must be triturated with any of the preceding substances, and iodine and bromine must not come in contact with oil of turpentine, nor phosphorus, nor sulphur.

The medicinal metallic salts, excepting **those of potassium**, sodium, lithium, magnesium, and calcium, are precipitated by ammonia and alkalies, and, not excepting the last two, by alkaline carbonates.

Chlorides are **decomposed by salts of lead and silver.**

Iodides and bromides are decomposed by nitric and by nitromuriatic acid; also by soluble salts of silver, lead, and mercury (☞ the precipitated mercuric iodide, formed by the action of corrosive sublimate on potassium iodide, dissolves in excess of the latter); also by strong sulphuric acid, by potassium permanganate, and by other energetic oxidizing agents.

Sulphides are decomposed by salts of heavy metals generally.

Sulphates are decomposed by lead solutions.

Carbonates are decomposed by acids and acid salts.

Phosphates are precipitated when phosphoric acid is introduced into alkaline solutions containing magnesium or calcium.

Hydrogen peroxide is decomposed by most substances; it may be mixed with ether or glycerin.

Chloral hydrate is decomposed by alkalies.

Arsenious acid and arsenites are incompatible **with magnesia**, lime water, tannin, and ferric hydroxide.

Antimonial preparations are **incompatible with acids**, especially **tannic** acid, and alkalies.

Cocaine solutions are precipitated by borax.

Antipyrine is incompatible with calomel and with sweet spirit of nitre.

IX.

Tables of Approximate Relative Weights and Measures in the Metric and Apothecaries' Systems.

Approximate Equivalents of Milligrammes in Grains.

Milligramme.	Grain.	Milligrammes.	Grain.	Milligrammes.	Grain.
0.1	=	1/600	1	=	1/60	8	=	1/8
0.2	=	1/300	1.2	=	1/50	9	=	1/7
0.3	=	1/200	1.6	=	1/40	10	=	1/6
0.4	=	1/150	2	=	1/30	12	=	1/5
0.5	=	1/120	3	=	1/20	16	=	1/4
0.6	=	1/100	4	=	1/15	20	=	1/3
0.7	=	1/90	5	=	1/12	30	=	1/2
0.8	=	1/80	6	=	1/10	60	=	1
0.9	=	1/70	7	=	1/8			

Approximate Equivalents of Centigrammes in Grains.

Centi-grammes.	Grain.	Centi-grammes.	Grains.	Centi-grammes.	Grains.
1	=	1/6	6	=	1	18	=	3
2	=	1/3	7	=	1 1/4	25	=	4
3	=	1/2	9	=	1 1/2	50	=	8
4	=	2/3	10	=	1 1/2	75	=	12
5	=	3/4	12	=	2	100	=	16

Approximate Equivalents of Grammes in Grains.

Grammes.	Grains.	Grammes.	Grains.	Grammes.	Grains.
0.001	=	1/60	11	=	176	27	=	432
0.010	=	1/6	12	=	192	28	=	448
0.100	=	1 1/2	13	=	208	29	=	464
0.200	=	4	14	=	224	30	=	480
0.500	=	8	15	=	240	31	=	496
0.750	=	12	16	=	256	32	=	512
1	=	16	17	=	272	33	=	528
1.50	=	24	18	=	288	34	=	544
2	=	32	19	=	304	35	=	560
3	=	48	20	=	320	36	=	576
4	=	64	21	=	336	37	=	592
5	=	80	22	=	352	38	=	608
6	=	96	23	=	368	39	=	624
7	=	112	24	=	384	40	=	640
8	=	128	25	=	400	50	=	800
9	=	144	26	=	416	100	=	1600
10	=	160						

Approximate Equivalents of Cubic Centimetres in U. S. Apothecaries' Fluidrachms.

Cubic Centimetres.	U. S. Fluid-drachms.	Cubic Centimetres.	U. S. Fluid-drachms.	Cubic Centimetres.	U. S. Fluid-drachms.
1	=	1/4	9	=	2 1/4	16	=	4
2	=	1/2	10	=	2 1/2	20	=	5
3	=	3/4	11	=	2 3/4	24	=	6
4	=	1	12	=	3	28	=	7
5	=	1 1/4	13	=	3 1/4	32	=	8
6	=	1 1/2	14	=	3 1/2	48	=	12
7	=	1 3/4	15	=	3 3/4	64	=	16
8	=	2						

X.

External Antipyretics.

a. **Cold** Sponging.
b. **Cold Compresses.**
c. **The Application of Ice.**
d. **The Cold Pack.**
e. **The Cold or Gradually-Cooled Bath.**
f. **Cold Affusion.**
g. **Iced-Water Enemas.**

---

a. COLD SPONGING.—The water may be of the temperature of the room or cooled with ice. A little alcohol or vinegar may be added to it, or Labarraque's solution. A sponge or wash-cloth may be used, and more or less moderate friction, according to the sensations of the patient. In all use of water great care must be taken to protect the bed.

Every part of the body is in turn bared, washed, dried, and again covered. The spongings may be repeated at intervals of two or three hours. They not only add greatly to the comfort of the patient, but also exert a favorable influence upon the nervous system and circulation of the blood, by causing it to flow more freely in the vessels directly under the skin. They lower the temperature only slightly, unless the water be very cold and the spongings frequently repeated.

b. COLD COMPRESSES.—For this purpose three or four thicknesses of old table linen or towelling, which is porous enough to hold a good deal of water, is most useful. The compress is wrung out of water of the required temperature and reapplied as it becomes warm. Or two compresses may be used alternately, each being cooled in turn by placing it on a block of ice in a basin or pan at the bedside. Cold compresses are often used for the head, and are commonly very acceptable to patients. They are without appreciable effect upon the general temperature. Very large cold compresses extending over the entire thorax and abdomen and frequently renewed exert a decided effect upon the internal fever. The compresses are sometimes allowed to remain continuously in position, a small quantity of cold water being from time to time added to replace that lost by evaporation.

Leiter's coils, which may be fitted to the head or applied over the heart or to other regions of the body in such a manner as to reduce local temperature by means of cold water flowing through them from a reservoir over the bed, exert an influence analogous to but not exactly the same as that exerted by the cold compress.

c. THE APPLICATION OF ICE.—Ice is commonly applied by means of a bladder or gum ice-bag. It must be cracked into pieces the size of a walnut and introduced into the bag with a little water, the bag being about half or two-thirds full. The air is then squeezed out and the stopper adjusted. If the bag be filled, or air enough left in it to distend it, it will not conform itself to the part to which it is applied. A much more effectual method of applying ice to the abdomen or over the heart is by spreading out a thick layer of finely-cracked ice between the folds of a coarse towel, which is then placed directly over the **skin.** This method requires constant watching, and is almost **sure to** wet the bedding. It is not available for prolonged use.

d. THE COLD PACK.—A blanket is spread evenly over a couch or bed; over this blanket is laid a coarse sheet wrung lightly out of water of the prescribed temperature and folded once. The patient is lifted upon the bed thus prepared and quickly wrapped in the wet sheet by the attendant in such a manner that it lies as smoothly as possible over every part of the body except the head. If the extremities feel cold before the packing, they must be warmed by friction, or else not included in the packing.

As soon as the damp linen is everywhere in contact with **the** body, the attendant folds the blanket over the patient in the same way, first drawing over and tucking one side smoothly under, and then the other, seeing that the chin is free and that the blanket is folded evenly, but without tension at the neck. Finally, the long end is drawn down and folded smoothly under the feet.

Three or even four thicknesses of wet sheets spread upon the blanket are necessary to reduce the temperature effectively.

The reduction of temperature from a single pack is usually transient, and repeated packings, even to the number of five or six, are often administered, the rise of temperature being slower after each. When the temperature does not rise above normal, or when shivering takes place, the packing must not again be renewed. When repeated packings are necessary, two couches are used side by side, and the patient is lifted directly from one pack on to the other. The same effect is produced, but less completely, by unfolding the blanket and sprinkling the sheet afresh with cold water.

The patient is allowed to remain in the last pack from three-quarters of an hour to an hour and a half; at the expiration of this time the skin generally becomes pleasantly warm, and in many cases outbreaks of perspiration take place.

During the packing the pulse is felt at the carotid or temporal artery and the temperature taken in the mouth.

e. THE COLD OR GRADUALLY-COOLED BATH.—The quantity of water used should be sufficient to wholly immerse the body of the patient. The tub must stand at the bedside. During the bath the skin should be gently rubbed. The temperature of the water should be about 90° F., or even higher than this, at the first bath. As the patient becomes accustomed to the bath it is gradually cooled by the addition of cold water to 85° F., or lower. Under no circumstances should it be cooled below 65° F. The average duration of the bath is fifteen minutes. But if shivering or great uneasiness occur, the patient is at once lifted into bed, placed upon a sheet previously made ready, and wiped dry, with brisk rubbing of the extremities and back. The moist sheet is then removed. The patient is covered up, and some hot soup or wine, or brandy and water, administered. The temperature is not always immediately reduced, but—as measured in the rectum—usually falls within an hour from one and a half to four or five degrees. In the course of some hours it rises again, and the bath is then repeated. If cold baths are not not well borne, good results in lowering the temperature often follow prolonged luke-warm baths. Sometimes it becomes necessary to repeat the bath four or five times in the course of twenty-four hours. A patient who is quietly sleeping, even if his temperature be high, should not be roused and immediately placed in the bath.

When young children are treated by this method, the temperature of the bath at the beginning should be warm, and a blanket spread over the tub, in which the little patient is gradually lowered into the water.

Not only is the temperature lowered by this means, but also a very favorable influence is exerted upon the state of the nervous system. The intellect clears up, the dulness diminishes.

f. COLD AFFUSION.—While the patient is in the tub, cold water —60° F.—is thrown by means of a sponge over his head, face, neck, shoulders, and chest. This is repeated once or twice just before he is removed from the bath. It is done rather for the sake of its good effects upon the nervous system in cases of great stupor and other evidences of serious nervous derangement than merely as a means of reducing high temperature. Cold affusions may be practised in bed, the mattress being suitably protected by water-proof sheets.

g. ICED-WATER ENEMAS.—Large rectal injections of iced water are sometimes followed by a fall of temperature. They are, when carefully administered, rather grateful than otherwise to patients. They are best given by means of the fountain syringe, the water being introduced into the bowel slowly, and the flow stopped for a few minutes by pressure upon the tube without withdrawing the nozzle, whenever a sense of pain or of desire to evacuate the bowel is experienced. In this way a large quantity of fluid may be injected. It is not often necessary to exceed three pints. This method of applying cold constitutes a useful addition to those in ordinary use, and may be advantageously employed in connection with them under suitable circumstances.

The patient's head and face must always be well bathed with cold water just before and during applications of cold to the general surface of the body. The occurrence of chill or rigor may be delayed by more or less vigorous rubbing or chafing of the body.

XI

Disinfectants.

The following list includes the disinfectants available for general purposes:

Dry and Moist Heat.
Fumes of Sulphur (Sulphur Dioxide).
Chloride of Lime (Calcium Hypochlorite).
Labarraque's Solution (Solution of Chlorinated Soda).
Corrosive Sublimate (Mercuric Chloride).
Sulphate of Copper (Cupric Sulphate).
Carbolic Acid.

DISINFECTION OF THE SICK-ROOM.—In the sick-room no disinfection can take the place of thorough ventilation and cleanliness. Complete disinfection of a room while it is occupied is impracticable. Much, however, can be done by washing the floor, window-ledges, and other surfaces with a solution of corrosive sublimate of the strength of one part in one thousand (1 : 1000), or a solution of carbolic acid, two parts in one hundred (2 : 100), or of chloride of lime, one part in one hundred (1 : 100), or of sulphate of copper, one part in one hundred (1 : 100). Among the manufactured articles sold in the shops for this purpose Platt's Chlorides is unequalled. It is to be diluted in the proportion of from one part in four to one part in ten of water. Compressed tablets of corrosive sublimate are sold by the chemists for the purpose of making the disinfectant solution. Each tablet contains seven and three-tenths grains, and the solution formed by dissolving one tablet in a pint of water is of about the strength of one part to one thousand (1 : 1000).*

Care must be taken to keep chemical disinfectants in **large** bottles or demijohns suitably and conspicuously labelled **and** marked POISON, and in a place entirely apart and away from **all** medicines, food, and beverages.

DISINFECTION OF APARTMENTS.—At the close of an infectious sickness the room may be effectually disinfected. For this purpose the more reliable gaseous disinfectants are the fumes of sulphur (sulphur dioxide) and chlorine. The agent first named is the best from a practical point of view, and is commonly used. The fireplace, windows, and doors are to be closed, the cracks being packed with paper, or covered with paper pasted on. Roll sulphur, broken fine, or the flowers of sulphur (sulphur sublimatum) may be used. A little fine sawdust mixed with the latter causes it to burn more freely. It may be placed in a shallow iron vessel or an earthenware pie-dish, which, to avoid the danger of fire, should be placed on the bottom of a high tin wash-kettle, or on tongs laid across a tub of water. It is ignited by a live coal or by first pouring over it a little alcohol. Three pounds of sulphur is the quantity to be used for every thousand cubic feet. A room fifteen feet long by twelve broad, with a ceiling ten feet high, contains eighteen hundred cubic feet ($15 \times 12 \times 10 = 1800$). As the fumes cannot be breathed even in diluted form, the door must be immediately and tightly closed. The following day all windows are widely opened, and allowed to remain so for twenty-four hours. Whitewashed walls are to be scraped and rewashed in addition to the fumigation.

DISINFECTION OF CLOTHING.—Boiling for half an hour will destroy the vitality of all known disease-germs, and there is no better way of disinfecting clothing that can be washed than to subject it to the ordinary operations of the laundry. Clothing may be disinfected by immersion for two hours in a solution of corrosive sublimate of the strength of 1 : 1000, or of sulphate of copper, 1 : 100, or of carbolic acid, 1 : 50, or of chloride of lime, 1 : 100. The bleaching properties of chloride of lime must not be forgotten. The clothing of the sick-room should not be allowed

---

* As suggested by Dr. C. M. Wilson.

to accumulate, but should go to the laundry as promptly as can be arranged. As an additional measure, and to lessen the risks of the laundry-women, it should be at once freely sprinkled with one of the above solutions. Articles of clothing that would be injured by boiling or by immersion in a disinfectant solution may be disinfected by exposure to dry heat in a properly-constructed "oven," such as are arranged in the hospitals of our large cities, and which may be used by the public. The separate articles must be freely spread out, as the penetrating power of dry heat is feeble. A temperature of 230° to 284° F. and an exposure of **three** hours are necessary. This heat is injurious to woollen **fabrics.** Finally, we must not forget the purifying effects **of fire.** Articles not readily disinfected by ordinary meas-**ures can be** destroyed by burning.

DISINFECTION OF THE PERSON.—The hands of those who nurse persons sick of infectious diseases should be occasionally washed in a solution of corrosive sublimate, 1 : 2000, or of carbolic acid, 1 : 50, or of Labarraque's solution, 1 : 10. This should invariably be done before taking food. If a solution of corrosive sublimate be employed, the hands must be afterwards rinsed with fresh water as a safeguard against mercurial poisoning, of which an early sign is soreness of the mouth and gums.

The above solutions are to be used for washing instruments and utensils that are exposed in the sick-room, except such as are used for eating and drinking purposes.

For bathing the patient's body weaker solutions must be employed,—corrosive sublimate, 1 : 5000; carbolic acid, 1 : 250; Labarraque's solution, 1 : 50. The dead should be wrapped in a sheet wet with strong disinfectant solutions,—corrosive sublimate, 1 : 500; carbolic acid, 1 : 20; or chloride of lime, 1 : 25.

DISINFECTION OF THE DISCHARGES, ETC.—Dissolve chloride of **lime in water in the** proportion of four ounces to the gallon; use one **quart** of **this** solution for the disinfection of each liquid stool in typhoid fever or cholera. If the discharge be very copious, it will be advisable to use even a larger amount. For the disinfection of solid fecal matter the above solution should be of double the strength. The matter to be disinfected must be exposed to the action of the solution for four hours, and solid masses are to be broken up by agitation of the vessel. Solutions of carbolic acid, 1 : 20, or of sulphate of copper, 1 : 25, may also be used for this purpose. But the best of all is a solution of corrosive sublimate of the strength of 1 : 500. This fluid should, on account of its highly poisonous properties, be colored red by the addition of potassium permanganate.

DISINFECTION OF WATER-CLOSETS, PRIVY-VAULTS, ETC.—No **stool** from **a** case of typhoid fever should be thrown into a closet without having been previously disinfected as above. Great care must be taken to prevent the contact of the discharges with the wood-work of the seat. The closet is to be thoroughly flushed several times a day, and in the intervals of its use a quantity of carbolic acid or chloride of lime solution should be allowed to remain in the hopper.

A privy-vault requiring disinfection may be treated with two or three pounds of corrosive sublimate dissolved in a large quantity of water and slowly poured into the vault. During an epidemic chloride of lime should be freely sprinkled over the surface of the contents of the vault every day.

XII

Medical Thermometry.

The art of taking and recording the temperature of the body is called Medical Thermometry. The instruments used are known as Clinical Thermometers. They are marked off into degrees upon the glass, and each degree is subdivided into fifths, so that the readings may conveniently be recorded in fractions of the decimal system.

The thermometers commonly used in the United States and Great Britain are marked in degrees of *Fahrenheit's* scale; those used in Europe are graduated according to the *Centigrade* scale. The scale of *Réaumur* is rapidly going out of use, but is still employed in some parts of Europe. On the scale of Fahrenheit the distance through which the mercury rises from zero to the boiling-point of water is divided into two hundred and twelve degrees, of which the thirty-second marks the melting-point of ice. Between the melting-point of ice and the boiling-point of water there are one hundred and eighty degrees ($32^\circ + 180^\circ = 212^\circ$ F.). The melting-point of ice is taken as zero in the Centigrade scale and in that of Réaumur, but in the Centigrade the boiling-point of water is at one hundred (100° C.), while in Réaumur's it is at eighty (80° R.).

The relation of the three scales to one another is, therefore,

F.	C.	R.
9	5	4

To convert recordings of the Fahrenheit scale into Centigrade degrees:

Subtract 32, multiply by 5, and divide by 9: thus, $98.6 - 32 = 66.6 \times 5 = 333.0 \div 9 = 37$. That is, 98.6° F. $= 37^\circ$ C.

To convert Centigrade degrees into Fahrenheit degrees:

Multiply by 9, divide by 5, and add 32: thus, $37 \times 9 = 333 \div 5 = 66.6 + 32 = 98.6$. That is, 37° C. $= 98.6^\circ$ F.

The Centigrade scale is better than that of Fahrenheit, and many physicians in this country prefer to use it. The following table of equivalents may therefore prove of use:

F.	C.	F.	C.	F.	C.
96.0° = 35.55°		101.3° = 38.5°		106.7° = 41.5°	
96.8° = 36.00°		102.0° = 38.88°		107.0° = 41.66°	
97.0° = 36.11°		102.2° = 39.00°		107.8° = 42.00°	
98.0° = 36.66°		103.0° = 39.44°		108.0° = 42.22°	
98.6° = 37.00°		103.1° = 39.5°		108.5° = 42.5°	
99.0° = 37.22°		104.0° = 40.00°		109.0° = 42.77°	
99.5° = 37.5°		104.9° = 40.5°		109.4° = 43.00°	
100.0° = 37.77°		105.0° = 40.55°		110.0° = 43.33°	
100.1° = 38.00°		105.8° = 41.00°		111.2° = 44.00°	
101.0° = 38.33°		106.0° = 41.11°			

As thermometers are liable after a time to give readings that are slightly too high, in consequence of the gradual contraction of the glass of which they are formed, it is necessary at intervals to compare them carefully with a standard instrument. This is done at the public observatories, to which any instrument maker will send them.

This contraction of the glass is called "seasoning," and goes on slowly. After two or three years it practically comes to an end, and the thermometer is then seasoned.

Clinical thermometers are maximum, or self-registering; that is, a small portion of the mercury is separated from the main bulk of it, or separates itself from it as it contracts, by reason of a device in the twist of the tube, in such a way that it remains in position in the tube, when the temperature falls, until shaken down, and thus indicates the highest temperature reached during the observation. The separated portion of the mercury is known as the "index." The reading is taken from the upper end of the index, which is then shaken down by a quick motion of the wrist, such as is made in cracking a whip, the thermometer being held by its upper end. Before taking the temperature the index should be below 95°. The best clinical thermometers are now made with a curved surface, which, acting as a lens, magnifies the width of the mercury; and with a flattened back, which lessens the danger of breakage from rolling.

Surface thermometers are clinical thermometers of **a special** shape, designed for measuring surface temperatures.

The object being to measure the internal temperature, the thermometer must be placed in such a position that the tissues of the body completely surround its bulb. The positions available are the armpit, or axilla, the mouth, the vagina, and the rectum. The fold of the groin, when the thigh is bent up or flexed over the abdomen, is in infants also occasionally used.

The axilla is usually selected. If very moist, it should be dried with a towel before the instrument is introduced; or if dry and harsh, it must be bathed with warm water and then dried. There is no difference in the temperature of the two armpits under ordinary circumstances. The bulb of the instrument must be placed deeply in the hollow, and the arm brought well across the chest. Care must be taken that no fold of clothing interfere with the contact of the instrument with the skin. The mercury rises rapidly at first, then more slowly. Allow five minutes for the taking of the temperature in the axilla or mouth. In the rectum or vagina less time is required,—not more than three or three and a half minutes. Time may be saved by rolling the bulb of the thermometer briskly between the palms of the hands, or with a piece of cloth or flannel, until the mercury reaches 95° or 96°.

In taking the temperature in the mouth, the bulb must be placed under the tongue and the lips closed about the stem, the patient breathing through his nose. Dip the instrument in water and wipe it with a clean napkin in the presence of the patient both before and after using it in the mouth. It is not safe to take the temperature in the mouth either in young children or in conditions of delirium. When the patient is in an insensible state, or when doubts arise as to the correctness of an axillary observation, the rectum or vagina may be used for applying the thermometer, and with self-registering instruments this plan involves no exposure of the person.

In restless children care must be taken to prevent the instruments from being broken, and in all cases to prevent a small thermometer from slipping entirely into the bowel. The temperature may be rapidly taken in unmanageable children by means of an old-fashioned thermometer which is not self-registering, by cautiously warming it until the mercury reaches a very high point, say 108°, and then quickly placing it in the armpit. The mercury falls rapidly to the temperature of the patient's body and then stops. After remaining stationary for half a minute, it may be read off.

The human body in health, like that of all warm-blooded animals, has a temperature of its own, which is nearly constant at all periods of life, in all seasons, and in every climate. This is known as the Normal Temperature, and as measured in the axilla is about 98.6° F. (37° C.) In the mouth it is about the same, but in the vagina and rectum it is fully half a degree F. higher. The surface temperature, being influenced by external causes, is lower, and varies in different parts of the body, the exposed and distant parts being coolest. The temperature of infants and children is a fraction of a degree higher and much more easily disturbed than that of adults, and after middle life the average temperature is somewhat lower than before that period. A diurnal variation independent of food or exercise, and amounting to one or one and a half degrees F., is observed in health,—the minimum being reached between 2 A.M. and 6 A.M., and the maximum being attained, after a gradual rise, between 5 P.M. and 8 P.M. This daily rhythmical fluctuation of temperature takes place not only in health, but also when in disease the whole range of the temperature is either abnormally depressed or elevated.

The temperature is usually elevated a fraction of a degree after taking food. Alcoholic drinks have a tendency to lower it. Very active exercise causes it to rise a degree or more, but when muscular exercise is carried to exhaustion a fall below the normal may be noted.

It is desirable to take the temperature at least twice daily, the best times being between seven and eight in the morning and about eight in the evening. The observations must be repeated at the same hours each day. In cases characterized by great or sudden variations of temperature or by very high temperature, or when the influence of treatment upon the fever is being closely watched, observations must be made at shorter intervals of time, and it may become necessary to take the temperature as often as every hour.

The temperature in disease may range below or above the normal. Sudden falls of temperature in fever are very significant; just as are abrupt rises from the temperature of health. The following terms are used to indicate the general condition of the patient in abnormal ranges of temperature

a. Temperature of Collapse	Below 96.5° F.
b. Subnormal Temperature	96.5° - 98° F.

Below the Normal {

c. Normal Temperature . . . . 98°–99.5° F.

Above the Normal.

d. Subfebrile Temperature . . . . 99.5°–100.5° F.
e. Moderate Febrile Temperature
   (Mild Pyrexia)   { 100.5°–102° F., A.M.
                   { 102.2°–103° F., P.M.
f. High Febrile Temperature   { 102°–104° F., A.M.
   (Severe Pyrexia)   { 104°–105.8° F., P.M.
g. Intense Febrile Temperature
   (Hyperpyrexia). . . . . 105.8°–110° F.

The range of deviation from the normal within the limits of which life can be well maintained is comprised between 92° F. and 110° F. A temperature of 95° on the one hand, or of 106° F. on the other, indicates great danger, especially if it be prolonged, and beyond these limits in both directions the danger to life speedily becomes extreme.

a. TEMPERATURE OF COLLAPSE, OR SHOCK.—A considerable and rapid fall of temperature attends the collapse which sometimes occurs during or towards the close of some of the essential fevers. In typhoid fever this condition may be produced by hemorrhage from the bowels, or by sudden peritonitis due to perforation of the wall of the bowel at some point of ulceration, or in consequence of sudden failure of the heart. The last of these accidents is liable to occur in any very grave case of fever, and occasionally follows the critical fall of temperature which occurs in pneumonia, in relapsing fever, and more rarely in other febrile diseases.

Very low axillary temperatures are met with in the stage of collapse in the algid or cold stage of cholera, the internal temperature as indicated by the vagina or rectum remaining extremely high. Great depression of the general temperature occurs in the collapse produced by various poisons, and especially by large quantities of alcohol. The temperature is apt to fall considerably below the normal in ordinary deep alcoholic intoxication, especially if the patients have been exposed to cold and wet.

b. SUBNORMAL TEMPERATURE.—This **condition attends** considerable losses of blood, starvation from any cause, the wasting of certain of the chronic diseases, such as cancer of various organs, some diseases of the brain and spinal cord, and the later stages of chronic diseases of the lungs and heart, especially when attended by dropsy.

The temperature is very apt to reach subnormal ranges in the morning for a few days at the termination of febrile disorders.

c. NORMAL TEMPERATURE.—If in the course of a continued fever, as typhoid, the temperature, which has been elevated, *suddenly* falls to normal or near it, though not below, this in itself is significant of something wrong, and may even acquire the importance of the "temperature of collapse," as indicating internal hemorrhage, perforation, or failure of the heart.

d. SUBFEBRILE TEMPERATURE.—Slight elevations of temperature often accompany trifling and transient disturbances of the general health, especially in children. They are also observed at the beginning of gradually-developing fevers, as typhoid, and at the close of slowly-subsiding febrile conditions.

e. MODERATE FEBRILE TEMPERATURE.—When the morning temperature reaches 101°–102° F. and the evening shows a further increase of one or two degrees, we have to do with actual fever.

f. HIGH FEBRILE TEMPERATURE.—When the temperature in the morning is above 102°–104° F., and in the evening reaches or ranges higher than 104.5°, the case becomes serious from the intensity of the fever alone. High fever is unattended by immediate danger to life if it be transient, but when prolonged it is ominous.

g. HYPERPYREXIA, OR INTENSE FEBRILE TEMPERATURE.—The temperature reaches 105.8° and continues to rise, or at all events does not fall. The condition is one of extreme and imminent danger to life. Hyperpyrexia often supervenes with great suddenness. It has been encountered after injuries to the brain and to the upper part of the spinal cord, in lockjaw, in sunstroke, and very often in the infectious diseases, especially scarlet fever and pneumonia. It sometimes occurs in rheumatic fever, especially after the intensity of the symptoms has begun to subside, or even when the patient is apparently almost well. Hyperpyrexia is often one of the indications of approaching death. In such cases a temperature of 110° to 112° is sometimes seen. The temperature sometimes continues to rise slowly for an hour or two after death.

The thermometer may be made to indicate a temperature much higher than that of the patient's body, by friction, or by being slipped against a poultice or hot-water bag, or into a cup of tea, when the attention of the nurse is given to other duties. These tricks are sometimes played by hysterical girls.

The temperature of a patient may be somewhat affected by excitement, fatigue, or exposure. Hence hospital patients often show for a few hours after admission a temperature higher than subsequently, or, if they have been exposed to cold, lower than really corresponds to their condition.

It is a peculiarity of the state of convalescence from the acute fevers that the temperature, though normal, is disturbed by trifling causes, and may be made to rise two or three degrees by the first visit of a friend, the first solid food, or even by sitting up. Such rises are usually very brief, the temperature quickly falling again to normal. They occasion uneasiness lest they be the beginning of a relapse. On the other hand, it occasionally happens that, though all the other symptoms have disappeared and the patient is almost well, the temperature remains subfebrile, and the patient is for that reason alone kept in bed. In more than one such case I have seen all traces of fever vanish upon cautiously allowing the patient to sit up an hour or so each day.

The attack of fever may begin suddenly, as in pneumonia, in which the temperature often rises rapidly and continuously to 104° F. or more. Such diseases are apt to begin with a more or less violent rigor or chill. Or it may be gradual, as in typhoid fever, in which the temperature rises little by little from the normal until the fourth or fifth day, when it attains about the height which, in the absence of complications, would be characteristic of the attack, 103°-104° F.

The fever having attained its height, remissions or falls of temperature follow. If these are not more than one or two degrees in extent, conforming to the diurnal variation in health, but at a higher range, the temperature is said to be continuous, or, more properly, subcontinuous, and the fever is a Continued Fever; if, however, the decline is greater than in health, the remissions being marked as compared with the rises or exacerbations, the fever is said to be of Remittent type; and, thirdly, when the remissions reach the normal or fall below it, we speak of the fever as being of the Intermittent type.

Remittent and Intermittent Fevers are grouped with the Periodical Fevers. When acute, they are usually of malarial origin. The symptomatic fever which accompanies chronic inflammatory disease, especially those of a tuberculous character, as pulmonary consumption, is of well-marked remittent or of intermittent type.

The daily exacerbation or increase of fever occurs, as a rule to which there are very few exceptions, in the afternoon or evening; the remissions or falls, in the morning. In rare cases of general tuberculosis, and still less frequently in typhoid fever, this order is reversed, the rise occurring in the morning and the decline in the evening. The fever is then said to be of " Inverse type."

The range of the temperature after it has reached its height is called the *fastigium*.

The decline of the fever is known as the *defervescence*. It is usually gradual, the remissions between the evening and morning exceeding the evening exacerbations until the normal is again established. This form of defervescence constitutes *lysis*. On the other hand, the decline of the temperature is sometimes abrupt, the temperature falling in the course of a single night or in a few hours from a considerable height to the normal or below it. This is known as a *critical defervescence*, or *crisis*. It is very often attended by some critical discharge, as of sweat or diarrhœa, and is liable to be followed by collapse.

Marked irregularity of the temperature-course of a fever usually indicates some disturbance or complication.

A gradual fall of temperature often precedes death; in some cases of fever, however, the temperature rises as death draws near (*preagonistic rise*), and it may even continue to rise for a short time after dissolution has taken place.

A transient rise in temperature after defervescence has taken place is called a *recrudescence*; a recurrence of fever with the other symptoms of the original attack, lasting several days or weeks, constitutes a *relapse*. Recrudescences are due to accidental causes, relapses to reinfection; the former are usually of trifling importance, the latter always serious. In order to detect at once these occasional recurrences of fever, the temperature ought to be systematically taken for at least a week after it has fallen to the normal range.

XIII

Urinary Tests.

(QUALITATIVE.)

Albumin.

1. Heat Test.

The following sources of error occur:

(a) The phosphates are precipitated, but are redissolved by the addition of dilute acid, whilst albumin is not.

(b) In highly alkaline urine the serum albumin may be converted into alkaline albumin not coagulated by heat. This error is avoided by acidulating the urine.

(c) In highly acid urine the albumin is converted into acid albumin not coagulated by heat. The addition of a drop of liquor potassæ converts the acid albumin into serum albumin, and coagulation occurs.

(d) There is occasionally a precipitate of uric acid. This precipitate may be recognized by its deep-brown color, and by the facts that it is never flocculent, and that it does not occur until the specimen begins to cool.

(e) When the urine contains resinous acids in considerable amounts, a precipitate is formed upon the application of **heat**. This precipitate is soluble in alcohol.

2. Nitric Acid Test. *(Heller's Test.)*

A small quantity of strong nitric acid is placed in the bottom of a test-tube, and then, by means of a pipette, an equal quantity of urine is floated gently upon the surface of the acid. If albumin be present, there will be formed at the line of junction a disk of coagulated albumin, not disappearing upon the application of heat.

Sources of error:

(a) In highly acid urines a disk of hydrated uric acid is formed, or

(b) A crystalline disk of nitrate of urea may be formed.

(c) In neutral urines a precipitate of amorphous urates is formed.

These precipitates disappear upon the application of heat.

(d) After the use of balsam of copaiba, a similar disk may be formed at the line of juncture.

3. Acetic Acid and Ferrocyanide of Potassium Test.

The urine is filtered. To the clear filtrate a large quantity of acetic acid (sp. gr. 1064) and a few drops of a ten-per-cent. solution of ferrocyanide of potassium are added. If serum albumin be present, a flocculent precipitate will form; if merely a trace, slight opalescence.

4. The Biuret Test.

The urine is treated with caustic potash, and a dilute solution of sulphate of copper is added, drop by drop. If albumin be present, a reddish-violet color will be developed; if peptones, the coloration will be red.

5. Potassio-Mercuric Iodide Test.

The solution employed in this test is made by mixing 1.35 grammes of perchloride of mercury, 3.32 grammes of iodide of potassium, 20 cubic centimetres of acetic acid, and 64 cubic centimetres **of water**. It is used by overlaying it with urine previously acidulated. If upon the application of heat the precipitate redissolves, it **consists** either of peptones, alkaloids, or urates.

6. The Picric Acid Test.

A saturated solution of picric acid precipitates serum, alkaline, and acid albumins, peptones, urates, alkaloids, oleoresins. The latter four are redissolved by heat.

256

Albumin (Continued).

7. *The Brine Test.*   The solution is made by adding a drachm of dilute hydrochloric acid to a pint of water and saturating the solution with common salt. It is employed by the overlaying process.

8. *The Sodium Tungstate Test.*   The solution consists of a mixture of equal volumes of a saturated solution of sodium tungstate and a saturated solution of citric acid, with a volume of water equivalent to the united bulk of these solutions. Overlaying process.

9. *The Terchloracetic Acid Test.*   If urine containing albumin be overlaid with a solution of terchloracetic acid, a precipitate without coloration will form at the line of junction. A delicate test, not precipitating peptones.

Blood.

One part in two thousand gives urine a smoky tint, and one in five hundred produces a bright cherry color.

The presence of blood **gives characteristic** reaction for proteids, as **serum albumin and** serum globulin, which **are always present.**

Spectroscopic Examination.

Microscopic Examination.

Chemical Examination.

The Guaiac Test.   Freshly-prepared tincture of guaiac; ozonic ether. The test is performed by placing a drachm of urine in a test-tube. Add a drop of the guaiac tincture, thoroughly mixing them, and gently shaking with as much ozonic ether as will equal the quantity of urine. If blood **be** present, the ozonic ether which separates will acquire a bright-blue color.

Sources of error :

(a) Saliva and nasal **mucus produce the** same blue line.

(b) Iodide of potassium **in the urine gives a** similar reaction.

Hæmoglobin.

The presence of hæmoglobin in the urine is established by the presence of blood coloring matter as determined by the spectroscope and the guaiac test, when at the same time the microscope reveals masses of brown pigment and very few or no red corpuscles.

Bile

Gives the urine various shades of color from **dark green to reddish brown.** Bile pigments **are recognized by the play of** colors, in which **green is distinctive. This play** of colors is **produced by several reagents:**

1. *Nitric Acid Test.*   A small quantity **of the** urine to be examined should be placed **on** a white porcelain dish, and **near** it a few drops of fuming nitric acid. The two fluids are gently brought into contact. If bile pigment be present, there will result a play of colors in which the green tint predominates

2. *Nitric and Sulphuric Acid Test.*   Equal volumes of the suspected urine and nitric acid are mixed in a test-tube. This mixture, upon being underlaid with sulphuric acid, shows, if bile pigment be present, the **green** tint and play of colors at the line of **junction.**

3. *The Hydrochloric Acid and Nitric Acid Test.*   If a mixture of equal bulks of urine **and** hydrochloric acid be underlaid with strong nitric acid, the presence of bile pigment will give the play of colors as above.

4. *The Iodine Test.*   If a small quantity of urine be floated upon the surface of tincture of iodine in a test-tube, the presence of bile pigment will develop a beautiful green color at the line of contact.

Glucose.

1. The Liquor Potassæ Test. (Moore's Test.)

This consists in a mixture of equal parts of the suspected urine and liquor potassæ in a test-tube, the upper layer of which is to be boiled. The presence of glucose develops a red-brown color in the heated portion, from the formation of glucic and melissic acids.

2. The Liquor Potassæ and Sulphate of Copper Test. (Trommer's Test.)

A drop or two of a weak solution of sulphate of copper is added to the urine, and then a volume of solution of potash equal to that of urine. Upon the addition of the potash solution, a blue precipitate of hydrated cupric oxide is thrown down. If sugar is present, this is dissolved on shaking the tube; a clear blue fluid results; on boiling the mixture **a** dense yellow precipitate of hydrated cuprous oxide is produced by the reduction of the cupric oxide by the sugar. This yellow precipitate afterwards undergoes a change to red.

3. Fehling's Test.

This **is a** modification **of that** of Trommer. The reagent employed is composed of—

(a) Cupric sulphate, 34.64 grammes, dissolved in 500 cubic centimetres of distilled water;

(b) Neutral potassium tartrate, 173 grammes, dissolved in 500 cubic centimetres of solution of caustic soda (specific gravity 1.12).

These should be kept in separate bottles, and mixed, when required, in equal proportions.

The strength of this solution is so adapted that 10 cubic centimetres are reduced by 0.05 gramme of glucose. The test is therefore of use in the quantitative estimation of sugar in the urine.

5. The Bismuth Test. (Böttger's Test.)

Equal volumes of urine and liquor potassæ are mixed in a test-tube. To this mixture is added a small quantity of bismuth subnitrate. If glucose be present, a precipitate of metallic bismuth will be thrown down upon the addition of heat. This precipitate will be gray if sugar be present in only small amount, and black if in larger quantity.

6. Fermentation Test.

Four ounces of urine are placed in an eight-ounce vial with a small fragment of yeast. In another similar bottle the same quantity of urine is placed without the yeast. The specific gravity is then taken. The two bottles are now set aside in a warm place for twenty-four hours, and the specific gravity of each is again taken. Each degree of specific gravity lost in the urine which contains the yeast indicates the presence of one grain of sugar in every fluidounce of urine. If metric measures are employed, each degree of specific gravity lost represents 0.22 gramme of sugar in every 100 cubic centimetres of urine.

Enteric Fever, Measles, Acute Tuberculosis.

The Diazo Reaction. (Ehrlich's Test.)

It is said to be characteristic of the urine in enteric or typhoid fever, measles, and acute tuberculosis to yield a deep-red color with diazo-benzol-sulphonic acid.

Ehrlich uses as a test not the diazo-benzol-sulphonic acid, but sulphanilic acid.

The procedure is as follows:

50 cubic centimetres of hydrochloric acid are made up to 1000 cubic centimetres with water, and sulphanilic acid added to saturation. To 200 cubic centimetres of the mixture 5 cubic centimetres of a half-per-cent. solution of sodium nitrite are added, and the resulting fluid is added to the urine in equal parts; or five or six times the volume of absolute alcohol is added to the fluid to be tested, and the reagent prepared as above is discharged, drop by drop, into the filtrate. Normal urine gives a yellow color, while the urine of fever patients turns scarlet.

XIV

Miscellaneous Tables.

A TABLE OF THE NUMBER OF **DROPS IN A** FLUIDRACHM.

The size of drops varies greatly, not only in different liquids, but also in the same liquid, according as it comes from different bottles. A bottle with a thick lip gives a larger drop than one with a thin lip, especially if the liquid be allowed to diffuse itself over the lip. "Droppers," as usually made, give a drop much smaller than that from a bottle, the size of the drop being dependent upon the size and bore of the point of the dropper. A dropper with a thick tip may give a very large drop. The average drop of watery solutions, *waters* or *liquors*, is about 60 to the fluidrachm; of *syrups*, except some which are very thick, about 60 to the fluidrachm; of *alcoholic solutions, tinctures*, 120 to the fluidrachm; of *volatile oils*, 110 to 120; of *ethers*, 75; of *vinegars*, 75; of *ether*, 150; of *chloroform*, 250. *Deodorized laudanum (Tinctura opii deodorata)* is really a watery preparation; hence, whilst **laudanum averages 120 drops,** deodorized laudanum averages 100 to the fluidrachm.

Acetum colchici	75	Oleum chenopodii	97
" destillatum	58	" cinnamomi	100
" opii	58	" cubebæ	86
" **scillæ**	75	" fœniculi	103
Acidum aceticum	73	" gau**theriæ**	102
" hydrocyan. dilut.	75	" menthæ **piperitæ**	103
" muriaticum	54	" olive	76
" nitricum	84	" rosmarini	104
" " dilutum	62	" sabinæ	102
" sulphuricum	90	" sassafras	102
" " aromat.	116	" tilii	80
" " dilutum	57	Spiritus ætheris **nitrosi**	90
Alcohol	118	" " **compositus**	90
" dilutum	58	Syrupus acaciæ	58
Aqua	54	" scillæ	85
" ammoniæ	49	Tinctura aconiti	118
Creasotum	91	" asafœtidæ	120
Chloroformum	250	" digitalis	120
Ether	150	" ferri chloridi	106
Glycerina	55	" guaiaci	120
Liquor iodi compositus	75	" iodi	144
" hydrarg. et ars. iod.	52	" opii	147
" potassii arsenitis	60	" opii camphorata	110
Oleum amygdala dulcis	59	" tolu	138
" anisi	85	Vinum antimonii	87
" carui	86	" colchici	75
" caryophylli	103	" **opii**	92

A glassful or cupful is estimated to contain about 4-6 fluidounces.

A wineglassful, about 1½-2 fluidounces.

A tablespoonful of liquid, about ½ ounce; **of powder, about** 2 drachms.

A teaspoonful of liquid, about **1 drachm**; of powder, about 2½ scruples.

A teaspoonful of magnesia, 10 grains; of powdered herbs, 1 scruple.

A teaspoonful of salts, sugar, sulphur, ½ drachm.

A teaspoonful of metallic oxides, 1-1½ drachms.

A drop of water and watery fluids, about 1℔.

A drop of oils and tinctures, about ⅔℔.

A drop of chloroform, about ½℔.

THE PULSE.

AVERAGE FREQUENCY AT DIFFERENT AGES—IN HEALTH.

Ages.	Beats per minute.		
In the fœtus *in utero*	between 150	and	140
New-born infants	" 140	"	130
During 1st year	from 130 down to		115
" 2d year	" 115	"	100
" 3d year	" 105	"	95
From 7th to 14th year	" 90	"	80
" 14th to 21st year	" 85	"	75
" 21st to 60th year	between 75	and	79
In old age	" 75	"	80

The pulse is generally more frequent *in females*, by 10-14 beats
per minute; *during* and *after exertion*, unless long continued;
during digestion or *mental excitement*; generally, more frequent in
the morning; and less frequent, in health, in the *nervous* as well
as in the *phlegmatic* temperament. It is temporarily accelerated
after sudden change of posture from the recumbent to the sitting,
and from either to the standing position, especially during convalescence and in other states where the action of the heart is
feeble.

RESPIRATIONS AT VARIOUS AGES.

	Number of respirations per minute.
First year	35
Second year	25
At puberty	20
Adult age	18

THE ORDER OF THE ERUPTION OF THE TEETH.

FIRST DENTITION.

As a rule, the teeth of the lower jaw precede those of the
upper, except in the case of the lateral incisors.

Central incisors	5th to 8th month.
Lateral incisors	7th to 9th month.
First molars	12th to 16th month.
Canines	16th to 20th month.
Second molars	20th to 36th month.

SECOND DENTITION.

First molars	5th to 7th year.
Central incisors	7th to 8th year.
Lateral incisors	8th to 9th year.
First bicuspids	9th to 10th year.
Second bicuspids	10th to 11th year.
Canines	11th to 12th year.
Second molars	12th to 13th year.
Third molars	17th to 21st year.

A TABLE OF THE APPROXIMATE RELATION BETWEEN THE HEIGHT AND WEIGHT UNDER NORMAL CIRCUMSTANCES.

A man of 4 ft. 6 in. to 5 ft. 0 in.	ought to weigh about			92.26 lbs.
" 5 ft. 0 in. to 5 ft. 1 in.	"	"	"	115.52 "
" 5 ft. 2 in. to 5 ft. 3 in.	"	"	"	127.86 "
" 5 ft. 4 in. to 5 ft. 5 in.	"	"	"	139.17 "
" 5 ft. 6 in. to 5 ft. 7 in.	"	"	"	144.29 "
" 5 ft. 8 in. to 5 ft. 9 in.	"	"	"	157.76 "
" 5 ft. 10 in. to 5 ft. 11 in.	"	"	"	170.86 "
" 5 ft. 11 in. to 6 ft. 0 in.	"	"	"	177.25 "
" 6 ft. 0 in.	"	"	"	218.66 "

(HUTCHINSON.)

A TABLE SHOWING THE "VITAL CAPACITY" FOR THE DIFFERENT STATURES IN HEALTH AND IN CONSUMPTION.

STATURE.	Capacity of Healthy Male.	Early Stage of Consumption.	Advanced Stage of Consumption.
	Cubic ins	Cubic ins.	Cubic ins.
From 5 ft. to 5 ft. 1 in.	171	117	82
" 5 ft. 1 in. to 5 ft. 2 in.	182	122	86
" 5 ft. 2 in. to 5 ft. 3 in.	190	127	89
" 5 ft. 3 in. to 5 ft. 4 in.	198	133	93
" 5 ft. 4 in. to 5 ft. 5 in.	206	138	97
" 5 ft. 5 in. to 5 ft. 6 in.	214	143	100
" 5 ft. 6 in. to 5 ft. 7 in.	222	149	104
" 5 ft. 7 in. to 5 ft. 8 in.	230	154	108
" 5 ft. 8 in. to 5 ft. 9 in.	238	159	112
" 5 ft. 9 in. to 5 ft. 10 in.	246	165	116
" 5 ft. 10 in. to 5 ft. 1. in.	254	170	119
" 5 ft. 11 in. to 6 ft.	262	176	123

(HUTCHINSON.)

OBSTETRIC CALENDAR.

The date in the upper line of each section 1, 1' being that of the first day of the last menstruation before conception, that corresponding in the lower line 3, 3' indicates approximately the commencement of labor; while the corresponding date in the middle line 2, 2' indicates the average but very variable time of the "quickening."